Max Weber is indubitably one of the very greatest figures in the history of the social sciences, the source of seminal concepts like "the Protestant Ethic" and "charisma." But, like that of his great forebears Adam Smith and Karl Marx, Weber's work always resists easy categorization. Prominent as a founding father of sociology, Weber has been a major influence in the study of ancient history, religion, economics, law, and, more recently, cultural studies. This *Cambridge Companion* provides an authoritative introduction to the major facets of his thought, including several (like industrial psychology) which have hitherto been neglected. A very distinguished international team of contributors examines some of the major controversies that have erupted over Weber's specialized work, and shows how the issues have developed since he wrote. The articles are both expository and critical, and demonstrate how our view of Weber has changed over the twentieth century.

THE CAMBRIDGE
COMPANION TO
WEBER

OTHER VOLUMES IN THE SERIES OF CAMBRIDGE COMPANIONS

THE CAMBRIDGE COMPANION TO

WEBER

EDITED BY

STEPHEN TURNER

University of South Florida

CAMBRIDGE
UNIVERSITY PRESS

PUBLISHED BY THE PRESS SYNDICATE OF THE UNIVERSITY OF CAMBRIDGE
The Pitt Building, Trumpington Street, Cambridge, United Kingdom

CAMBRIDGE UNIVERSITY PRESS
The Edinburgh Building, Cambridge, CB2 2RU, UK   http://www.cup.cam.ac.uk
40 West 20th Street, New York, NY 10011–4211, USA   http://www.cup.org
10 Stamford Road, Oakleigh, Melbourne 3166, Australia

First published 2000

Printed in the United Kingdom at the University Press, Cambridge

Typeset in Sabon 10/13pt   [CE]

A catalogue record for this book is available from the British Library

Library of Congress cataloguing in publication data

The Cambridge Companion to Weber/edited by Stephen Turner.
p.   cm.
Includes bibliographical references and index.
ISBN 0 521 56149 3. – ISBN 0 521 56753 x (pbk.)
1. Weber, Max, 1864–1920. 2. Sociology – History. I. Turner, Stephen P., 1951–
HM479.W42C36   2000
301′.09 – dc21   99–15846   CIP

ISBN 0 521 56149 3 hardback
ISBN 0 521 56753 x paperback

CONTENTS

CONTRIBUTORS

HAROLD J. BERMAN is Woodruff Professor of Law at Emory University and Ames Professor of Law, emeritus, at Harvard University, where he taught from 1948 to 1984. He is the author of many books on comparative legal history and legal philosophy, including *Justice in the U.S.S.R.* (1963), *Law and Revolution: The Formation of the Western Legal Tradition* (1983), and *Faith and Order: the Reconciliation of Law and Religion* (1993).

SVEN ELIAESON is Lecturer in Government at the University of Karlstadt. His *Bilden av Max Weber* is the basic book on Weber in Swedish. His forthcoming survey of the controversy over Weber's methodological writings is to be published by Polity. He has written extensively on issues related to Weber's political writings.

JON ELSTER is Professor of Political Science at Columbia University. In addition to books on rationality and rational-choice theory (*Ulysses and the Sirens* [1979], *Sour Grapes* [1983], *Solomonic Judgements* [1989]), he has written on Leibniz, Marx, and Tocqueville. A book on emotions, *Alchemies of the Mind*, is forthcoming from Cambridge University Press.

STANLEY L. ENGERMAN is John H. Munro Professor of Economics and History at the University of Rochester, and recently Pitt Professor at Cambridge University. Among his publications are: *Time on the Cross: the Economics of American Negro Slavery*, co-authored with Robert William Fogel (1974), and *The Cambridge Economic History of the United States*, co- edited with Robert E. Gallman (vol. I, 1996).

ALASTAIR HAMILTON is Professor of the History of Radical Reformation at the University of Amsterdam and the Dr. C. L. Thijssen-Schoute Professor of the History of Ideas at the University of Leiden. His publications include *The Family of Love* (1981); *William Bedwell the Arabist 1563–1632* (1985); *Heresy and Mysticism in Sixteenth-Century Spain* (1992); *Europe and the Arab World* (1994) and *The Apocryphal*

Apocalypse: The Reception of the Second Book of Esdras 4 Ezra from the Renaissance to the Enlightenment (1999).

PETER LASSMAN teaches political theory at the University of Birmingham, England. He has recently co-edited *Max Weber: Political Writings* (1994) and *Max Weber's "Science as a Vocation"* (1989).

JOHN LOVE has taught Sociology at the University of Melbourne and La Trobe University. He is the author of *Antiquity and Capitalism: Max Weber and the Sociological Foundations of Roman Civilization* (1991) as well as a number of articles on the work of Max Weber. He is currently working on a book on the sociology of contemporary capitalism.

WILFRIED NIPPEL is Professor of Ancient History at the Humboldt-Universität Berlin. His books include *Mischverfassungstheorie und Verfassungsrealität in Antike und früher Neuzeit* (1980); and *Public Order in Ancient Rome* (1995). He is the editor of *Max Weber, Die Stadt – Max Weber Gesamtausgabe I/22, 5* (1999).

CHARLES J. REID, Jr., is Research Associate in Law and History at Emory University School of Law. He has edited *Peace in a Nuclear Age: The Bishops' Pastoral Letter in Perspective* (1986) and has written on the development of rights in thirteenth-century canon law and the history of English land law.

GUENTHER ROTH, Graduate Professor of Sociology (retired from) Columbia University, edited and translated, with Claus Wittich, *Max Weber's "Economy and Society"* (1968) and, with Hartmut Lehmann, *Max Weber's "Protestant Ethic": Origins, Evidence, Contexts* (1993).

LAWRENCE A. SCAFF, Dean of the College of Liberal Arts at Wayne State University, has also taught at Pennsylvania State University, the University of Arizona and the University of Freiburg. In addition to many articles in social and political theory, his publications include *Fleeing the Iron Cage: Culture, Politics, and Modernity in the Thought of Max Weber* (1989).

WOLFGANG SCHLUCHTER is Professor of Sociology at the University of Heidelberg and Director of the Max Weber Center for Social and Cultural Studies at the University of Erfurt. His writings include: *Max Weber's Vision of History: Ethics and Methods* (together with Guenther Roth, 1979); *The Rise of Western Rationalism* (1981); *Rationalism, Religion, and Domination: A Weberian Perspective* (1989); *Paradoxes of Modernity* (1996).

ALAN SICA is Director of the Social Thought Program and Professor of Sociology at Pennsylvania State University. He edited the ASA journal, *Sociological Theory*, for five years and is the author of

Weber, Irrationality, and Social Order. He edited *Ideologies and The Corruption of Thought* (essays by Joseph Gabel), and *What Is Social Theory? The Philosophical Debates* (1998), and edited and introduced a book of essays on Weber by Paul Honigsheim (Transaction). His *Max Weber and the New Century* (Blackwell) will appear shortly.

ACKNOWLEDGMENTS

A great many people contributed to this volume, often in small ways. In several instances the help consisted of advice about potential contributors given generously and honestly by important and busy scholars for whom I was merely a voice on a telephone. The hospitality of the international community of letters, whose origins are usually associated with the Huguenot diaspora of the seventeenth century, still survives. Perhaps Weber, himself a distant product of this diaspora, would have appreciated its continued workings. Producing a book today requires rather different skills from those of the seventeenth century. Eileen Kahl, my research assistant, did the editing of the details in this volume, and there were a large number of details indeed. The Swedish Collegium for Advanced Studies in the Social Sciences supported me for some of the editing, for which I am very grateful. The volume goes into some uncharted waters: I especially thank those who stayed on board.

April 21, 1864	Born in Erfurt, Thuringia
1866	Ill with meningitis
1871	Foundation of the Second German Empire
1870–1872	Attends private Döbbelin school in Berlin
1872	Begins studies at Königliche Kaiserin-Augusta-Gymnasium in Charlottenburg
1872	Start of the *Kulturkampf*
1882	Studies at the University of Heidelberg: law, economics, history, philosophy, some theology
1883	Moves to Strasbourg to perform one year of National Service in the Army and studies at Strasbourg University; comes under the influence of his uncle Hermann Baumgarten
1884	Studies at Berlin University, including *Staatswissenschaft* (theory of the state), with Levin Goldschmidt and August Meitzen
1886	Takes the Bar exam; returns to his parents' house in Charlottenburg; begins work in the State Law and Agrarian History Faculty at Berlin University
1888	Doctoral student under Levin Goldschmidt; law clerk at the Royal District Court of Charlottenburg; third year of National Service; joins the *Verein für Sozialpolitik* (Social Policy Association)
1889	Graduates *magna cum laude* under Goldschmidt and Gneist with dissertation "Development of the Principle of Joint Liability and the Separate Fund in the Public Trading Company from the Household and Trade Communities in the Italian Cities"
1890	Dismissal of Bismarck
1891	*Habilitation* (teaching qualification dissertation) under

	August Meitzen, "Roman Agrarian History and its Importance for State and Civil Law"
1891–1892	Concludes inquiry into "The Conditions of the Agricultural Workers in East Elbian Regions of Germany," which brings academic recognition
1892	Extraordinary Professorship in Commercial and German Law at Berlin University
1893	Professor in Political Economy, University of Freiburg; marries Marianne Schnitger, his father's great-niece; commissioned by the *Kongress* to compile a second inquiry into the situation of German agricultural workers; joins the *Alldeutscher-Verband* (Pan-German League)
1894	Moves to Freiburg as Professor of Economics
1895	Gives inaugural academic lecture: "The National State and Economic Policy"
1896	Accepts Chair in Economics, University of Heidelberg
1897–1903	Period of mental illness beginning with the death of his father in 1897
1902	Resumes reading in art history, philosophy, and sociology; in intensive reading on the history, constitution, and economy of monasteries comes across the theme of "rationality," particularly in economic life
1903	Resigns teaching post at Heidelberg and becomes honorary professor
1904	Travels to United States to attend a scientific world conference at the World Exhibition in St. Louis; in the United States from August to December and at Columbia University library collects material for his work on *The Protestant Ethic and Spirit of Capitalism*; with Edgar Jaffé and Werner Sombart takes editorial control of the *Archiv für Sozialwissenschaften und Sozialpolitik* (Archive of Social Sciences and Social Policy); publishes "Objectivity in Social Science and Social Policy" introducing his concepts of "value freedom," "value relationship," and "ideal-type"
1905	Revolution in Russia
1905–1906	Publishes the *Protestant Ethic and the Spirit of Capitalism* in the *Archiv*
1906	Publishes "On the Situation of Constitutional Democracy in Russia"
1907–1908	Travels in Italy, France, and the Netherlands; develops interest in industrial work; publishes the *Agrarian Soci-*

ology of Ancient Civilizations; publisher Paul Siebeck gives him the task of continuing *Schönberg'sches Handbuch der Politische Ökonomie* and editorial control of the *Grundriss der Sozialökonomie*, which generates the texts eventually published as *Economy and Society*

1908	Participates in the conference of the National Liberal Party
1909	Co-founds *Deutsche Gesellschaft für Soziologie* (German Society for Sociology); identifies himself as a sociologist; at Vienna conference of the *Verein* speaks against Schmoller's support of bureaucratic social patronage of the workforce; suffers another relapse
1910	Speaks against racist ideology at the first conference of the *Deutsche Gesellschaft für Soziologie*
1911	Works on sociology of religion dealing with China, Japan, Judaism, and Islam; writes second part of *Economy and Society*
1912	Delivers a critical statement taking issue with the concept of "nation" at the Berlin sociology convention; resigns from the *Deutsche Gesellschaft für Soziologie* over disputes on the question of freedom from value judgment
1913	Adds "Conceptual Exposition" to *Economy and Society*; publishes "On Some Categories of Interpretive Sociology"; in Italy spends time with nature children, vegetarians, and other modern sects living under the influence of the ideas of Otto Gross and Erich Mühsam, an experience which softens his rigorous asceticism
1914	World War I begins
1914–1915	Serves as reserve officer and takes over functions of disciplinary officer on the Reserve Military Hospitals Commission; sets up and manages nine military hospitals
1915	Publishes first part of *The Economic Ethic of the World Religions*; takes position against the German policy of annexation
1916	Travels to Vienna and Berlin as a journalist for *Frankfurter Zeitung*; publishes *Religion of China: Confucianism and Taoism* and *The Religion of India: The Sociology of Hinduism and Buddhism*
1917	Publishes *Ancient Judaism*; gives lecture "Science as a Vocation"; publishes newspaper articles on a federal republican constitution for Germany. Russian revolution

1918	Accepts the Chair of Political Economy at the University of Vienna; joins German Democratic Party supporting constitutional monarchy. Lectures on "A Positive Critique of the Materialist Conception of History"
1919	Gives lecture "Politics as a Vocation"; nominated as a candidate for the National Assembly, but not elected; considered for Secretary of State for the Interior; serves on an unofficial committee advising the Ministry of the Interior on reform of the constitution; appointed to the official peace delegation to respond to the Allies' memorandum regarding Germany's war guilt; moves to Munich to take Chair in Economics; his mother dies
June 14, 1920	Dies in Munich

ABBREVIATIONS

AJ	*Ancient Judaism*, trans. and ed. Hans H. Gerth and Don Martindale, Glencoe, IL: Free Press, 1952.
ASAC	*The Agrarian Sociology of Ancient Civilizations*, trans. R. I. Frank, London: New Left Books; Atlantic Highlands, NJ: Humanities Press, 1976 [contains *Agrarverhältnisse im Altertum* and *Die sozialen Gründe des Untergangs der antiken Kultur*].
C	*The City*, trans. and ed. Don Martindale and Gertrud Neuwirth, New York: Free Press, 1966 [1958].
CS	*Critique of Stammler*, trans. Guy Oakes, New York: Free Press, 1977 [1907].
E&S	*Economy and Society: An Outline of Interpretive Sociology*, 3 vols., ed. Guenther Roth and Claus Wittich, Berkeley and Los Angeles: University of California Press, 1978 [1968] [continuous pagination].
FMW	*From Max Weber: Essays in Sociology*, trans. H. H. Gerth and C. W. Mills, New York: Oxford University Press, 1946.
GARS	*Gesammelte Aufsätze zur Religionssoziologie*, 3 vols. (1920/1), reprinted Tübingen: Mohr (Siebeck), 1988 [1920].
GAW	*Gesammelte Aufsätze zur Wissenschaftslehre*, 4th edn., ed. J. Winckelmann, reprinted Tübingen: Mohr (Siebeck), 1988 [1922].
GASS	*Gesammelte Aufsätze zur Soziologie und Sozialpolitik*, ed. Marianne Weber, Tübingen: Mohr (Siebeck), 1924.
GEH	*General Economic History*, New York: Collier Books, 1961 [1927], New Brunswick, NJ: Transaction, 1981.
GPS	*Gesammelte Politische Schriften*, Tübingen: Mohr (Siebeck), 1971.
MSS	*The Methodology of the Social Sciences*, trans. E. Shils and H. Finch, New York: Free Press, 1949.

MWG *Max Weber Gesamtausgabe*, Tübingen: Mohr (Siebeck).

PE *The Protestant Ethic and the Spirit of Capitalism*, trans. Talcott Parsons, New York: Scribner's, 1958.

PW *Political Writings*, ed. Peter Lassman and Ronald Speirs, Cambridge: Cambridge University Press, 1994.

R&K *Roscher and Knies*, New York: The Free Press, 1975.

R&SFM *The Rational and Social Foundations of Music*, trans. D. Martindale *et al.*, Carbondale, IL: Southern Illinois Press, 1958.

RC *Religion of China: Confucianism and Taoism*, New York: Free Press, 1964.

RI *The Religion of India: The Sociology of Hinduism and Buddhism*, New York: Free Press, 1958.

RR *The Russian Revolutions*, trans. G. Wells and P. Baehr, Ithaca, NY: Cornell University Press, 1995.

SWG *Gesammelte Aufsätze zur Sozial- und Wirtschaftsgeschichte*, reprinted Tübingen: Mohr (Siebeck), [1924] 1988.

TSEO *The Theory of Social and Economic Organization*, ed. Talcott Parsons, Glencoe, IL: The Free Press, 1947.

WL *Gesammelte Aufsätze zur Wissenschaftslehre*, 7th edn., ed. J. Winckelmann, reprinted Tubingen: Mohr (Siebeck), 1988 [1922].

WuG *Wirtschaft und Gesellschaft. Grundriss der verstehenden Soziologie*, 5th edn., ed. J. Winckelmann, Tübingen: Mohr (Siebeck), 1976.

STEPHEN P. TURNER

Introduction

Max Weber is widely regarded as the greatest figure in the history of the social sciences, and like Karl Marx or Adam Smith, who might be regarded as rivals to this title, Weber was much more than a disciplinary scholar. There is a demotic Weber, whose ideas have passed into common currency; a students' Weber, who is a founding figure of sociology or the theorist of modernity; a scholar's Weber, who is the creator of core ideas that have influenced the development of various specialties and whose specialized writings are is still debated within these specialties; a canonical "Weber" who is the subject of a scholarly industry, and, so to speak, a "deep" Weber, who has been the subject of the serious and continued reflection of several of the greatest intellectual figures of the century. Unlike Smith and Marx, there is no "ideological Weber": no one has turned Weber's thought directly into a political world view and set of policy recipes for the consumption of the general public. But there is a very important "political Weber" whose account of the morality of political life has influenced many politicians and political thinkers and remain central to questions about the nature of political responsibility.

The practiced ear can find echoes of Weber in the most diverse places – from the commonplace notion of "the Protestant Work Ethic" to the ubiquitous modern use of the term charisma, to the idea of bureaucratization. But the echoes can also be heard in many more recondite settings – from Harvey Mansfield's defense of George Bush as a particularly pure example of adherence to the ethic of responsibility in politics to Helmut Schmidt's earlier invocation of the same idea in German politics, to Octavio Paz who used the image of Weberian rationalization in attempting to understand the puzzle of the difference between the United States and Mexico. Weber, put simply, is one of the sources of our culture, and a source at the highest as well as the lowest level.

One can begin to gauge the significance of Weber by listing the huge variety of ideas and phenomena that the term "Weberian" has been used as a synonym for, or to modify. "Weberian" is widely used to signify such things as these: an approach to the study of social life and history in which institutions, particularly the state, are given causal significance and autonomy; as a synonym for interpretative or hermeneutic inquiries as opposed to positivist social science; as a name for the type which the modern rationalized western social order exemplifies and the world view of modernity with which it is associated; as a way of thinking about the subject matter of the social sciences by ordering the fundamental division between things that have histories and things that have natures in terms of the difference between what we can understand and what we can explain; as a way of seeing religion from the underside of its practical consequences in the everyday life and especially the economic life of individuals; as a way of seeing international politics as a struggle between competing interests and irreconcilable "ideal interests"; as a way of seeing political ethics and the morality of politics in terms of the distinction between responsibility and conscience; and as a way of seeing the state itself as an order resting, sometimes precariously, on legitimating beliefs.

The sheer diversity of these uses, the frequently subterranean character of the paths from Weber to their users, and the apparent but mystifying conflicts in the attitudes that inform them lead us to the puzzle of Weber himself. It might seem to be an easy task to tie up the various ideas into a more or less coherent package, and to discover a hidden essence that informs the whole of the work. This is the simplifier's Weber. Yet even the simplifications are not simple. Weber is pre-eminently a theorist of modernity and a modernist in his rational acceptance of the inevitability of rationalization. In this form Weber, through the American sociological theorist Talcott Parsons, is the source of much that figures in the conventional notion of "development" that the west has applied in the last fifty years to its "Others." Weber was certainly among the first to understand that the nineteenth-century alternatives of socialism and capitalism necessarily shared the same means, bureaucratic rationalization, and were thus more similar than different. But even Weber the theorist of modernity proves elusive. The "rationalistic" development of Weber's thought is matched by an anti-rationalist side. The notions of choice and commitment to world views that figure in existentialism and ultimately in post-modernism have sources in Weber's: the post-modern condition was well-described in his essay "Science as Vocation." Here Weber appears as a Cassandra and a critic of modernity.

The terrible inadequacy of this kind of simplification of Weber's thought is shown by the depth of reflection on Weber. His thought was the subject of long, and intellectually formative, reflection by such a diverse group of major figures of twentieth-century intellectual history as the existentialist philosopher, Karl Jaspers, the French sociologist and political commentator Raymond Aron (who, ironically, was the intellectual counterweight to another existentialist, Jean Paul Sartre), the doyen of post-war American foreign policy thinking Hans Morgenthau, Parsons and Edward Shils (each of whom developed his ideas in different directions). And he was also a subject of deep reflections by his opponents. Leo Strauss read and attacked Weber, but recognized at the same time that the challenge Weber posed to political philosophy was of the deepest significance – deeper than the ideology of the market or the ideology of opposition to the market. It goes without saying that only a thinker of extraordinary profundity could carry the weight of all this reflection. But merely listing these thinkers suggests that treating Weber "as a whole" and regarding portions of his work as portions of a doctrinal whole, that is to say treating him like a Leibniz or Descartes, would lead not to a single, deep understanding of Weber, but to a series of fundamentally incompatible deep interpretations.

I have not mentioned Weber the scholar, who as a young legal historian read thousands of medieval contracts in various languages to write a dissertation on medieval trading companies prior to the legal creation of the limited liability company, who in the middle of his life learned Russian in a few months in order to follow, and write on, the beginnings of revolutionary upheaval, and who, in his last decade, absorbed vast amounts of scholarship on the religions of Asia to write the relevant chapters for his *Economic Ethic of the World Religions*. This Weber is both the most impressive and the most difficult to know. Necessarily, the most central task that a *Companion* to Weber can address is to make sense of this Weber, the endlessly energetic working scholar. The sociologist Arthur Stinchcombe has commented that the best of Weber's companions was Max Rheinstein, who annotated a translation of the section of *Economy and Society* on the sociology of law. Rheinstein, he says, is

> clearly a mind of the same order of magnitude as Weber himself. He has treated Weber's text as a statement about the world, and . . . compared the text with the world. He is the only annotator who sometimes says, "Here Weber seems to be mistaken," and then goes on to say what the facts of the case are and what it means for the theoretical point under discussion.

In contrast, he notes, Parsons compares Weber only to other theorists, and members of the Weber industry treat "the text as a reflection of Weber's mind rather than the world . . . staying within the sacred tradition without saying how that tradition relates to the world."[1] These remarks set a high but not inappropriate standard for understanding Weber as a working scholar. But it is a standard that can be approximated today only by allowing for the fact that scholarship has moved on in the fifty years since Rheinstein worked, and the tasks of interpretation and commentary have become more rather than less difficult.

The problem of assessing Weber as a scholar, that is to say of saying whether he was right, is now inseparable from the problem of interpreting Weber and of interpreting and evaluating subsequent scholarship. Rheinstein himself was close enough to the intellectual world of Weber to be comfortable in the belief that he understood Weber. Today, to say whether Weber is right requires that one understand him, and this means both understanding a past world of scholarship and understanding the alternative ways in which the world has been described and interpreted since this world vanished. Connected to this problem is the difficult matter of specialization. A *Companion* needs to supply a guide to complex and sometimes exotic secondary literature rooted in disciplinary traditions that have long diverged. A difficult balance must be struck between the problem of interpretation and the problem of evaluation. It should be said that there are many excellent texts which are companions to Weber in a sense that is congruent with a long engagement with Weber's thought from, so to speak, the inside. These texts are valuable: it is absurd to think that a thinker who was the product of the previous century and a scholarly milieu that has long since disappeared can be adequately read as a contemporary. In any case, Weber scholarship is not easy to do on any other basis than long-term continuous engagement and reflection. Nevertheless, the reader who wishes to know whether Weber is right or wrong and wishes to form an independent understanding and evaluation of Weber needs something more: critical distance.

The goal of critical distance must, given the internal diversity of Weber's work and the disciplinary diversity of the secondary literature, be approached in a variety of ways. *The Cambridge Companion to Weber* is divided into sections reflecting general areas of concern: rationality, rationalization, and psychology; politics and culture; religions and their economic ethics; and law and economics, reflecting Weber's writings. But the chapters fall into several distinct types. Some chapters are explications of Weber's writings, either in their historical and biographical context or in relation to present concerns, or both. Some are presented "from the inside,"

---

[1] Arthur Stinchcombe, *Stratification and Organization: Selected Papers*, Cambridge and New York: Cambridge University Press, 1986, pp. 286–287.

others explicitly "from the outside." Jon Elster and Alan Sica consider, respectively, Weber's model of rational action and thesis of rationalization. Elster's perspective is contemporary and from the outside, from modern rational choice theory and its concerns with such themes as emotion; Sica makes some similar points from the inside, and from the perspective of the secondary literature on Weber. They show that Weber was as concerned about the limits of rationality and rationalization as he was about the processes themselves. Wolfgang Schluchter, writing from perhaps the most profound engagement with Weber of any living scholar, examines one of the most neglected aspects of Weber's career that is closely connected to this dual concern: his attempt to examine empirically the work process of a modern industry in terms of variables like fatigue. The importance and relevance of this aspect of Weber's work will be discussed below, for it points to a major error in the way Weber has been understood by some of his sociologist admirers.

In the next section, Peter Lassman and Lawrence Scaff provide basic overviews and explications of Weber's key concepts in the area of culture and politics. Guenther Roth examines Weber's thinking on ethnicity and nationality. Each of these essays is both historically sensitive and written with an eye to present relevance. Lassman and Scaff both abstract a set of core ideas from a number of diverse texts and show the consistency of Weber's thought on these topics. Roth shows the coherence of his thought on a major issue of the twentieth century, nationalism and ethnicity, and how these ideas appear in a range of contexts, from his explicitly academic writing to his political journalism and his private letters. This essay does a great deal to capture the flavor and texture of Weber's thought, and also shows the deep interrelations between his private thinking and his scholarly thinking on what remains a major issue in Europe and the world.

Weber's work has been a fecund source of controversy, and several of the remaining chapters are histories of these controversies, and this is another means of gaining critical distance. John Love, in two chapters, examines the complexities of the disputes over Weber's discussions of Asian religion and the economic ethic associated with it, and the separate dispute over ancient Judaism. These disputes are important to understanding Weber's mode of analysis, but they have been carried out in specialist settings that are for the most part inaccessible to the ordinary reader, and too often have been concerned not with what Weber actually said, but with caricatures of the argument. Sven Eliaeson examines Weber's political career and thinking by focusing on his extended meditation on the problem of creating constitutional structures that allow for political leadership, an area of especially important controversy that has been central to the political reputation of Weber in Germany.

Another type of chapter is concerned with specific areas to which Weber contributed, and is written by specialists in these areas. The subsequent development of these fields provides another means of gaining critical distance. The complex debate over Weber's *Protestant Ethic and the Spirit of Capitalism* and his writings on religion has continued in various forms and settings throughout this century. It is one of the greatest and longest running of all academic controversies. Alastair Hamilton's judicious analysis of the dispute shows why the issue has not died: despite the elusiveness of the thesis, it grasps a deep historical truth. Harold Berman and Charles Reid examine Weber as a historian of law – a topic that formed a large proportion of Weber's actual writing – and show some ways in which Weber was selective in his coverage, even in connection with issues which were central to him, such as the impact of Protestantism. Stanley Engerman examines Weber's troubled relationship to subsequent economic history, and shows where Weber anticipated later concerns. Finally, Wilfried Nippel examines Weber's relationship to the discipline of ancient history, in an essay combining explication and analysis of controversy with a discussion of Weber's influence on the area.

Several issues that have loomed large in past writing about Weber have been given less emphasis in this collection, because of considerations of space. The topic of Weber's sociology of economic institutions is indirectly touched on by several of the contributions but, as Stanley Engerman notes, is not developed in his chapter. An excellent survey of this topic is available, however, Richard Swedberg's *Max Weber and the Idea of Economic Sociology.*[2] Weber's occasional writing, and especially his political journalism on Russia, are not examined. The publication of texts, especially letters, in the *Max Weber Gesamtausgabe* has greatly clarified Weber's views on politics. But the sheer quantity and contextual complexity of this material make it difficult to handle in the format of a *Companion* volume.[3] There is also no direct discussion in the *Companion* of Weber interpreted as a fully realized normative political theorist, though this remains a vital part

[2] Richard Swedberg, *Max Weber and the Idea of Economic Sociology*, Princeton, NJ: Princeton University Press, 1998.
[3] Detailed discussions of Weber's political activity are available elsewhere. Wolfgang Mommsen, *Max Weber and German Politics, 1890–1920*, trans. Michael S. Steinberg, Chicago: University of Chicago Press, [1974] 1984 remains the definitive survey, and is also a highly accessible work. The newly published letters, to the extent that they add to or alter Mommsen's picture, have not been comprehensively surveyed, but Roth's chapter in this *Companion* does elucidate a key example of the kind of issues raised by these letters, as well as his political journalism and his practical political thinking.

of the Weber literature, as shown by Peter Breiner's recent *Max Weber and Democratic Politics.*[4] It must be said that Weber himself never wrote explicitly as a normative political theorist; consequently the issues in connection with these interpretations are somewhat different in character from cases in which there was a specific scholarly literature with which he was engaged and which responded to him.

Perhaps the most significant decision, however, was to omit any detailed discussion of Weber as a methodological thinker. A very large part of the critical literature on Weber, from the earliest commentaries, has focused on his account of the nature of what he called the "historical sciences," and treated Weber as a philosopher – a title he never claimed. Two major discussions of the large secondary literature on these topics exist, however, and, again, both are accessible to the general reader. Bruun's book on value in Weber's thought is still unsurpassed.[5] Sven Eliaeson will soon publish a comprehensive review of the literature on Weber's methodological thinking, *Max Weber's Methodologies,*[6] which will provide a comparable service for this very complex side of Weber's thought. Some acquaintance with Weber's methodological views and value theory is essential, however, and I will furnish a brief overview of them in the rest of this introduction, and attempt as well to shed some light on the core of his normative political thinking.

Weber applied to Weber

Understanding Weber and Weber's work today is an intellectual puzzle which Weber himself would have relished, for it illustrates his fundamental methodological argument, especially concerning the historically relative nature of social science thinking. In the remainder of the introduction, I will describe this argument and examine some of its premises. These premises have to do with values, and are the source of Weber's relativism. His applications of these ideas to the value choices faced by scholars and politicians are among the most telling and powerful of his writings. They appeared in a series of writings that were collected posthumously as the

[4] Peter Breiner, *Max Weber and Democratic Politics,* Ithaca, NY: Cornell University Press, 1996.

[5] H. H. Bruun, *Science, Values, and Politics in Max Weber's Methodology,* Copenhagen: Munksgaard, 1972.

[6] Sven Eliaeson, *Max Weber's Methodologies,* Cambridge: Polity Press, forthcoming. The recent book by Fritz Ringer, *Max Weber's Methodology: the Unification of the Cultural and Social Sciences,* Cambridge, Mass.: Harvard University Press, 1997, cannot be recommended. Criticisms of this book may be found in a review symposium in *The International Journal of Politics, Culture, and Society* 12 (2), 1998.

Gesammelte Aufsätze zur Wissenschaftslehre, and known as the *Wissenschaftslehre* (*GAW*). The most important of these are his essays "Objectivity in Social Science and Social Policy" and "The Meaning of 'Ethical Neutrality' in Sociology and Economics," collected and translated in *The Methodology of the Social Sciences* (*MSS*).

Weber's is perhaps the most vivid and coherent formulation of the problem of historical relativism as it arises in the social sciences (or, as he called them, the historical sciences). He posed the problem in this way: if the occupants of different historical epochs have different worldviews (*Weltanschauungen*), and if worldviews are compounded of or ultimately based on value choices that are themselves ultimate (in the sense that they are not subject to additional justifications that would be persuasive to those committed to other ultimate values), then to exist in a historical period and to conceive of one's world in accordance with its worldview is to have made an implicit value choice. If, in addition, worldviews have the function of constituting the objects of interest to us as analysts (that is to say, if they constitute the things that we want to explain, such as the early capitalist's act of saving), then the historical facts that are objects of explanation for us may well not be objects, or objects with the same significance or meaning, for others, in other historical epochs governed by other worldviews.

These apparently simple premises place the participant in the historical sciences, the analyst, in the following difficulty. If we are to explain the early capitalist's act as though it were our kind of act, that is to say, to give it the kind of meaning that those of us in a particular epoch would give it if we were to perform the act, we may be simply reinventing or reconstruing the act in such a way that it no longer has the meaning that it had to the person who performed it. The naive historian who does this will simply make the actions of figures in the historical past strange and unintelligible. But even the most sophisticated historian can be misled when an agent with a different worldview merely appears superficially to be acting in accordance with our way of thinking about what we do. In either case, there is a failure of historical understanding.

Our dilemma is that we have no alternative to the project of understanding people in, so to speak, our own terms. We have no other starting point than "our" way of constituting the objects of analysis. Of course, we can admit that we are trapped inside our worldview, and concede that there is nothing we can do to understand the early capitalist but to understand him in our terms, even if this perhaps means understanding in a way that has nothing to do with the way he and his contemporaries understood these actions. The other is to claim that we as historians *can* successfully enter into the mind of the early capitalist. But this claim seems inevitably to rely on intuition, and it is difficult to see how historical evidence can decide between rival intuitions. One way out of this dilemma would be scientistic: to dispense with "understanding," look for causal laws that provide explanations, and ignore questions about the significance or meaning of action, on the grounds that such questions are inherently valuative and therefore unscientific. Causal laws, however, do not come in our everyday terminology: just as in natural science, we would have to construct a new language of description, and new concepts of a type different from the concepts familiar to us from our own social experience.

Weber rejects each of these options. He dismisses the "no significance" alternative by considering the best case for it, and points out that even if this alternative were feasible and we could produce laws, as we can in the natural sciences, the results would be in the form of concepts that do not allow us to answer the kinds of questions that we as historical scientists or social scientists pose. We want to answer such questions as "why did modern capitalism emerge and come to dominate the world?" We have no idea what sorts of concepts the "no significance" social scientist might find to express her laws in, but "capitalism," for example, is not the kind of term she could use. The concept does not even arise in the worldview of, for example, people in subsistence economies, or even people in the past of Europe and the classical world. It is a term that arose, relatively recently, within our "worldview," and it is a category that has valuative significance, negatively or positively, to us.

We are trapped by the implicitly valuative and historically limited character of the kinds of questions we wish to ask. Nevertheless, if we recognize the existence of differences in worldviews, between, for example, the time of the Reformation and our own, we raise the possibility that these different worldviews can themselves be understood. We can construct models, both of human action and of worldviews, that we can systematically evaluate by comparing them to the evidence we have about the worldviews of others and about the course of their action. Assessing actions and modeling worldviews turn out to go together. To understand the actions of the early capitalist it is necessary to understand his values and the worldview that informs and embodies these values, such as asceticism. To fail to understand asceticism is to be cut off from our subject. But how can we understand it? We must begin with our own understood world, and with models of action behavior derived from our own social experience and employing the kinds of explanations we give of the actions of one another. In both the case of worldviews and the case of actions, we are compelled by the sheer complexity of the material to think in terms of typifications or models with which we can communicate our findings. We can construct these typifications explicitly, aiming at clarity, through abstractions that are necessarily also simplifications. We can then explain the typifications to our own contemporaries so that they can share a model of the early Protestant worldview.

So there is an activity of conceptualization and conceptual construction that is appropriate to the social sciences. The problem is that the significance of these models is readily misconstrued. The models of rationality we apply to economic actions may be historically very robust, that is to say they apply across and within a variety of contexts. We can show how the early capitalist's actions were rational, in the sense of being in accordance with a broader model of rational action, once we have identified his aims and connected them to his worldview. We may even be able to construct ideal-types that facilitate explanation, and they may be so clear and compelling that they outlast the very worldviews whose problems they were originally designed to solve. The models or typifications are simply tools that enable us, with our worldview and with the historical questions that can arise within it, to explain the actions of others. They have no foundation or claim to "correspond to reality" beyond these uses.

It was in this spirit that Weber offered his own conceptual constructions, such as his ideal-types of authority. Of course, they have proven to be applicable long after the academic milieu and political culture of elitist liberal pessimism that motivated their construction vanished into history. There is no assurance that they will be equally useful in the future. Though Weber's account of the worldview of the early capitalist motivated by religious anxiety was one of the most compelling, and controversial, reconstructions of a worldview ever composed, one may ask whether it will retain its utility indefinitely. Even now, it seems, audiences for whom religion has lost its significance have difficulty grasping Weber's account. This is, potentially, the fate of all such models: they serve particular audiences, for particular purposes of understanding; when these purposes change, their utility may vanish, and indeed so may their intelligibility.

Weber's texts themselves have the same difficulties for us that Weber believed actions have for the historical analyst generally. To understand them, we must reconstruct the contexts that motivated them, and to do this we must in some sense idealize and typify them, and also use these typifications to see what problems Weber thought his arguments solved. The problems they solved are not entirely alien to us. But neither are they precisely the same. This should be taken as a danger signal for interpreters. "Contextualism" is only a partial solution: Weber himself would have observed that appeals to context" are equally subject to the dangers of ideal-typical reification (c.f. *MSS* 96).

Weber's account of causality

This account of the distinctive task of the historian, in spite of its complexity on the one hand and the ease with which it fits with the actual character of historical analysis on the other, nevertheless has what the philosopher would consider a fatal flaw. Despite the usefulness of concepts across or between historical periods, the validity of the historian's insights appears to be essentially or ultimately relative. The historian, on this view, is motivated and constrained by the interests in historical phenomena that arise from his own time and place. These interests, it appears, might be satisfied by criteria of adequacy that themselves are also "local" or relative to time and place. This was not merely a theoretical possibility. In Weber's own time, some historical writers who were personally well known to him, such as Heinrich von Treitschke and Friedrich Gundolf, practiced history as a purposeful creation of edifying mythologies out of historical material.

These examples raise a quite interesting question. How objective can history be if it is entirely a matter of providing answers to questions that arise from historically specific interests in historical phenomena? History would seem to be no more objective than the cultural backgrounds or values that inform historical interests. Weber goes up to this point, and then draws a line. All historical inquiry, he argues, is ultimately in some respects causal. This fact thus constrains the historian's answers to questions.

The line Weber drew was the source of considerable controversy, for reasons that philosophers are most sensitive to. It raises a reflexive question: is the drawing of the line itself something that is done within a worldview, and thus relative to that worldview, or is it the case that, contrary to Weber's notion of the relativity of worldviews, this line is something outside of any worldview, or part of all worldviews? And there is also the question of the status of Weber's methodological thinking itself: Weber's own very specific formulation of the problem of causality, as it happens, derives from contemporary sources, namely a theory of legal causality which arose to address problems in jurisprudence which were important during the period of Weber's training as a young lawyer and shortly afterward. Is it merely the expression of a particular worldview? This issue produced a great deal of criticism of Weber, even by his close admirers, such as Karl Jaspers.

Weber adopted a view of causality based on the work of a colleague in Freiburg, Johannes von Kries, which was different from the standard Millian view that a cause is the "antecedent, or the concurrent of antecedents, which is invariably and *unconditionally* consequent."[7] The difficulty with the Millian notion of causality for lawyers is that it is unhelpful in determining liability, and this is a difficulty shared with historians. Both deal with unique events in their full particularity. For a particular event to occur in exactly the way it did, one might say, all of the particular conditions for the event had to in fact occur, and each condition is necessary and in this sense equally responsible for the outcome. If a bus driver, for example, transports a murderer to the scene at which the murder shortly occurs, the bus driver is causally responsible for the murder in the sense that his transporting the murderer is a necessary condition for the murder as it actually transpired. In criminal law one can distinguish between intentional and unintentional consequences and say that the bus driver made no contribution because the contribution, though causal, was unintentional or at least not criminally intentional.

In cases of liability and history, however, intentionality is not the same issue. One is liable for unintentional consequences of one's actions. One should not, however, be liable for consequences of actions that are ordinarily without bad consequences, such as freak accidents. Von Kries' probabilistic approach to this problem required him to analyze causality in terms of the probable outcomes of actions conventionally described in a particular way. These probabilities were at least theoretically calculable and the calculations could be grounded in empirical claims about the actual likelihood of a given consequence of an action of a particular type. Reckless driving, for example, has predictably bad consequences at a certain degree of probability; consequently reckless driving creates liability.

Weber saw that this problem was precisely parallel to the historian's problem of assessing the responsibility of historical figures for particular consequences of their action. He used the objective and numerical (though usually only theoretically calculable) consequences of standard actions as a standard for historical explanation. To say that any causal accounts in history, regardless of the worldview that constituted the problem, must meet this standard is to erect an objective, transhistorical, standard of adequacy for explanations. The fact that all explanations in the historical sciences have a causal aspect makes causal adequacy into a general criterion of validity, though as Weber formulated it, a rather weak and modest one.

---

[7] John Stuart Mill, *A System of Logic Ratiocinative and Deductive: Being a Connected View of the Principles of Evidence and the Methods of Scientific Investigations*, Books I–VI and Appendices, vols. VII and VIII in *Collected Works*, ed. J. M. Robson, Toronto and Buffalo, NY: University of Toronto Press and Routledge & Kegan Paul, 1974, Book III, ch. 5, p. 340.

Weber thus limited, at least in the domain of the explanation of action, the problem of historical relativism. An explanation of an action should be both adequate with respect to meaning, which is to say it should make the action intelligible to the relevant audience, and adequate with respect to cause, which is to say it should reach a minimum standard of probability. If this is "relativism," it is very far from arbitrariness: the audience-relative standard of intelligibility may be quite high and difficult to meet; the standard of causal adequacy at least prevents the historian from making a narrative out of improbable causal connections.

Much of what Weber says about idealization and typification, and about his notion of the ideal-type, arises from the problem of making these assessments: even to think of the hypothetical probability of an event requires us to think of it as an event of a certain type, that is to say of a class in terms of which one could imagine it falling and in which one could determine the relative frequencies of an outcome. For classifications that involve universal categories, such as living and dead, we can simply count. For most of the categories that interest us, such as "rational action," matters are more complex: the terms apply "more or less," and the notion of rationality in action is an ideal that is rarely if even fully attained. Yet it is through such concepts, and through other "meaningful" but culturally bound concepts, that we are best able to understand action.

Weber recognized that action explanations of the kind that are central to history, and were central to his conception of sociology, were only partial and limited. They operate essentially by supplying reasons for action, and Weber was well aware of, and highly sensitive to, the fact that conscious reasons explain only a small part of action and a small subset of the domain of human behavior. Other causal processes, biological or physical in character, always operate in concert with intentional action and at the margins of the category of intentional action, such as in the case of traditional conduct that was largely habitual and unconscious in character, and where there was an emotional base or component to action, such as moral feeling.

Weber was fascinated with these causal processes, but was at the same time wary of the kind of reductive generalization that was all too common among racial theorists of the time. He did not solve the problem of the relation of the biological to the realm of action, but offers many tantalizing remarks. The problem exemplifies the issue of the relationship between understanding and causal laws discussed earlier: action explanations operate in different terms, the terms of reasons and intentions, from biological causal explanations or psychophysical explanations, such as fatigue, or explanations of crowd emotion, such as contagion. The former are historical, governed by the exigencies of making particular acts intelligible for particular audiences; the latter are not.

Nevertheless, Weber says, the sociologist must be "well aware" of the "relative role," as he puts it, of "mechanical and instinctive factors, as compared with that of the factors which are accessible to subjective interpretation generally, and more particularly to the role of consciously rational action" (E&S 17). Not only are the biological factors "completely predominant" in the early stages of human development, "their continual interaction with [the factors that are understandable subjectively] is often of decisive importance. This is particularly true of all 'traditional' action and of many aspects of charisma, which contain the seeds of certain types of psychic 'contagion' and thus give rise to new social developments" (E&S 17). The two aspects of action, the subjectively meaningful (and paradigmatically rational) and that which is not, cannot easily be brought together in the same frame. But we can sometimes see that the type of action is underlain by, and corresponds to, these other factors and must be in "continual interaction" with them.

In the section of this *Companion* on rationality, rationalization, and psychology, the issues created by Weber's division of the usual domain of social science into meaningful and meaningless phenomena are discussed from several points of view. They point to a significantly different understanding of Weber's approach to action. Weber speaks of "the narrow limits to which [sociology understood as concerned with socially meaningful action] is confined" (E&S 17), and comments that rationalistic interpretation is only a "methodological device" the use of which "certainly does not involve a belief in the actual predominance of rational elements in human life" (E&S 17). These were not mere concessions to biological claims he did not accept: they represent a fundamental part of his conception of the human world and the place of intentional action within it.

Weber as an ethical thinker

Weber's devotion to the idea of the role of values and valuative worldviews in the constitution of the objects of inquiry in the historical sciences raises an important question about his conception of values. Values, especially those that derived from religion, were central topics in Weber's thought as a sociologist and especially in his massive studies on the economic ethics of the world religions. In some of Weber's writings the origins and character of values appear rather mysterious. In his most important methodological essay, "Objectivity in Social Science and Social Policy," he comments on the fact that all research in the social sciences is specialized, and tends to "lose its awareness" of the valuative roots of its modes of constituting its objects. "And it is well," he says: "that should be so. But there comes a moment when the atmosphere changes. The significance of the unreflectively utilized viewpoints becomes uncertain and the road is lost in the twilight. The light of the great cultural problems moves on" (*MSS* 112).

What does this mean? In the first place, it means that we are the products of our time and culture, and our time and culture are intrinsically valuative: they break the infinite manifold of events into chunks or categories which are meaningful for us, and this meaning is positive or negative. "Values" in this sense are non-optional and imposed upon us; they are not ordinarily at the level of full consciousness, much less "choice." They are, so to speak, in the background, and are the source of the changing light that presents the great cultural problems to us. But this notion of values as the pervasive, unreflective background to our thought does not fit very well with the notion of choice which Weber promotes in his two famous ethical writings, "Science as a Vocation" and "Politics as a Vocation," as well as in his discussion of the meaning of value neutrality, in which he is attentive to values in a conscious and explicit sense. Here he says that we can and indeed must, if we are to rise to full humanity, choose our values, and with his idea that values are "formed only in the struggle with other ideals which are as sacred to others as ours are to us" (*MSS* 57).

The "Vocations" essays can be read as fully congruent with the discussions of the valuative constitution of the objects of historical science in his other writings if we understand their shared roots. The common point Weber makes in both the case of an individual choice of a value and the case of the acceptance of a worldview (which is necessarily and pervasively valuative) is that these choices are necessarily baseless and fundamentally a matter of commitment, whether this commitment is conscious and explicit or semi-conscious and largely tacit. There is not, and cannot be, any sort of further rational justification of value commitments in either case. We cannot answer the question of the relative value of the great cultures of the world, for example, because we cannot mentally extricate ourselves from the influence of these cultures and occupy a standpoint independent of them. When faced with a choice between values, similarly, there is no external standpoint from which we can decide: our "reasons" necessarily refer back to other, more ultimate, valuative standpoints; in the face of ultimate values we must simply choose.

In this sense Weber is a relativist. But his "ethical" writings make it quite clear that our choices are far from being entirely unconstrained. The two "Vocations" texts have a parallel structure. They begin with a lengthy discussion of the institutional framework of the activity whose ethical significance they are about to discuss. Indeed, in each case the bulk of the essay is devoted to history, and addresses at length the practical constraints of activities and the practical constraints under which present institutions grew up: how modern democratic party politics came to be the exclusive form of politics in the west and how specialized university academic life became the dominant form for scholarship. The historical discussions are dry and say little about values. There is nothing about the moral significance of the "idea of the university" in the essay on science and nothing about the ideals of democracy and freedom in the essay on politics. The constraints imposed by administrative and practical political necessity on the form of political effort, however, are depicted as extremely tight. Similarly, the realities of life within universities are depicted as extremely constraining. It is only after Weber has established these realities that he looks at the various romantic interpretations of these activities to which his audience might be inclined. When he discusses them, he is brutally dismissive. To "the naive optimism in which science – that is, the technique of mastering life which rests upon science – has been celebrated as the way to happiness," his response is: "Who believes in this? – aside from a few big children in university chairs or editorial offices" (FMW 143). After these childish and absurd points of view are dismissed we presented with the serious alternative value choices, and these turn out to be very limited indeed.

Weber's mode of ethical argument in these essays consists of dividing the entire theoretically possible universe of values into three broad categories. The first category is what he calls other-worldly value choices. Such choices involve ends, such as salvation, that are not of this world. These choices themselves imply an "ethic," but in these cases it must be an ethic of "intention" or "conviction" because the only this-worldly guide to conduct that one can have in the pursuit of other-worldly goals is fidelity to one's convictions and purity of intention. The second category includes goals that are achievable within this world. These goals are mundane in the literal sense but may be very abstract and selfless, for example, the goal of the defense of one's country. The person pursuing these goals is governed by an ethic of responsibility or consequences: the only meaningful guide to conduct is the question "will my actions bring about the goal?" The third category consists of goals that are believed to be achievable in this world through particular means but which are in fact not achievable. The childish idea of science as a way to happiness is one example of this kind of confusion: the results of science are not unambiguously good. The attempt to be a this-worldly Christian pacifist is another example of an irretrievably confused project: renouncing violence in this world would make the violence of others pay, and thus produce violence. The peculiarity of religious traditions generally, and the western religious tradition in particular, is that they often occupy this third category, that is to say present what are other-worldly options as genuinely this-worldly options. The specific peculiarity of Christianity from this point of view is its recurrent attempts to bring about the kingdom of God on earth, mistaking an impossibility for a practical project.

Weber thought this third category was large, and in these essays was particularly concerned to identify and exhibit the defining feature of ethical viewpoints in this category: the illusions about the possibility of achieving desired ends with available means. Simply by identifying the actual institutional structures of politics and university life, Weber eliminated as unachievable and practically meaningless many of the idealistic value sentiments that his audiences had been exposed to. The idea of an unified worldview produced by an overarching reason, for example, which the heirs of the shattered worldview of Christianity sought to put in its place, was an impossibility simply because of the specialized nature of scholarship and the diversity of constitutive presuppositions for the various fields of scholarship. In politics, similarly, there could be no leaders of the type that many younger intellectuals hungered for, because, as Weber meticulously demonstrated, the processes of rising to power in the complex bureaucracies of modern democratic political parties would prevent the rise of the type of leader in question.

For Weber, there are few meaningful options left for the modern intellectual and the modern politician. The intellectual can return to Christianity, but today this can be done only at the price of sacrifice of one's intellect. The politician can cynically pursue power for its own sake within the democratic mass party system just as he could under past systems, but no serious person would want power as a goal in itself. The person seeking a serious non-illusory this-worldly political goal, however, faces a very small range of choices. Weber suggests that "the fatherland" is one such valuative choice (*FMW*, 126) and perhaps the only practical serious choice, because nationalism was the only plausible basis for a mass political party that could transcend the limitations of interest politics of the sort that characterized German parliamentary politics during Weber's lifetime (cf. "Parliament and Government in Germany under a New Political Order," *PW* 130–271).

Weber's reasoning serves to cut down the possible choices in these two spheres. By the end, it appears that there are no very appetizing choices that are not illusory. The tone is one of harsh realism, and "Realism" was indeed the term that his follower Hans Morgenthau used to characterize his own theory of international relations. Yet in each essay there is a different message, a message about passion. In the "Science" text, we are presented with the life of the specialized scholar, whose strange intoxication is bound up with the capacity to put on blinders, so that he can believe that the fate of his soul depends on whether or not he makes the correct conjecture at this passage of this manuscript. In the "Politics" text, Weber says that there is something especially moving about the mature individual who, says, with Luther, "Here I stand, I can do no other," who accepts defeat, but refuses to compromise his value commitments and takes responsibility for them. Only a person in whom the ethic of ultimate ends and the ethic of responsibility supplement one another is a genuine man, and thus capable of a political vocation.

What could these strange comments mean? Why is passion so important? Bertrand Russell once said that it is more difficult to live up to the demands of utilitarianism than it is to live up to the demands of Christianity. But in one respect the utilitarian has it easy: utilitarianism restricts this-worldly goals to the actually achievable, and thus the responsibility of the utilitarian is limited to the known. The utilitarian can be a bookkeeper of happiness: passion is unnecessary. In some domains, our limitations as knowers prevent us from always correctly drawing the line between that which is achievable in this world and that which is not. High politics, as Weber understood very well, is about decisions at the margins of achievability – where the possibility of failure is real, and uncertainty great. It is this vague margin beyond the predictably achievable and controllable which constitutes for Weber the domain of action that is of the greatest moral significance: in politics, the risks are mortal, both to the bodies of those under the care of the state and to the souls of decision makers. Here passion, as well as restraint, is essential. The lessons apply, *mutatis mutandis*, to the world of scholarship itself. Passion is essential, but it is not enough. The recipe for great scholarship is passion restrained by great intellectual self-discipline, particularly the discipline to face the facts. Few scholars have the two, and the delicate balance between the two, as long as Weber did, and to such effect.

PART I

Rationality, rationalization, and psychology

I

JON ELSTER

Rationality, economy, and society[1]

I. Introduction

The idea of rationality has a central place in Max Weber's *Economy and Society*.[2] In the years since it was written, rationality has also come to be one of the most important concepts in the social sciences – not only in economics, but also in political science and increasingly in sociology. In the present article I confront some central arguments in *Economy and Society*, notably from the first two chapters of Part I ("Basic Sociological Terms" and "Sociological Categories of Economic Action"), with what I believe to be the standard contemporary approach. Because I know much more about the modern theories than about Weber's writings – I am not a Weber scholar – my procedure will have to be somewhat schematic. In examining passages from Weber out of their historical context and without regard for the vast secondary literature, I obviously run the risk of anachronism, oversimplification, or worse. I can only hope that the analytical arguments will be useful to those with a better knowledge of the Weberian corpus.

The article is a personal essay, in the sense that it is colored by my own interests and preoccupations. For many readers of *Economy and Society*, the emphasis I give to emotions and social norms will come as a surprise. Yet although Weber's discussions of these topics are brief and often extremely condensed, I believe his treatment is very acute and worth highlighting. Also, as already indicated, I shall confront Weber's views about instrumental rationality with modern ideas from cognitive psychology and game theory that he could not possibly have anticipated.

I shall proceed as follows. In Section II I try to clarify the relation

---

[1] I am grateful to the editor and an anonymous referee for comments on earlier drafts of this article.

[2] All page references are to the English translation of this work (New York: Bedminster Press, 1968). Occasional changes that do not affect the meaning of the text are not indicated.

between rationality and rationalization. Although my task is to examine the former concept, I first need to disentangle it from the latter. In Section III I discuss Weber's view on the relation between three core ideas of modern economic theory: rationality, self-interest, and methodological individualism. In Section IV I present what I believe to be the standard model of rational-choice theory, as it is routinely applied by economists and other social scientists. In Section V I discuss Weber's fourfold typology of social behavior. In Section VI I consider what I believe to be some important omissions in Weber's theory of rationality. Section VII offers a brief conclusion.

II. Rationality and rationalization

Weber's main discussion of rational action and what differentiates it from other forms of social action occurs at the very beginning of *Economy and Society*.[3] Apart from these few dense pages, discussed in Section V below, the work contains few references to individual rational behavior. Almost all other references to rationality or to "rationalization" have to be taken in an institutional rather than in a behavioral sense. In particular, one should not confuse the distinction between instrumental rationality and value-rationality with the distinction between formal and substantive rationality.[4] When Weber refers to the rationalization of the modern world, he has mainly in mind the increasing importance of formally and substantively rational institutions. Although he also refers to the substitution of deliberate adaptation for unthinking acceptance of custom as an aspect of rationalization,[5] this individual-level statement is not typical.

Formal rationality is essentially a procedural concept. It is a property of economic, legal and bureaucratic systems that allow for calculability and predictability. In the case of economic action, formal rationality reaches its highest form in capital accounting.[6] Within the law, formal rationality requires that "in both substantive and procedural matters, only unambiguous general characteristics of the facts of the case are taken into account."[7] Within bureaucracy, formal rationality requires general rules, hierarchy, full-time officials, specialized training, and so on.[8] In law and bureaucracy, formal rationality is mainly characterized by the subsumption of individual decisions under general rules, not by ends-means reasoning. Because formal rationality in the economic field also requires formally

---

[3] *Ibid.*, pp. 24–26.   [4] *Ibid.*, pp. 85–86.   [5] *Ibid.*, p. 30.
[6] *Ibid.*, pp. 161–162.   [7] *Ibid.*, pp. 656–657.   [8] *Ibid.*, pp. 956–958.

rational law and administration,[9] subsumption under rules is in fact a general feature of formal rationality.

To be sure, Weber also maintains that formal rationality can itself be viewed as a means to an end, namely to the maintenance of "those who wield the economic power at any given time,"[10] whereas "the propertyless masses . . . are not served by the formal 'equality before the law' and the 'calculable' adjudication and administration demanded by bourgeois interests."[11] Yet the fact (if it is one) that formal rationality serves the interests of the economically powerful does not imply the absurd view that it has been instituted by that group for that purpose. Nor does it imply that formal rationality rests on ends-means reasoning, any more than the use of lot as an efficient mode of decision-making in certain contexts implies that the outcome of the coin toss is determined by efficiency. Formal rationality is not a consciously chosen means to anyone's end, nor is it itself a form of means-ends efficiency. It is neither a form of (class-restricted) rule-utilitarianism nor a form of act-utilitarianism.

Economic, legal and bureaucratic systems are substantively rational when they aim at creating a specific distribution of goods, income or life-chances,[12] or aim at bringing about some other substantive end. These systems are rational in the sense that they are not subject to individual caprice or favor, but are systematically oriented to a publicly defined purpose:

> Decisive is that this "freely" creative administration (and possibly judicature) would not constitute a realm of *free*, arbitrary action and discretion of *personally* motivated favor and valuation, such as we shall find to be the case among pre-bureaucratic forms. The rule and the rational pursuit of "objective" purposes, as well as devotion to these, would always constitute the norm of conduct. Precisely those views which most strongly glorify the "creative" discretion of the official accept, as the ultimate and highest lodestar for his behavior in public administration, the specifically modern and strictly "objective" idea of *raison d'état* . . . The [decisive point] is that in principle a system of rationally debatable "reasons" stands behind every act of bureaucratic administration, either subsumption under a norm, or a weighing of ends and means.[13]

As this passage shows, the substantive rationality of legal and bureaucratic institutions is a form of instrumental adaptation. Whereas individual value-rational action is oriented towards a specific behavior without regard for its consequences (see below), substantively rational action is guided by its consequences. Yet even though the formal or substantive rationality of

---

[9] *Ibid.*, p. 162.   [10] *Ibid.*, p. 813.   [11] *Ibid.*, p. 980.
[12] *Ibid.*, pp. 85, 812, 980.   [13] *Ibid.*, p. 979.

institutions must be sharply distinguished from the instrumental rationality or value-rationality of individuals, rational institutions (in either sense) may presuppose the rationality (in either sense) of the individual agents that make up the staff of these institutions. (i) As just noted, the substantive rationality of *raison d'état* presupposes individual agents endowed with instrumental rationality, i.e. with the capacity to choose the appropriate means to a given end. (ii) Formally rational *economic* action presupposes that the agents of the enterprise are instrumentally rational in the same sense. (iii) Whether an institution is based on formal or substantive rationality, its agents must be subjectively motivated to behave in the way the institution requires them to act. (iii a) This may come about through an attachment to *duty*[14] which is a form of value-rationality.[15] (iii b) It may also come about because the agents are aware of the sanctions they would incur if they failed to do what they are required to do, i.e. if they respond in an instrumentally rational way to career incentives. Although Weber does not discuss this link explicitly, it follows fairly naturally from what he writes in the "*Excursus* in response to Rudolf Stammler"[16] and elsewhere.

III. Rationality, self-interest, and methodological individualism

Economic theory and other social sciences that have adopted the economic approach to human behavior tend to rely on three principles. The first is that of methodological individualism: all social phenomena – including social structure and social change – can in principle be accounted for by explanations that refer only to individuals and their behavior. The second is that of rationality: individuals choose to perform the actions that best realize their desires, given their beliefs (see Section IV below for a fuller statement). The third is that of self-interest: the desires of the individuals are uniformly derived from their self-interest, often considered in the form of material self-interest. In expositions and discussions of rational-choice theory the relation between these three principles is often obscured. Some critics of methodological individualism wrongly assume that it implies rational-choice theory, and can be rebutted by rebutting the latter. Some critics of rational-choice theory wrongly assume that it implies an assumption of self-interest, and can be rebutted by rebutting the latter.

The correct relation, I believe, is the following. Methodological individualism is a form of reductionism, an injunction to explain complex social phenomena in terms of their individual components, much as modern biology tries to explain cellular phenomena in terms of their molecular

[14] *Ibid.*, pp. 264, 959.   [15] *Ibid.*, p. 25   [16] *Ibid.*, pp. 325–333.

components. Like the principle "every event has a cause," it is not a substantive theory, but (as the name implies) a methodological principle the negation of which is not so much false as obscure. The statement that people behave rationally is partly constitutive, partly methodological, partly substantive. It is constitutive in the sense that human beings are characterized by the *desire* to behave rationally.[17] It is methodological in the sense that we have to assume that other people are *by and large* rational if we are to make sense of what they say and do.[18] And it is substantive in the sense that *on any given occasion*, the assumption of rationality is open to empirical confirmation or disconfirmation. The assumption of self-interest is partly methodological, partly substantive. It is methodological in the sense that it is the simplest and most parsimonious motivational hypothesis. Given that it is always better to explain with less than with more, it is hence the natural starting point for any empirical investigation. It is substantive in the sense that on any given occasion, it is open to empirical confirmation or disconfirmation.

It is or should be obvious that methodological individualism does not imply rationality, but is consistent with any motivational assumption or even with the assumption that all individual behavior has a purely reflex character. It is or should be obvious that the assumption of rationality does not imply that behavior is self-interested, but is consistent with any motivational assumption, including those of altruism or envy. It is less obvious that the self-interest assumption fails to imply rationality. Yet a person may well be irrational and act out of self-interest, if he believes that all things considered he ought to choose an altruistic course of action and yet succumbs to weakness of will and chooses the action that best promotes his own interest.

Weber quite explicitly supports a version of methodological individualism when he writes that "for the subjective interpretation of action in sociological work [social collectivities such as states, associations and business corporations] must be treated as *solely* the resultants and modes of organization of the particular acts of individual persons,"[19] and that "for sociological purposes there is no such thing as a collective personality which 'acts.'" Yet his individualism is not a reductionism. Just as Durkheim argued against the view that sociology could be reduced to psychology, Weber writes that it is "erroneous to regard any kind of psychology as the ultimate foundation of the sociological interpretation of

[17] D. Føllesdal, "The Status of Rationality Assumptions in the Interpretation and in the Explanation of Action," *Dialectica*, 36 (1982), 302–16.
[18] Donald Davidson, *Essays on Actions and Events*, Oxford: Oxford University Press, 1980.
[19] Weber, *Economy and Society* (1968), p. 13.

action."[20] Weber did not, however, reject reductionism because he believed that social wholes or aggregates had independent explanatory power. Rather, he objected to the idea that action, and in particular rational action, could be understood in psychological terms:

> The source of error lies in the concept of the "psychic." It is held that everything which is not physical is *ipso facto* psychic. However, the *meaning* of a train of mathematical reasoning which a person carries out is not in the relevant sense "psychic." Similarly the rational deliberation of an actor as to whether the results of a given proposed course of action will or will not promote certain specific interests, and the corresponding decision, do not become one bit more understandable by taking "psychological" considerations into account. But it is precisely on the basis of such rational assumptions that most of the laws of sociology, including those of economics, are built up.[21]

This argument seems misleading. Even when the actual deliberation of the actor possesses the transparency of mathematical reasoning, the choice of premises – which factors to include and which to exclude in the calculation – is a contingent matter that can be illuminated only by empirical psychology. Also, as I argue in Section VI below, even transparent formal reasoning does not always yield a determinate result. Moreover, the advances in cognitive psychology and behavioral economics over the last twenty years show that the deliberation itself is subject to a large number of distorting influences. Weber recognized as much when he wrote that "in explaining the irrationalities of action sociologically, that form of psychology which employs the method of subjective understanding undoubtedly can make decisively important contributions,"[22] adding that this concession to psychology "does not alter the fundamental methodological situation." In my opinion, exactly the opposite is true. In light of the pervasive operation of bias and distortion in human reasoning, the "sociological interpretation of action" must rely on empirical psychology rather than on the idea of mathematical proof. It is because Weber adopted a disembodied notion of (instrumental) rationality that he wrongly concluded that methodological individualism in the social sciences could do without psychology.

Above I briefly sketched an argument for the methodological primacy of rationality over other motivational assumptions: to understand others we have to assume that they are by and large rational. Weber also offers an argument for this primacy, but of a very different kind:

> For the purposes of a typological scientific analysis it is convenient to treat all irrational, affectually determined elements of behavior as factors of deviation

---

[20] *Ibid.*, p. 19.   [21] *Ibid.*   [22] *Ibid.*

from a conceptually pure type of rational action. For example a panic on the stock exchange can be most conveniently analysed by attempting to determine first what the course of action would have been had it not been influenced by irrational affects; it is then possible to introduce the irrational components as accounting for the observed deviations from this hypothetical course. Similarly, in analysing a political or military campaign it is convenient to determine in the first place what would have been a rational course, given the ends of the participants and adequate knowledge of all the circumstances. Only in this way is it possible to assess the causal significance of irrational factors as accounting for the deviations from this type.[23]

This argument poses two problems. First, Weber seems to have an exaggerated view of the uniqueness of rational behavior, or, equivalently, to underestimate the problem of indeterminacy. I return to this question in Section VI below. Second, even assuming that rational-choice theory always and everywhere yields unique prescriptions and predictions, the proposed methodology is flawed. First, Weber ignores the possibility of multiple irrationalities that cancel each other out, with the result that the observed behavior coincides with the rationally prescribed one. To use an example from Kip Viscusi,[24] smokers as well as non-smokers process information about the dangers of smoking in ways that induce exaggerated risk perceptions. On the other hand, smokers are subject to a self-serving bias that induces them to discount the risks. Although the latter bias does not fully cancel the former, it does make the beliefs of smokers more nearly accurate than those of non-smokers. It does not, however, make the beliefs and the subsequent behavior more *rational*. Second – a more esoteric issue – Weber ignores the possibility of "non-standard causal chains" by which the beliefs and desires that would rationalize a certain action cause that action in "the wrong way." In a famous example offered by Donald Davidson,[25]

A climber might want to rid himself of the weight and danger of holding another man on a rope, and he might know that by loosening his hold on the rope he could rid himself of the weight and the danger. This belief and want might so unnerve him as to cause him to lose his hold, and yet it might be the case that he never *chose* to loosen his hold, nor did he do it intentionally.

Although Weber *defines* rationality as action that *is* generated by adequate mental processes, he *identifies* it as action in conformity with what *would be* generated by adequate mental processes. To use Weber's own analogy: if a mathematician reaches a true conclusion by means of

---

[23] *Ibid.*, p. 6.   [24] K. Viscusi, *Smoking*, Oxford: Oxford University Press, 1992.
[25] Davidson, *Essays on Actions and Events*, p. 79

false reasoning, Weber would presumably not call him rational. Nor should he or we assume that emotion and other irrational forces in decision-making are absent when the decision conforms with what a rational agent would have done. Weber goes wrong because he confuses an objective notion of rationality as *success* with the subjective notion of rationality as (roughly speaking) *acting for good reasons*.

Weber's views on the relation between rationality and self-interest are hard to disentangle. We have seen that bureaucratic systems may pursue non-self-interested goals such as *raison d'état* in an instrumentally rational fashion. Yet this does not imply that the agents of bureaucracy embrace these goals as their personal ends and pursue them in a rational manner. As noted above, two other motivational assumptions seem more plausible: a non-instrumental sense of duty and an instrumental concern for their own career. A case of non-self-interested instrumentally rational behavior would be provided by a private agent motivated by benevolence, who chooses among different charitable causes according to where his contribution would do most good. To my knowledge, Weber never discusses cases of that kind. Moreover, in one of his glosses on instrumental rationality[26] Weber seems close to identifying instrumental rationality with self-interest. Here, he repeatedly draws a contrast between instrumentally rational self-interested behavior and value-rational non-self-interested behavior, while entirely ignoring the possibility of instrumentally rational non-self-interested behavior. Yet as I argue in Section V below, that possibility is consistent with his general framework.

IV. Rationality: the standard model

Rational actions (choices, decisions) can be characterized in many ways. The approach taken in modern economics and decision theory, as well as in the other social sciences that take their lead, is resolutely subjective. Rational behavior is not behavior that is objectively optimal or adaptive, but behavior that is optimal from the point of the view of the agent and performed, moreover, because it is perceived to be optimal. Figure 1.1 is a schematic sketch of what I take to be the standard modern account. It is not offered for its own sake, but only as a benchmark for the discussion of Weber in the following sections.

The basic structure of rational behavior is set out in Fig.1.1. Here, the arrows have both a causal interpretation and a normative one. A rational action, for instance, is one that is both caused (in "the right way") by the

[26] Weber, *Economy and Society* (1968), p. 30.

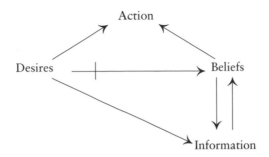

Fig. 1.1 Basic structure of rational behavior

desires and beliefs of the agents and optimal in the light of these desires and beliefs. The same dual condition obtains for belief-formation and information-acquisition. The blocked arrow, about which more later, indicates a causal link that is proscribed on normative grounds.

The model involves three distinct conditions. First, for an action to be rational, it has to be the best means of satisfying the desires of the agent, given his beliefs. In itself, this is a very weak requirement. If I want to kill a person and I believe that the best way of doing so is to make a doll representing him and stick a pin through it, then according to this weak definition I act rationally if I make the doll and pierce it with a pin. We would hardly be satisfied with this conclusion, however, not because the homicidal desire is irrational (it may be immoral, but that is another matter), but because the beliefs are transparently ill- founded.

Second, therefore, we need to stipulate that the beliefs themselves are rational, in the sense of being grounded in the information that is available to the agent. These may be beliefs about factual matters or about general lawlike connections. In particular, they will include beliefs about the *opportunities* available to the agent. In fact, rational-choice theory is often stated in terms of desires and opportunities rather than desires and beliefs. In that "reduced" version, the theory says that a rational agent chooses the most-preferred element in his opportunity set. Sometimes, this formulation is adequate enough. For some purposes, rational-choice theory can be summarized by saying that *people do as well as they can*. In general, however, we need to take account of the fact that the full set of objective opportunities available to the agent may not be known to him. Today, for instance, governments do not really know whether it is possible to develop commercially viable fusion power. Or, to take a more mundane example, an automobilist arriving in an unknown city without a map will not know the full set of routes that will take him through it. Applied to this situation, the theory says that *people do as well as they believe they can*.

In such cases, the agent must use whatever information he has to form some belief or subjective estimate of the alternatives. As noted, the fact that it is subjective does not in itself detract from its rationality. To be rational does not mean that one is invariably successful in realizing one's aims, only that one has no reason, after the fact, to think that one should have acted differently. Nor does a rational belief have to be true, only well-grounded in the available information. Beliefs are rational if they are formed by procedures that (are believed to) produce more true beliefs in the long run than any alternative procedure, but on any particular occasion the belief thus formed may not correspond to the facts. Beliefs are irrational when they are shaped by distorting influences of various kinds. Some of these are more in the nature of mistakes, as when people fail to observe simple principles of statistical inference. Others, however, belong to the category of *motivated irrationality*, as when the adding-up errors made by a salesman systematically (although non-intentionally) work out to his favor.

However, a belief is not made rational simply by being well grounded in the available information. If the automobilist is in a hurry, he should perhaps buy a map to acquire more information about the feasible routes. The third condition for rational behavior, therefore, is that the agent should acquire an optimal amount of information, or more accurately, invest an optimal amount of time, energy and money in gathering such information. Clearly, it will often be irrational not to invest any time in collecting information. If one is buying a house or a car, one should compare several options and investigate each of them in some depth. Equally clearly, there are occasions when there is a danger of gathering too much information. If a doctor makes too many tests before deciding on treatment, the patient may die under his hands. A general who insists on accurate information about the enemy's movement before attacking, can easily be taken by surprise. In between these extremes, there exists an optimal level of search, a "golden mean." Whether one can *know* where this optimum is located is another matter.

At any given time, an individual will have certain beliefs about the costs and value of acquiring new information. Once again, what he does must be assessed in the light of those beliefs, not in the light of what an external observer might deem optimal. The eye cannot see farther than its horizon. We can, therefore, give a third and final statement of rational-choice theory, as the principle that *people make the most out of what they have*, including their beliefs and their preferences.

As depicted in Fig.1.1, there are several factors which determine the amount of information that a rational agent will gather. The agent's beliefs about the expected costs and expected value of gathering the information will obviously matter. His desires – i.e. how important the decision is to him – will also enter into the calculus. Indirectly, therefore, the desires of the agents will enter into the process of belief formation. However, the blocked arrow from desires to beliefs in Fig.1.1 is intended to indicate that a direct influence, as in wishful thinking, is inadmissible. Although Hume said that "Reason is, and ought only to be, the slave of the passions,"[27] he did not mean that passion should be allowed to set itself up as an arbitrary tyrant. Even a slave needs some independence to serve his master well; beliefs born of passion serve passion badly.

Rationality thus defined can fail in two ways: by indeterminacy and by irrationality. On the one hand, any one of the optimality operations in Fig.1.1 might fail to yield a unique solution. On the other hand, even when the optimal outcome is uniquely defined, the agent might fail to conform to it, or might conform "in the wrong way." (Irrationality can also arise in cases of partial indeterminacy, but for present purposes there is no need to develop this point.) At the levels of belief-formation and information-acquisition, irrationality can arise either by "hot" mechanisms such as wishful thinking or by "cold" mechanisms that involve various (unmotivated) cognitive confusions. At the level of action or choice, irrationality can take the form of weakness of will or of spontaneous "visceral behavior"[28] in which ends-means reasoning is short-circuited.

V. Weber on action

Although extremely well known, Weber's taxonomy of action[29] is both so central to the present article and so briefly stated that a full reproduction seems appropriate:

Social action, like all action, may be oriented in four ways. It may be:

(1) *instrumentally rational (zweckrational)*, that is, determined by expectations as to the behavior of objects in the environment and of other human beings; these expectations are used as "conditions" or "means" for the attainment of the actor's own rationally pursued and calculated ends;

(2) *value-rational (wertrational)*, that is, determined by a conscious belief

[27] D. Hume, *A Treatise on Human Nature*, ed. L. A. Selby-Bigge, Oxford: Oxford University Press, 1970, p. 415.

[28] G. Loewenstein, "Out of Control: Visceral Influences on Behavior," *Organizational Behavior and Human Decision Processes*, 65 (1996), pp. 272–292.

[29] Weber, *Economy and Society* (1968), pp. 24–25.

in the value for its own sake of some ethical, aesthetic, religious, or other form of behavior, independently of its prospects of success;

(3)   *affectual* (especially emotional), that is, determined by the actor's specific affects and feeling states;

(4)   *traditional*, that is, determined by ingrained habituation.

A few pages later[30] Weber introduces some additional concepts, whose relation to these four categories is not entirely clear. First, there are "customs," or usages "based on long-standing practice." "The actor conforms with them of his own free will, whether his motivation lies in the fact that he merely fails to think about it, that it is more comfortable to conform, or whatever else the reason may be." If we rely only on the explicit definitions, the concept of customary behavior seems very close or even identical to that of traditional behavior, characterized as "a matter of almost automatic reaction to habitual stimuli which guide behavior in a course which has been repeatedly followed."[31] In a later passage (written earlier), Weber asserts that convention transforms custom into tradition: "It is by way of conventional rules that merely factual regularities of action, i.e., customs, are frequently transformed into binding norms, guaranteed primarily by psychological coercion. Convention thus makes tradition. The mere fact of the regular recurrence of certain events somehow confers on them the dignity of oughtness."[32] Custom is "devoid of any external sanction . . . conformity with it is not 'demanded' by anybody."[33]

Custom is maintained by two different mechanisms. On the one hand, "the stability of merely customary action rests essentially on the fact that the person who does not adapt himself to it is subjected to both petty and major inconveniences and annoyances as long as the majority of the people he comes in contact with continue to uphold the custom and conform to it."[34] In this sense, customs are what we may call *coordination equilibria* (not to be confused with conventions in Weber's sense: see below). On the other hand, the more action is determined by custom, "the more disquieting are the effects of any deviation from the customary. In this situation, any such deviation seems to act on the psyche of the average individual like the disturbance of an organic function."[35] Thus characterized, custom seems much more like *habits*, as exemplified by a person who feels upset when the morning newspaper doesn't arrive on time. In the following I only consider

---

[30] *Ibid.*, pp. 29–30.   [31] *Ibid.*, p. 26.

[32] *Ibid.*, p. 326. The word I have translated as "custom" (*Sitte*) is here rendered as "usage." Earlier in the work, however, Weber's distinction between "*Brauch*" and "*Sitte*" is rendered as a distinction between "usage" and "custom."

[33] *Ibid.*, p. 29.   [34] *Ibid.*, p. 30.   [35] *Ibid.*, p. 320.

customs in the sense of coordination equilibria. They differ from tradition in that deviation from the latter triggers expressions of disapproval rather than "inconveniences and annoyances."

Conventions – the mechanism that transforms custom into tradition – are in fact regularities of behavior whose "validity is externally guaranteed by the probability that deviation from it within a given social group will result in a relatively general and practically significant reaction of disapproval."[36] In my terminology,[37] what Weber here calls conventions are *social norms*. Sexual behavior, for instance, is conventionally regulated in this sense.[38] An example of pure customary behavior is not easy to find. The standard example of driving on the right side of the road is somewhat imperfect, since those who unilaterally drive on the left not only run the risk of an accident, but also expose themselves to the disapproval of other drivers. The reason – which holds quite generally for coordination equilibria – is that each actor not only wants to drive on the right as long as others do, but also wants others to drive on the right as long as he does. If one actor deviates, he may not only harm himself but also others, who will tend to react with disapproval. In some cases, however, the harm which the deviation imposes on others may be so small or hard to notice that the actor only incurs practical inconvenience without any disapproval. If I buy an unusual and (therefore) expensive brand of shoes, I may infinitesimally lower the demand for and raise the price of the customary brand which is produced more cheaply through economies of scale, but nobody will be affected enough to express disapproval on that ground. They may, however, express disapproval of my shoes on other grounds. As Weber notes, *fashion* is located "in the neighborhood of 'convention.' "[39] If I wear brown shoes with black dress, others may express their disapproval, although nobody is harmed. Some social norms may have their origin in the fact that deviations from the norm harm others, but not all do.

If customs, conventions and tradition are maintained by the disapproval or practical inconvenience that are incurred in the case of deviation, it might seem as if these categories of action can be assimilated to instrumental rationality. Suppose that an actor contemplates the choice between the conventional, customary or traditional option and a deviant alternative. If the disapproval or inconvenience is moderate and the advantages of the alternative are considerable, he might choose to deviate; otherwise the disapproval or inconvenience will deter him from deviating. This seems to

[36] *Ibid.*, p. 34.
[37] Jon Elster, *The Cement of Society*, Cambridge: Cambridge University Press, 1989.
[38] Weber, *Economy and Society* (1968), p. 607.   [39] *Ibid.*, p. 29.

be a matter of simple cost-benefit analysis, which does not call for any additional conceptual machinery. In the case of pure customary behavior, this conclusion seems justified. Annoyance avoidance is a straightforward principle of instrumental rationality. In the case of convention and tradition, however, the conclusion is not justified. In the first place, disapproval typically deters action through actual or anticipated *shame*, as noted by Weber in the case of sexual behavior.[40] As I argue elsewhere,[41] shame is a causal force capable of distorting judgment and affecting behavior over and above whatever impact it might have as a "cost." In the second place, we must ask whether the expression of disapproval by others is always instrumentally rational. In the general case, I believe, it is not.[42]

In his gloss on the category of affectual behavior, Weber notes that "action is affectual if it satisfies a need for revenge, sensual gratification, devotion, contemplative bliss, or for working off emotional tensions."[43] This is a rather unsatisfactory and hodge-podge list, confused by the fact that revenge (certainly) and sensual gratification (arguably) *are* ways of working off emotional tension. There is nothing to indicate that Weber had thought much or deeply about the role of emotion (the most important aspect of affect) in behavior, an exception being his analyses of shame and guilt in religious and secular life. According to modern psychological analyses of these two emotions[44] they differ in two main respects. On the one hand, shame is triggered by the thought "I am a bad person," whereas guilt is caused by the thought "I committed a bad action." On the other hand, shame induces a tendency to hide or disappear, whereas the action tendency of guilt is to confess or make reparations.

Weber was well aware of the link between shame and character. He refers to

> that distinctive type of "shame" . . . which characterizes modern secular man precisely because of his own *Gesinnungsethik* . . . Not that he has *done* a particular deed, but that by virtue of his unalterable qualities, acquired without his cooperation, he "*is*" such that he *could* commit the deed – this is the secret anguish born by modern man.[45]

Commenting on an episode in Herodotus, he writes that

---

[40] *Ibid.*, p. 607.
[41] Jon Elster, "Emotions and Economic Theory," *Journal of Economic Literature*, 36 (1998), pp. 47–74.
[42] Elster, *The Cement of Society*, pp. 132–133.
[43] Weber, *Economy and Society* (1968), p. 25.
[44] Summarized in Jon Elster, *Alchemies of the Mind*, Cambridge: Cambridge University Press, 1999, ch. III.
[45] Weber, *Economy and Society* (1968), p. 576. Here "*Scham*" is mistranslated as "guilt."

It is instructive to recall the attitude of the more rigorous Spartans toward a comrade who had fallen in battle in order to atone for an earlier manifestation of cowardice – a kind of "redeeming duel." They did not regard him as having rehabilitated his ethical status, since he had acted bravely for a specific reason and not "out of the totality of his personality," as we would term it. In the religious sphere, too, formal sanctification by the good works shown in external actions is supplanted by the value of the total personality pattern, which in the Spartan example would be an habitual temper of heroism.[46]

Although Weber does not use emotion terms here, his argument is essentially that shameful behavior – unlike guilt – cannot be undone by a punctual action, since it flows from the personality as a whole. He draws on this distinction in his analysis of Catholicism, where "it is particularly important that sins remain discrete actions, against which discrete deeds may be set up as compensations or penances. Hence, value is attached to concrete individual acts rather than to a total personality pattern produced by asceticism, contemplation, or eternally vigilant self-control."[47] Yet his argument is *not* that Catholicism instills guilt that can only be undone by confession or penance. Rather, it is that the institutionalization of these practices reduces the intensity of guilt in the sinner, and "spares him the necessity of developing an individual pattern of life based on ethical foundations."[48] The comment is profound, and may have far-reaching implications for emotion theory. It suggests that if norms and institutions are created to encourage the actions that tend to flow naturally from specific emotions, the situations that would normally produce those emotions may cease to do so.

According to Weber, affectual behavior and value-rational behavior "have a common element, namely that the meaning of the action does not lie in the achievement of a result ulterior to it, but in carrying out the specific type of action for its own sake."[49] Yet value-rational action differs from affectual behavior "by its clearly self-conscious formulation of the ultimate values governing the action and the consistently planned orientation of its detailed course to these values." Whereas an emotional person may literally ignore the costs of a risky action in the passion of the moment, the value-rational person may be fully aware of the costs while not letting them affect his decision. Weber observes, however, that not all emotional behavior takes the form of "uncontrolled reaction to some exceptional stimulus," as when we spontaneously strike out in anger upon receiving a particularly offensive insult. It may also take the form of "conscious release of emotional tension. When this happens it is usually

---

[46] *Ibid.*, p. 534.   [47] *Ibid.*, p. 561   [48] *Ibid.*
[49] All quotations in this paragraph are from *ibid.*, p. 25.

well on the road to rationalization, in one or the other or both of the above senses [instrumental rationality and value-rationality]." In feuding societies, for instance, emotionally charged revenge behavior has elements of both kinds of rationality. Revenge is an unconditional duty and to that extent value-rational; yet it is often carried out with great tactical and strategic skills and to that extent guided by instrumental rationality. There is ends-means reasoning, but revenge is the end, not a means to anything else.

This example points to an ambiguity in the notion of value-rationality. On the one hand, value-rationality may be oriented towards behavior that is within the immediate control of the agent, as in "Thou shalt not kill" or "Turn the other cheek." In such cases, instrumental rationality has no purchase. On the other hand, value-rationality may be oriented towards behavior that requires favorable external circumstances which the actor has to create. If a man insults my sister in my absence, I may have to deploy considerable ingenuity in tracking him down so that I can take revenge, yet this instrumental rationality in the choice of means does not make the behavior less value-rational.[50] Instrumental rationality may also be harnessed to the service of pure emotional behavior without any element of value-rationality, if the revenge is purely personal rather than embodied in a system of social norms and obligations. Revenge may also, of course, be nothing more than instrumentally rational behavior for purposes of deterrence. We see, therefore, how one and the same general type of behavior – harming those who harm oneself – may be (i) purely emotional, (ii) purely instrumentally rational, (iii) value-rational and instrumentally rational and (iv) emotional and instrumentally rational. If the situation is such that revenge is perceived as a duty and the agent is in a position to carry it out immediately, it may also be (v) purely value-rational.

Weber's notion of instrumental rationality emphasizes *efficiency* rather than *consistency*. In terms of Fig.1.1, he interprets the "desires" as "goals" rather than as "preferences." Although this approach makes good sense for the analysis of economic and political decisions, it is less suitable for consumer decisions. In modern economic theory, utility is not some kind of substantive objective function – analogous to profits – that the consumer tries to maximize. Utility is a simple shorthand for preferences, and rationality means nothing more than the choice of the most preferred option in the feasible set, subject to consistency constraints. Although the preference approach is more general than the ends-means approach, it might seem *too* general. If emotions and values are conceptualized as preferences, behavior based on these motivations is just as rational as

---

[50] *Ibid.*, p. 26.

normal market behavior as long as the consistency constraints are satisfied, and no further distinctions might seem possible or required.

Yet I believe it is possible to capture the specificity of value-rationality and emotional behavior within the preference approach. In the case of value-rationality, a distinction may be made on the basis of the absolute priority of the value in question over all other concerns. The appropriate tool for behavior guided by a dominant value is the idea of *lexicographic preferences*, which excludes the possibility of a trade-off between the value in question and other goods. In the case of emotional behavior, one might add that emotions do not only shape preferences: they also distort beliefs. In terms of Fig.1.1, emotions act on each of the proximate causes of action. Although emotional behavior might seem rational if we only consider its relation to the underlying preferences, it can easily appear to be irrational if we also take account of the impact of emotions on beliefs.

VI. Some omissions in Weber's theory of rationality

Weber's analysis of instrumentally rational behavior and its relation to other modes of behavior is for the most part clear and convincing. Yet in light of modern decision theory I think it is possible to assert that it contains several important omissions.

Weber ignores that since the rationality of action depends on the rationality of the beliefs on which it is based, a theory of rational behavior must include a theory of rational belief-formation and of optimal information-acquisition. Consider for instance the following passage: "From the standpoint of animistic symbolism's own basic assumptions its therapeutic methods might be regarded as rational, but they bear the same relation to empirical therapy as astrology, which grew from the same roots, bears to empirical computation of the calendar."[51] Weber does not ask the (for us) obvious question, viz. whether the cognitive assumptions themselves are rational or irrational. It is clear that they were *false*, but truth and rationality are two different matters. As Gerry Mackie has shown,[52] people may find themselves in a *belief trap* if they entertain false beliefs that cannot be revised because *the believed costs of testing the belief are too high*. From their point of view, the false belief is rational.

The most striking instance of this omission or neglect occurs in Weber's famous discussions of Protestant sects, in *Economy and Society* as well as

---

[51] *Ibid.*, p. 406.
[52] G. Mackie, "Ending Footbindings and Infibulation; A Convention Account," *American Sociological Review*, 61 (1996), pp. 999–1017.

in *The Protestant Ethic and the Spirit of Capitalism.* On the one hand, he asserts over and over again that the practitioners of "innerworldly asceticism" behaved rationally, in fact were paradigms of rationality.[53] On the other hand, he argues that underlying their rational effort was the belief that it would enable them to achieve *certitudo salutis.* Given their belief in predestination, they could not hold that rational effort would bring them salvation, but they could and did hold that it would give them the subjective certainty of salvation.[54]

This conflation of causal and diagnostic efficacy[55] is quite common. An even more explicit example than anything cited by Weber is given by E.P. Thompson:[56]

> It was not until 1770 that the Particular Baptists began to break out of the trap of their own dogma, issuing a circular letter (from Northamptonshire) which offered a formula by which evangelism and the notion of election might be reconciled: "Every soul that comes to Christ to be saved . . . is to be encouraged . . . The coming soul need not fear that he is not elected, for none but such would be willing to come."

The conflation is also, however, a paradigm of irrationality. One might say about the Protestant sects what Weber says about the animists: their behavior was rational, but only within their framework of magical thinking.

Thus Weber does not explicitly confront the issue that behavior cannot be more rational than the beliefs on which it is based. Nor does he confront the issue that the implications of rationality for behavior might be indeterminate because the rationality of the underlying beliefs is indeterminate. In particular, he entirely neglects *strategic behavior* as a source of belief indeterminacy. Elaborating on his methodology for determining the importance of irrational factors in behavior, Weber writes that

> in attempting to explain the campaign of 1866, it is indispensable both in the case of Moltke and of Benedek to attempt to construct imaginatively how each, given fully adequate knowledge both of his own situation and of that of his opponent, would have acted. Then it is possible to compare this with the actual course of action and to arrive at a causal explanation of the observed deviations.[57]

53 Weber, *Economy and Society* (1968), pp. 436, 479, 498, 575.
54 *Ibid.,* p. 115.
55 G. Quattrone and A. Tversky, "Self-deception and the Voter's Illusion," in J. Elster (ed.), *The Multiple Self*, Cambridge: Cambridge University Press, pp. 35–58; Elster, *The Cement of Society*, pp. 196–200.
56 E. P. Thompson, *The Making of the English Working Class*, Harmondsworth: Penguin Books, 1968, p. 38.
57 Weber, *Economy and Society* (1968), p. 21.

Weber does not seem to be aware of the need to "construct imaginatively" how each of Moltke and Benedek would try to "construct imaginatively" what the other would be doing, including their further constructive imaginings, and so on. Nor of course was he aware of the difficulties in doing so that have become increasingly apparent in recent years. In any complex social situation, multiple equilibria seem to be the rule rather than the exception. To take an extreme example, in some three-person games *any* behavior is an equilibrium, i.e. *no* behavior can be rejected as irrational.[58]

It would be absurd to criticize Weber for not having invented game theory. My point is only that because Weber – understandably – focused his attention on parametric rationality, he formed an exaggerated belief in the ability of the human mind to determine in all situations the uniquely rational course of action. If the rationality of behavior depends on the rationality of the beliefs underlying it, and if beliefs about the expected behavior of a strategic adversary are essentially indeterminate, then rationality, too, will often be indeterminate. We can add that Weber implicitly seems to have focused exclusively on decision-making under certainty and under risk, while ignoring decision-making under uncertainty – another source of belief-indeterminacy. To assess the rationality of the Los Angeles City Council with respect to earthquake prevention, we would have to know something about (what the council could rationally believe about) the probability of earthquakes of various strengths within a given time period. The fact is, however, that at present there is no scientific basis for assigning numerical probabilities to these events. In these situations of uncertainty, there is often a wide range of beliefs and behaviors that are consistent with the canons of rationality,[59] and hence it is often difficult to exclude any specific action as obviously irrational.

Conclusion

Weber's analyses of action and rationality display a stunning depth of insight. Although the crucial theoretical statements are extremely compact, a close reading shows that he was aware of the full range of human motivations and the ways in which they affect behavior. Among his main accomplishments I would list the following. (i) The analysis of the role of emotion in human behavior, including a distinction between spontaneous

---

[58] J. Sutton, "Non-cooperative Bargaining Theory: An Introduction," *Review of Economic Studies*, 53 (1986), pp. 709–724.

[59] K. Arrow and L. Hurwicz, "An Optimality Criterion for Decision-making under Uncertainty," in C. F. Carter and J. L. Ford (eds.), *Uncertainty and Expectation in Economics*, Clinton, NJ: Kelley, 1972, pp. 1–11.

emotions that short-circuit instrumental rationality and more durable emotions that can harness instrumental rationality to their ends. (ii) The analysis of three ways in which human behavior can be guided by general principles: by unconditional adherence to a value, by anticipation of disapproval caused by deviating from social norms, and by anticipation of practical inconvenience caused by deviating from a coordination equilibrium. (iii) The recognition of the role of emotions, notably shame, in regulating social norms. (iv) The discussions of guilt and shame, including their cognitive antecedents and their typical action tendencies. As noted initially, this enumeration may be somewhat idiosyncratic. Paradoxically, perhaps, I find Weber's analysis of irrational behavior (including value-rational behavior) more illuminating than his dissection of instrumental rationality.

This dissection does, in fact, seem to have some severe flaws. (v) Weber does not integrate his analysis of rational action with the analysis of rational belief-formation and information-acquisition. (vi) In particular, because of his neglect of strategic behavior he ignores the importance of *beliefs about beliefs* when several actors have to reach mutually interdependent decisions. (vii) Because of his focus on the probable consequences of behavior, he ignores cases of brute uncertainty in which it is impossible to attach numerical probabilities to the possible outcomes. (viii) For these various reasons, Weber exaggerated the uniqueness of what would be rational behavior in any given situation. (ix) From this mistake another mistake follows, namely the idea that the importance of irrational behavior in a given situation can be measured by first determining what the rational course of action would have been and then comparing it with actual behavior. (x) This idea is also invalid for another reason, namely that the rationality of behavior cannot be read off the behavior directly without knowledge of the way in which it was brought about.

The basic problem in Weber's writings on these issues is perhaps his failure to see how objective success and subjective rationality can deviate from each other. A person's behavior may be objectively appropriate and yet not be the end result of rational deliberations. Conversely, a person may act rationally if the beliefs on which he bases his decision are warranted *ex ante*, even if they are proved wrong *ex post*. Although Weber consistently emphasized the need to understand behavior as subjectively meaningful, he did not draw the full consequences from this idea. The closing pages of the *Protestant Ethic* suggest that he was influenced by the fact that *market competition* tends to generate objectively successful behavior, by its ruthless elimination of those who fail. To the extent that this is the case, we can explain behavior by invoking external necessity rather than by searching for its inner springs. It turns out, however, that the objective mechanism of competition is as indeterminate in its workings as the subjective rule of acting on good reasons.[60] Some inefficient firms survive, and some efficient ones go under. Whether approached from a subjective or an objective angle, the idea of rationality has less purchase on behavior than Weber thought.

[60] R. Nelson and S. Winter, *An Evolutionary Theory of Economic Change*, Cambridge, MA.: Harvard University Press, 1982.

2

ALAN SICA

Rationalization and culture

Current uses of Weber's rationalization theme

"Rationalization" is a sturdy device for appraising Weber's primary achievements. It is superior to other possible choices (charisma, value-freedom, ideal-types, status groups, bureaucratization), because Weber's best working years were spent exploring it. In addition, this key set of linked processes, unlike other phenomena he studied in detail, still seems to be enlarging its range of meaning in contemporary societies rather than becoming a part of inessential history. Paradoxically, rationalization might also be viewed as the simplest to understand of all Weber's principal innovations to social and economic thought. His discovery, if it can be so called, held that modern societies are forever striving to order what in its "natural" state is less ordered or even randomly occurring. Where people once noisily milled about, now they are put in rows or ranks of quiet obedience; where fiscal accounting was done from memory and rough approximation, now it is taken to the hundredth of one percentage point, or beyond; where music was the work of a single minstrel inventing melodies and lyrics as he strolled, now it requires an orchestra that plays perfectly in unison from a printed score, willful deviation from which is a cardinal sin. Weber realized that the organization of thought and action into regimented forms had virtually replaced religion as the unquestioned, motivating creed across much of "advanced civilization." And while he recognized in these developments admirable achievements, particularly in the production of material goods, he saw as well those seedbeds of pathology that affected individuals as much as the societies in which they struggled, vainly he thought, to maintain their individuality and freedom.

For Weber, rationalization processes were ubiquitous and unconquerable. This is so much the case that it, more than his other major themes, readily lends itself to popular expression in a number of forms. For example, the rationalization theme has inspired a sequence of memorable formulations as cinema. In 1973 when George Lucas was twenty-nine – long before he bequeathed lasting images to the iconography of popular culture, via his Star Wars movies, the Indiana Jones trilogy, and *Tucker* (about the visionary auto designer) – he wrote, directed, and edited the futurist anti-romance, *THX 1138*. In this moody, under-stated entry into the dystopian literature genre, the protagonist (Robert Duvall), for reasons unclear even to himself, cannot manage to ingest State-required quantities of daily sedatives. In this emotionless world of Lucas' devising, owing equal parts to *Brave New World* and the film, *2001*, passion is illegal, and interpersonal attachment literally unthinkable. When Duvall's character inconveniently wishes to maintain a longer involvement with his "computer-selected mate" than the State condones, paranoidal chase scenes and authoritarian terrorism bring the movie to an inevitably bleak ending. The film's audience – even if unaware of Huxley, Kafka, or Orwell as novelists – is by now thoroughly familiar with the principal motif: substantive irrationality accompanying cruel rationalization of social behavior, portrayed not only in *THX 1138*, but in numerous sister films, e.g., *Brazil*, the Mad Max series, and *Kafka*. The lone hero, constitutionally incapable of long-term obedience, rails against a social system that combines incomprehensibility, mean-spiritedness, and maddening benevolence of a purely cosmetic nature. But rebellion almost always fails, as state-sponsored order maintains its grim grip upon those whose desire for autonomy conflict with its demand for predictable and standardized social action.

In the slower but broader world of print, Weber's ideas about rationalized processes have been drawn upon in endless forms, sometimes almost in caricature. This was demonstrated some years ago when Ritzer in a short statement introduced his audience to the "McDonaldization" of social relations,[1] his inspiration being Weber. By invoking this term for sociological purposes, Ritzer hoped to show that practices common to US "fast food" chains had taken the rationalization of restaurant work to a previously unknown extreme. That his remarks grow ever more pertinent was demonstrated not long ago in three Associated Press stories. The first explained that with 20,160 US McDonald's restaurants operating as of September, 1996, having fed 95 percent of the nation's people at least once, almost no town of any size has escaped this company's version of culinary

---

[1] George Ritzer, "The McDonaldization of Society," *Journal of American Culture*, 6 (1983), pp. 100–107; see also Ritzer's *The McDonaldization of Society*, Newbury Park, CA: Pine Forge Press, 1994, and Ritzer, *Sociological Beginnings: On the Origins of Key Ideas in Sociology*, New York: McGraw-Hill, 1994, pp. 131–157 for an autobiographical account of Ritzer's interest in the problem, and his audience's enthusiasm for it, itself an interesting bit of quasi-Weberian data.

delight.[2] More intriguingly, an attached story revealed that political scientists have noted a correlation between the opening of McDonald's restaurants abroad and the beginnings of peaceful life in previously unruly societies. The "Golden Arches Theory of Conflict Prevention" reflects the restaurant's presence in 102 countries (along with its having achieved for the first time more brand recognition worldwide than Coca-Cola). In order to "qualify" for McDonald's presence, a nation must provide a steady supply of safe beef, reliable labor, construction companies of merit, and a lack of governmental red tape, all geared to the same, rationalized end: "McDonald's understands that its success lies in delivering consistency." And while the company is losing market share in the States, it is fast improving its balance sheet abroad (thus imitating the tobacco industry).[3]

Even more Weberian than these hamburger tales is the new development in the US, where McDonald's is trying to survive by lessening the time it takes to order and receive one's food. By using an array of robots, computers, and associated equipment, the restaurant can guarantee delivery of an order within ninety seconds at rush hour, or forty-five seconds at calmer moments, in those sixty-four experimental outlets where the technology is in place. The underlying assumption behind this extraordinary capital investment – that speed of delivery is more important to consumers than the nature of what is delivered – does not receive mention either by the journalist, nor the company's officials.[4] Perhaps surprisingly, there are still other serious students of "McDonaldization" who view the entire enterprise as a form of cultural fascism, which implants corrosive behavior and demand patterns, especially among children, that would be the envy of any authoritarian regime, e.g., "The benign nature of capitalist production portrayed by McDonaldland and Ronald McDonald is a cover for a far more savage reality."[5]

Even if the unblushing Americanization of Weber's global concept that is embodied in so-called "McDonaldization" – said to be viewed abroad as a credible snapshot of extant US culture – lacks the profundity and breadth

[2] Ted Anthony, "McDonald's Moves into All Segments of Society," Associated Press (July 15, 1997), from Coudersport, PA.
[3] Tom Hundley, "It's Been a Proven Fact [sic] : Peace Follows Franchise," Associated Press (July 15, 1997), from Kiev, Ukraine.
[4] Cliff Edwards, "Back to the McFuture: Technology Creates Faster Service, Tastier Food," Associated Press (July 21, 1997), from Colorado Springs, CO.
[5] Michael Raphael, "Professor Argues McDonald's Brainwashes Youth," Associated Press, Aug. 1, 1997 (State College, PA), reporting on Joe Kincheloe's "McDonald's, Power, and Children: Ronald McDonald (a. k. a. Ray Kroc) Does It All for You," a chapter in *Kinderculture: The Corporate Construction of Childhood*, Boulder, CO: Westview Press, 1997.

typical of Weber's own writing, it nevertheless has its uses (perhaps as "Weber lite"). For it points toward a cognate set of events and developments which first took hold in western societies, but has since spread over the globe, particularly among the richer countries. Like no other coherent grouping of changes in behavior, the rationalization of social and economic life has made the world a different place from what it was before the process became entrenched, affecting every aspect of private and public life for anyone who cannot or will not escape its grasp. Weber, of course, did not discover this all by himself, but he put the process under a special, comparative lens that only he knew how to grind to proper dimensions.

The range of alterations associated with rationalization is nearly synonymous with the most telling changes in world history over the last two centuries. The way war is waged, business is carried out, learning codified, and personal life experienced, then evaluated – to begin what could easily become an endless list – have endured a transformation so thorough that picturing a pre-rationalized world becomes ever more a feat of imagination granted only to the most gifted historians, novelists, and film-makers.

One way to visualize this is to examine antique college yearbooks, or, better yet, stroll through a vintage gymnasium, finding the hall of fame where yellowed photographs of yesterday's athletic heroes are mounted – say, those from around the turn of the century – and then to study their bodies carefully.

They are leaner, of course, often taller, and more muscular than was normal at the time. Yet very few look anything like the "sculpted" bodies expected within athletic programs today, where height, weight, body fat, muscularity, and all sorts of internally measured variables are analyzed by computer in order to find the "ideal" for any given athlete and the position they wish to play on a specific team. In fact, one of Weber's other gifts to theoretical terminology, the "ideal-type," finds almost perfect expression in the idealized model against which the individual athlete's physical condition and appearance are measured. Sports medicine, kinesiology, and all manner of related specializations, themselves only recently "rationalized," aim to protect, repair, and improve the athletic body – to produce a physical specimen impossible to better. Taken together, they amount to a rationalization of the haphazard in an almost pure form. Sports in the last century – in collegiate or family settings, whether for aristocrats or the lower orders, and for which one either had a "knack" or did not, and therefore pursued mainly for sociability and pleasure – are now entirely altered into global business opportunities, underwritten by electronic mass culture. And the professionals in charge of shaping bodies suitable for the highest level play, or of designing equipment that can speed up the game (e.g., wooden versus composite tennis rackets) have some time ago reached the status of quasi-science, all in pursuit of that winning millisecond.

In like manner, what since Ovid and Sappho were regarded as the "irrational" pleasures of sexual activity have lately found their sports analogues in the rationalized business that supplies therapists, instructional materials, and talk-groups, wherein one's inability to reach "the perfect game" are attacked frontally. The underlying assumption to this form of rationalization holds that golf strokes and sexual movements are both kinesiological phenomena, thus equally susceptible to deliberate analysis and improvement. The "mental aspect" of each, much harder to dissect and explain, eludes complete rationalization, but this, it is argued, is merely a temporary setback in the pursuit of complete understanding and inevitable perfectibility.

All of this, oddly enough, points toward something first noted in 1744 by the great iconoclast, Vico, in his *New Science*. As Momigliano explains:

> The basic difference between Vico and Gibbon was, of course, that Vico was interested in barbarism as the root of civilization itself and studied barbarism not as a problem of degeneration but as the matrix of language, poetry, law, and ultimately of reason. Conversely he realized – the first to do so – that too much reason could lead back to barbarism: there was such a thing for him as the *barbarie della reflessione*,

which, he believed, did not affect "the mind of the pagan *bestioni*" as it did the more civilized folk. "Vico did not dream of preferring barbaric law to Roman law. But reason was insufficient to keep control beyond a certain point. Barbaric laws had come as an unavoidable *ricorso*."[6] This foreshadows by centuries Karl Mannheim's observation (borrowed from Weber) that an excrescence of the formally rational, whether in social organization or in thinking, always leads to substantive irrationality.[7] Or, as acutely expressed by a former graduate student who studied Weber with Lawrence Scaff and myself, after spending six months in the "real world" of bureau-

---

[6] Arnaldo Momigliano, "Gibbon from an Italian Point of View," in G.W. Bowersock, John Clive, and Stephen R. Graubard (eds.), *Edward Gibbon and the Decline and Fall of the Roman Empire*, Cambridge: Harvard University Press, 1977, pp. 75–85, at 78–79. See also Momigliano's "Vico's *Scienza Nuova*: Roman 'Bestioni' and Roman 'Eroi,'" in his *Essays in Ancient and Modern Historiography*, Middletown, CT: Wesleyan University Press, 1982, pp. 253–276, as well as Mark Lilla, *G.B. Vico: The Making of an Anti-Modern*, Cambridge, MA: Harvard University Press, 1993, esp. pp. 209–217.

[7] Karl Mannheim, *Man and Society in an Age of Reconstruction: Studies in Modern Social Structure*, London: Routledge & Kegan Paul, 1940, pp. 39–75, "Rational and Irrational Elements"; see also *Rational and Irrational Elements in Contemporary Society*, L.T. Hobhouse Memorial Trust Lectures, No. 4; Mar. 7, 1934, London: Humphrey Milford/Oxford University Press, 1934.

cracy: "I'm beginning to think that George Orwell was the greatest prophet who ever lived."[8] If these juxtapositions – modern sports fetishization, Vico's concern about the *ricorso* to barbarism, interpersonal fascism in today's soft-voiced bureaucracy – seem forced or confusing, let us reduce the apparent lack of fit by viewing them through the conceptual apparatus which Weber built while he combined historical phenomena even more (apparently) incommensurable.

Weber's ideas themselves

The conventional wisdom about Weber, and those myriad textbook treatments which purvey and sustain it, argues that analyzing and describing "the rationalization process" inspired and organized his lifework, and therefore should serve as the master-key to the treasure chamber of the Weberian castle. One particularly strong version of this argument was first announced in Germany by Tenbruck, then distributed in the Anglophone market by others (e.g., Kalberg; Casanova).[9] Yet some noted Weber scholars (e.g., Hennis; Roth; Schluchter),[10] while disagreeing about much else, concur that this is not the best or most "correct" reading of Weber,

---

[8] The same former Weber student recently sent me new company guidelines from her redesigned workplace, where transparent cubicles have replaced walled spaces. These hortatory flyers instruct well-educated bureaucrats how to look at each other, how to speak, how to think, how to dress, and how to feel about what they have been instructed to do – all in the maternal tones of a kindergarten teacher, whose iron fist is gloved in silk, e.g., "If a coworker is too loud, kindly ask them to be sensitive to others in the area. They probably don't realize they are disturbing others . . ." Workers learn that "the new office design promotes a high-energy, creative team environment, that will allow employees to be more interactive and more efficient. There are many changes to adjust to in our new home, including color and interior design." One key innovation is to play "white noise" (i.e., static) throughout the work areas in order to mask regular office noises and music, but the volume is so high that it has driven workers to seek solace in restrooms, and causes headaches and earaches. Orwell, indeed!

[9] Friedrich H. Tenbruck, "The Problem of Thematic Unity in the Works of Max Weber," *British Journal of Sociology*, 31:3 (Sept., 1980), pp. 316–351; Stephen Kalberg, "The Search for Thematic Orientations in a Fragmented Œuvre: The Discussion of Max Weber in Recent German Sociological Literature," *Sociology*, 13:1 (1979), pp. 127–139, and "Max Weber's Types of Rationality: Cornerstones for the Analysis of the Rationalization Process in History," *American Journal of Sociology*, 85:5 (1980), pp. 1145–1179; José Casanova, "Interpretations and Misinterpretations of Max Weber: The Problem of Rationalization," in R. M. Glassman and V. Murvar (eds.), *Max Weber's Political Sociology: A Pessimistic Vision of a Rationalized World*, Westport, CT: Greenwood Press, 1984, pp. 141–154.

[10] Wilhelm Hennis, "Max Weber's 'Central Question,'" *Economy and Society*, 12:2 (1983), 136–180; Guenther Roth, "Rationalization in Max Weber's Developmental History," in Scott Lash and Sam Whimster (eds.), *Max Weber, Rationality, and Modernity*, London: Allen and Unwin, 1987, pp. 75–91; Wolfgang Schluchter, "The Paradox of Rationalization: On the Relation of Ethics and World," in Guenther Roth and Wolfgang Schluchter, *Max*

especially if an evaluative theory of history is attached to what Weber actually wrote. So the first question to resolve regarding Weber and "the problem of rationalization" is to discover to what extent knowing about this idea leads directly into Weber's theoretical core, or whether it is perhaps one of several crucial notions around which he created a chaotically brilliant portrait of social life, historical and contemporary.

One way of approaching this pivotal question is to retrace our steps to that graceful and lucid map of the Weberian continent drawn by the Alsatian scholar, Julien Freund. His geographical birthright – equal facility in Germanic density and French style – served him well while explaining Weber to the outside world. His dense summary of the rationalization process from "Weber's Vision of the World" is worth quoting, in part:

> Weber's rationalization is not to be confused with the notion of the rationality of history, which professedly directs human evolution on a course of universal progress . . . It is, rather, the product of the scientific specialization and technical differentiation peculiar to Western culture . . . sometimes associated . . . with the notion of intellectualization. It might be defined as *the organization of life through a division and coordination of activities on the basis of an exact study of men's relations with each other, with their tools and their environment, for the purpose of achieving greater efficiency and productivity.* Hence it is a purely practical development brought about by man's technological genius.
>
> Weber also described rationalization as a striving for perfection . . . as an ingenious refinement of the conduct of life and the attainment of increasing mastery over the external world . . . he analyzed its evolution in all major branches of human activity – religion, law, art, science, politics, and economics – while being careful not to go beyond the limits of what is objectively ascertainable . . .[11]

This is unobjectionably accurate and, when joined to other passages Freund dedicates to the topic, lands the naive reader generally in the right sector. Yet a look at Freund's sources within Weber's works illustrates one of the first problems confronting those who seek unambiguous familiarity with Weber's idea. Like most other exegetes, including many less talented than himself, Freund drew on a couple of famous passages in *From Max Weber,* unspecific reference to *The Rational and Social Foundations of Music* (though only regarding painting!), a minor speech Weber gave in 1910 about technology – and his exposition was complete. The approach

Weber's Vision of History: Ethics and Methods, Berkeley, CA: University of California Press, 1979, pp. 11–64.
[11] Julien Freund, *The Sociology of Max Weber,* trans. Mary Ilford, New York: Random House, 1968, p. 18. (Same pagination for paperback edition: New York: Vintage Books, 1969.)

to the question is unique only in Freund's sure grasp of the fundamentals and an extraordinary style, but his light reference to the original materials has become all too common among most writers trying to describe Weber's pivotal concept. And, to be sure, short of a full-scale intellectual biography, the fulcrum of which would be "rationalization," it is impossible to tell the whole story of how a political-economist and lawyer (1889–1897) converted himself into the foremost comparativist of his time (1904–1920). Yet perhaps within these few pages, we can make a practical start.

Attempts to explain, put to use, expand upon, correct, or reject Weber's rationalization thesis are legion and, when culled from a complete bibliography of Anglophone Weberiana that I compiled for another occasion,[12] it is easy to name dozens of valuable treatments, quite diverse in approach, intention, and subject matter.[13] One reason for this abundant work is that

[12] Alan Sica, *Max Weber and the New Century*, Oxford, and Cambridge, MA: Blackwell, forthcoming in 2000, which includes a 3000-item bibliography of secondary Weberian works in English, in addition to a complete listing of Weber's works in English translations.

[13] Representative works that elaborate Weber's notion of rationalization, chosen for their variety of approach, include the following (alphabetized by author): Martin Albrow, "The Application of the Weberian Concept of Rationalization to Contemporary Conditions," in Lash and Whimster (eds.), *Max Weber, Rationality, and Modernity*, pp. 164–182; Michael Banton, "Mixed Motives and the Processes of Rationalization," *Ethnic and Racial Studies*, 8:4 (Oct., 1985), pp. 534–547; Reinhard Bendix, "The Cultural and Political Setting of Economic Rationality in Western and Eastern Europe," in Reinhard Bendix, *et al.* (eds.), *State and Society: A Reader in Comparative Political Sociology*, Boston: Little, Brown, and Co., 1968, pp. 335–351; Roslyn Wallach Bologh, "Max Weber and the Dilemma of Rationality," in Ronald M. Glassman and Vatro Murvar (eds.), *Max Weber's Political Sociology: A Pessimistic Vision of a Rationalized World*, Westport, CT: Greenwood Press, 1984, pp. 175–186; Rogers Brubaker, *The Limits of Rationality: An Essay on the Social and Moral Thought of Max Weber*, London: George Allen & Unwin, 1984; Joseph M. Bryant, "From Myth to Theology: Intellectuals and the Rationalization of Religion in Ancient Greece," in William Swatos, Jr. (ed.), *Time, Place, and Circumstance: Neo-Weberian Studies in Comparative Religious History*, Westport, CT: Greenwood Press, 1990, pp. 71–85; Bruce Carruthers and Wendy Nelson Espeland, "Accounting for Rationality: Double-Entry Bookkeeping and the Rhetoric of Economic Rationality," *American Journal of Sociology*, 97:1 (July, 1991), pp. 31–69; Randall Collins, *Weberian Sociological Theory*, Cambridge: Cambridge University Press, 1983, especially ch. 2; Arnold Eisen, "The Meanings and Confusions of Weberian 'Rationality,'" *British Journal of Sociology*, 29:1 (Mar., 1978), pp. 57–70; Joseba I. Esteban, "Habermas on Weber: Rationality, Rationalization, and the Diagnosis of the Times," *Gnosis*, 3:4 (Dec., 1991), 93–115; Ferenc Feher, "Weber and the Rationalization of Music," *International Journal of Politics, Culture, and Society*, 1:2 (Winter, 1987), pp. 147–162; Franco Ferrarotti, *Max Weber and the Destiny of Reason*, trans. John Fraser, Armonk, NY: M.E. Sharpe, 1982; Ernest Gellner, *Reason and Culture: The Historic Role of Rationality and Rationalism*, Oxford: Blackwell Publishers, 1992; Andrew Goodwin, "Rationalization and Democratization in the New Technologies of Popular Music," in James Lull (ed.), *Popular Music and Communication*, 2nd edn., Newbury Park, CA: Sage Publications, 1992, pp. 75–100; Jukka Gronow, "The Element of Irrationality: Max Weber's Diagnosis of Modern Culture," *Acta Sociologica*, 31:4 (1988), pp. 319–331; Jürgen Habermas, "Max Weber's Theory of Rationalization," in *The Theory*

of Communicative Action, vol. I, trans. T. McCarthy, Boston: Beacon Press, 1984, pp. 143–271; Niles M. Hansen, "Sources of Economic Rationality," in Robert W. Green (ed.), *Protestantism, Capitalism, and Social Science: The Weber Thesis Controversy*, Lexington, MA: D.C. Heath, 1973, pp. 137–149; Heinz Hartmann, "On Rational and Irrational Action," in Geza Roheim (ed.), *Psychoanalysis and the Social Sciences: An Annual*, vol. I, New York: International Universities Press, 1947, pp. 359–392; Soma Hewa and Robert W. Hetherington, "The Rationalization of Illness and the Illness of Rationalization," *International Journal of Contemporary Sociology*, 30:2 (Oct., 1993), pp. 143–153; Richard A. Hilbert, "Bureaucracy as Belief, Rationalization as Repair: Max Weber in a Post-Functionalist Age," *Sociological Theory*, 5:1 (Spring, 1987), pp. 70–86; Barry Hindess, "Rationality and the Characterization of Modern Society," in Lash and Whimster (eds.), *Max Weber, Rationality, and Modernity*, pp. 137–153; Ludger Honnefelder, "Rationalization and Natural Law: Max Weber's and Ernst Troeltsch's Interpretation of the Medieval Doctrine of Natural Law," *Review of Metaphysics*, 49:2 [issue No. 194] (Dec., 1995), pp. 275–294; H. Stuart Hughes, "Weber's Search for Rationality in Western Society," in Green (ed.), *Protestantism, Capitalism, and Social Science*, pp. 150–169; David C. Jacobson, "Rationalization and Emancipation in Weber and Habermas," *Graduate Faculty Journal of Sociology*, 1:2 (Winter, 1976), pp. 18–31; Aleksandra Jasinska-Kania, "Rationalization and Legitimation Crisis: The Relevance of Marxian and Weberian Works for an Explanation of the Political Order's Legitimacy Crisis in Poland," *Sociology*, 17:2 (May, 1983), pp. 157–164; Bryn Jones, "Economic Action and Rational Organisation in the Sociology of Weber," in Barry Hindess (ed.), *Sociological Theories of the Economy*, London: Macmillan, 1977, pp. 28–65; Lutz Kaelber, "Weber's Lacuna: Medieval Religion and the Roots of Rationalization," *Journal of the History of Ideas*, 57 (July, 1996), pp. 465–485; Stephen E. Kalberg, "The Rationalization of Action in Max Weber's Sociology of Religion," *Sociological Theory*, 8:1 (Spring, 1990), pp. 58–84; Howard L. Kaye, "Rationalization as Sublimation: On the Cultural Analyses of Weber and Freud," *Theory, Culture, and Society*, 9:4 (Nov., 1992), pp. 45–74; Andrew M. Koch, "Rationality, Romanticism, and the Individual: Max Weber's 'Modernism' and the Confrontation with 'Modernity,'" *Canadian Journal of Political Science*, 26:1 (Mar., 1993), pp. 123–144; Ferdinand Kolegar, "The Concept of 'Rationalization' and Cultural Pessimism in Max Weber's Sociology," *Sociological Quarterly*, 5:4 (Autumn, 1964), pp. 355–373; M.M.W. Lemmen, *Max Weber's Sociology of Religion: Its Method and Content in the Light of the Concept of Rationality*, trans. H.D. Morton, Hilversum: Gooi & Sticht, 1990, 254 pages; Donald Levine, "Rationality and Freedom: Weber and Beyond," *Sociological Inquiry*, 51:1 (Winter, 1981), pp. 5–25; Karl Löwith, "Weber's Interpretation of the Bourgeois-Capitalistic World in Terms of the Guiding Principle of 'Rationalization',", in Dennis Wrong (ed.), *Max Weber* (Makers of Modern Social Science), Englewood Cliffs, NJ: Prentice-Hall, 1970), pp. 101–122; Valerie Ann Malhotra, "Weber's Concept of Rationalization and the Electronic Evolution in Western Classical Music," *Qualitative Sociology*, 1:3 (Jan., 1979), pp. 100–120; Gert H. Mueller, "The Notion of Rationality in the Work of Max Weber," *Archives européennes de sociologie*, 20:1 (1979), pp. 149–171; Benjamin Nelson, "Max Weber and the Discontents and Dilemmas of Contemporary Universally Rationalized Post-Christian Civilization," in Walter Sprondel and Constans Seyfarth (eds.), *Max Weber und die Rationalisierung sozialen Handelns*, Stuttgart: Ferdinand Enke Verlag, 1981, pp. 1–8; Donald A. Nielson, "The Inquisition, Rationalization, and Sociocultural Change in Medieval Europe," in William Swatos, Jr. (ed.), *Time, Place, and Circumstance*, Westport: Greenwood Press, 1990, pp. 107–122; Raul Pertierra, "Forms of Rationality? Rationalization and Social Transformation in a Northern Philippine Community," *Social Analysis*, 17 (Aug., 1985), pp. 49–70; George Ritzer, "Professionalization, Bureaucratization and Rationalization: The Views of Max Weber," *Social Forces*, 53:4 (June, 1975), pp. 627–634; Guenther Roth, "Duration and Rationalization: Fernand Braudel and Max Weber," in

in some ways, this topic rivals the "Protestant ethic thesis" as a favored route toward coming to grips with Weber at his most contentious and intriguing. Yet everyone who comments with scholarly authority on rationality and the behaviors which are, in historical hindsight, now thought to be its product agrees on at least one point: Weber was inconsistent in his technical use of terms, and there is no firmly delineable *locus classicus* to which the reader can turn for an unambiguous statement of Weber's global intentions.[14]

If one undertakes an "empirical" examination of the texts to which a range of Weber specialists has referred when offering their interpretations of the rationalization process, certain of his works, major and minor, do receive mention more than once. Yet this may be more an artifact of received wisdom or scholarly habit than a true measure of where one might

Guenther Roth and Wolfgang Schluchter, *Max Weber's Vision of History: Ethics and Methods*, Berkeley, CA: University of California Press, 1979, pp. 166–193; Mahmoud Sadri, "Reconstruction of Max Weber's Notion of Rationality: An Immanent Model," *Social Research*, 49:3 (Autumn, 1982), pp. 616–633; Wolfgang Schluchter, *The Rise of Western Rationalism: Max Weber's Developmental History*, trans. Guenther Roth, Berkeley, CA: University of California Press, 1981; Wolfgang Schluchter, *Rationalism, Religion, and Domination: A Weberian Perspective*, trans. Neil Solomon, Berkeley, CA: University of California Press, 1989; Alfred Schutz, "The Problem of Rationality in the Social World," in Dorothy Emmet and Alasdair MacIntyre (eds.), *Sociological Theory and Philosophical Analysis*, New York: Macmillan Co., 1970, pp. 89–114; Thomas W. Segady, "Rationality and Irrationality: New Directions in Weberian Theory, Critique, and Research," *Sociological Spectrum*, 8 (1988), pp. 85–100; Ronen Shamir, "Formal and Substantive Rationality in American Law: A Weberian Perspective," *Social and Legal Studies*, 2 (1993), pp. 45–72; Alan Sica, "Reasonable Science, Unreasonable Life: The Happy Fictions of Marx, Weber, and Social Theory," in Robert Antonio and Ronald Glassman (eds.), *A Weber-Marx Dialogue*, Lawrence, KS: University Press of Kansas, 1985, pp. 68–88; Alan Sica, *Weber, Irrationality, and Social Order*, Berkeley, CA: University of California Press, 1988 [revised paperback edn., 1990]; Joyce S. Sterling and Wilbert E. Moore, "Weber's Analysis of Legal Rationalization: A Critique and Constructive Modification," *Sociological Forum*, 2:1 (1987), pp. 67–89; J. J. R. Thomas, "Rationalization and the Status of Gender Divisions," *Sociology*, 19:3 (Aug., 1985), pp. 409–420; Bryan S. Turner, "The Rationalization of the Body: Reflections on Modernity and Discipline," in Lash and Whimster (eds.), *Max Weber, Rationality, and Modernity*, pp. 222–241; Stanley H. Udy, Jr., "'Bureaucracy' and 'Rationality' in Weber's Organization Theory: An Empirical Study," *American Sociological Review*, 24 (1959), pp. 791–795; Johannes Weiss, "On the Irreversibility of Western Rationalization and Max Weber's Alleged Fatalism," in Lash and Whimster (eds.), *Max Weber, Rationality, and Modernity*, pp. 154–163.

14 From the list in note 13, the most pertinent entries include Brubaker, *Limits of Rationality*; Kalberg, "Rationalization of Action"; Schluchter, *Rise of Rationalism*; Sica, *Weber, Irrationality*; to which should be added Randall Collins, *Max Weber: A Skeleton Key*, Beverly Hills, CA: Sage Publications, 1986, pp. 61–80, and Otto Stammer (ed.), *Max Weber and Sociology Today*, New York: Harper and Row, 1972, especially pp. 154–175, where several eminent Weberians answer Herbert Marcuse's famous attack on Weber's putative view of western history and politics.

go to find Weber's clearest, most embracing, or maturest formulation. This, at least, is what I have concluded after pedantically marching through representative treatments by Aron, Brubaker, Collins, Giddens, Habermas, Parsons, Löwith, and Ritzer, noting the Weberian sources of their stories.[15]

There apparently being no consensually identified textual sites to which all committed Weberians can turn in order to learn what he meant by the set of related events we call "rationalization," a measure of hermeneutic flexibility is introduced which might be put to good use. One unusually fruitful text was quoted by Reinhard Bendix in his fusillade against Marcuse thirty-five years ago, and comes from the famous "Technical Superiority of Bureaucracy" section of *Economy and Society*, chosen (and translated) by Bendix because it illustrates the consequences of rationalization in the everyday world of industrialized life. Opening with Weber's observation that "the second element mentioned, calculable rules, is the most important one for modern bureaucracy," the argument is developed thus:

> Bureaucracy in its fullest state of development also comes in a specific sense under the principle of *sine ira ac studio* (impartiality) [literally: *without anger and without partisanship*]. Its specific character, welcomed by capitalism, develops all the more completely the more it is "de-humanized." By "more completely" is meant, the more this specific character, which is seen as a virtue, succeeds in eliminating from all official business love, hate, all purely personal and all irrational elements of feeling, elements defying calculation. [The standard translation adds: "This is appraised as its special virtue by capitalism"; p. 975.] Instead of gentlemen of the old order, inspired by personal interest, favor, grace, and gratitude, modern culture requires, for the external apparatus which supports it, the more complicated and specialized it becomes, the less humanly concerned, strictly "practical *expert*."[16]

---

[15] Raymond Aron, *German Sociology and Main Currents in Sociological Thought*, vol. II, New York: Basic Books, 1967, no specific references; Rogers Brubaker, *The Limits of Rationality*, a detailed, unchronological, and eclectic usage, with particular attention to *E&S*, and several essays, including "'Author's Introduction' to *The Protestant Ethic*" and "Anticritical Last Word on *The Spirit of Capitalism*"; Randall Collins, *Weberian Sociological Theory* and *Max Weber: A Skeleton Key*, mostly attending to *E&S*, *GEH*, and *PE*; Anthony Giddens, *Capitalism and Modern Social Theory*, Cambridge: Cambridge University Press, 1971, heavily relying on *FMW*, *GEH*, and *E&S*; Jürgen Habermas, *Theory of Communicative Action*, the most sustained attempt at definitive exploration, putting to use several dozen passages from *E&S*, *FMW*, and *PE*; Karl Löwith, "Weber's Interpretation of the Bourgeois-Capitalistic World," in Wrong (ed.), *Max Weber*, the most unusual set of citations, including by far the most references to *MSS* and other essays regarding method, plus his political writings; George Ritzer, *Classical Sociological Theory*, 2nd ed., New York: McGraw-Hill, 1996 relying heavily on the essays of Stephen Kalberg and on Brubaker's short book, and citing material from *E&S*, *GEH*, and *PE*, in a standard textbook treatment which is surely seen by more novices than any of the previously mentioned literature.

[16] Reinhard Bendix, "Discussion on Industrialization and Capitalism" [in response to a paper by Herbert Marcuse], in Otto Stammer (ed.), *Max Weber and Sociology Today*, New York:

Despite obvious syntactical problems typical of Weber's fractured prose, the ideas are clear enough. But there are other routes toward understanding Weber's ideas in this general realm of theorizing.

Given the right semi-formal occasion, Weber could temporarily set aside his mandarin German and assume a bluntness of delivery that even today succeeds in animating his abstract arguments. A famous, biting example, first translated forty years ago by J. P. Mayer in *Max Weber and German Politics*, is this set of stenographically recorded remarks which Weber delivered to colleagues in the *Verein für Sozialpolitik* at their Vienna meeting in 1909 (which Mayer titled "Max Weber on Bureaucracy"):

> . . . the forward progress of bureaucratic mechanization is irresistible . . . When a purely technical and faultless administration, a precise and objective solution of concrete problems is taken as the highest and only goal, then on this basis one can only say: away with everything but an official hierarchy which does these things as objectively, precisely, and "soullessly" as any machine.
>
> The technical superiority of the bureaucratic mechanism stands unshaken . . . Imagine the consequences of that comprehensive bureaucratization and rationalization which already to-day we see approaching. Already now, throughout private enterprise in wholesale manufacture, as well as in all other economic enterprises run on modern lines, *Rechenhaftigkeit*, rational calculation, is manifest at every stage. By it, the performance of each individual worker is mathematically measured, each man becomes a little cog in the machine and, aware of this, his one preoccupation is whether he can become a bigger cog . . . it is strikingly reminiscent of the ancient kingdom of Egypt, in which the system of the "minor official" prevailed at all levels . . . we are proceeding towards an evolution which resembles that system in every detail, except that it is built on other foundations, on technically more perfect, more rationalized, and therefore much more mechanized foundations . . . it is still more horrible to think that the world could one day be filled with nothing but those little cogs, little men clinging to little jobs and striving towards bigger ones . . . The passion for bureaucracy . . . is enough to drive one to despair. It is as if in politics the specter of timidity – which has in any case always been rather a good standby for the German – were to stand alone at the helm; as if we were deliberately to become men who need "order" and nothing but order, who become nervous and cowardly if for one moment this order wavers, and helpless if they are taken away from their total incorporation in it . . . but what can we oppose to this machinery in order to keep a portion of mankind free from this parceling-out of the soul, from this supreme mastery of the bureaucratic way of life . . . I only wish to challenge the unquestioning idolization of bureaucracy.

Harper and Row, 1972, p. 159; Bendix translated this from *Wirtschaft und Gesellschaft*, vol. II, Tübingen, 1920, p. 662; for a different and standard English translation, see *E&S*, p. 975.

As Weber had become well aware, individuals, organizations, and societies at large, in their pursuit of private goals, profits, or predictability of performance, have come to trade efficiency and precision for human warmth and due regard for the personally unique. Or, as Benjamin Nelson observed at the same occasion in 1964 that inspired Bendix's pointed remarks:

> Professor Marcuse's insistent forthrightness in blaming so many of the ills of recent times on the "rationalism" which Weber, in his view, espoused in so undialectical a fashion, underscores a little known fact: Weber's renowned comparative studies from his *Protestant Ethic* (1904–05) to his *Wirtschaft und Gesellschaft* have yet to be understood in their true light. They are much more than they seem or are generally understood to be, comparative socio-logical investigations against a background of the history of Western civiliza-tion and culture. In a sense which many overlook, they are prophecies and warnings – prophecies about the menacing shape of things to come, warnings against the further expansion of the domain of conscienceless reason, even in the name of the most noble ideals . . . The noblest impulses only too often gave rise to the most baleful consequences. Thus the disenchanted world order of contemporary industrial "capitalist" society has been spurred on its fateful course by . . . high-minded altruistic religious impulses.[17]

The connections between Nelson's astute penetration of Weber's deepest motives and a host of related theoretical developments, some of them apparently quite distant from Weber's original concerns (e.g., Merton's famous argument about "unanticipated consequences of social action") are perhaps too obvious to require elaboration. But they do testify to the fertility of Weber's undemarcated "philosophical anthropology" as his ideas have circulated among serious social thinkers during this century.

Another astonishingly useful passage appears in a work to which none of the other specialists referred when handling the topic. "Parliament and Government in Germany under a New Political Order," which Weber wrote for a quasi-popular audience, first appeared as a set of five *Frank-furter Zeitung* articles between April and June in the anxious year of 1917. Weber was then being urged to participate in post-war German politics, and this essay reveals not only a topical study of problems facing his ruined country in the new, post-monarchical environment, but also manages to include some fairly dense theoretical pronouncements. I quote at length from the consolidated essay because within this thick passage there appear almost all of the truly important ingredients that went into Weber's rationalization schema:

[17] Benjamin Nelson, "Discussion on Industrialization and Capitalism," in Stammer (ed.), *Max Weber and Sociology Today*, pp. 167–168.

Historically, too, "progress" towards the bureaucratic state which adjudicates in accordance with the rationally established law and administers according to rationally devised regulations stands in the closest relation to the development of modern capitalism. The main inner foundation of the modern capitalist business is *calculation*. In order to exist, it requires a system of justice and administration which, in principle at any rate, function in a *rationally calculable* manner according to stable, general norms, just as one calculates the predictable performance of a *machine*. By contrast, it finds quite uncongenial what is popularly called "cadi [*khadi*] justice," where judgements are made on each *individual* case according to the judge's sense of fairness, or according to other irrational means of adjudication and principles which existed everywhere in the past and still exist in the Orient today. Equally uncongenial to capitalism is the patriarchal form of administration based on arbitrary decision and grace, but otherwise operating according to binding, holy but irrational tradition, such as one finds in the theocratic or patrimonial associations of rule (*Herrschaftsverbände*) in Asia and in our own past. The fact that this form of "cadi justice" and the type of administration that corresponds to it are very often *venal*, precisely because of their irrational character, allowed a certain form of capitalism to come into existence (and often to flourish luxuriantly thanks to these qualities), that of the trader and government contractor and all varieties of the *pre*-rational capitalism that has been in existence for four thousand years, specifically the adventurer and robber capitalism which was tied to politics, war, administration as such. *Nowhere* in such irrationally constructed polities, however, did or could there emerge the *specific* feature of *modern* capitalism that distinguishes it from those ancient forms of capitalist acquisition, namely the strictly rational *organization of work* on the basis of *rational technology*. These modern types of business, with their fixed capital and precise calculations, are far too easily damaged by irrationalities of justice or administration for them to have emerged under such circumstances. They could only emerge where law was practiced in one of two ways. *Either*, as in England, the practical shaping of law was in fact in the hands of advocates who, in the service of their clientele (men with capitalist interests), devised the appropriate forms for conducting business, and from whose ranks there emerged judges who were bound strictly by "precedent," and thus to *calculable* schemata. *Or where*, as in the bureaucratic state with its rational laws, the judge is a kind of legal paragraph-machine, into which one throws the documents on a case together with the costs and fees so that it will then spit out a judgment along with some more or less valid reasons for it; here again, the system works in a more or less *calculable* way.[18]

---

[18] *PW* 147–148, translated by Speirs; all emphases are Weber's own. The standard translation, under the title "Parliament and Government in a Reconstructed Germany: A Contribution to the Political Critique of Officialdom and Party Politics," is in *E&S* at pp. 1394–1395.

Careful hermeneutic analyses of these four excerpts, three from Weber, plus Nelson's, would constitute a small monograph – especially if carried out in line with the interpretative principles laid down by virtuosi such as Gadamer, Betti, de Man, Hirsch, George Steiner, Harold Bloom, and others who specialize in such labors.[19] Even without this ideal rigor, however, Weber's pointedly delivered vocabulary – a mixture of icy science and prophetic passion – leads the studious reader to several realizations that figure centrally in his overall understanding of rationalization.

From the beginning of Weber's realization that the Faustian bargain constituting modern western science and industrialization dazzled as well as blinded its beneficiaries – a lesson he may well have learned directly from Goethe during his enthusiastic boyhood reading[20] – his analysis had taken two antipodal forms. Benjamin Nelson openly admitted, Bendix often obscured, and Marcuse joyfully exploited this well-known "tension" in Weber: on the one hand, a clear-eyed portraiture of a civilizational condition from which he could not picture a likely escape, yet on the other a strong-voiced denunciation of those "de-humanizing" tendencies which were already well in place 100 years ago. Marx and many lesser thinkers offered utopian plans that promised redemption from the Faustian bargain – having one's cake while eating it, spoken in social theoretical language. In contrast, Weber understood precisely the benefits, political and economic, of rationalized life, and also recognized that this move away from the tailor-made, wisdom-based practices of *khadijustiz* that had served human-kind for millennia to the "legal paragraph- machine" judgeships of today could not be reversed, no matter how many miscarriages of "justice" might occur because of hyper-rationalized legal proceedings.

Another element of Weber's theorizing, one that pervades his detailed analyses of music, law, comparative religion, government, ancient history, and the lot, is his obsessively repeated opinion that modern life strains

---

[19] For bibliographic details, see Gary Shapiro and Alan Sica (eds.), *Hermeneutics: Questions and Prospects*, Amherst, MA: University of Massachusetts Press, 1988, paperback edn., pp. 293–307, 319–320. Especially enlightening in this context are Hans-Georg Gadamer, *Truth and Method*, rev. translation, New York: Continuum Publishing, [1989]1995; Emilio Betti, "Hermeneutics as a General Method for the Human Sciences," trans. in Josef Bleicher (ed.), *Contemporary Hermeneutics*, London: Routledge & Kegan Paul, 1980; Paul de Man, *Allegories of Reading*, New Haven, CT: Yale University Press, 1979; E. D. Hirsch, *Validity in Interpretation*, New Haven, CT: Yale University Press, 1967; George Steiner, *After Babel* (2nd edn., (New York: Oxford University Press, 1992; and Harold Bloom, *A Map of Misreading*, New York: Oxford University Press, 1975.

[20] For details of Weber's lifelong attachment to the imagery and ideas of Goethe, particularly with regard to Faust and the rationalization theme, see Sica, "Reasonable Science, Unreasonable Life."

toward rationality at every opportunity, and in so doing leaves behind an irrational or non-rationalizable past of primordial practices which were, until very lately in history, the chief indicators of humanness. Having written about this complex of ideas at length,[21] I will refer here only lightly to what I regard as the central paradox of Weber's rationalization theme, and its continuing importance to social and cultural theory today; and in a way that I think is consistent with Weber's sometimes unvoiced conclusions.

Western, modernized, rationalized humans have become childish in their demands upon each other and upon their environments, social and ecological, as have peoples in other parts of the world who have begun imitating this general model of behavior and social organization. When it suits their private short-term desires, they exhibit "rationality" in the purest economic meaning of the term. Yet after their material and status needs are more or less satisfied, at least temporarily, they turn for relief from regimentation and predictable tedium to those very realms of social life, those zones of solace, wherein rationality has the least play and the least likely future influence. That is, they rush to those few remaining human or animal intimates still available to them, to aesthetic realms of abandon which seem ever more important (perhaps the hallmark of "post-modern culture"), and to a revived yet only half-believed supernatural realm of doctrine and chant that requires, in order to work properly, a suspension of modern scientific principles that educated people find very difficult to manage – except those in dire psychological straits.

Taken together, this package of behaviors is not only schizoid, but also infantile. It requires a regulated, predictable, and unspontaneous "maturity" on the job site that is starkly alien to humanity's past, and rewards this intolerable condition with a range of "after-hours" children's amusements which intelligent adults from earlier times would likely consider imbecilic and demeaning. These are aspects of Weber's thoughts which, had he lived into the film and radio ages, might have formed the next chapter in *Wirtschaft und Gesellschaft*, where he would have been called upon to answer the question: "What is the next step for a culture which has lost its literacy and found its sedatives, both electronic and chemical?"

Weber has been vilified over the years for the carelessness of his prose. In fact, were it not for a team of selfless editors and transcribers headed by his wife, his vast posthumous output in the early 1920s would never have come together, and he would not now be remembered nearly so well. Only occasionally did he bother to work over a sentence or passage until it spoke

---

[21] See Sica, *Weber, Irrationality, and Social Order, passim.*

his true language, one that imitated his apparently riveting lectures. Perhaps the single most famous of his observations – so uncharacteristically poetic that some believe it was inspired by a great writer Weber admired (Goethe, Nietzsche, and Rilke have been proposed) – appears near the end of *The Protestant Ethic*. This concluding flash of brilliant pathos captures Weber's feelings about the rationalized life, and remains his most frequently quoted statement:

> No one knows who will live in this cage in the future, or whether at the end of this tremendous development entirely new prophets will arise, or there will be a great rebirth of old ideas and ideals, or, if neither, mechanized petrifica-tion, embellished with a sort of convulsive self-importance. For of the last stage of this cultural development, it might well be truly said: "Specialists without spirit, sensualists without heart; this nullity imagines that it has attained a level of civilization never before achieved."[22]

If one still needs to justify the study of Weber so many years after his death, this single paragraph, and all the theorizing that inspired it, is probably all that is required to make the case.

One criticism that could perhaps be leveled at Weber's rationalization theme today, might be that it gives moderns too much credit for seriousness and high-minded concern for their condition. After all, how many today could understand the meaning of Calvin's or Luther's writings? How many would be troubled by Nietzsche's attack on "philistine" thinking? How many would stare sleepless into the starry night after reading Goethe's *Faust* for the first time, and realizing there is no "comfortable" way out?

---

[22] *PE*, p. 182. As explained in note 20 above, I have argued at length that Weber's inspiration for this passage was Goethe.

3

WOLFGANG SCHLUCHTER

Psychophysics and culture*

Introduction

Max Weber engaged psychophysics directly and in detail on several occasions: the methodological article "Research Strategy for the Study of Occupational Careers and Mobility Patterns in the Workforce in Large Scale Industry," written for colleagues conducting a survey for the *Verein für Sozialpolitik*; the 1908/9 literature review "On the Psychophysics of Industrial Work," which includes a case study; the 1909 review "On the Methodology of Social Psychological Questionnaires"; a reader's letter concerning Marie Bernays; and an intervention in the debate at the annual conference of the *Verein für Sozialpolitik* in autumn 1911.

These "psychophysical writings," as Weber once described them,[1] have long been neglected by Weber scholars. Either they are ignored altogether, or treated as part of a purely empirical interest in working conditions. To be sure, Weber began his career as an economist with an empirical study of the social condition of agricultural workers, which implied also an interest in the social condition of industrial workers. When the *Verein für Sozialpolitik* turned in earnest to this later question, it was natural that Weber should be involved. Yet it has been claimed that after the study was conceived Weber's interest in the topic waned.[2] According to this view, the texts of 1908 and 1909 mentioned above represent a conclusion rather than a beginning. It is therefore understandable that until now they have played less of a role in the biography of Weber's work than in the history of

---

* Translation by Charles Turner.
[1] Early in 1909 Weber wrote Lujo Brentano: ". . . psychophysical writings remain – even after their appearance in the next edition of the *Archiv* – incomplete, preparatory works." Letter to Lujo Brentano, 13 April, 1909, BA Koblenz, N1, Brentano, Nr. 67, Bl. 85–86. These writings are published as vol. I/11 of the *MWG*.
[2] Compare Dirk Kaesler, *Max Weber: An Introduction to His Life and Work*, Oxford: Polity Press, [1979] 1988, pp. 66–73.

empirical social research in general and of industrial sociology in particular.[3]

To be sure, the texts also can be read with profit in this way. However, were they merely a contribution to empirical research, it would be hard to understand why Weber engaged so explicitly and *critically* with the experimental psychology of his day. Above all, it would be hard to explain why he counted the report into vocational selection and adaptation among his methodological writings, dealing as they did with the foundations of *interpretive* sociology. In other words, the texts are closely bound up with the theory of action being developed at the time. They are also part of his analyses of economic action under modern capitalism and linked to *The Protestant Ethic and the Spirit of Capitalism*. In this study Weber already referred to the discussion begun by Lujo Brentano on the relationship between labor time, wages, and productivity. Weber argued that a proletarian reserve army of labor makes for low wages, but hampers the qualitative improvement of the workforce, and in no way encourages the intensification of work. An appropriate level of commitment was not to be achieved through "mechanical financial operations" (*PE* 199), but could only be the product of a "long and arduous process of education" (*PE* 62). At the beginning of industrialization it had been very difficult to find appropriately qualified labor:

> And even present-day industry is not yet by any means entirely independent in its choice of location of such qualities of the population, acquired by longstanding tradition and education in intensive labor. It is congenial to the scientific prejudices of today, when such a dependence is observed, to ascribe it to congenital racial qualities rather than to tradition and education, in my opinion a very dubious procedure. (*PE* 199)

---

[3] Irmela Gorges, *Sozialforschung in Deutschland 1872–1914*, Königstein/Ts.: Anton Hain, 1980; Peter Hinrichs, *Um die Steele des Arbeiters, Arbeiterpsychologie, Industrie- und Betriebssoziologie in Deutschland 1871–1945*, Cologne: Pahl-Rugenstein, 1981; Horst Kern, *Empirische Sozialforschung. Ursprünge, Ansätze, Entwicklungslinien*, Munich: Beck, 1982; Anthony Oberschall, *Empirical Social Research in Germany 1848–1914*, Paris: Mouton, 1965; Friedrich Heckmann, "Max Weber als empirischer Sozialforscher," *Zeitschrift für Soziologie*, 8:1 (1979), pp. 50–62. On early industrial sociology see M. Rainer Lepsius, *Strukturen und Wandlungen im Industriebetrieb. Industriesoziologische Forschung in Deutschland*, Munich: Hanser, 1960, p. 9; Burkart Lutz and Gert Schmidt, "Industriesoziologie," in René König (ed.), *Handbuch der empirischen Sozialforschung*, 2nd edn, Stuttgart: Enke, 1977, vol. VIII, pp. 101–262; Christian von Ferber, *Arbeitsfreude*, Stuttgart: Enke, 1959, p. 14; Paul Lazarsfeld and Anthony Oberschall, "Max Weber and Empirical Social Research," *American Sociological Review*, 30 (1965), pp. 185–199; Gerd Schmidt, "Max Weber and Modern Industrial Sociology: A Comment on Some Recent Anglo-Saxon Interpretations," *Sociological Analysis and Theory*, 6:1 (1976), pp. 47–73.

The texts on the psychophysics of work expose this dubious character. While the studies on ascetic protestantism explained the emergence of modern capitalist work attitudes among entrepreneurs *and* workers in terms of the history of ideas, here the focus is on the "point of contact" at which the demands of capital on the worker, embodied in workplace organization, confronts his psychophysical endowment. At the center of this analysis lies not the capacity for rational orientation to work, but the non-rational operations of the organism.

Yet the analysis at this point of contact does have significance for the theory of action. Already in the series of essays from 1903 to 1906 on Roscher and Knies, Weber had dealt not only with two approaches to economics, the historical and the theoretical, but also with two forms of psychology, the explanatory and the interpretive. So the texts belong to several contexts indeed. One is doubtless the *Verein für Sozialpolitik* and its investigation of industrial work. The second is the experimental psychology of the time, with its interest in the psychology of work and questions of heredity. But a third is the logical-methodological, action-theoretic, and substantive context of the work as a whole. All are important. We will deal with them in turn.

The *Verein für Sozialpolitik* and the "Investigations into the Vocational Selection and Adaptation of Workers in the Various Branches of Large-Scale Industry"

The *Verein für Sozialpolitik* was founded in 1872 with the aim of encouraging social equality between owners and workers.[4] It turned against the dominant economic doctrines of Manchester liberalism, which was accused of giving no heed to the dispiriting effects of industrialization on the situation of workers. The *Verein* was to encourage a cross-party dialogue between theorists and practitioners, scholars and politicians.[5] Its

---

[4] On the *Verein*, Franz Boese, *Geschichte des Vereins für Sozialpolitik 1872–1932* (Schriften des Vereins für Sozialpolitik, 188), Leipzig: Duncker und Humblot, 1939, which describes the founding of the *Verein*; Dieter Lindenlaub, "Richtungskämpfe im *Verein für Sozialpolitik*," *Vierteljahresschrift für Sozial- und Wirtschaftsgeschichte*, 52, Parts I and II, Wiesbaden, Steiner, 1967; Else Kesten-Conrad, *"Verein für Sozialpolitik," Handwörterbuch der Staatswissenschaften*, 3:8 (1911), pp. 144–152; Irmela Gorges, *Sozialforschung in Deutschland 1872–1914*; Rüdiger von Bruch, "Bürgerliche Sozialreform in Kaiserreich," in Bruch (ed.), *Weder Kommunismus noch Kapitalismus. Bürgerliche Sozialreform in Deutschland vom Vormärz bis zur Ära Adenauer*, Munich: Beck, 1985.

[5] The industrialists soon withdrew from the *Verein* when consensus emerged on a solution to the worker question. On the relationship between the various groupings see Lindenlaub, "Richtungskämpfe," ch. 2.

aim was a "social reform"[6] with an emphasis on income distribution.[7] Those efforts towards a new social policy brought upon it the scorn of its liberal opponents and gave rise to the phrase "Socialists of the chair."[8] The new perspective was supported by the scientific analysis of neglected social policy issues through surveys, questionnaires, and reports.

Gustav Schmoller, who took over the chair in 1890, and who since that time had largely defined the *Verein's* direction, saw the conferences, meetings, and discussions of its members as fora for influencing public opinion. Added to this was an enormous publishing agenda. By 1907, when the attention on selection and adaptation began, the *Verein* had already published 120 volumes.[9] It had become an academic publisher, characterized by the "duality" of economic theory and social policy. This dual character led to internal tensions, which were openly displayed in 1905 during the annual meeting in Mannheim, at which the so-called dispute over value-freedom broke out. Schmoller had given a lecture entitled "The Relation of Cartels to the State,"[10] in which he argued for regulated competition and the control of large enterprises. Every joint-stock company with a certain volume of capital should grant a quarter of the votes on its board of directors to persons representing the interests not of entrepreneurs but those of state and empire. This led to heated debate as a result of which the meeting was extended for a day and to which Friedrich Naumann contributed.[11] Naumann opposed Schmoller's proposal with the argument that if the state carried out the desired reforms it would be subjecting large-scale industry to measures which made neither technical nor economic sense.

Friedrich Naumann's intervention met with enthusiastic and prolonged applause. Schmoller did not reply immediately, but used his closing remarks as president for the purpose. He denied Naumann's competence (he was known as a politician) to take part in a scientific discussion, and, in the face of the audience's agreement with Naumann, threatened his resignation.[12]

6 Schmoller, "Eröffnungsrede zur Generalversammlung," Sept. 30, 1907 *Schriften des Vereins für Sozialpolitik*, 125 (1908), pp. 1–3.
7 The *Verein* was not, however, party political. Schmoller put it thus: "neither extreme social reactionaries nor revolutionary socialists can feel at home in our association": cited in Boese, *Geschichte des Vereins für Sozialpolitik 1872–1932*, p. 267.
8 Wilhelm Lexis, "Kathedersozialismus," in *Handwörterbuch der Staatswissenschaften*, 5 (1910), pp. 804–806; Lindenlaub, "Richtungskämpfe," pp. 9, 39.
9 Boese, *Geschichte des Vereins für Sozialpolitik 1872–1932*, p. 305.
10 Schmoller, "Das Verhältnis der Kartelle zum Staate," lecture, Sept. 27, 1905, *Schriften des Vereins für Sozialpolitik*, 116 (1906) pp. 237–271.
11 Naumann, "Diskussionsbeitrag zur Verhandlung: Das Verhältnis der Kartelle zum Staate," *ibid.*, pp. 360–369.
12 Schmoller, "Das Verhältnis der Kartelle zum Staate," pp. 418–431, 433–434.

This led to a further discussion in which Max Weber took part. Weber objected to the fact that Schmoller had linked a substantive difference with Naumann, who by that time had left, to the question of the leadership of the *Verein*, which thereby made all discussion of controversial topics impossible. Naumann had treated Schmoller as a "normal" participant in debate, and his contribution had not addressed the policy of the *Verein* but was motivated by substantive concerns.[13]

The conflict almost led to the break-up of the *Verein*. It became clear that there was a conflict within the *Verein* over different conceptions of social policy and, perhaps more importantly, over different conceptions of economic theory. Weber's critique of Schmoller's conduct toward Naumann raised the question of how the opposition between the two wings might be treated in the future. The "left" and the younger generation objected to the idea of an ethical national economy by which the "right" and older generation was guided. They saw in it a threat to empirical research and therefore advocated the separation of judgments of fact from judgments of value. They believed that the conflation of "is" and "ought" had become "a habit of thought"[14] among the older generation, as a result of which it was unclear about the value judgments contained in its scientific work, while the older generation thought it methodologically impossible, and ethically and politically questionable, to avoid adopting an evaluative position in the human sciences.

It remained difficult, even after changes in the *Verein's* regulations, to satisfy the "left's" demand for a clear separation of theory-led economic and sociological research and evaluative social policy commitments. Therefore the representatives of the "left" began to think about a new organization, which would supplement but not replace the *Verein*. The result was the founding of the German Sociological Society (GSS) in Berlin in 1909.[15] Weber was a founding member, and immediately took upon himself a good deal of the initial organizational work,[16] attempted to persuade leading national economists to join,[17] and drew up "publicity

---

[13] Weber, "Diskussionsbeitrag zur Verhandlung: Das Verhältnis der Kartelle zum Staate" in *ibid.*, pp. 432–435.

[14] Weber, "Diskussionsbeitrag zu dem Wesen der volkwirtschaftlichen Produktivität," *Schriften des Vereins für Sozialpolitik*, 132 (1910), pp. 580–585.

[15] On Jan. 3, 1909. On the day of the *Verein's* first meeting, its executive consisted of: F. Tönnies, G. Simmel, W. Sombart, H. Beck, A. Ploetz, Ph. Stein, A. Vierkandt, G. v. Mayr, and M. Weber. See Dirk Käsler, *Die frühe deutsche Soziologie 1909 bis 1934 und ihre Entstehungsmilieus*, Opladen: Westdeutscher Verlag, 1984, esp. p. 294; Ursula Karger, "Institutionengeschichtliche Zäsuren in der deutschen Soziologie. Dargestellt am Beispiel der Deutschen Soziologentage," Dissertation, Bochum, 1978.

[16] See Marianne Weber, *Max Weber: A Biography*, New York: Wiley, 1975, p. 420.

[17] See the letters from Weber to Heinrich Herkner, 8 May, 1909, ZstA Merseburg, Rep. 92,

material"[18] on the efforts to institutionalize sociological research. He succeeded in having the GSS include in its statutes a ban on the pursuit of practical ideals, and recommended at the first annual meeting in Frankfurt in October 1910 surveys on a sociology of the press and a sociology of associations.[19]

But it was not only within the *Verein für Sozialpolitik* that bitter opposition emerged to the ethical school in economics. Opposition also came from the outside. Conservative economists in particular accused it of adopting a position sympathetic to workers. These included Richard Ehrenberg, an economist from Rostock, who had formulated his critique of the *Verein* long before the Mannheim congress. This was directed against the historical school as a whole, which, with its research based upon economic history and local and national archives, simply counterposed "the public interest" to the self-interest with which the English school set out. What was required was scientific economic research which made use of a precise comparative method: quantitative observation of the economic conduct of private enterprises, together with the logical principle of comparison drawn from the natural sciences, would make generalizations possible. To publicize his views he founded the Thunen archive in 1905, and following this the "association for exact scientific research" in 1910.[20]

Three camps thus can be identified which influenced discussion of economics and social policy within the *Verein* at the time the industrial labor surveys were being planned: the historically and ethically oriented economists around Schmoller, devoted to a patriarchal social policy; the economists and sociologists around Max Weber, who did theoretical as well as historical work but were committed to the postulate of value freedom and to a competitive balance between organized social interests; and the economists devoted to a natural-scientific model, who tied exact research to the postulate of value freedom and largely reduced questions of

N1. Max Weber, Nr.18, B1.14–18; 11 May, 1909, ZstA Merseburg, Rep. 92, N1. Max Weber, Nr.18, B1.19–20; to Lujo Brentano, June, 1909, BA Koblenz, N1. Brentano, Nr.67, B1.89, now in *MWG* II/6.

[18] Marianne Weber, *Max Weber*, p. 420.

[19] Weber also concerned himself with the funding of the research project on the press. See for example Weber's letter to the Heidelberg Academy of Sciences of May 9, 1910 (Lanz Foundation); also H.-Jörg Siewert, "Zur Thematisierung des Vereinswesens in der deutschen Soziologie," in Otto Dann (ed.), *Vereinswesen und bürgerliche Gesellschaft*, Munich: Oldenbourg, 1984, pp. 151–180.

[20] Richard Ehrenberg, "Die Ziele des Thünen-Archives," in Richard Ehrenberg (ed.), *Thünen-Archiv, Organ für exakte Wirtschaftsforschung*, vol. I/1, 1905, pp. 1–33.

social policy to the problem of devising an economic policy which would create the conditions for increased economic productivity.

This is the broader context within which the studies on industrial labor were conceived. The story of how the survey emerged is set down in the editorial report on Max Weber's essay "Investigations . . ."[21] As Heinrich Herkner, the head of the survey, later put it: "This choice of theme merely followed the tendency of the times. It dealt with the old question of the relationship between being and consciousness, life situation and fate, social relations and the soul of the factory worker, but with rigorous and partly new methods."[22]

The project was based upon a questionnaire, with supplementary questions and guidelines. In order to provide additional advice to the researchers, Weber wrote a commentary to spell out his own viewpoint, which was added to the material. Twelve thousand questionnaires were distributed.[23] However, the enterprise was hardly a roaring success. Qualified assistants were unavailable, and workers were unprepared to respond. In 1909 Herkner reported to the responsible committee: "The questionnaire appears to have been an unqualified success only in one case. Fräulein Bernays . . . has received 1,300 responses from workers in the München-Gladbach cotton mill and gained valuable information concerning the relationship between social origin and wage levels."[24] Although more acceptable results followed, the number of responses fell well below expectations.

In the following years Herkner reported regularly on work in progress. The final report for the general meeting and public discussion of the results were scheduled for the Nuremberg conference in October 1911. Reports and debates fell under the heading: "Problems of Worker Psychology according to the Perspective of the *Verein's* Inquiry." Herkner reported that "our inquiries reveal less a class division in the classical Marxist sense than an increasing differentiation within the working class itself and increased opportunities for an individual personal life."[25] Weber added that "*on the*

---

[21] For its reconstruction the author relied on the *Verein's* proceedings and documentation. The secondary literature is almost exclusively either too imprecise, too unspecific, or both.

[22] Heinrich Herkner, "Probleme der Arbeiterpsychologie unter besonderer Rücksichtnahme auf Methode und Ergebnisse der Vereinserhebungen," *Schriften des Vereins für Sozialpolitik*, 138 (1912).

[23] *Verein für Sozialpolitik*, Proceedings of the executive committee meeting, 26 and 28 Sept., 1909, p. 2.

[24] *Ibid.* Alfred Weber remarked on the difficulty of finding suitable research assistants, and on the desirability of a model study. He hoped that the work of Marie Bernays would be one. In fact, her first study, published a year after the first volume of the surveys, did serve as such. *Schriften des Vereins für Sozialpolitik*, 133 (1910).

[25] Herkner, "Probleme der Arbeiterpsychologie unter besonderer Rücksichtnahme auf Methode und Ergebnisse der Vereinserhebungen," *ibid.*, 138 (1912), p. 138.

basis of the material collected here and likely to be accumulated in the future there is *a very strong probability* that valuable and seminal results will be obtained."[26] In early 1915 the project closed.

The statements above are not untypical. Worker psychology was, theoretically and methodologically, placed between physiology and economics or sociology. It included questions of heredity and environment, or as Weber put it, life fate, and the relationship between laboratory experiments and mass observation. Weber was clear that whoever wished to pursue this in a non-essayistic manner must follow the path of scientific psychology.

Experimental psychology and the internal life of the worker

In the course of the nineteenth century psychological research oriented itself more and more closely to the model of the natural sciences. One major line of development is formed by two figures: Wilhelm Wundt and Emil Kraepelin.

For Wundt human life embraces two domains: bodily processes and the processes of consciousness. (It makes scientific sense to distinguish these conceptually and to ascribe them to physiology and psychology respectively.) Because in reality they belong together, these disciplines must be treated as complementary; but Wundt makes it clear that he is pursuing psychology. Physiological psychology is "fundamentally psychology, and, like every other branch of the science, aims *to investigate processes of consciousness in relation to one another.*"[27] Physiology is merely a means to this end.

The concept of "psychophysics" stems from Gustav Theodor Fechner, who argued that everything which can be perceived by introspection has an objectifiable organic correlate, so that stimulated physical changes would produce alterations in the activity of psychic perception. He attempted to formulate a mathematical relationship between these two series of events. His "exact theory of nature," published in 1860, marks the beginning of experimental psychology.[28] In his brilliant and moving speech marking the 100th anniversary of Fechner's birth, Wundt remarked with feeling that Fechner's precise empirical investigations into an external psychophysics ultimately served only to juxtapose science with speculations concerning an

---

[26] Weber, "Diskussionsbeitrag zur Verhandlung: Probleme der Arbeiterpsychologie unter besonderer Rücksichtnahme auf Methode und Ergebnisse der Vereinserhebungen," *ibid.*, 138 (1912).

[27] Wilhelm Wundt, *Grundzüge der Physiologischen Psychologie*, Leipzig: Engelmann, 1874; the fourth edition appeared in 1893 in two volumes, the fifth in 1902/3 in three.

[28] Gustav Theodor Fechner, *Elemente der Psychophysik*, Leipzig: Breitkopf und Hartel, 1860.

internal psychophysics, and a mystico-theosophical worldview resting on the assumption of an all-pervasive soul in nature and an ever-present God.[29] Wundt's physiological psychology was free from such notions, and concerned exclusively with "an investigation of empirically groundable relations between physiological and psychic processes."

Wundt's method involved systematically varying the intensity of stimuli and registering the perception of differences. Only through experiment did self-observation, hitherto the royal road of psychology, lose its subjective arbitrariness. However one judges the logical and methodological difficulties of Wundt's position, its influence was considerable. Wundt became head of a school which, as Kraepelin put it, "had the express aim of investigating, through controlled experiments, the law-like character of mental life in order to prepare the way for the gradual transformation of psychology into a science of experience."[30]

By the turn of the century physiological psychology had attained great national and international prestige. It influenced psychiatry via Emil Kraepelin, whose studies on the influence of drugs on elementary psychic processes laid the foundations for experimental psychopathology, establishing schools in Heidelberg and then Munich.[31] In 1896 the first volume of studies from the Kraepelin school appeared. Kraepelin opened it with a programmatic essay[32] in which he distinguished between two ways in which experimental psychology could be made useful to psychopathology: comparison of experimental results gleaned from normal and disturbed subjects; and the investigation of transitional stages between them through the controlled administration of alcohol, cocaine, morphine, hashish, bromide, tea, tobacco, and so on, to healthy subjects. In the course of these studies the problem of work capacity and fatigue increasingly predominated. Again and again bodily and spiritual overexertion, insufficient sleep and undernourishment "were identified as the primary or major cause of mental illnesses." For Kraepelin the central question was that of the causes of so-called psychoses of exhaustion and of "neurasthenia" then widely discussed. One assumes that Weber's interest in

[29] Wilhelm Wundt, *Gustav Theodor Fechner. Rede zur Feier seines hundertjährigen Geburtstages*, Leipzig: Engelmann, 1901, p. 49.

[30] Wilhelm Wundt, *Logik. Eine Untersuchung der Prinzipien der Erkenntnis und der Methoden wissenschaftlicher Forschung*, Stuttgart: Enke, 1893–1895, p. 168.

[31] Willy Hellpach described these studies, published in 1892, as "the cradle of experimental psychopathology." Hellpach, "Sozialpathologie als Wissenschaft," *Archiv für Soziologie und Sozialpolitik*, 21 (1905), p. 282.

[32] Emil Kraepelin, "Der psychologische Versuch in der Psychiatrie," *Psychologische Arbeiten*, 1:1 (1895), pp. 1–91.

Kraepelin's research into fatigue was not only scientific but also biographical in origin.[33]

Kraepelin followed a theory which assumed that psychophysical qualities were basic aspects of personality. Every human being possessed an individual apparatus "in which stimuli are worked through."[34] This apparatus is more fundamental than the content of experience, and must be taken into account in mental illness. This theory puts questions of psychic degeneration and psychopathic predispositions in a new light. To be sure, both of these concepts are dangerous because their use may absolve the investigator of the need to define mental processes precisely. Psychophysics is naturally more open toward the questions of degeneration and inheritance and more sensitive to biology than to "education and tradition" or culture. Yet Kraepelin did not advocate a "monadologic observation." In psychiatry, the theory of aphasia in particular had "led to a splitting of the soul into innumerable independent powers. Psychic abilities are represented here as the result of majority decisions by the lower house of perceptions and the upper house of memory images."[35] Thus Kraepelin assumes that the mental life of man consists of many intersecting processes, possesses no real fixity, and yet is determined by a number of basic physiological qualities. It is the task of psychological testing to isolate partial processes, to uncover their causes, and to evaluate their combined effect.

Kraepelin subscribed to the conventional view that mental and bodily performance changes over time, a change which can be represented in the form of a curve (his well-known work curve).[36] First, his measurements of performance showed that the course of the work curve varied enormously from one subject to another and in no way resulted in a simple model. It had numerous peaks within a given time span. Although it was immediately obvious to Kraepelin that exercise and fatigue were the most important determinants in the curve, a more precise analysis showed that others should be taken into account, above all habituation, stimulation, and strain. The work curve is thus a summation of curves.

Fatigue might be studied from a purely physiological point of view. Thus the Turin physiologist Angelo Mosso conceived of it as a reduction in muscle power, and tested this experimentally in the mid-1880s with the aid of a so-called ergograph, which represented the muscular performance of

---

[33] Lamprecht had spoken of the age of irritability, Hellpach of the specific irritability of the bourgeoisie. On the significance of this for a history of mentalities see Joachim Radkau, "Die Wilhelminische Ära als nervöses Zeitalter," *Geschichte und Gesellschaft*, 20:2 (1994), pp. 211–241.

[34] Kraepelin, "Der psychologische Versuch in der Psychiatrie," p. 46.

[35] *Ibid.*, p. 45.   [36] Kraepelin, *Die Arbeitscurve*, Leipzig: Engelmann, 1902.

the subject, such as the rhythmic lifting and letting fall the weight of a finger. The Kraepelin school employed a technically superior ergograph in which muscular performance was varied through the administration of medicines and drugs. Kraepelin's doctoral student Hans Walter Gruhle conducted tests with the ergograph in 1904/5, but was critical of the fact that it measured entire muscle groupings rather than individual muscles alone. In 1905 he moved to the psychiatric clinic of Heidelberg University, quickly came into contact with Max and Marianne Weber's circle, and advised Weber in his ventures into the terrain of experimental psychology.

Given the methods of a psychophysics of performance, its results can be applied to the field of industrial labor indirectly at best. The investigations were tied to the laboratory and studied activity that was largely irrelevant to actual work processes. Moreover, the relationship between objective and subjective qualities, between aptitude for and propensity to work, remained problematic. The environment was conceived primarily as the provider of stimuli, to which the "system" responded. Nevertheless, there would soon be an attempt to build a bridge to the psychology of work. Even before the turn of the century economists had discussed the "normal working day" in connection with worker protection legislation.[37] The experience of the reduction of the working day had shown that there was no proportional relationship between working time and efficiency. The same could be produced in a shorter working time. As mentioned above, Lujo Brentano reached the conclusion, shared by Weber, that increased wages and shorter working time led to an intensification of work, since under improved conditions workers were healthier, better nourished, and more willing to work.[38] The significance of subjective aspects was also recognized. Herkner in particular emphasized the influence of "worker satisfaction" on the performance of dependent wage labor.[39] Economists recognized that labor consisted of effort and struggle, and for the worker this meant "a sum of disagreeable sensations."[40]

Independently of Max Weber, then, economists were aware that the literature of experimental psychology could be instructive for the clarification of the objective and subjective aspects of industrial labor. The

[37] Wilhelm Stieda, "Normalarbeitstag," in Johannes Conrad et al. (eds.), Handwörterbuch der Staatswissenchaften, Jena: Fischer, 1900, pp. 987–995.

[38] Lujo Brentano, Über das Verhältnis von Arbeitslohn und Arbeitszeit zur Arbeitsleistung, 2nd edn., Leipzig: Duncker und Humblot, 1893.

[39] Heinrich Herkner, "Die Bedeutung der Arbeitsfreude in Theorie und Praxis der Volkswirtschaft," Jahrbuch der Gehe-Stiftung zu Dresden, (1905), pp. 3–36. Mention should also be made here of Karl Bücher's study of the influence of music and rhythm on work. Bücher, Arbeit und Rhythmus, Leipzig: Teubner, 1899, 2nd edn.

[40] Herkner, "Die Bedeutung der Arabeitsfreude," p. 10.

researchers on the *Verein*'s survey were asked to attend to the following points: "The length of the working day and other regulations, and their influence on the physical, psychic and ethical life of workers."[41] What needed to be recorded was "whether long-term work led to an increase in mistakes and decrease in relative output." Are there "differences between the performance of different workers? How can they be explained?" Further: "After what length of the working day does fatigue set in?"

Psychophysics had already influenced social science in a different way. Albert Schäffle based his organic social theory of the "construction and life of the social body" on psychophysical considerations.[42] Even if, like Max Weber, one fundamentally rejected organic analogies in economics and sociology, the asserted connection between psychophysics and socio-cultural processes could not be ignored. Darwin's theory of variation and selection had revolutionized creation theory and its secularized successors. Organic social theory and social Darwinism, though not identical, were connected in many ways. Organisms develop into ever more complex and thereby higher forms. Man as a higher form of being, like all organisms, has to seek an optimal adaptation to his life conditions. But in its "struggle for existence" association was more successful than isolation, so that sociality was "drummed into" him by nature. He formed into groups, which formed larger groups, which gave themselves an organizational form in order to defend their interests. The more complex a society becomes, the better can its organ of collective will formation, the state, defend its collective interests externally and represent them internally. In this way the development of human societies appeared a continuation of biological evolution.

It is no accident that Max Weber wrote to Heinrich Rickert in 1907 that he wished to criticize biologists' apparently value-free concept of development, according to which more differentiated or more complex meant higher.[43] But his conception of social science faced a greater threat from biological naturalism, which, were it adequately grounded, would make interpretive sociology and its theory of action impossible. If psychic, conscious human life was nothing more than the further development of the response functions of a simple organism, and if, furthermore, there

[41] "Work Plan for Investigation . . ." in Marie Bernays, *Auslese und Anpassung der Arbeiterschaft der geschlossenen Grossindustrie*, Leipzig: Duncker and Humblot, 1910.
[42] Albert Schäffle, *Bau und Leben des socialen Körpers. Encyclopädischer Entwurf einer realen Anatomie, Physiologie and Psychologie der menschlichen Gesellschaft mit besonder Rücksicht auf die Volkswirtschaft als socialen Stoffwechsel*, Tübingen: H. Lauppsche Buchhandlung, vol. I, 1875; vols. II–IV, 1878.
[43] Letter to Rickert, 3 Nov., 1907 in *MWG* II/5: 415.

existed a line of development from the simple actions of an unconscious being to the "conscious and considered" actions of a rational being, psychic life would be an epiphenomenon of physiological processes in the brain.

Psychophysics and action theory

The discussion so far has shown that Max Weber's confrontation with questions of psychophysics should in no way be seen solely in connection with the *Verein*. More general issues were at stake. Furthermore, it had a second component: ideological and scientific differences with his brother Alfred, which were compounded by the latter's return to Heidelberg from Prague.[44] The more general issues have two aspects: one logical-methodical,[45] one theoretical. With regard to logic and method, there are two questions. First, does the psychological origin of knowledge say anything about its validity? Second, do the propositions of economics, later called economic or sociological laws, require a psychological foundation? Theoretically, what influence should be ascribed to "upbringing and tradition" or culture, in relation to heredity and psychophysics?

Let me first turn to the methodological-methodical aspect from the point of view of its "prehistory" in Weber's work. Already in 1905, in his second article on "Roscher and Knies," Weber had engaged critically with the two leading representatives of experimental psychology, Wilhelm Wundt and Hugo Münsterberg, both of whom attempted to erect an idealist wall against psychophysical materialism. Weber thought the first volume of Münsterberg's *Foundations of Psychology*, in which he attempted to synthesize physiological psychology with Fichte's ethical idealism, a work of lasting significance.[46]

---

[44] Wolfgang Schluchter, "Max Weber und Alfred Weber. Zwei Wege von der Nationalökonomie zur Kultursoziologie," in Hans G. Nutzinger (ed.), *Zwischen Nationalökonomie und Universalgeschichte. Alfred Weber's Entwurf einer umfassender Sozialwissenschaft*, Warburg: Metropolis, 1995, p. 199.

[45] The term "methodological" used here follows Rickert, who distinguishes between constitutive and methodological categories. The boundary between the natural and the social sciences is not an epistemological but a methodological problem. The "methodical," on the other hand, refers to the investigation and handling of data. Whether to observe or interpret is a problem of method.

[46] Of interest here is Weber's assessment of Wundt and Münsterberg ten years after his discussion of their methodological writings. Following Münsterberg's death Rickert wrote an appreciation of his work. Max Weber responded. In a letter to Rickert he wrote that superficiality "is a quality inherent to all psychologists (apart of course from Jaspers and those like him) who are *not* strictly precise, including Wundt, Külpe e tutti quanti." But he expressly absolves Münsterberg of this charge. He continues: "I would gladly have read an *even* warmer appreciation (in tone if not meaning) of *Introduction to Psychology*. It is indeed the really consistent and philosophical culmination of Avenarius' work and in that

Weber was interested in two relationships: between values and knowledge, and between experience and knowledge. Wundt had defined the first relationship incorrectly; Münsterberg the second. Wundt's mistake was typical, Münsterberg's was critical, for here a representative of experimental psychology came remarkably close to the interpretive psychology of Wilhelm Dilthey, whose arguments had convinced historically oriented economists, but not Weber, who under the influence of Heinrich Rickert always remained critical of Dilthey.[47]

Weber began by disassembling Wundt's theory of creative synthesis and growth in psychic energy, through which the latter had identified cultural development with historical progress. He saw in this the residue of a metaphysical belief, reminiscent of Kant's belief in causality through freedom, but without Kant's formulation of it, which was "grandiose and, in its logic, ruthlessly perspicuous" (R&K 119). Weber had four arguments against such an idealist psychology: emergence occurred in natural as well as cultural processes; creative synthesis should be conceptualized as an epistemological, not a real, ground of knowledge, and grasped as a value relationship; processes of evaluation may be grasped physiologically, psychologically, biogenetically, sociologically or historically, but this said nothing about their validity; and a science of experience could not itself ground the value of the knowledge it produced, which was the result of a value judgment.

Münsterberg's mistake, according to Weber, was his tendency to polarize knowledge and experience. This led him to distinguish objectifying and subjectifying modes of observation. The objectifying and value-free analysis of natural processes, with its separation of subject and object, stood opposed to the immediate and value-related understanding of acts of will, in which subject and object are united. This entailed the idea that the category of causality was indeed applicable to natural processes, but not to acts of will. Against this Weber argued that the origin of knowledge should not be conflated with its empirical validity. He added that intuition played an important role in the origin of knowledge of culture as well as nature, and that where processes were understood, the evidence provided by the object of understanding was part of the psychology of knowledge. All

sense bound genetically to *your* own development, which itself once passed through that transitional stage, as you once put it so well. The psychologists are unaware of how seriously they ought to take it." Letter to Rickert, undated, DZA II, Mersburg Rep.92 N1. Max Weber Nr.25 B1.94.

[47] Cf. Weber's remark in a letter to Rickert of 3 Nov., 1907 in which he refers to the second edition of Rickert's *Philosophy of History*: "Dilthey gets off too lightly at the top of page 393: his essay is confused": *MWG* II/5: 416.

knowledge, including understanding, demands objectification. Even when that understanding is empathic, this does not lead to a division of the self: instead "first person experiences are replaced by reflection upon third person experiences which are conceived as an object" (*R&K* 166). This remains the case even when that object is feelings rather than thoughts. To be sure, the problem of indeterminateness, with which the cultural sciences alone have to struggle, arises here. But this is not a *logical* peculiarity. Certainly feelings remained relatively indeterminate even after their conceptualization, but this was not because they were feelings but because they were qualities. Weber states explicitly that the same applies to psychopathology. It too required, in order to be able to claim scientificity, a link between "the operation of empathically understanding mental processes or reproducing them in inner experience . . . and the concepts which have been produced by general 'observation'" (*R&K* 264).[48]

For Weber, psychology, of whatever type, is not foundational for the cultural and social sciences. It is a science of experience which specializes in certain problems and has its own epistemological goals. In so far as these problems confront it with meaningful processes, it, like all sciences of experience which objectify meaning, makes use of interpretation as well as observation. To put it in categories Weber developed later: it interprets either through direct observation, through explanatory understanding in terms of motivation, or reconstructively (*E&S* 8–9; *R&K* 152–154).

Despite this, Weber did not dispute the fact that alongside physiological and experimental psychology there could be an interpretive psychology. On the contrary: the fact that Karl Jaspers, under Weber's influence, developed one for psychopathology without its becoming a substitute for experimental psychology,[49] and then made it highly relevant to sociology,[50] shows that Weber had no reservations whatsoever towards a correctly understood interpretive psychology.[51] Jaspers himself insisted that such a

---

[48] Weber linked this to his reservations concerning psychoanalysis.

[49] Karl Jaspers, *Allgemeine Psychopathologie. Ein Leitfaden für Studierende, Ärzte und Psychologen*, Berlin: Springer, 1913.

[50] See Weber, "On Some Categories of Interpretive Sociology," *Sociological Quarterly*, 22 (1981), pp. 145–180.

[51] One candidate was obviously Freud's *Interpretation of Dreams*. But there were serious barriers to its reception, a fact about which Freud complained bitterly. Nevertheless, Freud played an important role in the work of psychologists around Weber. Thus Willy Hellpach: "However strong are my reservations towards many of Freud's exploratory and interpretive methods, I know of no work published in the last few decades, apart from the experimental psychology of the Heidelberg school, which can match the excitement of Freud's." Willy Hellpach, *Grundlinien einer Psychologie der Hysterie*, Leipzig: Engelmann, 1904, p. 38. Weber himself was aware of Freud's most important works, at least up to 1907. See W. G. Runciman, *Max Weber: Selections*, Cambridge: Cambridge University Press, 1978.

psychology had nowhere been "systematically developed." The best of it was to be found, "hedged about with aphorisms, philosophical observations, and characterological judgments in the writings of the most significant philosophical essayists," in Nietzsche, and, with certain reservations, in Freud.[52] Weber referred here to psychologists with spirit whom, dilettantish or not, one had to thank for valuable insights. But as far as hard questions of a science of experience were concerned, he held fast to experimental psychology.

Consequently Weber also rejected any undergirding of the economic theory of subjective values with "psychology." He took a critical stance towards "enlightened psychology," and any theory of concrete drives, or even self-interest. Yet the overcoming of the "simple psychology" by economics did not amount to theoretical progress, however much it was needed in order to avoid methodological confusions. Holding fast to the facts of everyday experience, economics postulated a majority of men "each of whom makes strictly rational use of those 'resources' and 'labor power' placed at his disposal either *de facto* or *de jure*, for the sole and exclusive purpose of achieving, in a peaceful way, an 'optimum' satisfaction of his *various* competing 'needs.'"[53] So it employs the concept of need, but uses it in its everyday, or in professional psychology's terms, vulgar, sense. The economist does not have to be familiar with abstractions employed by a psychologist in order to analyze the physiological and psychological qualities which are the basis of economic conduct. Economics is distinguished from psychology through the fact that it looks outward rather than inward, undertakes "not a psychological analysis of 'personality,'" but "an analysis of the 'objectively' given *situation*" (*R&K* 188).

In summer 1908, when Weber began to set down his essays on the Kraepelin school's research into exercise and fatigue, he employed this argument against the attempt to turn economics into applied psychology. Both historians and economists make use of causal analysis (*R&K* 164). But both remain as a rule at the level of everyday life. Where the historian demanded more, he stood in danger of achieving less. In the studies of ascetic protestantism Weber had already made this point with respect to cases of religious ecstasy. In the section on Pietism he mentioned cases which bordered on hysteria.[54] Yet attempts by professional psychology to throw light on the contents of this religious consciousness were premature to say the least. The battery of concepts which psychology had developed

[52] Jaspers, *Allgemeine Psychopathologie*, p. 153. On Freud, see p. 150.
[53] Weber, "Marginal Utility Theory and the Fundamental Laws of Psychophysics," *Social Science Quarterly*, 56:1 (1975), pp. 21–36.
[54] *Ibid.*

"do not at present go far enough to make them of use for the purposes of the historical investigation of our problems" (*PE* 244). The use of such concepts by the historian always stood in danger of creating "a false impression of scientific exactitude," and threatened impartiality towards the material (*PE* 244).

If one surveys Weber's writings up to 1908, it is clear that at this point the foundations of what he later called interpretive sociology were extensively laid. However, neither the theory of interpretation nor the theory of action were fully formulated. This was made possible through engagement with the psychophysics of industrial labor. It is above all two texts which warrant closer attention in this regard than is normally the case in the secondary literature: the report, also described as working directions, which Weber composed for the researchers on the survey for the *Verein*; and the essays on the psychophysics of industrial work, which did not arise in this connection but was the product of longstanding epistemological interests.

What can one learn from the two texts? Let us make Weber's two initial questions clear. First: why, in the analysis of economic activity, of industrial labor, is there no cooperation between the natural and the social sciences when such is in principle possible? Second: how might this be possible in the future? Are the questions and problems of these sciences the same? Weber's answer: In no way! If for experimental psychology the question is one of energy conservation, for economics it is one of cost reduction; if for the first physiological, for the second economic rationality. If the first relates to (psychophysical) *aptitude for* work, the second relates to (cultural) *attitude to* work. In Weber's view Kraepelin, despite his psychophysical assumptions, had difficulty incorporating psychic factors into his model of explanation. Stimulus and interest in work are heterogeneous concepts. And there was a divergence not only in questions and concepts, but also in method. Laboratory and factory were radically different contexts. There was still a yawning gap "between the most exact methods of calculation in industry and the experiments of psychologists."[55]

Nevertheless, in the light of Kraepelin's concepts, Weber thought it worthwhile, indeed necessary, to seek an equivalent for the measurement techniques of experimental psychology in the context of the factory. He found it in the wages books of firms, in which the performances of workers over time were set down. On the basis of this material a performance curve, which resembled Kraepelin's work curve, could be constructed. He illustrated how this might be done in individual cases through materials

---

[55] Weber, *Zur Psychophysik der industriellen Arbeit*, GASS 242.

from a weaving mill in Oerlinghausen belonging to relatives. Clearly, calculations from wages books are not a full equivalent for laboratory experiments, but in this way the methodical gap between experimental psychology and economics might at least be narrowed. Moreover, this was the only way "to gain a general picture of whether and at what points one has any chance at all of coming upon 'psychophysical' factors."[56]

Is what Weber says about method also true of concepts? Not wholly, for here it is not simply a matter of equivalence. There are concepts which are used in several disciplines. But their significance varies with the point of view from which they are applied. The concept of an "optimum," for instance, is common to physiology, psychology, and economics. But it signifies something different according to the "teleological 'functional value,'" the intellectual unity of the manifold to which it is related.[57] One might expect a narrowing of the conceptual gap between experimental psychology and social science. But Weber remained skeptical: theoretical points of view cannot be ordered according to Comtean hierarchies, nor are they simply complementary.[58] That which needed to be clarified through experiments, the relative contribution of disposition and individual or collective fate to performance, could not be:

> a wide gap would still separate us from an exact treatment of the "ultimate" questions – how far inherited dispositions on the one hand, life fate on the other, influence aptitude for work – even if the yawning gap between "exact" psychophysical observation and ours, which appeared in the above sketches, were closed, even if we believe ourselves to have achieved, in the treatment of these data, the degree of exactitude of a laboratory. [For the biologically oriented discussion of heredity in particular has] today in no way progressed so far that anything significant for our purposes might be gained from it.[59]

But Weber remained skeptical not only towards biological orientations in the social sciences, but also towards the demand for overexactitude,[60] a skepticism which had a private significance as well. It doubtless played a role in the ideological and scientific conflict which had broken out between

---

[56] Ibid., p. 294.   [57] Weber, "Marginal Utility Theory."

[58] See the formulation in the critique of Ostwald, where he wishes to make clear "what is always forgotten by modern doctrines of method: that the Comtean hierarchy of sciences is the lifeless schema of a grandiose pedant who is unaware that there are disciplines with heterogenous purposes all of which set out from everyday experience and which sublimate and work over this unscientific material from different independent standpoints": "Energetische Kulturtheorien," *Archiv für Sozialwissenschaft und Sozialpolitik*, 29:2 (1909), p. 586.

[59] Weber, *Zur Psychophysik der industriellen Arbeit.*

[60] As von Bruch notes, Schmoller made this claim to exactitude for part of his research. Rüdiger von Bruch, "Bürgerliche Sozialreform in Kaiserreich."

him and his brother Alfred. As mentioned earlier, Alfred Weber had accepted the call from the University of Heidelberg and moved from Prague to Heidelberg in winter 1907/8. He was working at the time on publication of a theory of industrial location, the most important reason for his appointment.[61] During his time in Prague, about which little is known, he clearly had a close relationship to Christian von Ehrenfelt and was impressed by the latter's apparently exact evolutionary research and his biologically grounded anti-bourgeois sexual ethics. Within the family circle he was regarded after his return as a "naturalist" with "antimoralistic preoccupations," dominated by a belief in the god-like character of the natural sciences.[62] This occasioned often violent disagreements between the brothers.

In his text on psychophysics Weber warns repeatedly against the premature treatment of observed individual and collective qualities and modes of conduct as inherited, a warning directed at those working on the survey, at other members of the *Verein*, and especially at Alfred Weber. In a letter to Alfred he observed one must "underline *still* more thickly the warnings against dilettantism, and maintain absolute skepticism towards the chances that *today* something essential can be concluded on this point." To be sure, Weber also spoke against the bracketing out of questions of heredity. One could "not *remain silent* about the fact that *somehow* and *somewhere* these problems are relevant."[63]

That Weber's warnings were also directed at his brother becomes clear from a letter to Hans Gruhle. Weber had written his review of the literature on the psychophysics of work not least "in order to demonstrate to my *brother*, who will *lead* the investigation (of the *Verein*) . . . the *great* (though surmountable) difficulties of approaching the problem of *heredity* in *this* way."[64] Weber must also have expressed this view to Eduard Gothein, who noted a conversation with him in summer 1908: ". . . then I discussed with Weber the program of investigation into industrial psychology he has been working on. His postulates are brilliant and carefully formulated, and perfectly designed to pour cold water on the premature enthusiasm of his brother,"[65] who was delivering himself of "psychiatric

[61] Alfred Weber, *Über den Standort der Industrien. Part I: Reine Theorie des Standorts*, Tübingen: J. C. B. Mohr (Siebeck), 1909.

[62] See the letters from Marianne to Helene Weber of 7 Jan., 1908 and 26 June, 1908, Max Weber–Schafer collection. Marianne informed her mother, who was frequently concerned over Alfred's mental state, about the occasional meetings and discussions she and Max had with him. See also the letter from Max to Helene of 14 Aug., 1908 in *MWG* II/5.

[63] Weber to Alfred, 19 Sept., 1908 in *ibid.*, p. 661.

[64] Weber to Gruhle, 13 Oct., 1908 in *ibid.*, p. 675.

[65] Gothein to Marie Louise Gothein of 28 and 29 Aug., 1908. Universitätsbibliothek Heidelberg, Handschriftenabteilung.

chatter about tiredness thresholds, inherited ability, stress."[66] Alfred himself had another view of the matter. During the preparation of the survey he objected to Max Weber's objectifying mode of observation: "During the investigation, my interest, which was directed towards the personal fate of the workers, was thwarted or drowned out by the perspective presented by my brother, which he set down in his essay 'The psychophysics of industrial labor.' Here everything is an objective analysis of the enterprise in relation to the physiology and the psyche of the workforce."[67]

The emergence of interpretive sociology

The largely negative results of Max Weber's venture into psychophysics and the theory of heredity had positive effects on his interpretive sociology. Through Kraepelin's work he made clear to himself "how infinitely complex is the way, from an 'energetic' point of view, in which psychic factors influence the psychophysics of work,"[68] and how mistaken is a purely physiological, but also purely culturalist interpretation of the psychic. Moreover: precisely through Kraepelin's work one could learn something of the psychophysical context of practice and habituation.

But there was a further important result. The conduct of workers was neither solely determined by their psychophysical apparatus nor regulated by maxims. There existed something else "in between," which was connected with states of mood, knowledge of which was of fundamental significance for interpretive sociology. In the essays on psychophysics there is a passage which, in view of later developments, is remarkably instructive. The following factors affect work performance:

> Firstly, on the one hand, rational considerations: again and again we will come upon the fact that workers regulate, increase or decrease their performance *planfully* according to "material" (i.e. economic) *purposes*, or, when more than one performance is required, alter the combination. Through pragmatic interpretation we can "clarify" the "maxims" which such purposeful regulation follows. On the other hand, performance changes quantitatively and qualitatively through changes in the psychophysical apparatus, changes which under certain circumstances enter consciousness according to the psychic effect – facilitation or hampering of performance – but *not* according to the psychophysical process which "lie behind" it; but which very

66 *Ibid.*
67 Alfred Weber to Christian von Ferber, 8 Mar., 1952. Private collection of Christian von Ferber.
68 Weber, "Energetische Kulturtheorien."

often remain wholly hidden and only become visible as the effect: alteration of performance. We can attempt to *explain* the causes of these components with the aid of so-called external experience and as a special case of rules arrived at through experiment. Then there are components which occupy a *specific* intermediate position . . . these are processes in which "states of mood" enter consciousness and influence performance *without* the origin of this influence . . . being consciously experienced: these processes can be *understood* "psychologically."[69]

If one places this alongside the passage from the critique of Stammler concerning the difference between purpose- and norm-maxims, and adds the remarks on exercise and habituation, one has virtually all the foundation stones for a method for interpretive sociology and a typology of action orientation: the distinction between pragmatic understanding, psychological understanding, and observational explanation; the distinction between reactive and meaningful conduct and, within the latter, between habitual or traditional, affectual, purpose-rational and value-rational action. In this way Weber made clear not only the barriers between experimental psychology and interpretive sociology, but also the benefits of their cooperation. Even the worker performance curves were made up of components which were not the business of a single discipline.

But it was not only the theory of understanding and action which benefited from the studies of the psychophysics of industrial labor. The theory of personality too took on sharper contours. To be sure, study of the psychophysical qualities of the personality did not lead Weber to abandon his basically dualist and hierarchical concept of personality, according to which the organism, the vegetative underground, must be culturally domesticated. But engagement with the psychophysical literature made it clear that this underground is not a formless material which takes on form only through being stamped with culture. The psychic *habitus* is formed from both "sides."[70]

In his later works too Weber remained close to the insights gained from his encounter with psychophysics. This manifested itself, not only in the basic categories of sociology, but also in the preface to the sociology of religion. The problem for a comparative sociology of religion was "the

---

[69] Weber, *Zur Psychophysik der industriellen Arbeit.*

[70] Friedrich Albert Lange once called for a physiological reading of Kant. Weber read Kant value theoretically. But the physiological and the value theoretical readings were not wholly contradictory. Weber came remarkably close to Lange in the texts on psychophysics. See Friedrich Albert Lange, *Geschichte des Materialismus und Kritik seiner Bedeutung in der Gegenwart*, 2 vols., Leipzig: Friedrich Brandstetter, [1875] 10th edn., 1921, vol. II, p. 389. On the significance of physiological neo-Kantianism see Hubert Treiber, "Zur 'Logik des Traumes' bei Nietzsche," *Nietzsche Studien*, 23 (1994), pp. 1–41.

special peculiarity of occidental rationalism, and within this field that of the modern occidental form" (*PE* 26). One might assume that "the most important reason lay in differences of heredity." Wholly in the spirit of the psychophysical studies, he insisted that he considers biological heredity to be of great significance for cultural history. But he saw no way "of exactly or even approximately measuring either the extent or, above all, the form of its influence on the development investigated here." Furthermore, it

> must be one of the tasks of sociological and historical investigation first to analyze all the influences and causal relationships which can satisfactorily be expected in terms of reactions to environmental conditions. Only then, and when comparative neurology and psychology shall have progressed beyond their present and in many ways very promising beginnings, can we hope even for the probability of a satisfactory answer to that problem. (*PE* 31)

The same opinion had been expressed to him some years before by an "eminent psychiatrist" (*PE* 186). Who was that? If I am not mistaken, it was Emil Kraepelin.

PART II

Politics and culture

4

PETER LASSMAN

The rule of man over man: politics, power and legitimation

Man is born free, and everywhere he is in chains. One believes himself the others' master and yet is more of a slave than they. How did this change come about? I do not know. What can make it legitimate? I believe I can solve this question.

(Rousseau)[1]

In place of "Sociology," a theory of the forms of rule (*Herrschaftsgebilden*). In place of "Society," the culture complex, as my chief interest.

(Nietzsche)[2]

Just like the political associations which preceded it historically, the state is a relationship of rule (*Herrschaft*) by human beings over human beings, and one that rests on the legitimate use of violence (that is, violence that is held to be legitimate). For the state to remain in existence, those who are ruled must submit to the authority claimed by whoever rules at any given time. When do people do this, and why? What inner justifications and what external means support this rule?

(Weber [*PW* 311])

Politics, power and the rule of man over man

The idea that the "rule (*Herrschaft*) of man over man" is an inescapable fact of human existence is a central theme of Max Weber's social and political thought (*E&S* 939).[3] A discussion of the forms of rule (*Herrschaft*) constitutes the core of his most important work, the unfinished and

---

[1] Jean-Jacques Rousseau, *The Social Contract*, in *The Social Contract and other Later Political Writings*, edited and translated by Victor Gourevitch, Cambridge: Cambridge University Press, 1997, p. 41.

[2] Friedrich Nietzsche, *Werke. Kritische Gesamtausgabe*, vol. VIII/2, ed. Giorgio Colli and Mazzino Montinari, Berlin: De Gruyter, 1970, p. 6136.

[3] Cf. Wilhelm Hennis, *Max Weber: Essays in Reconstruction*, trans. Keith Tribe, London and Boston: Allen & Unwin, 1988, p. 182.

incomplete *Economy and Society*.[4] For Weber, the idea of a world free from "the rule of man over man" is utopian. So too is any escape from the struggle for power through a unity of interests within classes, political parties, states or nations.

Few political thinkers have been committed to the idea of the "permanence of the political"; in some ways Weber was obsessed with it.[5] For Weber, man's unavoidable fate is to be a political animal, but politics does not and cannot offer a road to either happiness, justice, perpetual peace or redemption. "Anyone who goes in for worldly politics must, above all, be free of illusions and acknowledge one fundamental fact: to be resigned to the inevitable and eternal struggle of man with man on this earth" (*GPS* 29). The "rule of man over man" is the inevitable concomitant of this struggle. Struggle requires leaders who, in turn, require the "apparatus of a human following."[6] Consequently, it is not surprising that the religious prophet and the political demagogue play a central role in Weber's thought.[7]

The nature of the "rule of man over man" varies historically. The dominant form of rule in the west has changed from a regime based on personal to one based on impersonal relations. But the central questions remains the same: "The problem of men capable of exercising it: where do they come from, how are they selected, what are their leading ideas, what is their formative power?"[8]

The concept of the political

Weber proceeded, especially throughout *Economy and Society* (*Wirtschaft und Gesellschaft*), by defining his terms. The systematic "conceptual exposition," which appears as the first section of *Economy and Society* (although it was in fact written after those chapters which follow it in the published text), can be taken to represent Weber's mature view of these questions. Here, Weber's definitions of his basic concepts exhibit a marked concern with the sheer inescapability of relations of power, struggle, competition, selection and force in the social life of mankind.

"Politics," for Weber, means:

---

[4] Guenther Roth, "Introduction," *E&S*, p. lxxxviii.
[5] Joseph Schwartz, *The Permanence of the Political*, Princeton, NJ: Princeton University Press, 1995; Sheldon Wolin, *Politics and Vision*, Boston: Little Brown and Company, 1960.
[6] Karl Jaspers, "Max Weber: Politician, Scientist and Philosopher," in *Descartes, Leonardo, Max Weber: Three Essays*, London, Routledge, 1965, p. 217.
[7] Cf. Hennis, *Max Weber: Essays in Reconstruction*, p. 183.
[8] *Ibid.*, pp. 182–183.

Striving for a share of power or for influence on the distribution of power, whether it be between states or between groups of people contained within a single state. Essentially, this corresponds to ordinary usage. If one says that a question is a "political" question, or that a minister or official is a "political" official, or that a decision is determined "politically," what is meant in each case is that interests in the distribution, preservation, or transfer of power play a decisive role in answering that question, determining this decision or defining the sphere of activity of the official in question. Anyone engaged in politics is striving for power, either power as a means to attain other goals (which may be ideal or selfish), or power "for its own sake," which is to say, in order to enjoy the feeling of prestige given by power. (PW 311)

But if this text is read in the light of the conceptual distinction between the state and civil society which provided a background to much contemporary German political thought then it appears that Weber had a purpose in formulating his definitions in this way. He carefully distinguishes between those social relationships and associations which are based on similarities of interest and ideals, such as those exemplified in a religious sect, and those relationships and associations which are concerned with ruling and being ruled, most significantly in the form of the modern state. In so doing Weber is asserting that neither set of relationships is reducible to the other: although politics takes place within a social and cultural context it must also be understood in terms of its autonomy. Civil society is the arena for the conflict of "ideal" as well as material interests. But Weber does not attribute to the state any special capacity, in the manner of Hegel or of much political theory of his own time, for transcending these struggles. The state is regarded in a demystified way as nothing other than an "enterprise" or as a set of practices (*Betrieb*).[9] The "modern state is an 'organization' (*Betrieb*) in exactly the same way as a factory; indeed that is its specific historical characteristic" (PW 146).

Weber describes the modern state as being nothing other than an "enterprise" or a "business" (*Betrieb*) because, as with other major institutions, it has become "disenchanted." Nevertheless the most significant political conflicts and problems still raise deep questions concerning ultimate values. Indeed he argues that the ubiquity and intensity of conflicts of value are a consequence of disenchantment, and especially of the loss of the "blinding" effect of the Christian ethic.[10] Political questions are not

[9] Reinhard Bendix, *Max Weber: An Intellectual Portrait*, New York: Anchor Books, 1962 [1960]; Theodor Schieder, *The State and Society in our Times*, London: Thomas Nelson, 1962.

[10] Max Weber, "Science as a Vocation," in Peter Lassman, Irving Velody, and Herminio Martins (eds.), *Max Weber's "Science as a Vocation,"* London: Unwin Hyman, 1989, p. 24.

susceptible to definite resolution: "different gods struggle with each other and will do for all time."[11] Weber was intensely skeptical of all attempts to attain a permanent harmony of values either by means of the construction of a "moral science" or by means of political practice. In other words, Weber's conception of the realm of the political is inseparable from his theory of value. He insists that we live in a world in which the reality of rule and the struggle for power, the effects of which will be heightened by the permanent existence of relative scarcity of resources, will be given direction and substance by the inevitable struggle of irreconcilable values.[12]

Rule and legitimation

Although "*Herrschaft*" is a, if not the, central organizing concept in Weber's political thought, it is a term which has been surrounded by confusion. It has variously been translated as "domination," "rule," "authority," "leadership," and even as "imperative coordination," to mention only some of the more well-known examples. It is sometimes argued that Weber's concept of "*Herrschaft*" is untranslatable or that it defies easy translation. It is often asserted that, for example, there is no equivalent word in English. This has not, as has been indicated, prevented various interpreters and translators of Weber from offering their own preferred version.

One obstacle to understanding is the peculiar reception history of Weber's work. Much of post-Second World War social science has worked with a rather simplified and misleading account of Weber's intentions, and often, until very recently, as a result of the incomplete character of translation, with a fragmentary knowledge of his work. Consequently, Weber's central concepts have frequently been assimilated to the language of the modern social sciences in an uncritical manner. In particular, it has often been assumed that Weber's concepts are contributions to an unproblematic and politically neutral "value-free" theoretical discourse. This is, of course, a massive simplification of his thought. This simplification results from the fact that many commentators on Weber have not paid sufficient attention to the intellectual and historical context. Many have also assumed that the meaning of Weber's terms could be unproblematically derived from their usage in ordinary language. But it is now apparent that Weber was using the concept of "*Herrschaft*," as well as his other related

---

[11] *Ibid.*, p. 23.
[12] Michael Zängle, *Max Weber's Staatstheorie in Kontexte seines Werkes*, Berlin: Duncker and Humblot, 1988.

political concepts, in a highly deliberate manner. Weber was contributing to an intellectual debate which had political implications. In considering Weber's political ideas, therefore, the much misunderstood demand for "value-freedom" or "neutrality" ought to be set aside. Weber's discussion of the basic forms of political and social association is itself an expression of a political position.[13] Most importantly, Weber's "determined realism" was taking aim at the "state metaphysics" of von Gierke and his followers with its stress on *"Genossenschaft"* (cooperation, fellowship) at the expense of *"Herrschaft."*[14]

Intellectual context is only part of the story, however. The concepts, generalizations, and interpretations which constitute the core of Weber's *Economy and Society* are themselves informed by an implicit theory. The coherence of the work derives from his idea of the significance of the political: his understanding of the nature, inner development, direction and unavoidability of relations of power and rule which pervade all complex structures of human relations. When Weber makes judgments concerning the "utopian" character of political programs he is presupposing a conception of social and political reality understood in terms of his belief in the inescapability of "the rule of man over man."

The discussion of the concepts of "legitimate order" and of "struggle" which occupy a strategic position in Weber's exposition illustrate some of the problems of interpretation. The concept of "legitimacy" refers to the acceptance of the validity of an order of rules. This definition is not concerned with the normative question of whether or not that body of rules ought to be considered legitimate, that is to say the question of the beliefs which justify acceptance. This is a point where many of Weber's critics argue that he has unjustifiably altered the generally accepted meaning of the concept.[15] Weber ignores the argument that a concept such as "legitimacy" has implicit normative implications and cannot, therefore, be used in a "neutral" manner. According to Weber's critics to describe a regime as

[13] Melvin Richter, *The History of Political and Social Concepts*, Oxford: Oxford University Press, 1995, pp. 58–70; Hennis, *Max Weber: Essays in Reconstruction*, pp. 152–172; Otfried Höffe, *Political Justice*, Oxford: Polity Press, 1995; Gangolf Hübinger, *"Staatstheorie und Politik als Wissenschaft im Kaiserreich*: Georg Jellinek, Otto Hintze, Max Weber," in H. Maier *et al.* (eds.), *Politik, Philosophie Praxis: Festschrift für Wilhelm Hennis zum 65. Geburtstag*, Stuttgart: Klett- Cotta, 1988.

[14] Otto Hintze, *Soziologie und Geschichte. Gesammelte Abhandlungen*, vol. II, Göttingen: Vandenhoeck & Ruprecht, 1964, p. 142.

[15] David Beetham, *The Legitimation of Power*, London: Macmillan, 1991; R. Grafstein, "The Failure of Weber's Concept of Legitimacy," *Journal of Politics*, 43 (1981); John H. Schaar, "Legitimacy in the Modern State," in William Connolly (ed.), *Legitimacy and the State*, Oxford: Basil Blackwell, 1984; Hannah Fenichel Pitkin, *Wittgenstein and Justice*, Berkeley: University of California Press, 1972.

legitimate must be to refer to a valued achievement other than the contingent fact that its citizens appear to obey its laws or just happen to believe it to be legitimate. Worse still, Weber's use of the concept of "legitimacy" would appear to remove the possibility of saying that some states simply are "illegitimate" even though its citizens or subjects obey its commands or laws. Weber's intention, presumably, was to avoid the difficulties involved in arguments of this kind. Legitimacy, for him, was to be regarded simply as a precarious political achievement. No regime can survive for long if it is based on force alone. As a result, all rulers must strive to attain legitimacy, understood here simply as a successful claim, in a world of permanent political "struggle." Legitimacy is, in effect, defined in terms of legality, with the proviso that the laws must in fact usually be obeyed.

Here the difficulties with the notion of neutrality become apparent. Weber was, in many ways, influenced by both legal positivism and post-Nietzschean skepticism. He was not concerned with the problem of which regimes are normatively legitimate, but with a different question. If one accepts, as he did, that no appeal to a transcendent standard for judging the legitimacy of regimes was credible in the modern disenchanted world, the question becomes "how can modern regimes legitimate themselves or be held to be legitimate?" Modern mass democratic states could fall under the influence of unprincipled demagogues or worse who would lack the constraints provided by formerly legitimating beliefs.[16] But Weber would not have arrived at this problem without having already made a negative "political" judgment about the credibility of present normative political beliefs.

The theme of the distinctiveness of the political domain is stressed throughout his work: not all forms of "struggle" are necessarily political struggles in the strict sense, and neither are all "associations of rule" necessarily concerned with political rule. In this respect Weber is quite unlike recent thinkers who wish to see all relations of "dominance," including those in the personal realm, as "political." "Political associations" are distinguished by their use of force and the threat of force:

> An association of rule shall be called a *political* association only inasmuch as its existence and the validity of its ordinances within a definable geographical *territory* are continuously guaranteed by the application and threat of physical compulsion on the part of the administrative staff.   (*E&S* 54)

[16] Tracy B. Strong, "Max Weber and the Bourgeoisie," in Asher Horowitz and Terry Maley (eds.), *The Barbarism of Reason: Max Weber and the Twilight of Enlightenment*, Toronto: University of Toronto Press, 1989.

In contrast, a "hierocratic association" is also an "association of rule," but the basis of its rule is found in the application of forms of psychological compulsion (*psychischer Zwang*) and the distribution or denial of religious benefits. A church is a "hierocratic association" with an administrative staff which is able to claim successfully the monopoly of the legitimate use of such forms of coercion.

In a similar fashion Weber distinguishes between power (*Macht*) and rule (*Herrschaft*). He defines power as "every chance of imposing one's own will within a social relation, even against resistance, regardless of what this chance is based upon." Rule (*Herrschaft*) is defined as "the chance of having an order with a specific content obeyed by specifiable persons." In order to specify the distinctiveness of political rule Weber contrasts "rule" in an economic context from "rule" in a political context. The purest form of the former is a monopolistic control of a market while the purest form of the latter is provided by the rule of a prince or patriarch. As far as Weber is concerned the concept of "rule" (*Herrschaft*) is to be used in the narrow sense to refer to the power to command and not, in a more general sense, to all kinds of control including those forms which emerge from market-based economic exchange (*E&S* 946).

An "association of rule" is a political organization if its order and existence take place within a particular territory and this order is backed by the threat and the application, by an administrative staff, of the use of physical force. A state is that particular kind of political organization which, in addition, is able, through its control of the means of administration, to maintain a monopoly of the legitimate use of physical force and violence. This definition brings together the essential characteristics of the state: physical force, legitimation, and administration.

It is especially important that the essential feature of territoriality in Weber's account is not overlooked.[17] The territorial dimension is stressed in Weber's discussion of "political communities." (*E&S* 901–940). The meaning of "political" is apparent here. He argues that a "political community" is to be distinguished from any kind of economically structured social grouping in that the "specific pathos" of a "political community" is that it, more than any other form of association, produces among its members a "community of political destiny." Experience of common political struggles produces deep feelings of a shared fate which can transcend other social and cultural ties.

The state, and Weber is focusing primarily on the modern form of the

---

[17] Thomas Baldwin, "The Territorial State," in H. Gross and R. Harrison (eds.), *Jurisprudence: Cambridge Essays*, Oxford: Clarendon Press, 1992.

state, is to be identified with those means rather than the ends which are peculiar to it. The essential characteristic of political rule in the modern state, for Weber, is, therefore, that it is that form of rule which is supported by the use of or threat to make use of physical force. From this set of dry conceptual distinctions, Weber arrives at one of the most striking images of the state in the history of political thought:

> In the past the most diverse kinds of association – beginning with the clan – have regarded physical violence as a quite normal instrument. Nowadays, by contrast, we have to say that a state is that human community which (successfully) lays claim to the *monopoly of legitimate physical violence* within a certain territory, this "territory" being another of the defining characteristics of the state. For the specific feature of the present is that the right to use physical violence is attributed to any and all other associations or individuals only to the extent that the *state* for its part permits that to happen. The state is held to be the sole source of the "right" to use violence. (*PW* 310–311)

Rule and legitimacy

In Weber's view, the stability of any form of rule depends on the requirement that those who are ruled accept or submit to the authority of those who rule. Weber was here influenced to a large degree by the tradition of "*Staatslehre*" and, in particular, the work of his friend and colleague Georg Jellinek. Jellinek had discussed the forms of justification of the state in his "*Allgemeine Staatslehre*."[18] Weber adapted Jellinek's "empirical types," such as "religious-theological" and "legal-theoretical" forms of justification to create his "ideal types" of legitimation. It is directly in keeping with his concern with the structure of ways of life (*Lebensführung*) that Weber thought it to be of supreme importance to ask why the ruled submit to be ruled: "What inner justifications and what external means support this rule?" (*PW* 311).

Weber puts the question of legitimation at the center of his account of the relations of rule. He takes it as a basic fact of social life that any inequality in the distribution of power and any form of rule will need to justify itself and seek legitimacy. All relations of privilege and inequality between different groupings require doctrines or myths which serve to justify their existence and continuation. Under relatively stable conditions these legitimating doctrines are generally accepted by the masses, who, according to Weber, are normally politically passive, but, during periods

---

[18] Georg Jellinek, *Allgemeine Staatslehre*, Berlin: O. Häring, 1900, pp. 184–220.

when the inherent inequalities of social existence become visible, legitimating ideas are questioned, with intense and possibly violent struggles as a consequence.

Legitimate rule can be described in terms of three ideal-typical forms. Firstly, there is the authority of "the eternal past," of *custom*, hallowed by the fact that it has held sway from time immemorial and by a habitual predisposition to preserve it. This is "traditional" rule, as exercised by the patriarch and the patrimonial prince of the old type. Then there is the authority of the exceptional, personal *"gift of grace,"* or charisma, the entirely personal devotion to, and personal trust in, revelations, heroism, or other qualities of leadership in an individual. This is "charismatic" rule, as exercised by the prophet or, in the field of politics, by the chosen war-lord or the plebiscitarian ruler, the great demagogue and leader of a political party. Finally, there is rule by virtue of "legality," by virtue of belief in the validity of legal *statute* and the appropriate (*sachlich*) juridical "competence" founded on rationally devised rules (*PW* 311–312).

Despite the detailed attention given to traditional and legal rule Weber was fascinated by the phenomenon of charismatic rule. Weber, revealingly, frequently states that he is interested "above all" in the character of "rule by virtue of devotion to the purely personal 'charisma' of the 'leader' on the part of those who obey him." Furthermore, it is here "where the idea of *vocation* (*Beruf*) in its highest form has its roots" (*PW* 312).

Weber's classification seems to be a radical modification of the traditional typology of six forms of constitution which had been a preoccupation of political theorists since the ancient Greeks and which, in the form set out by Aristotle, had been dominant throughout the history of western political thought. The radicalism of Weber's approach is revealing. Although he insists that his forms of state are ideal-types and as such they cannot exist in reality he has, nevertheless, reduced the number of types to three. This is to a large extent the consequence of his decision not to base his classification on the two Aristotelian criteria of the size of the ruling body and its ability or inability to contribute to the public good but, instead, simply on the possible formal bases of command and of claims to legitimation.

The order in which Weber presented the three types of rule, in its later versions, was deliberately meant to discourage any interpretation which could see them as constituting an evolutionary progression.[19] In *Economy and Society* he discusses rational, legal rule with a bureaucratic staff first, followed by traditional rule, and last, but certainly not least, charismatic rule. Nevertheless, to define legal bureaucratic rule as the specifically

---

[19] Wolfgang Mommsen, *The Age of Bureaucracy*, Oxford: Basil Blackwell, 1974, pp. 1–21.

modern form is to admit that although there may be no warrant for a deterministic evolutionary account this "universal" set of categories does possess an implicit historical as well as a more systematic dimension.

All forms of rule are combined with specific forms of administration. The pure type of legal rule is best represented by a bureaucratic form of administration. The essence of legal rule is contained in the idea that legitimacy is derived from acceptance of the authority of a system of abstract rules. The administration of law consists in the application of these rules to particular cases. The institutional structure which is most formally rational, and the form which characterizes the modern western state, rests primarily on this type of legitimacy. The cultural significance of this form of rule lies in the fact that the individual obeys an impersonal order. The legal form of rule implies the existence of a rule-governed way of conducting government and administration.

Bureaucratic administration is hierarchical in form. The administrative staff of such an organization consists of officials who have been produced by a specialized training. Administrators of this type are completely separated from ownership of the means of administration just as the modern proletarian is separated from ownership of the means of production. Weber, in discussing this form of rule in so much detail, was not primarily interested in the internal mechanics of this form of organization but, rather, in the political and cultural implications of the rule of "officialdom."

It would be a mistake to interpret Weber as saying that either the bureaucracy rules alone or that this form of rule amounts to the "rule of law" which is central for modern liberal constitutionalism. In keeping with his commitment to the centrality of command Weber is consistent in pointing out that the head of an administration is not an administrator. For example, the head of a legal bureaucratic order could be a president or a monarch. The real problem, in Weber's view, occurs in the tendency of bureaucracy to extend its role beyond its legitimate province and to transform what Weber considered to be the genuine politics of leadership into routine administration. In a modern state in which strong political leadership is lacking, the probability is that the higher ranking officials are likely to win their battles with their nominal superiors, such as cabinet ministers, simply because of their possession of the specialist knowledge which bureaucracy contains. As far as the rule of law is concerned Weber does not deny its importance but, for him, it operates as a façade covering the reality of relations of power and rule which are the foundation of all political regimes. The significance of bureaucracy also lies in the fact that, for Weber, the development of the modern state is synonymous with the development of modern officialdom and bureaucratic organization, in the same way as the development of modern capitalism is bound up with the increasing bureaucratization of the economic enterprise (*GAW* 477).

The technical superiority of bureaucracy over all other forms of administration guarantees its progressive development in the modern world. It is symptomatic of Weber's whole approach, and of the way in which his typology cuts across more conventional ways of discussing political forms, that the encroachment of bureaucracy is common to both capitalist and socialist economies. In fact, as far as Weber was concerned, a socialist economy was far more likely to be subject to bureaucratic rule than was a capitalist economy. The tension between formal and substantive rationality is built into the operation of all forms of modern bureaucracy. The extension of bureaucratic rule under conditions of socialism is, for Weber, an important example of this unavoidable and insoluble conflict between formal and substantive rationality. In this case Weber meant that the substantive aims and ideals of socialism, such as equality, community and distributive justice, are in a state of permanent tension with the formal, hierarchical character of bureaucracy whose ability to produce the highest degree of formal rationality and economic calculability necessary for economic planning is indispensable for its survival. Bureaucracy has become indispensable for the modern state whatever its economic arrangements.

The growth of bureaucracy has several implications. Most significant among these is the tendency towards social leveling, a related "plutocratization" based on the length of time required to gain the necessary technical training and qualifications, and the predominance of a culture of formalist impersonality. The "spirit" of bureaucratization, with its leveling tendencies and its undermining of traditional privileges of status (*Stände*), possesses an "elective affinity" with the culture of "mass democracy." This can be observed in the bureaucratization of political parties. Democratic mass political parties cease to rely on the personal leadership of "notables" and become bureaucratically organized under the leadership of party officials. Nevertheless, Weber argues that in order to grasp the affinity between democracy and bureaucracy the true nature of modern democracy must be understood. There is no real sense, in Weber's view, in which the masses can be said to govern directly in the modern democratic state. Formal democratization does not produce any real change in the way in which the masses are ruled. Democracy is simply a mechanism whereby leaders are selected. There is, however, a fundamental and ironic tension between the logic of democracy and the logic of bureaucracy. The growth of bureaucracy is, to a large extent, the unintended consequence of the democratic struggle against rule by notables while the democratic principle requires that the power of administrators be curbed. Modern mass democracy cannot function without bureaucracy. There is a fundamental tension between the two principles even if democracy is understood not in the sense of direct democracy, but as the rule of elected party leaders. The indispensability of bureaucracy has another implication: genuine revolutions are increasingly unlikely to be successful in modern states.

Legal rule with a bureaucratic staff supplanted traditional forms of rule in western states, those which were legitimated by beliefs in the sacred character of the social order. In contrast with bureaucratic rule, forms of rule which rest upon an appeal to tradition produce regimes of personal loyalty rather than obedience to a set of abstract rules. The most important and "pure" form of traditional legitimation is represented by "patriarchal rule." The administrative staff of a ruler of this type are not officials but personal retainers. While rulers of this type are bound by traditional "rules," they have a great deal of freedom of action: in contrast to the rationality and predictability of bureaucratic rule, traditionalism permits a high degree of arbitrariness.

It has been argued that "in the ultimate analysis" the central theme in Weber's *Economy and Society* is the "never-ending struggle of charisma as a particularly powerful social force, which Weber more or less identified with individual creative activity, on the one hand, with the routinizing forces of bureaucratization and routinization on the other."[20] Charisma is, as Weber points out, not a new concept: He adopted it from the vocabulary and contemporary study of early Christianity. Its original meaning is "gift of grace." Weber took the concept and, in a way which some have found controversial, extended its domain of reference so that it might be used in the analysis of politics. He defined charisma as:

> the quality of a personality, held to be out of the ordinary (and originally thought to have magical sources, both in the case of prophets and men who are wise in healing or in law, the leaders of the hunt or heroes in war), on account of which the person is evaluated as being gifted with supernatural or superhuman or at least specifically out of the ordinary powers not accessible to everybody, and hence as a "leader." (*E&S* 241; *MSS* 140)

Weber's stress on charisma and its struggle with the forces of rationalization and bureaucratization is a reflection of a deeper underlying theme in his work. The emphasis placed on the role of charisma, which seems at first sight to be out of all proportion to its historical occurrence, is under-

---

[20] *Ibid.*, pp. 19–20.

standable when it is seen to reflect a central theme, much influenced by Nietzsche, in Weber's thought; the tension between ethics and the world.[21]

The importance given to the concept of charisma in Weber's classification of forms of legitimation is itself highly revealing. Why does charisma play such a central role in Weber's work? Underlying all of Weber's political thought is the problem of the continuing existence of the free human being under modern conditions of rationalization and disenchantment.[22] Despite the intended and superficially "value-free" nature of the vast structure of *Economy and Society* and his other major works, Weber frequently reveals his own value-laden standpoint. Behind all debate about the forms of rule, whether they take a bureaucratic or a charismatic form, there is the question of which type of human being will predominate: the *"Kultur-mensch"* (the cultured man) or the *"Fachmensch"* (the expert specialist, the technician) (*E&S* 1002).

One of the consequences of this account of legitimacy and of forms of rule, which many of Weber's critics have found troubling, is the way in which it treats democracy. For Weber there is no form of democratic legitimation as such. Democracy is one of those political forms which do not seem to fit easily into his classification of forms of legitimation. Weber discusses modern democracy under the heading of charismatic rule and not as an example, as one might expect, of legal rule. Democracy in the modern state primarily takes the form of plebiscitary democracy which Weber sees as itself being a version of charismatic "Leadership Democracy" (*Führer-Demokratie*). Weber argues that in this type of regime legitimacy is only formally derived from the will of the ruled. In fact, the leader, in this case a demagogue, rules on the basis of the devotion and trust of his followers.

Modern mass democracies are plebiscitarian democracies in which parties are involved in a continuous parliamentary struggle for power. Legitimacy resides simply in the ability of a charismatic party leader to maintain the support of his followers and of the masses. There is no attempt by Weber to appeal to any other standard of legitimacy. This concentration on relations of rule and the struggle for power as the central reality of politics reveals a tension in Weber's account. Despite his insistence on the need in the modern parliamentary state for "politically responsible and mature" citizens who understand rather than unreflectively follow the policies of strong leaders Weber was unable to confer any deep significance on public debate and deliberation as an essential component of democratic

---

[21] Zängle, *Max Weber's Staatstheorie*.
[22] Hennis, *Max Weber: Essays in Reconstruction*, p. 101.

legitimation. To do so would be to appeal to those ideas he had called "utopian" and, therefore, lacking in credibility.

The problem created by Weber's account of democratic politics is illustrated further by the way in which he discusses the ancient Greek city state, the *polis*. It could be argued that Weber's account of the modern democratic state is simply a realistic description which does not, in fact, rule out the possibility that in other states or in earlier times genuine democracy, representative or direct, could exist. In fact, it seems that, because the Greek *polis* was neither a traditional nor a rational bureaucratic form, Weber had, according to the logic of his classification, to place it within the category of charismatic rule, as an example of a "plebiscitarian democracy." According to his critics the justification for doing so was "extremely thin and casual."[23] Weber characterizes political life in the Greek *polis* in terms of a competition between demagogues resting on emotional appeals to the masses. There is a marked tendency to disregard any notion of political community constituted on the basis of citizenship and public debate which is indicative of the total "neglect of the civic dimension of politics," which "is a central feature of . . . [his] political theory."[24] The evidence, however, in support of Weber's interpretation is, to say the least, weak. "To dismiss the Greek *polis* in general and Athens in particular as irrational does not advance our understanding."[25] Nevertheless Weber was compelled to characterize it in this way by his scheme of classification with its roots in his vision of politics as struggle which takes place, most dramatically, between charismatic political leaders and ultimate value-standpoints.

Politics and legitimation in a disenchanted world

Despite the seeming, but ultimately unsustainable, impartiality and detachment of his mode of presentation, Weber was in fact recasting the traditional question of political legitimation. Weber's account can be understood in terms of his interpretation of the fundamental problem created by the inevitable tension between the universal operation of power and the universal need for its legitimation for the rulers and the ruled. This problem has become increasingly important because, in Weber's view, the defining

---

[23] Moses Finley, *Ancient History: Evidence and Models*, London: Chatto & Windus, 1985, p. 94.

[24] Rune Slagstad, "Liberal Constitutionalism and Its Critics: Carl Schmitt and Max Weber," in John Elster and Rune Slagstad (eds.), *Constitutionalism and Democracy*, Cambridge: Cambridge University Press, 1988, p. 128.

[25] Finley, *Ancient History: Evidence and Models*, p. 103.

characteristic of modernity is its relentless advance of the forces of rationalization and "disenchantment" which have the combined effect of undermining those ideas and beliefs on which we have relied for so long to provide the grounds for our ideas of legitimacy. This is especially true, Weber argues, with the demise of natural law and all other "metajuristic axioms" (*E&S* 874).

This theme in Max Weber's thought can be considered in the light of what Wilhelm Hennis has argued constitutes Weber's "central question." According to Hennis the fundamental theme which runs throughout all of Weber's thought is a concern with the relationship between forms of *Lebensführung*, the ways in which men attempt to give meaning to their existence, and the constraints imposed by the logic of power, politics and the inescapable "rule of man over man."[26]

Although he was suspicious of all philosophies of history which claimed to find some direction, meaning, or purpose in the course of world history it has often been pointed out that Weber's own work itself rests on an interpretation of epic proportions of the cultural transformation of the modern west. The historical uniqueness of western society and of the modern western state is described in terms of its experience of "disenchantment." In Weber's words:

> The fate of our age, with its characteristic rationalization and intellectualization and above all the disenchantment of the world, is that the ultimate, most sublime values have withdrawn from public life, either into the transcendental realm of mystical life or into the brotherhood of immediate personal relationships between individuals.[27]

This account of the disenchantment of our ultimate values has serious implications for the problem of legitimating political power in the modern world. While our culture is being radically transformed by the forces of rationalization and disenchantment the reality of power and of "the rule of man over man" has remained and will continue to remain a constant throughout human history.[28] In fact, Weber argues, it is precisely in the modern disenchanted world that the problem of legitimation will become even more difficult to resolve. One of the consequences of rationalization and disenchantment is the undermining of our sense that our ultimate values are supported by secure foundations while our appreciation of the reality of plural, conflicting, and irreconcilable values is heightened. In fact, the modern predicament seems to indicate that an age of relative certainty,

---

[26] Hennis, *Max Weber: Essays in Reconstruction*.
[27] Max Weber, "Science as a Vocation," p. 30.
[28] Sheldon Wolin, *Politics and Vision*.

if there ever was one, was simply an interlude between eras of uncertainty. Thus it is not surprising that Weber argues that the modern disenchanted world bears comparison with that of the pre-Socratic Greeks:

> For here, too, different gods struggle with each other and will do for all time. It is just like in the old world, which was not yet disenchanted with its gods and demons, but in another sense. Just as Hellenic man sacrificed on this occasion to Aphrodite and on another to Apollo, and above all as everybody sacrificed to the gods of his city–things are still the same today, but disenchanted and divested of the mythical but inwardly genuine flexibility of those customs.[29]

The idea of a fundamental conflict of values, which deepens under modern conditions, is central for an understanding of Weber's political thought. It is the fate of modern man to live with a "polytheism" of conflicting values.

In this sense there is, as has often been noted, a similarity, which is not accidental, between the political ideas of Weber and Machiavelli.[30] Weber was familiar with Machiavelli's work and frequently refers to him. Both Weber and Machiavelli share a belief in the autonomy of the political domain. Politics and government are characterized by their own logic, methods, paradoxes, and fate. Furthermore, Weber's depiction of political leaders is similar to that of Machiavelli. In short, for Weber all political life is centered around the fact of power; politics is struggle; political struggle requires leaders; genuine political leaders must be guided by a sense of responsibility for their actions; political leaders, if they are to be successful, require a following and an organizational apparatus; and the political leader is always constrained to a varying degree by the requirements of his or her following. As with Machiavelli the political world is described in terms of an endless and, often tragic, struggle between the powers of "*virtù*" and "*fortuna*"; individual charisma and fate (*PW* 355).[31] To put it even more directly, fundamentally for Weber "all politics is violence – even, in its own fashion, democratic politics."[32] In keeping with this account those who engage in politics are involved with "diabolical" forces (*PW* 75). Ultimately, Weber's vision is bleak: that it is our common fate to be condemned to live in and to try to make sense of a world where the "rule of man over man" is an inevitable reality.

[29] Max Weber, "Science as a Vocation," p. 23.
[30] Carlo Antoni, *From History to Sociology: The Transition in German Historical Thinking*, trans. Hayden White, Detroit, MI: Wayne State University Press, 1959; Mommsen, *The Age of Bureaucracy*.
[31] Niccolò Machiavelli, *The Prince*, Cambridge: Cambridge University Press, 1988, pp. 84–7.
[32] Maurice Merleau-Ponty, *Adventures of the Dialectic*, London: Heinemann, 1974, p. 26.

5

LAWRENCE A. SCAFF

Weber on the cultural situation of the modern age

Max Weber's life and work unfolded across one of the decisive turning points in western culture. He experienced the consolidation of modern capitalism, the dynamism of a new urban and technological civilization, and the numerous avant-garde challenges to the inherited cultural traditions of the nineteenth century. He followed the cultural movement of the *fin de siècle* with interest, even becoming personally entangled with some of its more extreme representatives. His scholarly interests then combined with his personal experience to produce a distinctive body of reflection on the cultural crisis of the times in science, politics, art, economy, ethics, and religion.

Weber's greatest work was always motivated by historical questions bearing on the present, but oriented toward the comparison of world civilizations: "Universal historical problems" and a "universal history of culture," as he wrote in the introduction to the *Collected Essays on the Sociology of Religion* (*PE* 13, 23).[1] His response to the changing cultural milieu took an astonishing variety of forms and was articulated with an historical depth and universal scope rarely matched in scholarship, from complex reflections on the underlying dynamics of the orders of life and value in different societies, to numerous unfinished projects in cultural sociology. Through all of these studies he aimed for a kind of genetic and morphological account of the modern age, an assessment of what Weber himself liked to call "the fate of our times."

There is a temptation to see the *fin de siècle* cultural situation in which he was placed as one of flux, confusion and multiplicity, and then to cast Weber as the anguished questioner of rationalism and the defender of pathos and a tragic sense of history. But such a view would be far too simplistic and, in the end, self-defeating. The reason Weber's writings on

---

[1] References are to the English language translations of Weber's work, when they exist, and otherwise to the German texts; in the interest of textual accuracy I have sometimes altered the translation according to the original.

the cultural situation of our age are so compelling is because of the complexity of his commitments to science and the reasoned ambiguities in his vision of the "cultural significance" of modern life.

Recent scholarship, especially the editing of Max Weber's extensive correspondence in the collected works, the *Max Weber Gesamtausgabe*, now allows a renewed appreciation of his thought as a decisive, tension-ridden meeting point for the contending forces of the modern world. Historians and sociologists have added a more differentiated picture than was available previously of the oppositional cultural milieu and counter-cultural movements that connect Weber's *fin de siècle* to our own.[2] Others have taken up the modern cultural issues in more specific contexts, such as music, cultural criticism, literature of the avant-garde, and science itself.[3] The combined effect of this body of critical and historical scholarship has been an increasingly complex and intriguing perspective on the cultural biography of Weber's scholarly projects, one that encourages an improved understanding of the significance of the cultural issues for Weber's thought.

The coda to the Protestant ethic: the problem of modernity

In the concluding section of *The Protestant Ethic and the Spirit of Capitalism*, Max Weber turned his attention to the cultural implications of his ideas about religious asceticism and economic rationalism. Declaring that "The Puritan wanted to work in a calling; we are forced to do so," he observed that the modern capitalist economy now rests on mechanical rather than moral or "spiritual" foundations. Today we "are born into this mechanism," and our lives, choices, opportunities, and cultural values are constrained by the "iron cage" of material goods and acquisitiveness. "Victorious capitalism" can dispense with its ascetic orientation or ethos and rely instead on opposite norms – hedonism, gratification, consumption, greed – thus creating the most obvious and significant of what Daniel Bell

---

[2] Thomas Nipperdey, "War die wilhelminische Gesellschaft eine Untertanengesellschaft?," in *Nachdenken über die deutsche Geschichte*, Munich: Deutsche Taschenbuch Verlag, 1990; Wolfgang Mommsen, *Bürgerliche Kultur und künstlerische Avantgarde: Kultur und Politik im deutschen Kaiserreich 1870 bis 1918*, Frankfurt: Propyläen, 1994; Hubert Treiber and Karol Sauerland (eds.), *Heidelberg im Schnittpunkt intellektueller Kreise*, Opladen: Westdeutscher Verlag, 1995; Klaus Lichtblau, *Kulturkrise und Soziologie um die Jahrhundertwende. Zur Genealogie der Kultursoziologie in Deutschland*, Frankfurt: Suhrkamp, 1996.

[3] Music: Christoph Braun, *Max Weber's Musiksoziologie*, Laaber: Laaber-Verlag, 1992; cultural criticism: Edith Hanke, *Prophet des Unmodernen: Leo N. Tolstoi als Kulturkritiker in der deutschen Diskussion der Jahrhundertwende*, Tübingen: Niemeyer, 1993; literature: Edith Weiller, *Max Weber und die literarische Moderne: Ambivalante Begegnungen zweier Kulturen*, Stuttgart: Metzler, 1994; science: Wilhelm Hennis, *Max Webers Wissenschaft vom Menschen: Neue Studien zur Biographie des Werks*, Tübingen: Niemeyer, 1996.

has referred to as the "cultural contradictions of capitalism."[4] For Weber the main contradiction had to do with the very *idea* of duty to calling or vocation, which "prowls about in our lives like the ghost of dead religious beliefs," and the *actual* unreflective and ethically "unjustified" pursuit of wealth. "In the field of its highest development, in the United States," he observed shortly after his American travels of 1904, "the pursuit of wealth, stripped of its religious and ethical meaning, tends to become associated with purely mundane passions, which often actually give it the character of sport" (*PE* 181–182).

These passages about the mechanization of modern life may be the most famous Weber ever wrote. They culminate in a rare prophetic pronouncement, Weber's version of those "last men who invented happiness" pilloried in Nietzsche's prologue to *Zarathustra*: "For at the last stage of this cultural development, it might well be truly said: 'Specialists without spirit, sensualists without heart; this nullity imagines that it has attained a level of civilization never before achieved'" (*PE* 182). Such potent language bears the imprint of *fin de siècle* pessimism about the cultural dynamics and prospects of the modern socio-economic order, a view our contemporaries sometimes share with the criticisms found in these passages. Weber's language can also be understood as a way station on the path to subsequent critical assaults, such as Horkheimer and Adorno's denunciation of the "culture industry" in *Dialectic of Enlightenment*.[5] Such pessimism seems to envisage no future for culture in a world characterized at its core by the moral and cultural "irrationality" of economic "rationalism."

But there is another, quite different aspect to Weber's questioning of the modern age, as becomes apparent even in the last paragraph of *The Protestant Ethic*. Having completed his first study of economics and religion, and censured the lifeless specialists and the torpid sensualists, Weber notes that the next and more demanding task for science will be to investigate the "significance of ascetic rationalism" across the entire range of cultural phenomena, from social groups to the state, from "scientific empiricism . . . to spiritual ideals . . . to the other plastic elements of modern culture." We want to know how modern culture came about. But typically, he adds, we are incapable of endowing "the contents of religious consciousness with the significance for the conduct of life, culture, and national character that they actually have had" (*PE* 183). We are thus predisposed to overlook the constructive socio-cultural effects of an ethos

---

[4] Daniel Bell, *The Cultural Contradictions of Capitalism*, New York: Basic Books, 1976.
[5] Max Horkheimer and Theodor W. Adorno, *Dialectic of Enlightenment*, trans. John Cumming, New York: Continuum, [1972] 1987.

enshrined in religious ideals. Furthermore, Weber notes, to understand our world fully we must pose another question as well: namely, how has ascetic rationalism itself been shaped by "the totality of socio-cultural conditions, especially the *economic*?" (*PE* 183).

Now this perspective on the formation of modern culture is found in Weber's own social scientific investigations and quest for historical knowledge. It recalls his earlier work of the 1890s, which addressed the transition from traditional forms of labor, production, and social organization, to modern capitalist forms in the agrarian sector of the eastern German provinces. What Weber noticed in tracing the developments in class structure and economic relationships was the emergence of the underlying values of individual freedom, choice and initiative – the humanly understandable desire for improvement in a person's way of life and life opportunities (life "chances" or "fate" in his terminology). Put simply, peasants wanted freedom, even if it meant the loss of traditional social bonds and new risks. The same kind of dynamism and energy fascinated Weber about American social life. There, it was dynamism nourished by a still active strain of ascetic rationalism, a peculiar ethos of worldly striving and accomplishment in the national character. These commonalities suggested that America could be seen as the paradigm of "the modern." And Weber's later work focused not only on social and economic action and their institutional settings, but also on the internal consequences of rationalism for personality, the conduct of life, and the contents of cultural expression – including the essential features defining the landscape of aesthetic culture itself.

The theme is truly monumental in scale and importance, figuring powerfully not only in his topical writings on science and politics, but also in a theory of modernity constructed around a thesis about the unique characteristics and cultural effects of western rationalism. Yet the thesis is often elusive. Weber's thinking about the cultural situation of the modern age exhibits several contrasting, yet partially overlapping tensions: the tension between the moral or spiritual order (for example, religious asceticism) and the material order (for example, the "iron cage" of mechanization and materialistic norms), between the morality of self-control and the morality of self-gratification, between aesthetic culture and social modernity, between pessimism about cultural development and affirmation of modern culture and its "goods." Content conflicts within Weber's work.

How should we understand these polarities and tensions in Weber's thinking, especially as they bear on the modern present? How did Weber judge the modern cultural situation? How did he respond to the nostalgia for traditional social orders and powers that is so much a part of the cultural pessimism of his time?

Five theses about modernity

For Weber "the modern" is always contrasted with tradition and tradition-alism. Examples of the contrast abound in his work, from the Pomeranian laborers on the great rural estates of the east to the young Pietistic women recruited for factory piece-work in the west. Weber employs the latter example in *The Protestant Ethic* because it is especially instructive about the character of the new ethos: the "ability of mental concentration . . . absolutely central feeling of obligation to one's work . . . a cool self-control and frugality." One does not work to live, but one lives to work and achieve; labor becomes "an absolute end in itself, a calling" (*PE* 62–63). In this instance, the ethos is supported by an ascetic salvation religion, and this turns out to be characteristic: the unities and natural cycles of a settled traditionalism – the kind of reconciled organic communal existence depicted so powerfully in Tolstoy's epic novels, and one source of Weber's fascination with the Russian literature of his time – are disrupted and left behind by such a new outlook.

It is to Weber's credit that he realized that challenges to the "organic" cycle of life and its sense of "wholeness" can lead to a search for alternatives, for counter-cultural routes of escape from the iron cage of modern forms. Such challenges, acutely perceived by Tolstoy and Dos-toevsky, tend to result especially in the turn to what we can call "aesthetic modernity." At one level Weber set out to understand the conditions generating this kind of search. At another he wanted to trace the paths followed by social groups and individuals in their confrontations with the mechanization of life.

The peculiar feature of modernity is that it does not tend toward a new unity. Modernity has two sides: material progress, but also the manipula-tion of subjectivity and individual choices, which subverts the achievements and spiritual basis of modernity itself. In Weber's usage, "modernity" contains the idea of "progress" through production and accumulation of wealth and the mastery of nature (that is, "social modernity"), as well as the idea of emancipating the rational subject. The nature of specifically *modern* culture is to subvert not only the traditional or pre-modern, but also those accomplishments that come to characterize "modern culture" itself. The difficulty, however, is that one aspect of modernity eventually comes into conflict with the other: the conditions for subjective freedom run up against the conditions for objective control, such that "modernity" as a general socio-cultural phenomenon comes to be divided against itself. Stated schematically, Weber's general view is that the cultural situation of the present is characterized and shaped fundamentally by five large-scale historical considerations amounting to "theses" about the present-day cultural situation.

Foremost among these considerations is the notion that capitalism has transformed the material conditions of modern life in such a way as to affect dramatically the nature of cultural forms and cultural production. Speaking of capitalism as "the most fateful force in our modern life" (*GARS* 17), Weber tends with his *capitalism thesis* to convey a sense of the irreversibility of the developmental sequence unleashed by the new forms for systematically organizing the factors of production. Much of his most famous work, such as *The Protestant Ethic* and the extended essays on comparative world religions, but also the less familiar writings on the economy of antiquity, took up precisely the question of how, why, and when traditionalism was overtaken by the revolutionizing dynamics of a new *ethos* of labor, continuous profit-oriented production and exchange, and the benefits of rational calculation. The contemporary "social question" was itself generated by modern capitalism, as were the various forms of socialism and their ideologically inspired efforts to conceive a distinctive alternative culture, politics, art, and way of life. Indeed, from Weber's perspective organized socialism was above all a "cultural movement," as he repeatedly reminded Robert Michels, one of its best-informed critics, and it thus had to be understood as a proposed cultural alternative to the actually existing social relations of the capitalist age.

Second, Weber developed the thesis that modernity is characterized above all by the increasing dominance of a specific kind of rationalism which must be understood in terms of means-ends categories, purposive or goal-oriented actions, and "instrumental" standards. The notion of purposive or instrumental rationality (*Zweckrationalität*) intruding into the everyday lifeworld and all spheres of culture, including those aspects of art and morality where claims to a protected "autonomy" had prevailed previously, is often considered Weber's most distinctive and original contribution to an understanding of modernity. Interpreted in its most consequential form, this *rationalization thesis* maintains that the essential driving mechanism of purposive or instrumental rationality is "intellectualization" or the increasing dominance of abstract cognitive processes. Rationalization can thus include pervasive features of modern life such as standardization, commodification, measurement in terms of efficiency, cost-benefit analysis, legalistic administrative procedures, and bureaucratic coordination and rule. The last of these features – the tendency toward "bureaucratization" in public affairs, which Weber tends to characterize as "inescapable" and an "objectification of mind" – therefore becomes an exceptionally obvious example of a more general and deep-rooted cultural development.

The encroachments of "instrumental reason" into the spheres of modern culture are significant for contributing to the process Weber calls the "disenchantment of the world." The *disenchantment thesis* holds that modernity represents a loss of the sacred sense of wholeness and reconciliation between self and world provided by myth, magic, tradition, religion, or immanent nature. It ushers in the disruptive sense of disengagement, abstraction, alienation, homelessness, and the "problem of meaning" that begins to gnaw at the vital core of modern experience and social philosophy. It signifies the loss of that "oceanic feeling" which Freud places at the center of *Civilization and its Discontents*. As both Weber and Freud recognize, reflection on what is perceived as lost or missing, or efforts to cope with the sense of loss, tend to become synonymous with modern thought itself, leading sometimes to therapies aimed at *re*enchanting the world.

Yet disenchantment is simultaneously the path to knowledge and freedom, for it also means that "there are no mysterious incalculable forces that come into play, but rather that one can, in principle, *master* all things by *calculation*" (FMW 139; his italics). The notion of mastery or rule over nature, the liberatory aspiration of western science, carries with it the burdens of responsibility for our own history as well. As Weber asserts in one of his most moving passages, the fate of our modern epoch

> which has eaten of the tree of knowledge is that it must know that we cannot learn the *meaning* of the world from the results of its analysis, be it ever so perfect; it must rather be in a position to create this meaning itself. It must recognize that world views (*Weltanschauungen*) can never be the products of advancing empirical knowledge, and that therefore the highest ideals, which move us most powerfully, are formed for all time only in the struggle with other ideals which are just as sacred to others as ours are to us. (MSS 56)

Beginning as a gloss on Genesis 2–3, Weber's post-Kantian view ends by affirming the limits of intellectualization and the consequent priority of value-conflict in coping with our new freedom to impose meaning on the world.

The fourth thesis emerged after the turn of the century, as Weber became increasingly impressed by the crisis in the received liberal culture of his time and the approaching ascendancy of a new "aesthetic culture" of feeling, emotion, authenticity, self-expression and interiority. Referring at one point to ours as "an age of subjectivist culture" (*GASS* 420), he groups within this *thesis of subjectivist culture* all those elements in the critique of morality and "values," latent in the larger questioning of western rationalism from Nietzsche onward, that nowadays are typically assigned to the awkward category "post-modern." The many misappropriations of Nietzsche and Freud exemplified the tendency in Weber's own time, as did the uneasy challenges – mounted most visibly within the counter-cultural *Lebensbewegung*, sexual reform and youth movements – to "instrumental reason" and science's project of rational mastery of self and world. Weber was well aware of these efforts through acquaintance with figures like the renegade Freudian, Otto Gross, the off-beat communal projects at Ascona,[6] or events like the Lauenstein conference of artists and intellectuals orchestrated in 1917 by Eugen Diederichs, impresario publicist for the avant-garde. In fact, the whole of "Science as a Vocation" can be understood as his reply to the new subjectivism.

Finally, especially in his writings on Russia[7] and the later political writings Weber takes note of the trend toward "democratization" in the modern age. His *democratization thesis* is complicated, but in general it includes the notions of an extension of formal rights of citizenship, mobilization of citizens, and a "leveling" of traditional systems of social stratification. At the end of "The Right to Vote and Democracy in Germany" (1917) he pens a characteristic summation:

> "Democratization" is a fact in the sense of the leveling of distinctions among status groups in the *bureaucratic state*. There is only the choice between either "administering" the mass of citizens deprived of rights and freedoms like a herd of cattle in a bureaucratic "authoritarian state" with pseudo-parliamentarianism, or else including the citizens as *participants* in the state.[8]

Weber then makes clear that only the latter course is possible for a modern nation-state committed to preserving its power and viability over the long term. In passages like these he seems to share Alexis de Tocqueville's concern for the relentless march of social equality ending in "mass society." Yet for Weber, the process carries no necessary implications for the advance of political democracy in the sense of increasingly effective citizen control, higher levels of participation, or more rigorous practices of representation and accountability. Countervailing forces challenge such outcomes. When addressing fundamental "constitutional" questions, he tends to cite the

6 Martin Green, *Mountain of Truth: The Counterculture Begins, Ascona, 1900–1920*, Hanover, NH: University Press of New England, 1986.
7 *Ibid.*, p. 420.
8 Max Weber, *Zur Politik im Weltkrieg: Schriften und Reden, 1914–1918* (*MWG* 396).

efficacy of the "principle of small numbers" and the indispensability of strong leadership in the mass politics of the modern age. Democratization becomes the dialectical counterpart to bureaucratization – both unintentionally contributing to its advance because of the shared norm of "equal treatment," but also opposing bureaucratization as a potential threat to rights and freedoms.

Culture and the question of meaning

How did Weber reconcile these potentially conflicting theses about modern culture? At the risk of moderate oversimplification, it can be said that he adopted two approaches. One involved an interpretation of the significance or meaning of different modes of activity and cultural engagement "within the total life of humanity," as he stated the idea at a crucial juncture in "Science as a Vocation" (*FMW* 140). The second found expression in his efforts to advance the cause of *Kulturwissenschaft* or "cultural science," both in aspects of his own work and in the new German Sociological Society that he helped organize, together with Simmel, Ferdinand Tönnies, and Werner Sombart.

Weber's reflections on the tendency toward rationalization, intellectualization or disenchantment, and his concern with the ubiquitous search for "meaning" are closely connected with a subtle line of reasoning about the nature of modern experience – a point of view that is often distorted and misinterpreted. Misunderstanding comes about partly because of the unusual form of presentation of the leading idea: in the "Intermediate Reflection"[9] (or "The Religious Rejections of the World and their Direction") he gives a synthetic ideal-typical treatment of cultural "spheres" in terms of the conflicting life-orders and value-spheres of the modern world of specialized, vocational humanity; but in "Science as a Vocation" he offers a genealogy of western science's self-conscious answers from Plato through Nietzsche and into our modern present to Tolstoy's central query addressed to the modern individual: "What shall we do and how shall we live" (*FMW* 143, 152–153)?

Reduced to its most essential features, Weber's standpoint in these writings holds that the world as we experience it is separated into different, even radically opposed "orders of life" or "spheres of value" that operate

---

[9] This important summation of Weber's views, literally entitled "Intermediate Reflection: Theory of the Stages and Directions of Religious Rejections of the World," appears at the end of the first volume of *GARS*, thus after the studies of the Protestant ethic and the religion of China, and before the manuscripts on the religion of India and ancient Judaism; it is translated in *FMW*, pp. 323–359.

according to their own internally constructed, law-like and autonomous principles. Weber uses these two nouns interchangeably – literally, "life-order" and "value-sphere" – to identify a level of suprapersonal social forces or "rules" that tend to define the kinds of actions, choices, roles, and norms available to us as participants in a particular form of life. As we enter these orders or spheres and act within them, with full consciousness and consistency of purpose, we find ourselves constrained by their requirements – their distinctive "means" and autonomous "ends." We also find ourselves compelled to choose among the orders themselves: either science or faith, moral goodness or worldly power, eros or asceticism, art or life – or, at the symbolic extreme, either "god" or the "devil."

In the "Intermediate Reflection" Weber complicates the pattern of life-choice enormously by following his famous typology of salvation religions – ascetic or mystical, this-worldly or other-worldly – with a sharply defined contrast between a life devoted to an "ethic of brotherliness" and radically different commitments to the economic, political, aesthetic, erotic, or intellectual orders of life. Though he uses the notion of an *irreconcilable struggle among the orders of life* in different ways, Weber's general intention is to show that the classical assumption, persisting into the nineteenth century, of a "unity" of action and experience among science, art, morality, and politics has been shattered by the powerful forces of rationalization and differentiation. His claims about the "warring gods" are thus a consequence of the overcoming of traditionalism through the dynamic of western rationalism and its leading protagonist: the order of intellect, knowledge or science.

However, in "Science as a Vocation" Weber then enters his own plea for science or the pursuit of knowledge and its core values – "self-clarification" and "intellectual integrity" – against the enchantment promised by the Augustinian plea: *credo non quod, sed quia absurdum est* – I believe in it, precisely because it is opposed to reason. The dialectical route to his affirmation of integrity and understanding is strewn with richly illustrative commentary and an insistence on the *limits* of science. The central paragraph bears quoting at length:

> The impossibility of "scientific" pleading for practical standpoints . . . is meaningless in principle because the different value spheres of the world stand in irreconcilable conflict with each other. . . . we realize again today that something can be sacred not only in spite of its not being beautiful, but rather *because* and *in so far* as it is not beautiful. You can find evidence for this in the fifty-third chapter of Isaiah and in the twenty-second Psalm. Since Nietzsche, we realize that something can be beautiful, not only in spite of the aspect in which it is not good, but rather in that very aspect. You will find this

expressed earlier in the *Fleurs du mal*, as Baudelaire named his volume of poems. It is an everyday saying to observe that something may be true although it is not beautiful and not sacred and not good. But those are only the most elementary cases of these struggles of the gods of the particular orders and values. I do not know how one might wish to decide "scientifically" between the *value* of French and German culture: for here, too, different gods struggle with one another, now and for all times to come.

(*FMW* 147–148)

Claims for the superiority of one value-sphere or culture over another rest on illusory notions of "progress" or arguments such as the assertion that "differentiation" is a "progressive" feature of modern culture (*MSS* 28). The very idea that scientific rationality or progress is the essence of modernity is a case in point: to embrace scientific rationality or a particular notion of technical progress is to make a *value* choice. But in the modern situation there are always other values equally compelling to others, and no single value-sphere that can be foundational. Our age of "culture wars" and the "clash of civilizations" illustrates the impasse, for what modernity reveals after traditional authority has been swept away is an incommensurable and irresolvable battle among opposed ultimate value-standards and world-views. From Weber's perspective, such a condition means that

We live as did the ancients when their world was not yet disenchanted of its gods and demons, only we live in a different sense: as the Hellenes at times sacrificed to Aphrodite and at other times to Apollo, and, above all, as everybody sacrificed to the gods of his city, so do we still nowadays, only our bearing has been disenchanted and denuded of its mystical but inwardly genuine plasticity. Fate and certainly not "science" holds sway over these gods and their struggle ... Who will take upon himself the attempt "to refute scientifically" the ethic of the Sermon on the Mount – for instance, the sentence "resist not evil," or the image of turning the other cheek? And yet it is clear, in mundane or this-worldly perspective, that this is an ethic of undignified conduct. One must choose between the religious dignity that this ethic confers and the human dignity that preaches something quite different: "Resist evil – otherwise you are co-responsible for an overpowering evil." According to the ultimate standpoint the one is the devil and the other the god, and the individual must decide which is god *for him* and which is the devil. And so it goes through all the orders of life. (*FMW* 148)

On the other hand, we must recognize that salvation religions and the inner-worldly asceticism of the sects, still very much with us today, particularly in American public life, have settled these disputes for themselves in favor of a unified, consistent moral order, an experience that is also a part of our cultural genealogy. In Weber's words,

> The grandiose rationalism of an ethical and methodical conduct of life which flows from every religious prophecy has dethroned this polytheism in favor of "the one thing that is needful." Faced with the realities of outer and inner life, Christianity has deemed it necessary to make those compromises and relative judgments, which we all know from its history. Today the routines of everyday life challenge religion. Many old gods ascend from their graves; they are disenchanted and hence take the form of impersonal forces. They strive to gain power over our lives and again they resume their eternal struggle with one another. What is hard for modern man, and especially for the younger generation, is to measure up to *workaday* existence. The ubiquitous chase for "experience" stems from this weakness; for it is weakness not to be able to countenance the stern seriousness of our fateful times.   (*FMW* 148–149)

Weber wants to emphasize that today a unified and consistent life-order can exist only within the confines of sectarian belief or revealed religion. But our *experience* of the contemporary everyday world in its ordinariness, including the aspects Simmel referred to as "objective culture," speaks to us with a cacophony of voices staking rival claims to our lives, to our choices about what to do and how to live. This is what he means by saying that immersion in the pure experience of modernity leads to "polytheism," whether it provokes a quest for primary "life experience," exalted spirituality, transcendental being, or the latest technological gimmickry. For over a millennium the reality of this struggle over how to conduct our lives was held in check by what Weber refers to as the "grandiose rationalism" and "pathos" of Christian ethics with its methodical, practical effects on everyday life. In his modern vision, however, the "fate of our culture," fragmented and dispersed, has now accelerated onto another path.

These lines from "Science as a Vocation" are an historical and cultural *tour de force*, a sketch of three millennia from Isaiah to Nietzsche, from ancient religion to modern science, ending in our modern age. In Weber's view ours is surely a post-Nietzschean age, yet one having a resemblance to Old Testament Hebrew and Greek cultures: like the former, we have come to recognize the irreconcilable conflict among value-spheres, and like the latter, we have fallen under the spell of sacrificing to the different orders of life. But the orders and spheres are now governed by conflicting *intellectualized* and *impersonal* forces: think of processes like state administration, global economic rationalization, technological innovation, or abstract "rational" principles like efficiency, equity, ecological harmony, gratification, growth, planning, productivity and work. These conflicts are no longer held in check by a single moral order. Instead they become more deeply entrenched and intractable.

Weber warned against mistaking his analysis for a comprehensive moral and political doctrine, an argument favoring "relativism," or a simplistic decisionism. The warning is an indication of the difficulty we have in grasping his views. According to his perspective, historical observation and the sociology of world religions provided the touchstone for diagnosing the modern human condition. For in the last analysis Weber remained self-consciously committed to the scientific project of a search for "historical truth," the last words in *The Protestant Ethic and the Spirit of Capitalism*. Furthermore, with regard to practical standpoints he held that Tolstoy's question could not be given a single, definitive answer on the basis of a rational scheme of knowledge. But that was not to say the question had no reasonable answers at all. Answers could still be reached with clarity and conviction in the individual's conscience and within the dignity of the human "soul." The important question was *which* "gods" would humanity choose to serve. Oriented by such an intentionally archaic and sacred vocabulary, could we grasp the significance of choice among gods and demons as applied to our own modern experience and profane culture? Could we fight clear of our moral confusions about *who* or *what* was worthy of our deepest loyalty and commitment, and *why* it should be the case? The twentieth century has recorded a highly ambiguous and problematic response to such queries.

Culture as a subject of science

Weber's other important line of thinking about modern culture followed a different path. It was worked out in a continuing effort to conceive social science as a cultural science, or a science of the "contents of culture." Surprisingly, much along this dimension of Weber's contribution is still poorly understood, even though it is essential for revealing the sense in which he proposed engaging in sociological analysis and cultural inquiry.

The most far-reaching plans Weber ever developed for investigating crucial aspects of contemporary culture were those worked out in connection with the fledgling German Sociological Society (GSS). Starting with discussions among colleagues in 1909, he essentially proposed three areas for large-scale collaborative projects, sponsored by the Society and private foundation funding, that promised to take a comprehensive look at major aspects of contemporary life: a sociology of the modern press, a sociology of modern forms of associational activity, and a sociology of the leading modern professions (*GASS* 431–449). Alongside the 1890s studies of agrarian labor and the later report on the "Psychophysics of Industrial Work" of 1908–1909, these projects stand out as Weber's most serious efforts to encourage investigation of empirical socio-cultural phenomena. Unfortunately, for various reasons, including the intervention of war and Weber's own work on the monumental *Outline of Social Economics*, the GSS proposals produced only limited actual results.

Weber's formulation of the topics is instructive, nevertheless. His initial outline of questions focused on the effect of the mass-circulation newspaper on the thought, personality, interests and even the "mode" of reading conditioned in the modern reader by daily exposure to "all aspects of cultural life, from politics to theater and everything else imaginable" through contact with printed news media.

> The press undoubtedly induces powerful shifts in habits of reading, and thus powerful alterations in character, in the entire manner in which modern persons adapt themselves outwardly. The incessant change, the attention to massive changes in public opinion, all the universal and inexhaustible possibilities for viewpoints and interests weigh enormously on the peculiar nature of modern humanity. But how? . . .
>
> We must investigate, first: what does the press contribute to the character of modern humanity? Second, how will the objective, supra-individual cultural values be influenced? Which of them will be set aside? What will be destroyed forever and then recreated in terms of mass beliefs, mass hopes, the "feeling for life" (as one says today), or the possible positions toward life?
>
> (*GASS* 440–441)

Questions similar to these concerning the news media motivated Weber's interest in the comparative study of associations and the professions – all aspects of an appreciation for the evolving dynamics of "civil society" under modern conditions.

Weber is usually remembered for the formal categories of *verstehende* sociology and notions related to the "subjective interpretation of action," as set forth at the beginning of *Economy and Society*. But the excursion into cultural sociology revealed in this aspect of his work is compelling not because of the emphasis on "understanding" and its methodological presuppositions, but because of the relationship it postulates between an objective aspect of the life orders and the subjective aspect of character or personality – a relationship between "structure" and "agency," in today's fashionable terminology. Cultural sociology for Weber thus investigates the structural determinants of the modern print media or associational activity, for example, not simply for their own sake, but in order to probe the effects of modern forms of communication and association on the identity of the individual person. The connection between social structure and character was actually a Weberian theme from the 1890s. In this later cultural sociology the theme is redirected toward selected aspects of social modernity and the tensions within the self arising from the increasing scale, expanding variety, and accelerated rhythms of modern life.

In addition to these socio-cultural investigations, several aspects of modern "aesthetic" culture inspired Weber's greatest enthusiasms – especially music, architecture, painting, sculpture, and literature. In only one of these – music – did his ambition to think through the implications of "rationalization" and "disenchantment" come to fruition, and then in a difficult and radically incomplete form. But in passages scattered through his major works – the "methodology" essays, the "Intermediate Reflection" of 1913–1915, or the 1920 "Introduction" to the *Collected Essays on the Sociology of Religion* – and in asides like his comments at the GSS meetings, Weber's remarks are sufficient to indicate the direction of his thinking about "the specific and peculiar rationalism of Western culture" and the "significance of ascetic rationalism" (*PE* 26, 183) that he believes to be determining for the dynamics of contemporary civilization.

Consider, for example, his brief comparative generalizations about innovation in architecture and its implications for the other arts, such as painting or sculpture, which is only one element in a connected series of comments on "rationalism" in a universal history of cultural forms in the 1920 introduction to *The Protestant Ethic* and the collected essays on world religions:

> Pointed arches have been used elsewhere as a means of decoration, in antiquity and in Asia; presumably the combination of pointed arch and cross-arched vault was not unknown in the Orient. But the rational use of the Gothic vault as a means of distributing pressure and of roofing spaces of all forms, and above all as the constructive principle of great monumental buildings and the foundation of a *style* extending to sculpture and painting, such as that created by our Middle Ages, does not occur elsewhere. The technical basis of our architecture came from the Orient. But the Orient lacked that solution of the problem of the dome and that type of "classic" rationalization of art as a synthetic whole – in painting by the rational utilization of linear and aerial perspective – which the Renaissance created for us. (*PE* 15)

As a careful student of the history of culture, Weber seems to have in mind the kind of "technical rationalism" that provides answers both to technical problems in the construction of space and spatial relationships – Brunelleschi's triumphal dome on Florence's *Duomo*, or Masaccio's brilliant perspectival integration of human and architectural form – and then to aesthetic problems resolvable through the invention of a style. As an example of the latter, he notes the interesting case of the unnamed innovators who "swung sculpture in the direction of a 'feeling for the body' which was stimulated primarily by the new methods of treating space and surface in architecture" (*MSS* 30). Moreover, in a well-developed field like modern architectural theory, it is striking that Weber's independent formulation of the issue of technical rationalism and style finds resonance and confirmation within the community of practitioners itself.[10]

It is one of the ironies of the "contents" of culture that art in general is perceived as attempting to take a stand against rationalism, carving out a protected zone of exclusion for itself, or cultivating a posture of redemption from mechanization or the merely technically rational through art. This is especially true of music, "the most 'inward' of all the arts," that can appear as "an irresponsible *Ersatz* for primary religious experience" (*FMW* 342–343)[11] and thus serve as the crucial test case for the idea of an aesthetic value-sphere. In Weber's view, however, rationalization in music follows the same course as architecture and painting: it develops as "technical" solutions to problems of artistic expression, following the path of tempered intonation, harmonic composition, use of the triad and chromatics, a rational system of notation, specific instrumentation (with the nucleus of the string quartet), technical improvements in instruments and tuning, experimentation with dissonance, and the modern tendency toward "dissolution of tonality" (*MSS* 30–32; *PE* 14–5; *R&SFM* 102).[12] Music is not different from the other arts. Its development can also be understood from the perspective of that "specific and peculiar rationalism" which Weber ascribes to western culture as a whole.

In literature the equivalent appeal to "interiority" is found in lyric poetry, and for Weber that meant primarily the work of Stefan George and his circle, or contrasting figures like Ricarda Huch, Rainer Maria Rilke, or Emile Verhaeren. Weber's relationship to literary modernism in the George Circle was no doubt characterized by "ambivalence" and a clash of cultures.[13] But the reasons lay deep within Weber's interpretation of the modern art-form in the context of urbanism and the effect on the individual of those impersonal, disenchanted forces seeking control over the self. Lyric poetry could be understood as both a mirror of the metropolis, its rhythms and pace, and an effort to criticize and overcome its limitations. Such "ecstatic" symbolist poetry presented itself, in Weber's view,

[10] L. A. Scaff, "Social Theory, Rationalism and the Architecture of the City: Fin-de-siècle Thematics," *Theory, Culture & Society*, 12 (1995), pp. 63–85.

[11] Cf. M. Paddison, *Adorno's Aesthetics of Music*, Cambridge: Cambridge University Press, 1993, p. 139.

[12] C. Braun, *Max Weber's Musiksoziologie*, Laaber: Laaber-Verlag, 1992, pt. 2; L. A. Scaff, "Life *contra Ratio*: Music and Social Theory," *Sociological Theory*, 11 (1993), pp. 234–240.

[13] See Weiller, *Max Weber und die literarische Moderne*, esp. pp. 61–162.

partly as a protest, as a specific means of escape from this [mechanized] reality – that is, escape through the highest aesthetic abstractions or the deepest dream-states or more intense forms of excitation – and partly as a means of adaptation, an apology for its own fantastic and intoxicating rhythmics. Lyric poetry like Stefan George's – that is, poetry characterized by such intense consciousness of the last impregnable fortress of purely artistic form, yet aware of the frenzy produced by the *technique* of our lives – could not be written at all without the poet allowing the experience of the modern metropolis to flow through himself, even though these impressions devour him, shatter and parcel out his soul, and even though he may condemn them to the abyss. (*GASS* 453)

This portrait of the artist is a paradox: a mirror of the times, yet a rebellious figure; a defender of *l'art pour l'art*, but a proponent of art in the service of personal redemption and social criticism.

The cultural sociology of the George Circle demonstrates the possibility of successfully creating a separate protected zone of authenticity, but only by adapting to the most basic of all Weberian forms of secondary association: the ascetic religious sect. That was both its strength and its weakness, and in either case an illustration of the ambiguities and paradoxes of rationalism in aesthetic modernity.

Conclusion

The implications of Weber's work for the cultural situation of the modern age are manifold: his major writings identify the wayward path we have followed through nearly three millennia, our conflicted relationship to our history and traditions, and the difficult "universal historical problems" we now face as a diversified world civilization. They also give us access to the cultural biography of western "rationalism," to its devolution into competing life orders and spheres of value, into small-scale "rationalisms" whose results conflict. Indeed, in many ways Weber's great achievement is to trace the adventures of the *logos* through a universal history of culture. As he emphasized in one key statement of purpose in *The Protestant Ethic*, "Something is never 'irrational' in itself, but only from a particular 'rational' *point of view* . . . If this essay makes any contribution at all, may it be to bring out the complexity and variety in the only superficially unambiguous concept of the 'rational'" (*PE* 194). This limited claim could be restated for the work as a whole. It is a claim, moreover, containing a teaching modern humanity would do well to remember.

Today's contests and confusions over "rationalism" and culture often seem to play themselves out on the terrain Weber charted for us. One effort attempts to overcome the separation among the orders of life or the spheres of value. Another tries to breathe life back into the forms of community and the structures of meaning. Still another challenges the imposing narratives of rationalism and unmasks the will to power lurking behind the project of knowledge. And beyond the community of science lie the numerous attempts to fashion new myths, invent new modes of redemption, enact new therapies of enchantment, or simply return to the venerable old churches and world religions.

Ours is indeed a world Weber would quickly recognize, a world wracked by the "great substantive problems of culture" so characteristic of our century. But Weber was neither a prognosticator, nor a classical utopian, nor simply an unmasker of pretense and power. As a guide through the maze of modernity his work offers engagement with the forces and phenomena of the world as it has come to be – our actually existing world that is historically so and not otherwise. And that is its strength: analysis, diagnosis and interpretation not of "the impenetrable mists of the future" (*RR* 110), but of the lucid and comprehensible vistas of our historical present.

6

GUENTHER ROTH

Global capitalism and multi-ethnicity: Max Weber then and now

We live in an era of capitalist globalization and renewed ethnic conflicts. Universalist and particularist forces contend with one another. In this setting capitalism and ethnicity can be connected positively as well as negatively. I would like to reconsider Max Weber's views about the relations between nation-state and ethnic groups (nationalities) and between various kinds of capitalism and ethnicity.[1] I would like to suggest that some of his theoretical and policy statements remain useful for illuminating: 1, the persistence of modern and traditional components in contemporary capitalism; 2, the multi-ethnic components of capitalism; 3,

---

* I would like to thank Michael Matthiesen (Göttingen) and Hubert Treiber (Hanover) for help on various points.

[1] In his (in)famous inaugural speech at the University of Freiburg in 1895 Weber approximated the term "nationality" to the present sense of ethnicity, although with a different rationale. He gave the speech under the title "Nationality in the National Economy" ("Die Nationalität in der Volkswirtschaft"). In print it appeared as "The Nation-State and Economic Policy" ("Der Nationalstaat und die Volkswirtschaftspolitik") (*MWG* I/4:537; for an English translation see *PW* 1–28). In the middle of the 1890s Weber still linked nationality to "physical and psychic racial qualities" (*MWG* 548), as they had perhaps emerged over many generations (*MWG* 554). In *Economy and Society* he anticipated the present understanding in terms of fictionality: "The concept of 'nationality' shares with that of the 'people' (*Volk*) in the conventional 'ethnic sense' the vague connotation that whatever is felt to be distinctively common must derive from common descent. In reality, of course, persons who consider themselves members of the same nationality are often much less related by common descent than are persons belonging to different and hostile nationalities" (*E&S* 395). Weber considered "the catch-all term 'ethnic' unsuitable for a really rigorous analysis. However, we do not pursue sociology for its own sake . . . The concept of the 'ethnic' group, which dissolves if we define our terms exactly, corresponds in this regard [concerning its heterogeneous components] to one of the most vexing, since emotionally charged, concepts: the nation, as soon as we attempt a sociological definition" (*E&S* 395). In spite of Weber's reservations about the utility of the term "ethnic" he comes so close to equating nationality and ethnicity that the terms can be used interchangeably. Both systematic attempts in *E&S* remained fragmentary (see pp. 393–398 and 921–926).

the course of capitalism, democracy and ethnicity in Russia and eastern Europe.

Introduction

The present globalization of capitalism, which is facilitated by electronification, should not make us overlook that only recently have we attained again the level of world market integration that existed before 1914. This makes that period, as well as Weber's theoretical and practical understanding, particularly suitable for a comparison. The integration of the world market remained intact until August 1914 in spite of nationalism and imperialism, tariff barriers and "protection of national labor" because Great Britain in particular kept its markets open. Only recently have we entered again a new era of free mobility and easy availability of capital, information and personnel. A new cosmopolitan elite is emerging at the apex of tremendous international migration.

Although Weber disclaimed an "inner sympathy" with capitalism, as against the champions of older laissez-faire doctrines, he defended, as a "rather pure bourgeois," the imperatives of the capitalist market place against its many detractors from the right and left. It is important to understand that he affirmed market- and profit-oriented acquisitive capitalism and opposed *rentier* capitalism, especially in the form of the entailed estate. Shortly before sailing to the United States in 1904 he declared that "feudal pretensions cannot substitute for the spirit of relentless bourgeois labor. I consider it more than questionable that we can keep up in the long run with the great hard-working peoples (*Arbeitsvölker*) of the world, especially the Americans" (*GASS* 331, 390f.; *MWG* I/8: 184). Weber took the didactic line, especially toward well-meaning but naive Protestant reformers, that it should not matter whether one loved or hated capitalism: "Not a policy operating with anticapitalist slogans . . . but . . . the resolute insistence on promoting our bourgeois-industrial (*bürgerlich-gewerbliche*) development is the only economic policy feasible in the long run in the age of capitalism, whether you love it or hate it" (*MWG* I/4:672f.). Weber, then, recognized no superior alternatives, whether restorative or revolutionary, to market-oriented industrial capitalism.

It has often been pointed out that Weber's stance put him into the camp of "social imperialism" and economic nationalism, but it should not be overlooked that his principled recognition of international capitalism and of an integrated world economy profited from a cosmopolitan family experience which I would like to recall briefly.

Weber was descended on the maternal side from one of the wealthiest

Anglo-German merchant families of the nineteenth century, the Huguenot Souchays and their relations.[2] The great family fortune on the maternal side was accumulated in the era of pacifist capitalism in Manchester and London through cotton trade and merchant banking. In his youth Weber became familiar with the turbulent development of railroad capitalism in the United States and Germany through his paternal friend Friedrich Kapp and his own father, who had connections with German and American railroad interests.[3] He witnessed Bismarck's conservative turn after 1879, which included Prussian railroad socialism – "the cause of the misery of our whole constitutional situation."[4] Since his father was for many years head of public construction in Berlin, Weber early understood the benefits of competition between private (largely English) and public utilities in Europe's most rapidly expanding metropolis. For many years father Weber was a member of the key budget committee in the Reichstag and the Prussian diet. As a member of the committee on taxing the exchange he fought the agrarians in 1881, when they inflamed the widespread "hostility against free acquisition on the part of the urban bourgeoisie."[5] Among Weber's relatives were the Prussian minister of agriculture Lucius von Ballhausen and the minister of trade Adolf von Moeller – both rich capitalists with investments inland and abroad. Weber's cousins Ernest and Edouard Bunge in Antwerp were leading importers of Argentine wheat and Congo rubber and belonged to the highest circles of the Belgian bourgeoisie. His relatives in Bielefeld and Örlinghausen made him familiar with

---

[2] For my accounts of the family history see Guenther Roth, "Zur Entstehungs- und Wirkungsgeschichte der 'Protestantischen Ethik,'" in Bertram Schefold (ed.), *Kommentar zur Faksimile-Ausgabe*, Düsseldorf: Verlag Wirtschaft und Finanzen, 1992, pp. 43–68; "Weber the Would-Be Englishman: Anglophilia and Family History," in Hartmut Lehmann and G. Roth (eds.), *Weber's "Protestant Ethic": Origins, Evidence, Contexts* (Cambridge: Cambridge University Press, 1993), pp. 83–121; "Between Cosmopolitanism and Ethnocentrism: Max Weber in the Nineties," *Telos*, 96 (1993), pp. 148–162; "Heidelberg–London–Manchester. Zu Max Webers deutsch-englischer Familiengeschichte," in Hubert Treiber and Karol Sauerland (eds.), *Heidelberg im Schnittpunkt intellektueller Kreise*, Opladen: Westdeutscher Verlag, 1995, pp. 184–209; "Max Weber in Erfurt, Vater und Sohn," *Berliner Journal für Soziologie*, 3 (1995), pp. 287–299.

[3] Friedrich Kapp (1824–1884) emigrated to the United States after the failure of the 1848 Revolution and became a leading Republican figure in New York. He returned to Germany after its unification in 1870/1 and served in the Reichstag as one of the leaders of the National Liberals. At Christmas 1875 he gave to the eleven-year-old Max Weber his German edition of Benjamin Franklin's autobiography. (Kapp's son Wolfgang – 1858–1922 – is infamous for the failed Kapp Putsch against the Weimar Republic in 1920, which Max Weber condemned in the strongest terms, but his own younger brother Arthur supported.)

[4] Letter to Johann Plenge, June 5, 1909 (*MWG* II/6:142).

[5] Max Weber, sen., campaign speech for re-election to the Reichstag, reported in the *Magdeburger Zeitung*, Oct. 21, 1881. I would like to thank Hubert Treiber for making this source accessible to me.

the export problems of the Westphalian textile industry. Finally, Max Weber sen. and Max Weber jun. belonged loosely to the circle around Georg von Siemens and the Deutsche Bank – the group most actively oriented to investments in the Anglo-Saxon realm.

The epoch of the two world wars witnessed the decline of the capitalist world economy and the rise of the *Wirtschaftsstaat*[6] under nationalist, fascist and Communist aegis. Weber viewed the beginnings of this development with grave concern. After the outbreak of the First World War he was increasingly worried that even a military victory could not undo the damage done to German finance capital and Germany's position on the world market.[7] These practical concerns have been largely ignored in the sociological literature, which has focused on Weber's developmental theory of capitalism. But here too a re-examination is in order.

Modern and traditional components in contemporary capitalism

Weber's categories of capitalism can still benefit the analysis of present-day constellations if we treat them typologically rather than developmentally. It is well understood that his basic dichotomy of capitalism – rational versus traditional (or irrational) – had a developmental rationale and was meant to serve genetic rather than functional analysis. But insofar as we are interested in the present, we must focus on the manifold combinations of modern (rational) and traditional (irrational) elements. Here it is important to notice that Weber himself does not equate modern with contemporary capitalism. It is true that the "most modern" capitalism consists in rationally organized, bureaucratized large-scale enterprises, but these employ every trick of political and adventure capitalism in order to maximize their profits. This is as true of his time as of ours. Just as in Imperial Germany Krupp never concluded a foreign deal without bribery, so in the Federal Republic every big corporation facilitates foreign (and domestic) deals with bribery.[8] This may appear rational from the perspec-

---

[6] The *Wirtschaftsstaat*, no longer a familiar term, referred to the state's increasing public ownership and public regulation. See the inaugural lecture at the University of Bonn by the constitutional historian Ernst Rudolf Huber, "Das Deutsche Reich als Wirtschaftsstaat," 1931, which anticipated a permanent decline in the liberal order.

[7] As late as 1917 Weber declared that Germany's economic future may be forfeited "no matter how gloriously the war might end" (*MWG* I/15:212).

[8] On Krupp see the famous pre-First World War memoirs by Wilhelm Muehlon *Ein Fremder im eigenen Land: Erinnerungen und Tagebuchaufzeichnungen eines Krupp-Direktors 1908–1914*, Bremen: Donat, 1989. In 1996 the Clinton administration extracted a hesitant agreement from its European partners in the OECD to eliminate the tax deductibility of foreign bribes. In the same year the Singapore government suspended the Siemens corpora-

tive of the popular "rational actor," but for Weber bribery is a traditional component of capitalism.[9] Thus, in his understanding capitalism does not become ever more modern (or modern-rational) by leaving the old elements behind. Rather, the secular trend is in the direction of more political, adventure and robber capitalism. Trusts, cartels and conservative state socialism – not yet the radical variety – are the big threats to the liberal order. In Weber's perception the period of pacifist capitalism is being displaced by imperialist as well as autarkist currents that produce grave dangers for Germany and the world economy.

Weber's insistence on clear conceptual distinctions led him, however – and indeed misled him – to construe dichotomies that made causal assessments more difficult. A striking illustration is the passage on the German-born railroad tycoon Henry Villard (1835–1900) and the Northern Pacific Railroad in the charisma fragment of *Economy and Society* (1118); there the analytical distinction overwhelms the explicitly recognized combination of elements:

> The antagonism between charisma and everyday life arises also in the capitalist economy, with the difference that charisma does not confront the household but the enterprise. An instance of grandiose robber capitalism and of a spoils-oriented following is provided by Henry Villard's exploits. [In 1881] he organized the famous "blind pool" in order to stage a stock exchange raid on the shares of the Northern Pacific Railroad; he asked the public for a loan of fifty million pounds without revealing his goal, and received it without security by virtue of his reputation. The structure and spirit of this robber capitalism differs radically from the rational management of an ordinary capitalist large-scale enterprise and is most similar to some age-old phenomena: the huge rapacious enterprises in the financial and colonial sphere, and "occasional trade" with its mixture of piracy and slave hunting. The double nature of what may be called the "spirit of capitalism," and the specific character of modern routinized capitalism with its professional bureaucracy, can be understood only if these two structural elements, which are ultimately different but everywhere intertwined, are conceptually distinguished.

The facts, which Weber no longer remembered correctly, don't make Villard's 'blind pool' a convincing example of entrepreneurial charisma, and the dichotomy of modern bureaucratized capitalism (*Alltagskapitalismus*) and grandiose booty capitalism makes it hard to recognize that

---

tion and four other multi-national firms from public contracts for five years because of proven bribery.
[9] On the typological classification of bribery and extortion in capitalist and socialist systems, see *E&S*, pp. 194–205.

Villard's railroad firm was a rational and efficiently organized enterprise that still could not be profitable – no English or American railroad company ever was in the long run.[10] The railroads, the greatest industrial projects of the nineteenth century, almost always lost money for the investors.

Weber could draw on the example of Henry Villard and American railroad capitalism because he knew the financier through his father. When Villard completed the transcontinental link in September 1883, he launched an international publicity campaign in order to attract more migrants and more capital.[11] Thus, it came about that among other dignitaries Max Weber sen., semi-officially representing the city of Berlin, and Georg Siemens, director of the Deutsche Bank, traveled for one month coast to coast in Villard's private train.[12]

American railroad capitalism combined not only modern and traditional features (in Weber's sense) but also had a multi-ethnic component. It depended on international capital, mostly English and German, employed a multi-ethnic workforce, including tens of thousands of Chinese coolies, and expected its profits to come primarily from land sales to immigrants.

Whereas we do not know what father Weber wrote back to his family – the letters have been lost – we know that the son read the newspaper accounts of participating journalists, especially Paul Lindau's (1990). They vividly describe the multi-ethnic social scenery. On a basic level, however, the multi-ethnic realities of contemporary capitalism were already familiar to him through his Huguenot and Anglo-German family background.

[10] It is intriguing to notice that the event stayed magnified in Weber's mind and that he exaggerated the numbers. Only 8 million dollars were raised "blindly"; 50 million dollars (not pounds) was the final pool. Investors did not act irrationally. Villard's Oregon Railroad and Navigation Company paid good dividends and the purpose of his request could be guessed.

[11] Cf. Sig Mickelson, *The Northern Pacific Railroad and the Selling of the West*, Sioux Falls, SD: Center for Western Studies, 1993.

[12] Among the English guests was James Bryce, not yet a famous author. By the time the trip ended and the German guests gave Villard a farewell dinner at Delmonico's in New York, the Northern Pacific was bankrupt and Villard, abandoned by most investors, retreated to Berlin to seek support in Kapp's circle of relatives and friends. Siemens eventually rescued the NPR in alliance with the London Rothschilds, the Frankfurt Cohens and the New York Speyers and Morgans. When Villard's enterprise failed again in the depression of 1893, he was in the midst of promoting German interests at the Chicago World Fair and had just given $50,000 in travel grants to young German technicians, artisans and scientists. It was at this time that Max Weber jun. made detailed plans to follow in his father's tracks to Buffalo and Chicago, but it took him another decade to make the trip.

Capitalism and multi-ethnicity

In the age of the cosmopolitan bourgeoisie capitalism was nothing but multi-national and multi-ethnic. Today historians of English industrialization such as Stanley Chapman[13] discover the significance of its multi-ethnic presuppositions. In Lancashire and London, Huguenot and Jewish families from Frankfurt, Lutheran ones from Hamburg and, later, orthodox Christians from the Ottoman Empire organized production and trade with the help of multi-ethnic labor, including thousands of German clerks and tens of thousands of Irish workers. In its cosmopolitan mentality this family capitalism was a precursor of today's multi-national corporations. These corporations are today more than ever multi-ethnic, since communications technology no longer requires geographic concentration. The old locational theories (such as Alfred Weber's *Standorttheorie* of 1909) have lost much of their explanatory value.

An early example of Weber's interest in the multi-ethnic aspects of industrial capitalism is a travel letter that has escaped notice in the literature. It illustrates not only the symbiosis of the most modern capitalism and traditional corruption but also the link between capitalism and multi-ethnicity. A few weeks after his father's death Weber reported at length to his mother about a visit to the multi-national Orconera company near Bilbao. In her biography Marianne Weber cited the letter,[14] but she passed over its subject (just as she omitted in other contexts their visit to the Villard family in New York in 1904 or the identification of the Prussian minister of trade as "my esteemed cousin Möller" from the discussion in the *Verein für Sozialpolitik*, 1905). The iron ore mine near Bilbao was a joint undertaking by "Krupp, two English and two or three Spanish firms of similar caliber"; it mined a million tons of ore and employed several thousand workers.

> There is nothing in the world as magnificent as these mines. No safety regulations restrain the engineer's boldness . . . The unskilled labor is done by Galicians, skilled work, such as drilling, by Basques, who are much in demand and paid higher wages, even comparable to German ones . . . A large amount of capital is invested in blast furnaces and foundries, even in some tool factories and water-driven mills – the latter two still somewhat backward

---

13 Stanley D. Chapman, *Merchant Enterprise in Britain: from the Industrial Revolution to World War I*, Cambridge and New York: Cambridge University Press, 1992.
14 Of Sept. 18, 1897; Marianne Weber, *Max Weber: A Biography*, trans. Harry Zohn, with an Introduction ("Marianne Weber and her Circle") by G. Roth, New Brunswick, NJ: Transaction Press, 1988 [1926], p. 234.

– and in all conceivable areas of production. The tremendous power derived from so much capital concentration exploits the wretched state of the Spanish administration to a monstrous degree. The gentlemen with whom I talked take the venality of the governor, the ministers and of all public officials for granted.[15]

(Weber apparently gained access to a German engineer and director through the German consul in Bilbao, who turned out to be a fraternity brother.) But the Basque communities, which practice "strictly democratic self-administration," were also corrupt, because the propertied are accustomed to pay "bribes instead of taxes." The workers were regarded "as sober and easily satisfied etc. . . . The extent of their exploitability – more political than economic – rests of course primarily on the fetters of traditionalism maintained by the church (*Klerus*)." Weber's conclusion: "On this basis the most modern capitalism unfolds with tremendous energy."[16]

It is obvious that for Weber this capitalism has a multi-ethnic basis: German and English engineers, Basque skilled workers and Galician hands are put to work by mobile, international capital. He is also aware that there are no significant motivational differences between Catholic and Protestant workers. Since he is best known for his developmental theory of *The Protestant Ethic and the Spirit of Capitalism* – a secular theory focused on the seventeenth and eighteenth centuries – it should be emphasized that in his view doctrinal differences did not affect the course of industrialization in the nineteenth century. Indeed, he recalled his Spanish visit a decade later in a passage of "The Psychophysics of Industrial Work" in order to clarify this point:

> We want to reiterate as clearly as possible that, as far as the modern industrial workforce is concerned, religion (*Konfession*) as such no longer creates differences in the way in which this seems to have been true for the bourgeoisie in the era of early capitalism. Rather, the intensity of religious influence, whether Catholic or Protestant, on conduct (*Lebensführung*) is important. Contemporary Catholicism, which differs so much in its thrust from medieval Catholicism, is today as useful a means of domestication as any kind of "Protestant asceticism." This is demonstrated, among other examples, by recent developments in northern Spain, where the entrepreneurs take advantage of Jesuit education. (*MWG* I/11:362)

Weber's analytical recognition of the multi-ethnic aspects of capitalist development and the relative motivational indifference of religious affilia-

[15] Bayerische Staatsbibliothek Munich, Deposit Max Weber-Schaefer, Ana 446.
[16] *Ibid.*

tion was awkwardly combined with his well-known ethno-centric bias, especially toward the Poles. In fact, Weber ambitiously entered German politics in the 1890s with a shrill demagogic rhetoric that tried to combine a rational strategy of economic development with an economically irrational policy of Germanization. He received "stormy applause," for example, in Karlsruhe in 1897 for this kind of demagogic razzle-dazzle:

> Whoever makes it possible for an alien race, Polish or Italian, to accommodate itself to lower wages in Germany, thus acting against the justified desire of German workers to earn a living appropriate to German expectations, is an enemy of *Deutschtum*. We shall always fight him, be he a professor, journalist or minister – not as professors but as Germans, to the death (*bis aufs Messer*" (*MWG* I/4:833).

(Prudently, Weber never gave concrete meaning to the phrase *Deutschtum* he so frequently employed.) Weber, then, hoped to raise industrial wages to English levels by slowing the internal (German and Polish) migration from eastern to western Germany, and thus to promote a unionized labor aristocracy that would be a bulwark against the Social Democratic labor movement (cf. *MWG* I/4:572). For this reason he wanted to curtail the competition from cheap seasonal workers, primarily Italians and Russian Poles, by closing the frontiers.

The centerpiece of the Germanization policy was the "homesteading act" of 1886, which was devised by the minister of agriculture, Lucius von Ballhausen, and by Max Weber sen., who sat on the drafting committee of the Prussian diet. Thus, the son's opposition to employing Italian and Polish seasonal labor had partly a concrete economic rationale, but his policy of ethnic exclusion derived partly from the nationalist utopia of the National Liberals and the exigencies of the *Kulturkampf*, in which the Poles appeared as an ethnic-religious obstacle.[17] Economic developments, however, soon undermined the effort to create an ethnically homogeneous, culturally Germanized nation state. It never made economic sense to settle (west) German peasants as self-sufficient producers in mixed German–Polish areas. Weber himself pointed out that on the eve of the First World War Germany had already a million foreign laborers (cf. *MWG* I/15: 72).

The story is made more complex by the fact that the young Weber, like

---

[17] Max Weber, sen. and his brothers-in-law Hermann Baumgarten and Julius Jolly, prime minister of the state of Baden from 1868 until 1876, were deeply committed to the *Kulturkampf*, the struggle with the papacy and its allies, the Catholic Center party and the Poles. Max Weber jun. recognized the reasons for its ultimate failure, but never abandoned his opposition to Catholic and orthodox Lutheran authoritarianism. See esp. Weber's letter to his uncle Hermann Baumgarten, April 25, 1887 : Max Weber, *Jugendbriefe*, Tübingen: Mohr, 1936, p. 234.

his father, still viewed Germany as an emigrant country burdoned with the "grave problem of population growth, which prevents us from being eudaemonists and from assuming that peace and prosperity (*Menschen-glück*) lie in the womb of the future" (*MWG* I/4:558) – Weber's familiar Social Darwinist fanfare. His father viewed the homesteading act, which was intended to displace Polish Prussians, not seasonal laborers, as a realistic alternative to the popular colonial fantasies, the economic irrationality of which Friedrich Kapp had vigorously attacked before his early death in 1884.

The issues posed by population growth and emigration motivated the young Weber to intervene strenuously in the great debate between the partisans of the industrial and the agrarian state. At the Protestant–Social Congress of 1897 and on similar occasions he stressed time and again that the international division of labor and production was inescapable. This included his defense of finance capital, the stock exchange, rational speculation and commodity futures. Weber advocated tariffs against cheap imports and especially Argentine wheat, with which his cousin Edouard Bunge swamped the European markets, but he opposed tariffs that impaired the crucially important trade with the most advanced industrial countries.

It is well known that Weber's political failure at the end of the 1890s went together with his psychosomatic collapse. Tariffs were raised higher than he considered prudent. Restrictions on the exchange damaged the German position on the world market. The Junkers managed for a time to outlaw wheat futures and to uncouple wheat prices from the world prices. The homesteading law proved a costly failure, which benefited mostly the Junkers and the Poles. The capitalist estate owners retained Polish seasonal labor. Disgusted, Weber resigned from the Pan-German League because it had capitulated to the Junkers.

The retreat to the status of a capitalist *rentier* gave Weber a chance, however, to deepen his grasp of the relation between capitalism and nationality (or ethnicity). In 1904 he enriched his familial knowledge about the United States through personal observations. Immediately afterwards, and still with fresh impressions from his American journey, the Russian revolution made him seriously examine for the first time the issues of constitutional reform, capitalism and nationality in the Tsarist Empire. It was his political hope that the increasing Germanophobia in Russia could be mitigated by better comprehension on the German side and especially by an understanding with the Russian liberals (cf. *MWG* I/10:503). I will, however, focus here not on Weber's analysis of the liberal constitutional proposals and the governmental reactions to the Revolution, but on some aspects of the nationality problem and of capitalist development.

Eastern Europe and Russia

Weber was no cultural pessimist in the conventional sense – he did not join the chorus of those who decried the decline and decadence of the west – but he was skeptical about the chances of democratizing Tsarist Russia and downright pessimistic about the cultural and even physical survival of the Jews and the Germans. What strikes me from today's vantage point is the fact that Weber set aside the condition of the Germans and the Jews. He excluded "the situation of the Germans in the Baltic provinces," in part because "I as a German could not remain unbiased in view of the cultural devastation first perpetrated from above and later from below" (*MWG* I/10:150). At the same time he bemoaned the situation of the "terribly mistreated inhabitants of the Russian ghettos" (*MWG* I/10:302) and the "Bialystok massacre" (*MWG* I/10:658, *Judenmetzelei*, cf. p. 314). "The problem of Russian Jewry" appeared to him "downright desperate" (*MWG* I/10:151): "The problem posed by the fate of these five to six million people cannot be described adequately in its terrible seriousness within the sketch I am presenting here" (*MWG* I/10:362).[18]

Weber was also skeptical about the developmental relationship of democracy and capitalism. Key passages have often been cited, such as this comparison of Russia and America:

> It is utterly ridiculous to attribute elective affinity with democracy or even freedom (in any sense of the word) to today's advanced capitalism – that "inevitability" of our economic development – as it is now imported into Russia and as it exists in the United States [Weber thinks primarily of the trusts and Rockefeller]. Rather, the question can be phrased only in this way: How can democracy and freedom be maintained in the long run under the dominance of advanced capitalism? (*MWG* I/10:270; cf. *RR* 109)

More precisely, at issue was the persisting domination of Tsarism with the help of "arch-reactionary big capital" and "the absolutely reactionary attitude of the few big entrepreneurs" (*MWG* I/15: 249, 241).

Weber pointed, however, not only to the compatibility between advanced capitalism and authoritarian government, but also considered it possible that a successful democratization of Russia could strengthen imperialism: "If successful, the Russian revolution too will produce an iron age and a tremendous increase in armaments, especially in Germany" (*MWG* I/10:503). Weber's expectation was guided by a historical rule of experience

---

[18] This sentence and the references to the desparate situation of Russian Jewry and the situation of the Germans in the Baltic provinces do not appear in the abridgment translated by Gordon Wells and Peter Baehr (*RR*, cf. pp. 62, 124, 163).

that ranged from the democratic imperialism of ancient Athens to the "land-grabbing wars of the democratic Union against Mexico etc."[19] After all, Weber also considered the three great military monarchies of Russia, Prussia and Austria to be responses to the liberation message of the French Revolution.

In comparing the United States and Tsarist Russia, Weber saw them connected via Europe. In his first Russian chronicle he employed the image of the two "communicating population reservoirs" (*MWG* I/10:273; cf. I/11:110). From one side there was "the mighty immigration of Western ideas," from the other "the tremendous immigration of European, especially of east European people into the United States, where it weakens the old democratic traditions." More explicitly he spoke elsewhere of illiterates and "immigration from the 'uncivilized' (*unkultivierten*) regions of Europe" (*MWG* I/15, 748). His concern about mass emigration from "uncivilized" areas and his advocacy of protective tariffs against countries with cheap production costs was based on the conviction that "the presumption of an international cultural equality was completely unrealistic" (*MWG* I/4:302). He accused the freetraders in Eugen Richter's Progressive party, the Social Democrats, and the Ethical Culture movement of adhering dogmatically to this presumption. The problem of cultural inequality seemed more serious for the United States than Germany. Like so many of his American contemporaries, he underestimated the enormous integrative powers of that immigrant society.[20] Still, he remained upbeat about the United States after his 1904 visit: "In spite of all, a marvelous people, and only the Negro question and the terrible immigration form the big black clouds."[21]

In spite of his misgivings about culturally unequal groups Weber was

---

[19] Letter to Helene Weber, Dec. 6, 1885: Max Weber, *Jugendbriefe*, p. 192.

[20] Marianne Weber was highly impressed by the efforts of educated women in the Settlement movement to Americanize the immigrants. In a newspaper report written immediately after her return she wrote: "Private charity is confronted with gigantic tasks because a flood of 800,000 immigrants from the poorest and least civilized (*kulturloseste*) strata of the European proletariat pours into the ports. Irish, Italians, Greeks, Armenians, Poles and thousands of Galician and Russian Jews, for whom there is no place and no hope in their homeland, seek a decent life over there. Whereas previously they were without any political rights, now they can acquire voting rights after five years. Since the majority learns to make proper use of their rights slowly, there is constant danger to the culture of the United States. To ward it off, all idealist energies must be employed for the rapid socialization and Americanization of these foreign masses. American women participate in this task of mass education to an outstanding degree." "Was Amerika den Frauen bietet. Reiseeindruecke," *Centralblatt des Bundes deutscher Frauenvereine*, 6 (Feb. 15, Mar. 1, Mar. 15, 1905), Mar. 1, p. 178.

[21] Marianne Weber, *Max Weber: A Biography*, p. 302.

able, during the First World War, to modify the old nationalist position he had taken in his inaugural lecture at Freiburg in 1895. On Christmas day 1915 he changed his tune:

> A state must not necessarily be a 'nation state' in the sense that its policies are oriented exclusively to the interests of a single, predominant nationality. The state can serve the cultural interests of several nationalities . . . In view of the changed historical condition we must demand in the very cultural interest of the German nationality that our state turn increasingly toward this task.[22]

At the time, it was, of course, Weber's tactical consideration to replace the repressive Germanization policy toward the Prussian Poles in favor of tying the projected Polish state politically and economically to Germany. At the moment of the German empire's collapse, he regretted that German diplomacy had not played the nationalities card: "We could have founded our policy on the nationalities principle, on a union of free peoples allied with Germany culturally and economically" (*MWG* I/15:754).

The task of creating a union of free peoples remains on the historical agenda today. It is complicated by the enormous gradient in living standards from west to east, by the migration pressures and the very transformation of capitalism. Undreamed-of advances in communications technology have seriously weakened bureaucratic capitalism and powerfully promoted speculative capitalism. Weber's dictum no longer holds that "the whole developmental history of modern *Hochkapitalismus* is identical with the bureaucratization of the enterprise" (*GAW* 477). Full development is followed by devolution. The "most advanced forms of capitalism" are today subject to debureaucratization and the decentralization of innovation, production and service.

It appears to me that international cultural equality is in economic respects no longer so unreal as Weber assumed for his time. He himself had to revise his assessment regarding the "economic intelligence and capital prowess" of the Poles (*MWG* I/4:553). The world-wide availability and mobility of know-how, information, organization, capital and personnel facilitates a critically important homogenization. Structural features of the First and Third Worlds overlap not only because of the migration of people and capital but because of an internal differentiation that tends to exacerbate social inequality.

In my judgment Weber's voice should still be heard because he refused to take an easy stand of blind optimism or hopeless pessimism. After the collapse of the Soviet Union and the end of the Cold War people in east and

---

[22] *Frankfurter Zeitung*, Dec. 25, 1915; *MWG* I/15:91.

west have been given another chance to "work while it is day."[23] I believe, therefore, that after ninety years Weber's challenge remains valid:

> What is not won for broad masses of individuals now, in the course of the next generations, as an "inalienable" sphere of personal rights and liberties (*Persönlichkeits- und Freiheitssphäre*) – as long as the economic and intellectual "revolution," the much reviled "anarchy" of production and the equally reviled "subjectivism" continue undiminished and make possible the individual's autonomy – will perhaps never be accomplished, insofar as our feeble eyes can penetrate the thick mists that envelop the future of human history.
>
> (*MWG* I/10:272; cf. *RR* 110)

[24] *New Testament*: John 9:4.

7

SVEN ELIAESON

Constitutional Caesarism: Weber's politics in their German context

Max Weber's true calling was to become a politician. In an often quoted letter to Mina Tobler, he refers to politics as his secret love.[1] Yet Weber was acutely aware of his own limitations and why they excluded him from politics. He recognized his inability – vividly evident in his life as a scholar – to compromise, as well as his unsuitedness to the "slow, strong drilling through hard boards, with a combination of passion and a sense of judgment," that he believed politics to require (*PW* 369). Nevertheless, he waited in the background for circumstances to hand him a political role. But his moment never came.

Weber's unhappy passion for politics had long and complex consequences. He was one of the few figures in German intellectual life to have a well-developed conception of politics that (also) rose above party-political interests. The members of his circle, such as Karl Jaspers, took up the task of the political education of Germany in the few moments in which events provided an opening, such as the early years of the Weimar Republic, the period just before its demise, and the period immediately after the Second World War, when democracy was reintroduced at bayonet tip. Weber was treated retrospectively as a substitute "founding father" for the Federal Republic of Germany by his close admirers in Germany. And this political mythologization of Weber produced a powerful scholarly reaction that has ever since colored perceptions of Weber's politics, notably by emphasizing the ways in which Weber was unlike liberal democrats elsewhere.

Weber's career as a policy scientist, advisor, and sometime politician

Weber was actively involved in public policy questions throughout his life, as well as with elective politicians. He grew up in a political household: his father was a member of parliament. As a youth, he had unusual access to

[1] Letter of Jan. 17, 1919: *MWG* I/16:19.

the political and intellectual elite, e.g. Theodor Mommsen. As a young scholar he secured the directorship of a policy study on the East Elbian farm workers, sponsored by the *Verein für Sozialpolitik*, and used the study to make a controversial recommendation: to halt the import of cheap migrant Polish labor on grounds of national interest (the main theme in his famous *Freiburger Antrittsrede, PW* 1–29). This recommendation was inimical to the interests of the Prussian Junkers, whose estates depended on this labor, but established Weber as a provocative voice, issuing policy recommendations based on facts.[2]

He gained a platform with the Christian politician Friedrich Naumann, whose "national social" movement, an evangelical reform group, sought to enter parliament.[3] In 1897 Weber himself was close to becoming a candidate for the *Reichstag* in Saarbrücken – but he declined an invitation to be placed on the ballot because he had just been appointed Professor in Political Economy at Heidelberg. Instead he became an informal counselor to Naumann, a role that he continued to play throughout his life. Between 1893 and 1898 he flirted with Hugenberg's[4] conservative and nationalistic Pan-German League, but soon left it. It is important to keep in mind that Weber, despite his more conservative inclinations in his youth, was by the standards of his time "left" in politics, i.e. a liberal (of a sort) pleading for democracy (of a sort).

In 1904 he traveled to the USA together with Ernst Troeltsch[5] (and hundreds of other German scholars). This trip had a deep impact on Weber, who made numerous references to features of American politics (the spoils system, party caucuses, political machines) in his political writings. In 1905 he learned Russian, and wrote extensively on the pre-revolutionary situation in Tsarist Russia. During the war Weber continued to write in the dailies, notably the *Frankfurter Zeitung* (a liberal paper closed during the Nazi regime). He formed a one-man "loyal opposition" critical of the personal rule of the Kaiser. He commented upon matters of war aims,

---

[2] Rita Aldenhoff, "Nationalökonomie, Nationalstaat und Werturteile. Wissenschaftskritik in Max Weber's Freiburger Antrittsrede im Kontext der Wissenschaftsdebatten in den 1890er Jahren," *Archiv für Rechts- und Sozialphilosophie*, 43 (1991), pp. 79–90.

[3] The Christian social reformer Naumann is probably best known for launching the concept *Mitteleuropa*, the idea of central Europe as a political entity, in a book published in 1916.

[4] Hugenberg was a conservative media owner who later paved the way for the Nazi takeover in 1933.

[5] The theologian Ernst Troeltsch is a key figure among Weber's colleagues, defining much of his methodological problem horizon (in *The Crisis of Historicism*), also being Weber's semidetached suburban neighbor in Heidelberg (they lived in the same villa, in Zigelhäuser Landstraße 17). See also Hans Rollmann: "'Meet me in St. Louis': Troeltsch and Weber in America," in Hartmut Lehmann and Guenther Roth (eds.), *Weber's "Protestant Ethic": Origins, Evidence, Contexts*, Cambridge: Cambridge University Press, 1987.

submarine warfare, the nature of the conflict with the west, and most important, on constitutional reform.[6]

In 1917–1919 these efforts entered a new and more intense phase, in which Weber stood on the verge of offering himself as a political leader. In the aftermath of the revolutionary transition after the war Weber delivered his famous lecture "Politics as a Vocation" (his "swan-song," as Golo Mann once put it), and a lecture on "Socialism" for Austrian officers. At the end of the war Weber participated in the work on the first draft for the Weimar constitution as the only external (politically independent) expert and joined the German delegation to the Versailles peace conference. For a period he was also a member of the workers' and soldiers' council in Heidelberg and, at a mass rally, urged a national revolution – even guerrilla warfare if necessary – against the provisions of the Versailles treaty. He was touted as a secretary of state for the interior,[7] participated in the formation of a liberal party, and was once again on the verge of becoming a candidate for parliament.

As a witness to the Munich revolution (*Räterepublik*) and its aftermath, he testified in favor of sparing the lives of two of its prominent participants after it collapsed, and evoked the wrath of rightist students who opposed punishment for the assassination of Kurt Eisner, the prime minister in Bavaria.[8] However, in the last year of his life Weber withdrew from all politics.

Weber's views on politics: introductory remarks

The most problematic feature of Weber's political thinking is his frequent reference to the "Caesaristic" element in modern politics. The term alludes to the ancient practice whereby soldiers elect their victorious leader as ruler. In modern terms, it is a sort of democracy, but one in which

---

[6] Many of Weber's texts are not as yet translated to English. The *PW* from 1994 is incomplete as compared to *GPS*.

[7] Wolfgang Mommsen, *Max Weber and German Politics, 1890–1920*, trans. Michael S. Steinberg, Oxford: Blackwell, 1984 [1974], p. 301.

[8] His testimony is thought to have saved the life of the playwright Ernst Toller and perhaps also that of Otto Neurath the philosopher (later to play a major role in logical positivism), who was secretary of finance in the revolutionary government after the murder of Eisner. Weber was also well acquainted with Schwabing bohemians and anarchists such as Toller and Erich Mühsam. When Anton Graf von Arco assassinated Eisner, a Prussian Jew and social democrat whom Weber detested, he received a mild sentence. Weber wanted him executed in order to avoid similar political murders. Judicially tolerated political killing became common in the early Weimar Republic, the most notable victim being Walter Rathenau.

democracy is combined with unrestrained power on the part of the leader.[9]

Caesarism was, so to speak, a toxic cure for those diseases of the German political order that Weber was most sensitive to, and understanding the peculiar context for his political activity is essential. The context is often characterized as the German *Sonderweg*, or "special path." The notion of a German *Sonderweg* is controversial. In its less controversial form it refers to Germany's delayed development to a centralized nation-state and to the policies which enabled it to catch up with France and Great Britain, policies that required a strong and interventionist state.[10] Weber saw the political problems of this path through the problem of the career and legacy of Otto von Bismarck and particularly through the problem of leadership that Bismarck's career revealed.

Bismarck's legacy

Bismarck succeeded in leading Germany not only to unification, but through an era of rapid economic development and expanded power.[11] In a few decades, the production of coal and iron had multiplied and Prussia had developed the first modern welfare state, pioneering the creation of social policy institutions, insurance, and retirement schemes. Bismarck understood the need to make the growing working and bourgeois classes part of development, and did so by giving them a stake in the economic success of the rapid industrialization. But he did this in the interest of the state and its stability, for the purpose of preventing opposition and revolution. This successful development "from above" contributed to an apolitical and obsequious stance among the bourgeoisie that enjoyed the fruit of economic development: one does not bite the hand that feeds. It was a hindrance to labor agitation, since the workers had already achieved some of the reforms that were part of the international socialist agenda without having had to fight for them.

Bismarck effectively curtailed the power of the German parliament. For a time, this worked well. But there was no real opportunity for a new

[9] On the ancient roots of Weber's plebiscitary democratic dictator, see Gustav Schmidt, *Deutscher Historismus und der Übergang zur Parlamentarischen Demokratie: Untersuchungen zu den politischen Gedanken von Meinecke, Troeltsch, Max Weber*, Hamburg: Matthiesen, 1964, and Weber himself, *PW* 331.

[10] Friedrich (Frederick) List, one of the intellectual inspirations for the economic policies of the state, was a critic of laissez-faire, and argued that, for instance, protectionist tariffs would be beneficial for the development of infant industries.

[11] Cf. Thorstein Veblen, *Imperial Germany and the Industrial Revolution*, New York: Agustus M. Kelley, [1915] 1964.

political leadership to mature and develop under his rule, and thus there was a succession problem. When Bismarck's "resignation" was accepted by the young Wilhelm II, Germany was left with a vacuum that turned out to be difficult to fill. The weaknesses of the constitutional structure also became obvious. The lack of a parliamentary check on the selection and appointment of leaders became a handicap when the central functions of the state were no longer in the hands of people with political instincts rather than bureaucrats. The difficulty of filling the power vacuum with competent leaders continued for the rest of Weber's life, and provides his political writings with a complex theme.

What reforms did Weber promote, and why? The pressing issue at the beginning of his career was the post-Bismarckian power vacuum. The weakness of the constitutional structure was made obvious by Wilhelm II, who became Kaiser in 1888. His reign was a catastrophe, especially in foreign policy, because of his lack of consistency and propensity for stirring up Germany's neighbors by heavy-handedness and bluster. The contrast with Bismarck was very striking. Bismarck had been adept at controlling the monarch, and staged the drama of German nation-building, defining Germany's role in world politics and making an ally of Austria, a former antagonist. Diagnosing the problems revealed by the succession led eventually to Weber's development of the notion of plebiscitary leadership democracy, democracy with charismatic or Caesaristic leadership, as a path toward a democratic or popular state (*Volksstaat*).

"Caesarism" proved to be more dangerous a notion than Weber had anticipated. But the problem it was designed to solve was equally difficult, and needs to be understood on its own terms, and to understand Weber's attraction to Caesarism one must understand his diagnosis. Weber saw that any change in constitutional structure had to accord with various political realities that were specific to the German situation. The main reality was the weakness of the bourgeoisie. As a consequence of Bismarck's policies, Junker-dominated Prussia and Berlin became the center from which German economic and administrative modernization was generated. This kind of modernization would not ordinarily lead to modern constitutionalism. The social basis of modern constitutionalism in every society in which it has flourished has been the bourgeoisie. In Germany, the bourgeoisie had a limited role: they participated in economic modernization without participating in the power structure.

Weber was a pessimist (or even an alarmist) concerning the sociological infrastructure on which a stable German government could be built. When he considered possible leading classes, he found each of them wanting. The Junkers formed the dominant basis for recruiting both officers and state officials, but their self-interest as a class was anti-modernist and backward-looking. Their prosperity depended on protective custom tariffs and cheap immigrant labor in order to survive American competition in the grain market. Weber regarded them as a drag on the nation: he sardonically remarked that they were good for a card game or a hunting party.[12]

The German bourgeoisie, however, was not a promising alternative. The bourgeoisie tended to be apolitical, owing in part to a long tradition of Romantic skepticism about the Enlightenment, and in part to a sense of impotence resulting from the failure of the liberals in 1848 to unify Germany. They benefited from Bismarckian economic interventionism, but did not gain self-assurance as a result of it. Weber's verdict is this:

> if I ask myself whether the German bourgeoisie has the maturity today to be the leading political class of the nation, I cannot answer this question in the affirmative *today*. The bourgeoisie did not create the German state by its own efforts, and when it had been created, there stood at the head of the nation that Caesarist figure made of distinctly un-bourgeois stuff. (*PW* 23)

The Caesarist figure is of course Bismarck. Weber had little positive to say about the working class either: "They are wretched minor political talents, lacking the great power instincts of a class with a vocation for political leadership" (*PW* 26). Moreover, their leading strata (the labor aristocracy, Lenin would call them) were imprinted rather by bourgeois ideals than by an alternative of their own. Weber actually saw this as a reason to regard their demands for more of a stake in running the government as legitimate. The journalists who liked to regard themselves as leaders of the labor movement were, Weber thought, *poseurs*. The combination of Bismarckian anti-socialist laws and equal suffrage to the German parliament had successfully promoted a domesticated revisionist/reformist labor movement which lacked political drive, and parliament became a sanctuary for "revolutionaries."

Liberal constitutionalism as a technique

For an Anglo-American reader, this formulation of the problem should already seem strange. Liberalism means "freedoms," enshrined politically as "rights" and protected by various institutional methods which limit state authority or the powers of the agents of the state, self-rule, and egalitarianism, at least with respect to political participation. The core problem of liberalism is state power: limiting it, controlling it, or alternatively of

[12] Paul Honigsheim, *On Max Weber*, New York and London: Free Press and Macmillan, 1968, p. 3.

justifying its positive role, a role which is to be determined by constitutions and by democracy or more broadly by consent arising through discussion. Weber, however, was far removed from all of this. He had no sentimental attachment to either democracy or parliamentary forms. "Rights" barely exist as a concept in his texts, and when they appear they do so as a valuable residue of past fanaticism (*E&S* 6). He dismissed Mill's famous defense of the tolerance of the expression of opinions on which government by discussion depends as resting on a metaphysics he did not share.[13] Indeed, he showed little affinity even with German liberalism, which made its own distinctive contribution to the liberal tradition with the idea of the *Rechtsstaat*, the ideal of a state of laws not of men, that is to say of discretionary power in the hands of officials.[14] Weber hardly uses the word *Rechtsstaat*. The explanation for this is that the word itself has natural-law connotations. And natural law was alien to Weber, who was very pronounced in favor of what we might call legal positivism – or, maybe better, legal realism, since there were lingering elements of natural law in the legal positivism of his day, which is a notorious source of confusion when trying in retrospect to see the historical adequacy of certain debates.[15] Weber was an enemy of these confusions, and opposing them is difficult to distinguish from opposing liberalism as such.

He was a liberal in the sense of being deeply concerned about the individual as an autonomous cultural being, a value that was not shared by contemporary socialism. But he did not defend this as a universal principle, much less design a state that made the protection of individual autonomy into a general goal for the population as a whole. Indeed he did not think that this was feasible for ordinary people, governed by the necessity of making a living, though he did attempt to preserve the possibility of autonomous action and autonomous life for the few who could work out the material conditions for autonomy. This was an aristocratic notion of autonomy rather than a principled universalistic one.

Weber's lack of interest in liberal "principles" was not unique. Many liberals, including Weber's father, Max Weber sen., accommodated to the Bismarckian political order, and this placed them in a strangely subservient position in which "principles" were something of an embarrassment.

---

[13] Marianne Weber, *Max Weber: A Biography*, New York: Wiley, 1975, p. 325.

[14] Cf. Stephen P. Turner and Regis A. Factor, *Max Weber and the Dispute over Reason and Value*, London and Boston: Routledge & Kegan Paul, 1984, pp. 17–22; 72–74.

[15] The Swedish "nihilist" philosopher Axel Hägerström and his followers in the school of Scandinavian legal realism responded in a similar way to the lingering natural-law elements in contemporary "legal positivism," making a point of either writing "rights" in quotation marks or by qualifying the term by adding "or the realities such a concept is supposed to represent."

Bismarck denied the principle of parliamentarian responsibility and regarded himself as responsible only to the Kaiser. By *de facto* accepting this, German national liberalism accepted the primacy of the pragmatism of power, and a liberalism of results in which material vested interest played the dominant role.

The political weakness of the bourgeoisie meant that the "modernizing" political ideas elsewhere associated with the bourgeoisie had much weaker support. The important ideas pointed in a different direction. A strong intellectual tradition established in the reaction to the French Enlightenment and Revolution assured that rationalistic liberalism was seen as alien. And the fact that Germany defined itself as "other," other than France in politics and other than England with respect to the economic role of the state, together with this tradition, led to a situation in which the political peculiarities of Germany themselves came to have a complex valuative or cultural significance, which took the form of the idea that Germany had a unique cultural mission.

The idea behind this was vague but widespread. Germany's cultural mission in world history was as the bearer of unique cultural ideals that were threatened on the one side by Russian barbarism and on the other by Anglo-Saxon individualism and selfishness or "utilitarianism" in politics and French rationalism. These ideas are easier to define in terms of what they were not, and what they conflicted with in German political culture. Utilitarianism as such was in dissonance with German idealism about the state, for example, and negative freedoms were despised in favor of positive freedoms. These vague but powerful political ideas were themselves a hindrance to a "normal" route to modern mass democracy. The successes of the Bismarckian Prussia-dominated *Obrigkeitsstaat* or "obedience state" confirmed and supported the idea of a special German political mission, which was closely linked to the actual geographical location of Germany between East and West, and between great military powers on each side.

Weber shared much of this, notably the sense of a distinctive national cultural mission that required a strong state. But he was scrupulously unsentimental about it, and did not romanticize the state, though perhaps he romanticized leaders, especially leaders faced with difficult and dangerous choices. He focused instead on the practical political matter of the deficiencies of the executive. Germany was well administered, by a highly professionalized class of devoted bureaucrats, but the chancellors after Bismarck were politically inept and weak. Ineptitude could not be dealt with constitutionally because parliament had no check on the selection and appointment of leaders, who served at the pleasure of the monarch. Their ineptitude was primarily political. They did not understand power, as Bismarck had, and they especially failed to understand the problem of democratic legitimacy, which Bismarck understood intuitively, namely that to be free to act, leaders needed to have popular backing and trust. This led Weber to the problem of legitimacy and the role of popular support in a modern constitution, and to his apparently strange characterization of this in terms of Caesarism, and of such figures as Bismarck as Caesars.

Charisma, Caesarism, and plebiscitary democracy

Conceiving of the problem of constitutional forms as a technical problem is helped by employing a terminology that is appropriate for technical problems, that is to say a vocabulary free of emotional attachment. The German constitutional tradition and the tradition of German liberalism did not provide the right terminology, and the terminology of western liberalism was repellent. The will of the people for me is a fiction, Weber wrote, and as we have seen he dismissed the notion of the rights of man, though not the practices they supported.[16] "*Rechtsstaat*," as we have seen, he avoided. This is not surprising. These terms all had normative associations. Weber, in contrast, had a clearly "functional" view of democracy and was a relativist in constitutional matters. In a particularly revealing letter to Hans Ehrenburg on 16 April 1917, Weber wrote that "as far as I'm concerned, forms of government are techniques like any other machinery . . . The governmental form is all the same to me, if only politicians govern the country and not dilettantish fops like Wilhelm II and his kind."[17] So it is perhaps not surprising that Weber employed distinctive terms, or used commonplace terms in a distinctive way. Some of these terms appear and are defined in his explicitly scholarly writings, some of which appear primarily in his political writings, and some appear in both. The three key terms are "legitimacy," "Caesarism," and "Plebiscitary."

In *Economy and Society* we find the ideal-types of legitimacy carefully defined. We do not find the other two terms. Caesarism is found in Weber's political writings but rarely in *Economy and Society*.[18] But the definition of

---

[16] The much-quoted remark in full is "Such notions as the 'will of the people', the true will of the people, ceased to exist for me years ago; they are *fictions*" (letter to Michels of 4 Aug. 1908, here quoted from Mommsen, *Max Weber and German Politics*, p. 395).

[17] Mommsen, *Max Weber and German Politics 1890–1920*, p. 396.

[18] The concept of "Caesarism" is nevertheless occasionally used there. See *E&S*, p. 1451 where Weber actually deals with parliamentary control. But it is debatable what status the latter parts of *Economy and Society* have, and what status Weber himself ascribed to them. It is telling that we will not find *Economy and Society* at all in the text-critical edition *Max Weber Gesamtausgabe*, where it is broken down into its composite parts.

types of legitimacy comes with a proviso. The types – charismatic, rational-legal, and traditional – are ideal-types rather than simple classifications, and consequently, as Weber makes clear, we will not find them in reality: the historical cases are all mixed cases. Plebiscitary and Caesaristic are similar, as Weber uses them. In real politics there are Caesaristic or plebiscitary elements rather than pure forms.

Charisma is a relational concept. It refers to *personal* influence, resulting from personal qualities, and is unrestricted by formalities. Plebiscitary derives from a plebiscite or referendum, a vote of all of the people rather than of their representatives. But in Weber it refers to a political technique: the method of defeating one's rivals or enemies by making demagogic appeals directly to the masses and mobilizing their devotion (*E&S* 268). *Caesarism* refers to a method for the continuous exercise of power, characteristically by using the referendum or the threat of it as a means of intimidating office holders, such as parliamentary representatives, from acting against the leader's will. The plebiscitary leader, that is to say one who has come to power on the basis of a plebiscite or more generally of popular support, might become a Caesar, a more exclusive category, by ruling successfully and increasing their power on the basis of such threats. The plebiscitary category is exemplified by populist leaders such as Huey P. Long; typical Caesars are Napoleon (I and III), Cromwell, de Gaulle, Hitler, and of course Julius Caesar himself. But all of these cases are mixed. The "charismatic" rule of Hitler, for example, had many legal-rational as well as traditional elements, and the elements balance one another: although Weber believed that the Caesaristic plebiscitary element was important in democratized hereditary monarchies, such as Victorian Britain, it was greatly tempered by the monarchical elements (*PW* 221, from "Parliament and Government . . .").

These terms have a common feature. They are terms taken from the classical world that are used to characterize a distinctively modern situation, the situation of mass democracy. Weber saw democracy itself as a technique, a technique for the production of legitimation, for which there were various possible forms. Direct democracy was one.[19] Weber dismisses it: what might work in Athens and Glarus (a Swiss canton) – smaller units, communities so small that they could gather in a square – would not function in a large country, and even in smaller communities were not without dysfunctions. An oligarchy of well-known and established families tended to get the upper hand and rule in the name of the people. Moreover, complex matters like a modern budgetary process could not realistically

---

[19] Terminological note: direct democracy could also refer to referendum.

arise from a process of direct democracy (*PW* 128). Another technique is pure corporatism, a system in which professional groups become the realigned estates of the parliament. Weber rather hastily dismisses this option as well. He concludes that a representative government with national caucuses or mobilizing "machines" (nation-wide electoral organizations), i.e. modern political parties as we recognize them, in a representative democracy in which professional politicians compete for office, is unavoidable. There is no alternative to a parliamentary system (*PW* 205).

Weber does not bother to develop an ideal-type of *democratic* legitimacy, democracy being a subspecies of charismatic rule, which in its turn is a transitional phase between traditional and legal-rational rule. As Breuer suggests,[20] Weber probably toyed with the idea of developing such a fourth type of legitimacy; we probably should be grateful to him that he abstained – his political sociology would have risked losing its distinctiveness. Yet something like the idea of consent was not far from his thinking. Weber speaks of political parties as a fruit of mass democracy. But from the way he phrases this it seems clear that he is referring to the actual historical process that had taken place during the nineteenth century, rather than implying the thesis that only democracy is truly legitimate, or that democratic legitimacy is the highest form of legitimacy.

Instead, he regarded mass democratization with parties as the organizing structure in which the struggle for power can take place and as an inevitability to be adjusted to: "the most modern forms of party organization . . . are the offsprings of democracy, of mass franchise, of the need for mass canvassing and mass organization, the development of the strictest discipline and of the highest degree of unity in the leadership" (*PW* 338). Weber saw linked development of mass democracy and party organizations as inevitable but without enthusiasm, much like Tocqueville. Nor was this an error. Though he did not foresee that parties might provide the organizing structure for totalitarianism, as in Stalin's Soviet Union or Mao's China, his description of modern parties fits the mass parties in totalitarian one-party systems as well.

The democratic party system was not always friendly to leadership, and one of the themes of Weber and his pupil Michels was the complex interaction between the leader and his means, the machine of mass organization. Characteristically, for Weber, the problem was seen as a matter of choice in which there were few genuine options:

---

[20] Stefan Breuer, "The Concept of Democracy in Weber's Political Sociology," in Ralph Schroeder (ed.), *Max Weber, Democracy and Modernization*, London and New York: Macmillan and St. Martin's Press, 1998, p. 2.

> . . . the only choice lies between a leadership democracy with a "machine" and democracy without a leader, which means rule by the "professional politicians" who has no vocation, the type of man who lacks precisely those inner, charismatic qualities which make a leader. Usually this means what the rebels within any given party call rule by the clique.   (*PW* 351, cf. *FMW* 113)

This is one of the most quoted passages in "Politics as a Vocation." Weber invests his hopes in the form of rule that allows for charismatic leaders, which he saw as the only way to avoid irreversible petrification of rule by the clique, famously characterized by Michels as the Iron Law of Oligarchy. It was with this choice in mind that Weber became involved with the Weimar constitution.

Weber and the Weimar constitution

Weber became involved in constitutional matters in a formative way at a formative moment: the creation of a new constitutional order in the wake of German defeat. In a sense, this was the call that Weber had long waited for, though it was not precisely the call that he expected or desired. Nevertheless, he played a significant part in the writing of the constitution, especially in the way in which the powers of the president were defined, as reflected in Article 41, about the president being elected directly by the people instead of by parliament, and Article 48, which granted the president extraordinary powers in times of crises. Weber's role in relation to Article 48 is a matter of dispute while his role in promoting Article 41 is accepted knowledge.[21]

One of the basic goals for Weber was the creation of a working parliament (*PW* 177), as contrasted to the "negative politics" that the Bismarckian constitution had produced. The sole power of the parliament in the former system was to veto government bills and approve expenditures, and this power was repeatedly flouted by Bismarck, and also constitutionally limited – the budget of the Prussian army, for example, was not under the control of the German federal government. Weber envisioned a parliament which could require access to files, conduct on-the-spot inspections, cross-examine under oath those called in as witnesses for the parliamentary commission, etc. (*PW* 179). On this point Weber's parliamentarianism is clear and unambiguous. One purpose of a strong parliament was to balance the power of the bureaucracy. As Weber wrote towards the end of the war, Wilhelmine Germany had been a

---

[21] For reasons of space, I have not dealt with the crucial topic of German federalism and the problem of Prussian hegemony, though this problem was important to Weber and for the demise of democracy in the Weimar Republic.

dreamland for unrestrained bureaucracy. "The monarch believes he is governing personally, whereas in truth officialdom enjoys the privilege of exercising power without control or responsibility, thanks to the cover he provides" (*PW* 164). If parliament was to avoid this, it needed to organize itself in commissions with the power to review the activities of government.

The second major goal was a strong, popularly elected president, and in retrospect this was the crucial, and subsequently also the most controversial point. Towards the end of the Weimar era a less parliamentarian and "semi-presidential" rule appeared, as though in fulfillment of Weber's ideas. But a stable form of semi-presidential rule controlled by parliament did not emerge. Instead, the Weimar parliamentary system collapsed, and the President, Hindenburg, appointed Hitler Chancellor, using his emergency powers under Article 48.

The fact that Weber simultaneously supported parliamentarian democracy and plebiscitary rule raises many questions of interpretation. Weber did not see competition between the principle of parliamentary rule and the plebiscitary principle as a problem that might threaten the constitutional order itself, but he was a pioneer in discussing the two competing principles of leadership selection: he saw the strong leader as a guarantee of the people's will against bureaucracy, state or party. He envisioned balance, much like in a monarchical system. "The President of the Reich" (especially the final passages; see *PW* 308) leaves us in no doubt about Weber's democratic creed. Here Weber described the power capabilities of the popularly elected president much in line with a monarch and as a means of *strengthening* parliamentarianism, by preventing the system from undermining itself.

However, the extraordinary power capabilities of a president with a plebiscitary mandate of his own turned out to be disastrous in July, 1932, when Chancellor von Papen had Hindenburg fire the Socialist Prussian government and in January, 1933, when Hitler was appointed Chancellor, quite in accordance with constitutional rules. The main flaw in the old imperial constitution was the lack of a unity of executive power, which resulted in a lack of democratic accountability. The Weimar constitution was very democratic but did not foresee the dangers of enemies of the system taking over "from the inside." There were loopholes in the constitution that could allow for popular opponents of democracy to come to power: this became a danger with the loss of a pro-democratic majority, resulting in weak governments with a fragile power basis, so to speak sitting on the knees of the formally very strong president, who in reality was not much more than a wooden war monument.

The combination of proportional representation and a weak democratic political culture put extraordinary demands on the shoulders of a senile president steeped in the traditions of the older and outmoded form of state, attitudes that Weber wished to supplant by rearranging constitutional powers. Weber's potentially Caesaristic president turned out to be "the wolf looking after the sheep." Article 48 meant that the President could legally have the basic laws suspended, and in the end this meant that parliamentary control ceased to function. In this sense Weber does have co-responsibility for the Nazi take over, though the result was an *unintended* consequence of his constitutional design.[22] And this co-responsibility assured controversy, for the chain of consequences is both complex and made of links that are themselves controversial.

The controversy: Wolfgang Mommsen vs. Karl Loewenstein

In 1959, Wolfgang Mommsen published *Max Weber and German Politics*. The book was a solid historical dissertation, much admired even by the vehement critics of its stringent conclusions. It changed the image of Weber "from a kind liberal to an ugly nationalist." The most controversial chapter is the tenth: "From a Liberal Constitutional State to Plebiscitary Leadership Democracy," with its famous formulation about Weber's charismatic leadership democracy serving: "to make the German people inwardly willing to acclaim Adolf Hitler's leadership position."[23] In the second edition Mommsen accepted a modification suggested by Ernst Nolte, and reformulated this to say that the concept of charismatic leadership democracy served "if only marginally, to make the German people receptive to support of a leader, and to that extent to Adolf Hitler." Mommsen comments upon the ensuing debate in an "Afterword" to the second edition as well as in new footnotes.

The crucial chapter in Mommsen's book deals with several issues: the elitism espoused in Weber's letters to his young protégé Michels, the British examples of Caesaristic leadership, as well as his "functional" view of constitutional forms (illustrated by his rather sudden shift from support of parliamentarianism to support of strong presidential rule), and Weber's rejection of natural law in favor of legal positivism. The pivotal point in the debate is the role assigned to parliament and Weber's failure to fully grasp the risks of plebiscitary leadership. These themes were not new. Karl

---

[22] Arnold Brecht, *The Political Education of Arnold Brecht. An Autobiography 1884–1970*, Princeton, NJ: Princeton University Press. Abridged version of *Lebenserinnerungen* I–II, from 1966–1967, Stuttgart: Deutsche Verlags-Anstalt, 1970, pp. 157ff.

[23] Mommsen, *Max Weber and German Politics*, p. 410.

Löwith, J. P. Mayer and Georg Lukács[24] had already touched upon them. But in Germany a different image of Weber as a western-style liberal, promoted by Theodore Heuss, had prevailed. The construction of this image was motivated by the lack of "founding fathers" for the recently established Federal Republic of Germany. But the western-style liberal past it attempted to connect with was a fiction. In the ensuing controversy Karl Loewenstein, an émigré constitutional scholar, emerged as the most active and formidable critic of Mommsen. He raised objections to Mommsen's most substantial point: that the ease with which Weber shifted his plea for parliamentarian democracy to one advocating presidential rule represented a plea for a new and adventurous kind of leadership democracy. But in his rejoinders Loewenstein actually seems to engage in a debate with himself over the proper understanding of Weber.

The influence of the British example on Weber is important to both Mommsen and Loewenstein. "What he had in mind for Germany was true parliamentarianism, if possible after the British model," Loewenstein writes.[25] But this passage is illustrative of the ambiguous partly normative and partly empirical character of the British example. Among Weber's "orthodox defenders" there is a tendency to resolve this ambiguity on the side of the normative, as shown by such phrases as "true parliamentarianism." Weber would not have used such a term. But he might have derived his expectations about the possibility of demagogic leadership, and of parliament's response to it, from the careers of Gladstone and Lloyd George.

Loewenstein wrote that "Max Weber repeatedly stressed that the British Parliament has been the model school of an elite political leadership," and a few lines later: "In the British political milieu there is no room for a non-parliamentary demagogue."[26] This suggests that Weber considered the role of parliament as a nursery for political talent to be paramount, and that the British model shows that parliamentarianism and demagogy do not conflict. But elsewhere even Loewenstein acknowledges that the parliamentary principle and the plebiscitary principle have a more complex and potentially problematic relationship. "As Max Weber has shown," he wrote, "there is an inseparable link between the plebiscitary selection of leaders

---

[24] Georg Lukács, *The Destruction of Reason*, London: Merlin, 1980 [1953]; Karl Löwith, "Max Weber und seine Nachfolger," *Mass und Wert*, 3 (1939/40), pp. 166–176; J. P. Mayer, *Max Weber and German Politics*, London: Faber & Faber, 1944.

[25] Karl Loewenstein, "Max Weber als 'Anherr' des plebizitären Führerstaats," in *Kölner Zeitschrift für Soziologie und Sozialpsychologie*, 13 (1961), p. 282.

[26] Karl Loewenstein, *Max Weber's Political Ideas in the Perspectives of our Time*, Cambridge, MA: University of Massachusetts Press, 1965, p. 45.

and the demagogism inherent in mass democracy" and "England, among the older constitutional democracies, has exemplified the plebiscitary trend for nearly a century"[27] and further: "In this sense mass democratization brings with it a method of selecting political leaders which is supplementary to and, in some cases, a *substitute* for the parliamentary designation."[28] This raises the question of which case Weber had in mind, and the possibility that parliamentarianism was for him largely supplementary to plebiscitarianism. And this in turn raises the question of whether if parliament is necessarily the ladder which demagogic leaders climb, it is a ladder they can kick away.

The question is one that arises from the term Caesarism itself, for Julius Caesar himself embodied the risks for constitutional orders that arise in the course of conflict between charismatic leaders and representative bodies. When the plebiscitary leader develops into a Caesaristic leader, his power resting primarily on popular rather than parliamentary support, then we move away from the ideal-typical parliamentary system. The plebiscitary leader has his support and prestige in parliament as a result of his popular appeal and demagogic talents, while the Caesar simply is above the legal aspects of constitutional forms and somehow carries his own legitimacy with him – being able to say, as de Gaulle did, "La France, c'est moi" – and have this accepted by the people.

The seemingly unresolved tension between two principles, parliamentary control and (Romantic) charismatic leadership of the people, occurring not within but over the heads of parliamentary representatives, has two aspects, because the two principles really deal with two distinct functions of the constitution, the problem of selecting and eliminating leaders and the problem of control. Weber writes about both the control function of parliament, which he treats as a very basic function, and the problem of succession (*PW* 227–28). Yet Weber's characterization of the actual role of parliament, and especially of the secondary role of the British parliament in times of crises, gives one the clear sense that parliament is not intended to be the locus of power. The problem is to have a parliament that is sufficiently powerful, not merely legally but also politically, to perform the functions that it must perform, such as dealing with the removal of failed leaders.

Weber's basic idea of how leaders who failed should be treated is clear enough: accountability and democratic control are central. Weber met with Ludendorff after the war in order to convince him to give himself up to the Allies. The two men had an exchange over democracy and Weber told

---

[27] *Ibid.*, p. 64.   [28] *Ibid.*, p. 63, emphasis supplied.

Ludendorff that the ruler rules and the people obey. "I could like such a democracy," was Ludendorff's reaction. Weber added that thereafter the people can rule and say "to the gallows with the leader." Turning this rather vivid characterization into a working set of institutions is another matter. Granting parliament powers is not enough, since the leader could avail himself of Article 48 and act against parliament. Removal of a failed leader determined to stay in power requires a "people" with a capacity to act assertively to send leaders to the gallows, as Weber characteristically overstates the matter. But this is a capacity which Weber did not believe the German people had – on the contrary, their lack of political maturity, symbolized by their failure to have executed a king, as the French and British had, was one of the problems that concerned him the most. So what did Weber really have in mind, and specifically what role was parliament actually expected to have?

Did Weber really hold the position that the powers of parliament would remain, no matter what kind of leadership emerged? In one way this might appear as a contradiction. Weber certainly knew that parliament would be powerless against a charismatic leader claiming exclusive legitimacy who had a gift for electrifying the masses. One of the talents of the charismatic leader, especially in its Caesaristic variation, is precisely his ability to break through the restrictions of the formal constitution and, in a sense, be above the law. But elsewhere there are indications that Weber simply did not believe that charismatic prowess of this sort was possible in the modern world, and that consequently it was no threat. It is also clear that Weber – even though his comments about parliament as "nevertheless not worthless" are rather condescending – wished to preserve parliamentary control to the extent of enabling parliament to fire leaders. But although the problem is emphasized it is not really scrutinized.

The author who devoted much of his thought to resolving the constitutional ambiguities that Weber bequeathed to German posterity was Carl Schmitt. Schmitt had the actual experience of Weimar parliamentarianism before him, and could see with great clarity that Weimar parliamentarianism could not withstand conflicts between totalizing *worldview* parties, such as the Communists and National Socialists, which had nothing but contempt for parliamentary discussion. He drew from this the fatal conclusion that necessity required accepting the rule of a totalizing party – the National Socialists. The presidential leader, Hindenburg, came to a parallel conclusion, and used Article 48 to install Hitler in power. Schmitt, in short, filled the lacunae in Weber's constitutional thinking. How Weber himself might have filled it will forever remain unclear.

The name of Schmitt was used, for example by Jürgen Habermas in the

1964 centennial for Weber held in Heidelberg, as a means of intimating Weber's guilt by intellectual association with Nazism, and it has been used in this way ever since. But Schmitt's relation to Weber and to Nazism, and Schmitt's thought as a whole, is more complex than this crude intimation allows. In the introduction to this volume, Stephen Turner shows how Weber applied a distinctive form of reasoning to the issue of political decision-making, in which the genuine choices were precipitated from the list of apparent choices by showing that many of the apparent choices were unachievable, and notes that Weber understood that great political achievement ordinarily involved risky choices, choices at the limits of achievability. Schmitt formalized this kind of thinking, which he called necessitarian, and distinguished between the contingent and the necessary.[29] His acceptance of Nazism, in his own mind, was an acceptance of necessity.

Risks may be calculated, but in the end there is no assurance that they have not been miscalculated. Perhaps Schmitt miscalculated the "necessity" of Nazism; perhaps Weber can be said to have miscalculated the risks of Caesarism. If so, the lesson is that politics as rational calculation may prematurely foreclose genuine and preferable possibilities, and the case of Schmitt is a salutary reminder that not only risks but the "necessities" that provide the framework for the calculation of risks can themselves be the subject of error. But the calculations may not have been erroneous. And nothing about the evil of the results implies that they were, for as Weber would have been the first to say, there is no principle that says that evil outcomes are always avoidable. Blame, in any case, should attach first and foremost to those who rejected and undermined Weimar democracy: their blindness was not the result of miscalculation, but of mutual hatred.

[29] Cf. Kari Palonen, Das "Webersche Moment." Zur Kontingenz des Politischen, Opladen and Wiesbaden: Westdeutscher Verlag, 1998.

PART III

Religions and their economic ethics

8

ALASTAIR HAMILTON

Max Weber's *Protestant Ethic and the Spirit of Capitalism*

The background

The intensity of the debate which followed the publication of Max Weber's *Protestant Ethic and the Spirit of Capitalism* in 1904–1905 shows how relevant the essay was considered at the time. The subject interested many of Weber's contemporaries – economists, historians, social scientists and philosophers. What, they were asking, were the origins of capitalism? What were its characteristics in its modern form? How far was it affected by religion and, more particularly, by Protestantism? The prosperity of Holland and England in the seventeenth century, attended by the economic decline of Italy and Spain, had long fascinated scholars and suggested that there was some relationship between the Reformation and economic progress. In order to confirm this theory they could turn to far earlier sources – the seventeenth-century political economist William Petty, the great exponent of the Enlightenment Montesquieu, and the historian Henry Thomas Buckle writing in the mid-nineteenth century.[1] But they were also in search of a more modern analysis of the true nature of the relationship. In his study on suicide which appeared in 1897, the French sociologist Emile Durkheim observed that Protestants, and above all German Protestants, divorced more and killed themselves more than the members of any other confession. Such primacies, he maintained, indicated an industrial society in a particularly advanced stage, with a high standard of education and living.[2] This, in turn, raised the question of the extent to which Protestantism might have contributed to this advance and to the development of the class on which such a society rested, the bourgeoisie.

---

[1] For a discussion of earlier ideas on the subject see Paul Münch, "The Thesis before Weber: an Archaeology," in Hartmut Lehmann and Guenther Roth (eds.), *Weber's "Protestant Ethic": Origins, Evidence, Contexts*, Cambridge: Cambridge University Press, 1993, pp. 51–71.

[2] Emile Durkheim, *Le Suicide. Etude de sociologie*, Paris: Quadrige/Presses Universitaires de France, 1995, pp. 147–173.

The corollary that Catholicism was an obstacle to progress was substantiated by a work which served as the starting point for Weber's essay: a doctoral dissertation composed by one of Weber's pupils, Martin Offenbacher. *Konfession und soziale Schichtung. Eine Studie über die wirtschaftliche Lage der Katholiken und Protestanten in Baden* (Confession and Social Strata, a Study on the Economic Position of Catholics and Protestants in Baden), was published in 1901. The Grand Duchy of Baden, in which Heidelberg, Weber's town of residence, was situated, had a population some 60 percent of which was Catholic and the rest Protestant. Offenbacher, providing abundant statistics (which have since been challenged), compared the situation of the two confessions. The Catholics, who were mainly rural, showed little ambition to further their somewhat basic education. If they did find employment in industry, they hardly ever gained promotion beyond the simplest jobs. The Protestants, on the other hand, were attracted by a professional training, tended to predominate in the towns, and occupied senior positions in the management. As businessmen they showed a spirit of enterprise altogether lacking among the Catholics and consequently attained an ever greater prosperity.

Religion interested Max Weber for most of his life. It intrigued him as a universal phenomenon which shaped men's mentality and affected their behavior in a variety of domains. Although he concentrated primarily on the connection between religious faith and attitudes to economics, it was this interest that prompted him to study in a more general context the religions of the world. He started with Christianity and later proceeded to the religions of the east, Confucianism, Taoism, Hinduism, Judaism and Buddhism. But Weber also had his own religious commitment. For much of the last decade of the nineteenth century he was a participant in the Protestant Social Congress and he continued, certainly until the First World War, to express himself on ecclesiastical matters. Within the wide spectrum of Protestantism at the time he was a liberal Protestant, and a number of the convictions of liberal Protestantism in early twentieth-century Germany emerge from his essay – impatience with the traditional attitudes of the Prussian church, a consequent hostility towards Lutheranism and a tendency to idealize Calvinism, especially in its later forms.[3]

The Protestant Ethic and the Spirit of Capitalism was written in 1902 and 1903 at the Calvinist university of Heidelberg where Weber spent much time with colleagues who shared the Reformed faith of his mother's family rather than the Lutheranism of his father. To their influence can be

[3] See Friedrich Wilhelm Graf, "The German Theological Sources and Protestant Church Politics," in Lehmann and Roth (eds.), *Weber's "Protestant Ethic"*, pp. 27–49.

added a study by a Swiss theologian which had appeared in 1855, Matthias Schneckenburger's *Vergleichende Darstellung des lutherischen und reformierten Lehrbegriffs* (Comparative Examination of the Lutheran and Reformed Doctrines). Although Weber used the term "Protestant Ethic," he in fact drew a sharp distinction between Lutheranism and Calvinism. He overlooked the great achievements of Lutheranism – the religious toleration to which Lutherans had contributed, their pioneering work in the domain of ecclesiastical history and Biblical criticism, the bold social experiments of groups of Pietists. Like many liberal Protestants he associated Lutheranism with a combination between authoritarianism and passivity which, he believed, characterized the Wilhelmine Empire. He had studied the situation of farm labor, particularly in the east of Germany, in the early 1890s, and he had there encountered Lutheranism in its most conservative form, xenophobic and intolerant, still savoring of the feudal system in which it had developed over three centuries previously, resistant to change and to the more liberal influences emanating from the cities. Even the main revivalist movement of the nineteenth century, the "Awakening," was very largely a movement of reaction, according a prominent part to poorly educated laymen.[4]

Weber's inquiry into agrarian society had led him to undertake a broader investigation of the entire social structure of Germany. Many of the defects which he detected were, he felt, peculiar to his own country and the result of a particular type of mentality. He was struck by the contrast with other nations where commercial activity had been far more successful. He looked above all at the system in England and concluded that the economic success both of England and America could be traced back to a Puritan or Calvinist tradition. For Weber Calvinism stood in contrast to Lutheranism. With a flexible structure and little hierarchy, it had been exported ever since the mid-sixteenth century with extraordinary success and had functioned admirably in Switzerland, France, Scotland, the Netherlands, parts of Germany and other areas in central and northern Europe. Weber saw it as a dynamic faith eminently suited to the progress of the modern world, the advance of the bourgeoisie, and the evolution of capitalism.

Later, in the introduction he wrote to his collected essays on religion published in 1920, Weber stated a further object behind *The Protestant Ethic*. He then said that a common purpose of all his studies on the religions of the world was to examine what he described as "rationalism," a feature prominent in western civilization and less so in the east. He

---

[4] Cf. Nicholas Hope, *German and Scandinavian Protestantism 1700 to 1918*, Oxford: Clarendon Press, 1996, pp. 354–399.

regarded this rationalism – which he perceived in western art (music, sculpture and painting), science and mathematics – as particularly evident in capitalism. His intention was not to analyze the purely material causes of capitalism, historical and economic, but to search for something deeper – something inherent in western beliefs and religious outlooks, and equally lacking in eastern ones. He argued that capitalism in its modern western form, which he clearly detached from its medieval form, was profoundly indebted to one particular, somewhat late, development of Christianity.

But what was capitalism in its modern western form? It should be distinguished from "the impulse to acquisition" which "exists and has existed among waiters, physicians, coachmen, artists, prostitutes, dishonest officials, soldiers, nobles, crusaders, gamblers, and beggars. One may say that it has been common to all sorts and conditions of men at all times and in all countries of the earth, wherever the objective possibility of it is or has been given" (*PE* 17). Modern western capitalism was very different. It had nothing violent about it; it was a far cry from the buccaneering principles of the past and indeed the present. It differed from Jewish capitalism (which Weber defined as "pariah capitalism") (*PE* 165–6). The capitalism Weber had in mind "*may*," he suggested, "even be identical with the restraint, or at least a rational tempering, of this irrational impulse" (*PE* 17). It was by definition disciplined and rational and was accordingly associated with the rational organization of formally free labor.

Such, Weber admitted, was not the only peculiarity of western capitalism which differentiated it from the capitalism of the east. In his introduction and in his other writings, he added further factors of importance which contributed to its formation and to its unique nature. But in his *Protestant Ethic* he examined what he himself called "one side of the causal chain" (*PE* 27): the spirit of capitalism.

The essay

The spirit of capitalism was best described in terms of those who harbored it. Weber defined its holders as "men who had grown up in the hard school of life, calculating and daring at the same time, above all temperate and reliable, shrewd and completely devoted to their business, with strictly bourgeois opinions and principles" (*PE* 69). In order to convey his idea still better Weber posited an "ideal-type" of capitalist. Since this was one of the most original aspects of his essay but was also widely criticized we should look more closely at what Weber meant.

Weber explained the function of the ideal-type in a note to a passage on the early continental textile industry, a description of the life of the "putter-out" who received the cloth from peasants and sold it on to a middleman. In his footnote he wrote that the

> picture has been put together as an ideal-type from conditions found in different industrial branches and at different places. For the purpose of illustration which it here serves, it is of course of no consequence that the process has not in any one of the examples we have in mind taken place in precisely the manner we have described.   (*PE* 200)

The ideal-type, therefore, did not necessarily correspond to any particular individual. In the case of the capitalist it was pieced together from a variety of quotations without too much heed being paid to their context. The writers who furnished the quotations could rarely be defined as capitalists themselves, and the period from which the quotations were selected could well be later than that which Weber ascribed to the association between capitalism and Protestantism.

The ideal-type of the capitalist was a man who

> avoids ostentation and unnecessary expenditure, as well as conscious enjoyment of his power, and is embarrassed by the outward signs of the social recognition which he receives. His manner of life is ... often ... distinguished by a certain ascetic tendency ... He gets nothing out of his wealth for himself, except the irrational sense of having done his job well.   (*PE* 71)

His was a disciplined spirit of enterprise, from which all joy was absent. The resulting profits were immediately reinvested in the business. For Weber this spirit was best embodied by Benjamin Franklin, and it is from a quotation from Franklin's *Advice to a Young Tradesman* that the ideal type was mainly derived (*PE* 32). Such a mentality had an essentially ascetic element, and Weber thus started off by investigating the association between asceticism and labor.

In the middle ages the ascetic, who could also serve as an intermediary between man and God, was to be found primarily within a monastic order. He lived an existence segregated from the world. His whole life was an expression of what Weber called "otherworldly asceticism." The desire for gain, which existed as it had always existed, met with no ideological approval. Great fortunes were indeed made, but they never received the official sanction of the church. Weber here quoted Thomas Aquinas who defined financial profit as *turpitudo*. There was a tendency among the rich to bequeath wealth to religious institutions "as conscience money" or to return it to former debtors to compensate for *usura* taken from them (*PE* 73–74).

The first results of the Reformation led only to a partial change. Although the world was still regarded as reprehensible, Luther rejected the monastic status and introduced the idea of "calling," the divine vocation to pursue a particular path in the world where the duties imposed by God were to be fulfilled. Weber admitted that, despite Luther's conservatism, there was one thing about the calling that was unquestionably progressive: "the valuation of the fulfillment of duty in worldly affairs as the highest form which the moral activity of the individual could assume" (*PE* 85). This was a first step towards the "worldly asceticism" which was to characterize Calvinism. Otherwise Weber described Luther as a "traditionalist," whose approach actually represented a step backwards from the mystics of the middle ages – Weber referred to Tauler's "equalization of the values of religious and worldly occupations, and the decline in valuation of the traditional forms of ascetic practices" (*PE* 86). Lutheranism was, by definition, submissive. For the Lutheran the calling was "a fate to which he must submit and which he must make the best of" (*PE* 160); he accepted "the lot which God has irretrievably assigned to man" (*PE* 162).

As long as the idea of the calling remained the prerogative of orthodox followers of Luther it had few consequences. Only with the Calvinists, and some of the sectarians influenced by them, do we find the implication that the successful practice of the calling was a sign of divine approval. For the Calvinists brought with them the notion of election and predestination. Although implicit in the works of Luther this idea never assumed a central position for him. It was deliberately skirted by Melanchthon. With Calvin, on the other hand, its significance increased, but, Weber admitted, only assumed a role of true importance after his death (*PE* 102).

The result of the rise of the teaching of predestination was "a feeling of unprecedented inner loneliness of the single individual" (*PE* 104). There were no longer any sacraments to which he could turn for assistance. Nor was there any church to which he could turn for consolation, for the church could not fathom the divine decree of whether he was damned or saved. God was ineffably distant and unintelligible. So how could the individual obtain any degree of certainty about whether he was among the elect or the reprobate?

Calvin himself restricted knowledge about the judgment of the individual to God. Only He could know who was saved and who damned, and the creature was doomed to remain in ignorance. This changed with Calvin's successors – even with Beza. Later in the sixteenth and early in the seventeenth century the idea that election was recognizable grew and the doctrine of predestination implied that the individual himself could indeed have some certitude of his destiny. Good works, successfully rewarded, became a sign of divine approval (*PE* 114–115). "In practice," wrote Weber, this means that God helps those who help themselves. Thus the Calvinist, as it is sometimes put, himself creates his own salvation, or, as would be more correct, the conviction of it. But this creation cannot, as in Catholicism, consist in a gradual accumulation of individual good works to one's credit, but rather in a systematic self-control which at every moment stands before the inexorable alternative, chosen or damned. (*PE* 115)

The self-control and discipline once required of the medieval monk was now expected of every Christian in the world. "Worldly asceticism" came into its own. Rather than a disconnected series of actions which would ultimately add up to the believer's credit, "the God of Calvinism demanded of his believers . . . a life of good works combined into a unified system" *PE* 117). In this system there was a new rationality, a method, which emerges from the spiritual autobiographies in which the Christian would chart his own progress.

The Calvinist teaching of predestination, grace and salvation had wide consequences, according to Weber. It was the starting point of English Puritanism, and by way of the Puritans affected the German movement known as Pietism. Weber mentioned August Hermann Francke, for whom "labor in a calling was also the ascetic activity *par excellence* . . . That God Himself blessed His chosen ones through the success of their labor was as undeniable to him as we shall find it to have been to the Puritans" (*PE* 133). German Pietism, however, was vitiated both by its adoption by the Lutherans and by its emotionalism. Weber's final verdict was unfavorable:

> We may say that the virtues favored by Pietism were more those on the one hand of the faithful official, clerk, laborer, or domestic worker, and on the other of the predominantly patriarchal employer with a pious condescension . . . Calvinism, in comparison, appears to be more closely related to the hard legalism and the active enterprise of bourgeois-capitalistic entrepreneurs.
> (*PE* 139)

Much the same could be said of Methodism. Although it assimilated some healthy Calvinist influences through George Whitefield, it was adversely affected by emotionalism and Lutheranism under Wesley (*PE* 142).

The Baptists presented a different problem. Their Anabaptist origins meant that, from the outset, they were ideologically opposed both to Lutheranism and to Calvinism and that they rejected predestination. Nevertheless Weber attributed to them a different form of asceticism which was later to prove highly fruitful. "In so far as Baptism affected the normal workaday world the idea that God only speaks when the flesh is silent evidently meant an incentive to the deliberate weighing of courses of action and their careful justification in terms of the individual conscience" (*PE* 149). Excluded from public office, the Mennonites in Holland and the

Quakers and other descendants of the Baptists in England concentrated on business and trade, and, thanks to their "worldly asceticism," prospered in both fields. Their behavior was always exemplary; their belief that "honesty is the best policy" made them ideal trading partners. Thus the importance they attributed to the conscience as the revelation of God to the individual "gave their conduct in worldly callings a character which was of the greatest significance for the development of the spirit of capitalism" (*PE* 151).

The one movement which unreservedly accepted the Calvinist heritage and on which Weber concentrated in his last chapter as the prime example of the spirit of capitalism was English Puritanism. As the best statement of Puritan belief Weber chose the Westminster Confession of 1647; as the spokesmen of the ideas of the Puritans he singled out John Bunyan, who carried the idea of "God's book-keeping" "to the characteristically tasteless extreme of comparing the relation of a sinner to his God with that of customer and shopkeeper" (*PE* 124), and above all Richard Baxter. In Baxter's vast work Weber found one of the very few quotations which seemed to support his thesis of a direct connection between the virtuous practice of the calling, financial profit and salvation:

> If God show you a way in which you may lawfully get more than in another way (without wrong to your soul or to any other), if you refuse this, and choose the less gainful way, you cross one of the ends of your calling, and you refuse to be God's steward, and to accept His gifts and use them for Him when He requireth it: you may labor to be rich for God, though not for the flesh and sin.   (*PE* 162)

Among the English Puritans Weber discovered all the features of the ascetic capitalist described in Benjamin Franklin's *Advice to a Young Tradesman*. One of these was the condemnation of "enjoyment" for enjoyment's sake which could be classified as the "irrational use of wealth." In describing the Puritans Weber introduced the idea of "comfort" – "der Begriff 'des comfort'" – "comfort" significantly remains in English in the German original (*GARS* 191). Comfort "characteristically limits the extent of ethically permissible expenditures." It divided the modern western capitalist from his medieval predecessors and indeed from his Catholic (or Mediterranean) counterparts. As for the Puritans, "over against the glitter and ostentation of feudal magnificence which, resting on an unsound economic basis, prefers a sordid elegance to a sober simplicity, they set the clean and solid comfort of the middle-class home as an ideal" (*PE* 171). (In the German "home" too remained in English.) This was the most perfect expression of the "rational bourgeois life" (*PE* 174). Wealth was not acquired for its own sake (something which was condemned), but it was acquired in pursuit of the calling.

> In conformity with the Old Testament and in analogy to the ethical value of good works, asceticism looked upon the pursuit of wealth as an end in itself as highly reprehensible; but the attainment of it as a fruit of labor in a calling was a sign of God's blessing. And even more important: the religious valuation of restless, continuous, systematic work in a worldly calling, as the highest means to asceticism, and at the same time the surest and most evident proof of rebirth and genuine faith, must have been the most powerful conceivable lever for the expansion of that attitude toward life which we have here called the spirit of capitalism. (*PE* 172)

The same spirit could also be observed in Holland. Even if Weber admitted that it had only really been dominated by strict Calvinism for seven years, "the greater simplicity of life in the more seriously religious circles, in combination with great wealth, led to an excessive propensity to accumulation" (*PE* 172–173). And it could be clearly perceived in America. Indeed, in America the Puritan spirit – "the specifically middle-class outlook of the Puritans" – was thrown into relief by the contrast with the mentality of the luxury-loving adventurers who colonised other areas of the continent (*PE* 173–174).

Yet the glorious age when piety and capitalism were so intimately connected would seem to have been short-lived. Within a brief period "the intensity of the search for the Kingdom of God commenced gradually to pass over into sober economic virtue; the religious roots died out slowly, giving way to utilitarian worldliness" (*PE* 176); Bunyan's pilgrim was replaced by Robinson Crusoe. For a time the benefits alone of the system were evident. Not only had the mentality described produced enterprising businessmen but it had also provided the disciplined and rational work force without which modern capitalism would be impossible. The capitalist thus had a body of "sober, conscientious, and unusually industrious workmen, who clung to their work as to a life purpose willed by God" (*PE* 177). But as the "religious root" died "the utilitarian interpretation crept in unnoticed." Materialism started to increase its hold and form the type of system which Weber observed in his own day and deplored.

> Since asceticism undertook to remodel the world and to work out its ideals in the world, material goods have gained an increasing and finally an inexorable power over the lives of men as at no previous period in history. Today the spirit of religious asceticism – whether finally, who knows? – has escaped from the cage. But victorious capitalism, since it rests on mechanical founda-tions, needs its support no longer . . . No one knows who will live in this cage in the future, or whether at the end of this tremendous development entirely

new prophets will arise, or there will be a great rebirth of old ideas and ideals, or, if neither, mechanized petrification, embellished with a sort of convulsive self-importance. For of the last stage of this cultural development, it might well be truly said: "Specialists without spirit, sensualists without heart; this nullity imagines that it has attained a level of civilization never before achieved."   (PE 181–182)

The Protestant Ethic and the Spirit of Capitalism was printed in volumes 20 (1904) and 21 (1905) of the *Archiv für Sozialwissenschaft und Sozialpolitik* (Archives for Social Science and Social Policy), the journal published in Tübingen of which Weber himself had been appointed associate editor in 1903. It was not Weber's only statement about the connection between Protestantism and capitalism. In 1906 he first published a brief article entitled "The Protestant Sects and the Spirit of Capitalism" which he was later to expand and in which he studied the economic behavior of some of the American sects he had been so struck by during his visit to the United States in 1904. What interested him was the fact that members of a sectarian Church – Baptists, Methodists, Quakers and others – were credited with complete financial reliability. Weber traced this idea back to the origins of the sects, and, indeed, of the Calvinist churches, when only those who were known to be virtuous were admitted to communion. The decision to admit members was no longer in the hands of the clergy but in those of the laity. The fact that a church member could take communion meant that his fellows were sure of his integrity.

> The member of the sect (or conventicle) had to have qualities of a certain kind in order to enter the community circle. Being endowed with these qualities was important for the development of rational modern capitalism . . . In order to hold his own in this circle, the member had to *prove* repeatedly that he was endowed with these qualities. They were constantly and continuously bred in him'   (FMW 302–322, esp. 320)

The same situation was reproduced in the contemporary American club, groups of people, voluntarily united, who knew each other sufficiently to vouch for one another. The community was responsible for the individual; the individual had to prove himself to the community; and the community would foster, and sometimes select, his best qualities. When put into practice these qualities would, in turn, redound to the honor of the community. "The capitalist success of a sect brother," Weber concluded, "if legally attained, was proof of his worth and of his state of grace, and it raised the prestige and the propaganda chances of the sect" (FMW 322).

Weber returned to the subject of Protestantism in his work on economics, in his later studies on the religions of the world, and in the articles he wrote answering his critics, but he never altered the substance of his thesis. To it he clung with extraordinary obstinacy. He repeated it in his posthumously published *Economy and Society* (pp. 586–589, 615–623) and in his *General Economic History*, the series of lectures which he delivered in 1919–1920 (*GEH* 365–369). He made a few small additions to the main text of his original essay. He brought about some stylistic changes and added new footnotes responding to objections and attacks. But however much he embroidered on his original theme, *The Protestant Ethic and the Spirit of Capitalism* remained his fundamental text on the subject. In one of the additional footnotes he stated: "I have not in revision left out, changed the meaning of, weakened, or added materially different statements to, a single sentence of my essay which contained any essential point" (*PE* 187).

The debate

If we judge a text by its capacity to provoke reaction – positive, negative, above all enduring for almost a hundred years – then Max Weber's *Protestant Ethic and the Spirit of Capitalism* must be regarded as one of the most important works of this century. Even if few historians writing at the moment would incorporate his ideas in a study of seventeenth-century Calvinism, Weber still has a distinguished and influential follower in Christopher Hill and the debate about the thesis itself seemed, certainly until a few years ago, to be raging as intensely and as emotionally as it did when his essay first appeared.[5] It has been joined by so many scholars that it has become an object of study in itself. To it have been dedicated monographs, bibliographies, anthologies and conferences. Because Weber replied to the main objections to his thesis made in his lifetime, and because relatively little has in fact been added to these objections since, the debate serves as an effective illumination of some of his ideas and indicates the sort of research which he stimulated.

The reactions to Weber's essay were immediate. Many of Weber's contemporaries accepted his thesis with enthusiasm. It was greeted warmly by the cultural historian Eberhard Gothein, by the economic historians Gerhard von Schulze-Gaevernitz and William Cunningham, and by the church historian Hans von Schubert. Weber's colleague Ernst Troeltsch,

---

[5] Among the many publications on the debate see Philippe Besnard, *Protestantisme et capitalisme. La Controverse post-wébérienne*, Paris: Armand Colin, 1970. For a later discussion accompanied by a thorough bibliography, see Gordon Marshall, *Presbyteries and Profits: Calvinism and the Development of Capitalism in Scotland, 1560–1707*, Oxford: Clarendon Press, 1980, pp. 3–12, 14–27, 320–329. More recent still is Malcolm H. MacKinnon, "The Longevity of the Thesis: A Critique of the Critics," in Lehmann and Roth (eds.), *Weber's "Protestant Ethic"*, pp. 211–243.

Professor of Systematic Theology at the University of Heidelberg, accepted most of Weber's ideas and provided further material to support them. As a result the thesis was sometimes known as the Weber–Troeltsch thesis.

The criticisms ranged from those by friends of Weber, such as Werner Sombart, a fellow editor of the *Archiv für Sozialwissenschaft und Sozialpolitik* who simply proposed slightly different theories of his own, to the more direct attacks of H. Karl Fischer, the Kiel historian Felix Rachfahl[6] and the political economist Lujo Brentano.[7] One of the main objections to Weber missed the point of his essay. This concerned the antiquity of capitalism and its first causes. That capitalism in its original form was far older than the emergence of Calvinism Weber never doubted, and he was in fact prepared to attribute it to many of the factors suggested by his critics. Yet his essay provoked a series of alternative explanations some of which still retain their historical validity.

Werner Sombart, who had already posited a connection between religion, especially Protestantism, and economic development in his *Modern Capitalism* of 1902, was stimulated by Weber to explore the roots of capitalism still further. In *Die Juden und das Wirtschaftsleben* (The Jews and Economic Life) he concluded that the spirit of capitalism should be sought among the Sephardic Jews expelled from Spain and Portugal at the end of the fifteenth century. Many settled in Amsterdam and Hamburg, and, having derived their own particular ethos from the Talmud, were more responsible than any other single group for fashioning capitalism. And the role of the Jews led Sombart to emphasize the economic significance of immigration.[8] This remained a popular theme among Weber's critics. Brentano too referred to the tendency among Catholic capitalists to emigrate north after the Reformation – his own family, originally from Lake Como, was an example – but did these capitalists then become Protestants? No, they remained Catholic, and up to his own day pious Catholics could still be found among the great capitalists of the north.

In the longest – and according to Weber the rudest – response to his essay, "Kalvinismus und Kapitalismus" of 1909 (directed against both Weber and Troeltsch),[9] Rachfahl also touched on the importance of

---

[6] The attacks by H.Karl Fischer and Felix Rachfahl, together with Weber's rejoinders, are published in Max Weber, *Die protestantische Ethik, II, Kritiken und Antikritiken*, edited by Johannes Winckelmann, Gütersloh: Mohn, 1968, henceforth quoted as *Kritiken und Antikritiken*.

[7] Contained in Lujo Brentano, *Der wirtschaftende Mensch in der Geschichte: Gesammelte Reden und Aufsätze*, Leipzig: Felix Meiner, 1923.

[8] On Weber and Sombart see Hartmut Lehmann, "The Rise of Capitalism: Weber versus Sombart," in Lehmann and Roth (eds.), *Weber's "Protestant Ethic"*, pp. 195–208.

[9] *Kritiken und Antikritiken*, pp. 57–148.

immigration in his formulation of a theory which was to be developed by later historians. After the Reformation, capitalists were repelled by countries in which religion had invaded the entire apparatus of the state and ended up by inhibiting the free spirit of commerce – Spain and parts of Italy. But they were no more attracted by places dominated by Calvinist or Puritan fanaticism. They were drawn, rather, by lands where toleration prevailed and where there was a separation between church and state.

And to immigration Weber's critics added other causes for the advances and transformation of capitalism. In his inaugural address as rector of the University of Munich in 1901 Brentano had concluded that capitalism, even if it was as old as trade itself, developed in its modern form in Italy in the wake of the Crusades and was always assisted by Roman law which flourished at the same time.[10] In his "Puritanismus und Kapitalismus,"[11] his main critique of Weber's essay, he pointed out that justifications of financial gain could already be found in the writings of Thomas Aquinas, one of whose scholastic followers, Franciscus Maironius, even justified interest. The true ideological "emancipation" of capitalism, however, was the work of Machiavelli. With the Reformation life – and above all work – in the world was at last preferred to the monastic ideal of the middle ages, but of none of the Reformers could it be said that they in any way exalted the acquisition of riches or justified capitalism. If anything the contrary was true, and Brentano saw the advance of capitalism in seventeenth-century England as being due to various factors including the victory of the Machiavellian spirit over the Puritans and the rise of empirical philosophy. While Rachfahl attributed the progressive alteration of Protestantism and its adaptation to the open spirit of Locke and the Enlightenment partly to the influence of the Anabaptist tradition which affected Calvinism in England in the seventeenth century, he also ascribed it to the rational libertinism which remained in the debt of the humanists and above all of the man whom he contrasted with Calvin, Desiderius Erasmus.[12]

Then there was Weber's evaluation of the relationship between religion and the spirit of capitalism. It was to this that one of his very earliest critics, H. Karl Fischer, objected in an article that appeared in 1907 in the same review which had published Weber's own essay, the *Archiv für Sozialwissenschaft und Sozialpolitik*.[13] Fischer maintained that neither the

---

[10] Lujo Brentano, "Ethik und Volkswirtschaft in der Geschichte," in Brentano, *Der wirtschaftende Mensch*, pp. 34–76.

[11] Brentano, "Puritanismus und Kapitalismus," in *ibid.*, pp. 363–425.

[12] *Kritiken und Antikritiken*, pp. 134–136.

[13] H. Karl Fischer, "Kritische Beiträge zu Professor Max Webers Abhandlung 'Die protestantische Ethik und der Geist des Kapitalismus,'" in *Kritiken und Antikritiken*, pp. 11–26.

capitalist spirit nor the ideas on duty Weber associated with it could necessarily be said to have been affected by religious beliefs or writings. Ideas about duty may have had their root in psychological causes altogether independent of religion, while the capitalist spirit was more likely to be due to political and social elements. That the reverse might be true, on the other hand, Fischer was ready to admit. Some of the Reformers would thus have adapted their ideas to the existing economic circumstances, or to capitalism.

Rachfahl too was dissatisfied. He claimed that Weber had not provided sufficient evidence to substantiate his own thesis and had thus failed to formulate the relationship between Protestantism and capitalism correctly. What really happened in those areas which Weber singled out as examples of the triumph of the spirit of capitalism? How Calvinist were the capitalists? In Holland not only had capitalism developed well before the introduction of Calvinism but many of the great capitalists remained Catholics (albeit indifferent ones) or, at a slightly later date, became Arminians. They were ready to make profit where they saw the chance. They were prepared to trade with Spain while the true Dutch Calvinists fulminated against such lack of scruples. In England, where capitalism had also existed long before the arrival of Puritanism, Rachfahl doubted the extent to which those capitalists who were indeed Puritans or Quakers were truly motivated by religion in their attitude to commercial transactions. Weber had certainly provided no evidence to prove conclusively that they were. In America, that highly heterogeneous collection of societies harboring both the Puritans and the descendants of Catholics and cavaliers, it was, according to Rachfahl, impossible to find traces of the ideal-type of Weber's capitalist. Great fortunes were indeed accumulated, but there was no sign of a prevailing Puritan influence in the process.[14]

For both Rachfahl and Brentano, Calvinism and Puritanism led not to a justification of high earnings but rather to a middle-class ambition to earn adequately – to what Rachfahl called "*der mittlere Wohlstand.*"[15] "The Puritan ethic," wrote Brentano, "is the traditional economic ethic of the petite bourgeoisie which reflected the development of the spirit of the craftsman of the second half of the middle ages."[16] The statements among the Puritans regarding profit should be seen as a reflection of the capitalist world in which they lived rather than as the result of theological convictions. The first reaction of those Puritans who did enrich themselves was to

---

[14] *Kritiken und Antikritiken*, pp. 93–105.
[15] *Ibid.*, pp. 118–119.
[16] Brentano, *Der wirtschaftende Mensch*, p. 420.

abandon Puritanism. The idea that work was pleasing to God, which Weber seemed to restrict to the Puritans, was a commonplace to be found in the New Testament, the Church Fathers and the great Schoolmen

Weber's ideal-type of capitalist was also criticized. Where could it be found? However sober their attire, after all, the jovial figures portrayed in Dutch paintings of the seventeenth century did not correspond to the dedicated ascetic described by Weber any more than the humorless products of Calvinist discipline depicted in the Anglo-Saxon world at a later date could be associated with any particular financial prosperity. Not only, as Fischer pointed out, could capitalists be found in Catholic countries but capitalists in Holland lived in full enjoyment of their wealth.[17] Rachfahl, who also dwelt on the Dutch love of pleasure, argued that capitalists were less single-minded than Webers' ideal-type. Their motives were usually mixed. The capitalist spirit could be combined with the ambition of power or honor, with a desire to serve one's neighbor or the community and the country, with care for one's own family, even, perhaps, with a wish to enjoy life. The spirit of capitalism as Rachfahl defined it was no more than an instinct of acquisition which went beyond the immediate satisfaction of needs. It resulted in the accumulation of capital and gains from its further investment. It was attended by speculation and exploitation of the economic situation of the moment and a mathematical calculation of the relationship between the available means and the likely result.[18]

The criticism to which Weber was to remain most vulnerable was his use of sources. Rachfahl had accused him of superficiality and had questioned his interpretation of Baxter's writings and Cromwell's thought. Brentano went into the matter more deeply. Few people, he said, were more opposed to capitalism than Calvin, and the same applied to the Puritans whom Weber quoted as examples of his ethos, Bunyan and Baxter. But the man whom Weber had misunderstood most was Franklin. The quotation which he provided, Brentano correctly observed, should be understood ironically. Other works by Franklin show that he held the ideas of Aristotle and argued persuasively for a virtuous pleasure, moral rather than physical.[19]

Brentano, finally, added another objection which was to be taken up by later critics such as H. M. Robertson.[20] Weber's idea that the notion of the "calling" was peculiar to Lutheranism was altogether incorrect. The calling was in fact of equal antiquity to Christianity itself. It was to be found in the

---

[17] Fischer, "Kritische Beiträge," pp. 23–24.
[18] *Kritiken und Antikritiken*, p. 81.
[19] Brentano, *Der wirtschaftende Mensch*, pp. 403–418.
[20] H. M. Robertson, *Aspects of the Rise of Economic Individualism. A Criticism of Max Weber and His School*, Cambridge: Cambridge University Press, 1933.

New Testament and throughout the Middle Ages. Consequently all of Weber's argumentation which depended on the novelty of the Protestant calling could be dismissed.[21]

In spite of their criticisms Fischer, Rachfahl and Brentano were all prepared to grant Weber certain points. Fischer conceded that "there is undoubtedly a close connection between religious confession and capitalist development."[22] Rachfahl too agreed that "there can be no doubt of an inner relationship between Calvinism and capitalism."[23] As formulated by Luther, and still more by Calvin, Protestantism unquestionably assisted the development of capitalism. But the reciprocal influence should not be exaggerated. Brentano admitted that the Puritan teaching of grace, in areas where capitalism already existed, could contribute to the spread of the capitalist spirit among the religiously minded by removing certain inhibitions. He also confirmed the theories in Weber's "Protestant Sects and the Spirit of Capitalism" according to which a businessman could only profit from joining a sect whose first principle was honesty and in which "trust magnates" might assuage their consciences by spending their earnings on works of charity – even if there were cases of communities which refused to accept such a situation and excluded the capitalist from their midst.[24]

After Weber's death Brentano's objections were elaborated upon by R. H. Tawney, Professor of Economic History at London University from 1931 to 1949, a man presented alternately as a critic and as a follower of Weber. Together with the American sociologist Talcott Parsons, who translated Weber's essay into English in 1930, Tawney did much for the future of Weber's ideas in the English-speaking world. His *Religion and the Rise of Capitalism*, first published as a book in 1926, was based on the Holland Memorial Lectures delivered at King's College, London in 1922. Besides the objections already advanced by Brentano Tawney added a number of his own. He felt that many more causes should be adduced for the rise of capitalism – geographical discoveries, technological progress, the operations of the great trading companies. Capitalism, he agreed, had existed well before the Reformation. Like Brentano he drew attention to those intellectual movements which had functioned quite independently of religion – the political thought of the Renaissance, the ideas of Machiavelli, not to mention the numerous speculations of economists on prices, money and foreign exchanges. He believed that Weber oversimplified Calvinism. It was misleading to ascribe to the English Puritans Calvin's own views of

---

[21] Brentano, *Der wirtschaftende Mensch*, pp. 391–399.
[22] *Kritiken und Antikritiken*, p. 25.
[23] *Ibid.*, p. 93. Cf. pp. 125, 140–141.
[24] Brentano, *Der wirtschaftende Mensch*, pp. 420–421.

"social duties and expediency." Numerous other elements had intervened to form the spirit of Puritanism.

Tawney nevertheless admitted that Weber made some outstandingly important points.

> What is true and valuable in his essay is his insistence that the commercial classes in seventeenth-century England were the standard-bearers of a particular conception of social expediency, which was markedly different from that of the more conservative elements in society – the peasants, the craftsmen, and many landed gentry – and that that conception found expression in religion, in politics, and, not least, in social and economic conduct and policy.[25]

This was the line which Tawney himself chose to pursue in his study. The Puritans became the representatives of a new ethos which was to have an immense effect on economic development and was to transform countless aspects of English life and thought. In order to prove this Tawney referred to many of the sources and quotations which had already been used by Weber. Despite his disagreements, he came so close to Weber in his conclusions that the thesis, after being associated with Weber and Troeltsch, came sometimes to be known as the Weber–Tawney thesis.

Other historians were more critical of Weber. Both Hugh Trevor-Roper in the 1950s and Herbert Lüthy still later revived the charges of Rachfahl and emphasized the fact that the great capitalists of the sixteenth and seventeenth centuries (whom Trevor-Roper placed in the tradition of Erasmus) found their commercial activities inhibited in the absolutist states of the Counter-Reformation. They made for more tolerant areas in Europe, such as Holland, which happened to be Protestant. The various Reformations, Lüthy suggested, may have been beneficial to capitalism "by default" – because Protestantism never managed to dominate the state in the way that Catholicism had done. Yet, just as Trevor-Roper believed in "a solid, if elusive, core of truth in Weber's thesis,"[26] Lüthy, in his analysis of Calvinist Geneva, admitted that Calvinism "gave the capitalist a legitimate place in the Christian city as a prominent agent in the work of glorifying God, not through pious endowments and legacies, nor through renouncing his possessions, but through the actual exercise of his economic function."[27]

Some of the sharpest criticisms of Weber have been on theological grounds. The recent attack by Malcolm H. MacKinnon is an example.

---

[25] R. H. Tawney, *Religion and the Rise of Capitalism*, Harmondsworth: Penguin Books, 1969, p. 313.

[26] *Ibid.*, p. 6.   [27] Lehman and Roth (eds.), *Weber's "Protestant Ethic."*

Weber, he said, took as his point of departure for the doctrine of predestination in England the Westminster Confession of 1647. Yet by then not only
did the "calling" to which Weber referred apply exclusively to divine
matters, but Calvinism had introduced the idea of the covenant and thus of
the certainty of salvation for those who worked for it. "This development,"
wrote MacKinnon, "effectively robs Weber of the religious sanction and its
ultimate use by the Puritan to transform the world in the name of God. In no
way did seventeenth-century Calvinism sanctify a worldly calling, unintentionally or otherwise. As Weber conceives of it, therefore, his Protestant
ethic makes no contribution to capitalist development."[28]

Effective though this critique of Weber's theory might sound it was not
accepted by all scholars. If anything, it added further fuel to the controversy.[29] And while the debate about Weber's thesis continued among
historians and theologians, the methodology used by Weber, and above all
by his pupil Offenbacher, was both criticized and applied by sociologists. In
a radical attack on Weber, *Religions and Economic Action*, which first
appeared in Stockholm in 1957, Kurt Samuelsson pointed out that the
tables drawn up by Offenbacher and based on average figures for the years
from 1885 to 1895 took no account of the extent to which the confessions
were represented in those school districts in which Protestants predominated in the schools. Samuelsson found that in fact there were more
Protestants than Catholics who lived in areas where higher educational
institutes were available. This altered the evidence and allowed Samuelsson
to conclude that Offenbacher used only those statistics which suited his
pre-existing beliefs,[30] and that Weber's method was "unwarrantable."[31]
Other sociologists followed Offenbacher in investigating the connection
between religious faith and social status. Does Protestantism, they asked,
develop a special work ethos in the believer? And does such an ethos lead

---

[28] Malcolm H. MacKinnon, "Part I: Calvinism and the Infallible Assurance of Grace," *British Journal of Sociology*, 39 (1988), pp. 143–177, esp. 144–145. See also "Part II: Weber's Exploration of Calvinism," *British Journal of Sociology*, 39 (1988), pp. 178–210.

[29] It has been rejected out of hand by David Zaret, "The Use and Abuse of Textual Data," in Lehmann and Roth (eds.), *Weber's "Protestant Ethic"*, pp. 245–272, and criticized by Kaspar von Greyerz, "Biographical Evidence on Predestination, Covenant, and Special Providence," in *ibid.*, pp. 273–284. Although Von Greyerz agrees to some extent with MacKinnon about Baxter (who, MacKinnon argued, could not be regarded as a Puritan prototype and was himself highly skeptical about the doctrine of predestination), he is far less convinced by his arguments about covenant theology and questions the effect that technical doctrine might have had on the "average committed layperson."

[30] Kurt Samuelsson, *Religion and Economic Action*, Stockholm: Svenska Bokförlaget, 1961, pp. 137–147.

[31] *Ibid.*, p. 150.

to greater professional success than that of the Catholics?[32] The results of this research have been conflicting and inconclusive.

Conclusion

However we may judge it the Weber controversy has produced books and essays of the highest quality. It has also stimulated research in relatively new fields.[33] Yet one fact emerges from the debate: it is just as difficult to demolish Weber's thesis as it is to substantiate it. Many of Weber's critics have tried to invalidate his essay by advancing further causes of capitalism and showing that it existed long before the Reformation. To those who did so in his lifetime Weber replied that he had never suggested that Protestantism was actually a cause, let alone the sole cause, of capitalism. "We have no intention whatever," he wrote in *The Protestant Ethic*,

> of maintaining such a foolish and doctrinaire thesis as that the spirit of capitalism . . . could only have arisen as the result of certain effects of the Reformation, or even that capitalism as an economic system is a creation of the Reformation . . . On the contrary, we only wish to ascertain whether and to what extent religious forces have taken part in the qualitative formation and the quantitative expansion of that spirit over the world.   (PE 91)

[handwritten margin note: Argument against arguments of Weber]

Although the exact chronological boundaries of modern capitalism in its connection with Protestantism are by no means always clear in Weber's essay, he said he was well aware that the religious element was limited in time and that utilitarian and other currents soon replaced it. When it came to ascertaining what the causes of capitalism actually were Weber referred, both in his introduction to *The Protestant Ethic* (PE 22–25) and elsewhere, to other factors, many of which had been put forward by his critics: the separation of business from the household; rational book-keeping; scientific progress; the tradition of Roman law; and the development of the western city.

Those who, like Rachfahl, provided an alternative definition of the spirit of capitalism and an alternative explanation of its success were told that they were unable to distinguish between the spirit and the system of capitalism.[34] Weber claimed to agree with Rachfahl's theory of the impor-

---

[32] A survey of such studies is provided by Besnard, *Protestantisme et capitalisme*, pp. 99–110.

[33] Many of Weber's critics pointed out that Scotland was neglected by him and could in fact be used to contradict his thesis. In seventeenth-century Scotland the doctrine of predestination was, after all, accepted far more widely than in England, yet Scotland remained poor and backward. This prompted Gordon Marshall to write *Presbyteries and Profits*.

[34] *Kritiken und Antikritiken*, p. 172.

tance of toleration. But toleration, he said, only furthered trade and capitalism, allowing for immigration. It had nothing to do with the spirit of capitalism as he understood it.[35] The *spirit* of capitalism, and the ideal-type who possessed it, were creations of Weber's own.[36] He made a highly eclectic (and subjective) use of quotations which, put together, could indeed amount to an expression of his own definition of the spirit of capitalism, or of the ideal-type, even if none of the figures quoted actually harbored such a spirit or corresponded to such a type. He was attempting to describe a singularly evasive object, a mentality. To do so he provided his own premises. Here, as Brentano had pointed out, his argumentation was a *petitio principi*.[37] Against a theory which assumes the acceptance of the premises posited by its author it is difficult to argue.

So how are we to assess Weber's thesis now?[38] It is still debated but is seldom actually applied by historians. Does this mean that Weber's critics have come into their own? Subsequent research, certainly, has invalidated a number of the points Weber made. He was unquestionably extreme in his dismissal of Lutheranism, and Rachfahl could rightly point to the prosperity of Lutheran Hamburg. Nor, it is generally agreed, did Weber do justice to Catholicism, especially in its later forms. With characteristic reluctance to admit himself in the wrong, Weber said that it was Brentano who had failed to understand Benjamin Franklin rather than he (*PE* 192–193), yet few scholars would deny that Weber misrepresented Franklin and that he was equally arbitrary in his treatment of many of his other sources, such as Bunyan and Baxter.[39] Some of the greatest historians of the century, such as Henri Pirenne, have proved that Weber was mistaken about Calvinist influence in Holland, and there has been much skepticism about his analysis of Puritan influence in America.

Weber has been justly rated for representing the Lutheran idea of the "calling" as so novel and distinctive, for his interpretation of the "calling" at a later date, and for the importance he attributed to the doctrine of predestination in seventeenth-century England. For to what extent did the

---

[35] *Ibid.*, pp. 156–157. Cf. *PE* 243.

[36] Against Rachfahl's objections Weber maintained that the ideal-type which he described was not supposed to correspond to anything more than a single component of the spirit of capitalism – "a particular constitutive component of the *lifestyle* which stood by the cradle of modern capitalism. To modern capitalism, together with countless other elements, it contributed." *Kritiken und Antikritiken*, p. 169.

[37] Brentano, *Der wirtschaftende Mensch*, p. 384.

[38] Cf. Anthony Giddens' assessment in his introduction to Weber, *Protestant Ethic*, London: Counterpoint, 1985 pp. xx–xxvi.

[39] For a recent critique of Weber's use of Baxter see William Lamont, *Puritanism and Historical Controversy*, London: UCL Press, 1996, pp. 103–128.

English Puritans described by Weber really believe in predestination? From a recent analysis of contemporary diaries and autobiographies it would appear that neither predestination nor covenant theology were of much concern to English laymen. The true preoccupation would seem to have been with special providence or God's presence in their lives. God was thus by no means as remote for the Puritan as Weber made Him out to be.[40] And then, who were the Puritans? The borders between the various shades of Anglicanism and the various shades of Puritanism in England now appear vague and fluid. The clear definitions that existed in Weber's day have been called in doubt as has the primacy attributed by Weber, and later by Tawney, to the Puritans as the custodians of progress. Above all, however, scholars have questioned the extent to which Calvinism in any of its forms actually served to justify the accumulation of wealth and a behavior which can be defined as capitalist. Weber's quotations in support of his thesis, wrenched out of context as they are, can hardly be accepted as conclusive proof and no historian has come up with anything more convincing.

Although a number of historians have agreed that Protestantism, albeit not necessarily as Weber saw it, did have some relationship with economic progress and modern intellectual developments and that Weber made a contribution to the study of this relationship, there is in fact not much in the various parts of Weber's thesis which stands up to examination. The "core of truth" which Trevor-Roper found appears less solid and more elusive than ever. One of the drawbacks of the debate provoked by Weber's essay, however, is that excessive weight has been laid on Weber as a historian. But is it fair still to judge Weber's text by what it has to offer historians today? It is surely more fruitful to examine *The Protestant Ethic and the Spirit of Capitalism* not only as a part of Weber's vision of society but as an expression of the ideas prevailing in early twentieth-century Germany, to assess the extent to which Weber was presenting the notions of liberal Protestantism, and to study the essay in association with other contemporary works on the same subject.

---

[40] Von Greyerz, "Biographical Evidence on Predestination, Covenant, and Special Providence," p. 275.

9

JOHN LOVE

Max Weber's Orient

What was it that drove Weber, arguably even to this day the foremost theoretician of modern *western* society and its historical evolution, to embark on a far-reaching series of investigations of *non-western* cultures? The question arises inevitably when one considers the sheer scale of Weber's writings on the world religions, all but encyclopedic in scope and displaying an extraordinary capacity of the part of their author in ordering and synthesizing the detailed historical materials involved (a task made all the more impressive given the technical difficulties arising from the undeveloped state of the documentary and scholarly sources at the time).[1] Was all this effort required to establish the correctness of the Protestant ethic thesis? Or, was something further involved that went beyond the earlier problematic and transformed it?

In what follows we shall assume that Weber's studies of the orient, along

---

[1] Weber's reflections concerning the orient are largely to be found in two of his three large-scale studies of religion, *The Religion of China* and *The Religion of India*; though many of his other works, especially *Economy and Society* (containing *The Sociology of Religion*), have extensive discussions as well. In grappling with Weber's perspective it is instructive to realize that the first two works just mentioned were first published under the umbrella title of "Die Wirtschaftsethik der Weltreligionen" ("The Economic Ethics of the Word Religions") in the *Archiv für Sozialwissenschaft und Sozialpolitik* from 1916 to 1919. (They were subsequently republished in 1920/1 with some modifications, and with the inclusion of *The Protestant Ethic* plus several important linking essays, as a three-volume work entitled *Gesammelte Aufsätze zur Religionssoziologie* (*GARS*) [*The Collected Essays on the Sociology of Religion*].) These works present a number of difficulties both as studies in their own right and in relation to Weber's other writings. In recent years Weber scholars have looked increasingly to this body of work as a key to understanding his fundamental concerns. In what follows we largely accept Wolfgang Schluchter's view that Weber's "later program aimed at enlarging the developmental history of modernity which he had begun with his study of Protestantism and embedding it in the developmental history of the whole West. In this respect Weber had only a limited interest in the history of other civilizations, and therefore his later analysis had asymmetric features which were accentuated by the later program": W. Schluchter, *The Rise of Western Rationalism: Max Weber's Developmental History*, trans. Guenther Roth, Berkeley, CA: University of California, 1981, p. 149.

with his *Ancient Judaism*, constitute key parts of what was a major expansion and enhancement of the Protestant ethic thesis and concerned the daunting task of grasping the rationalization of the modern world in the context of universal history. Whilst the original umbrella title of the monographs he began to publish in 1915, *The Economic Ethic of the World Religions*, suggests Weber remained preoccupied with demonstrating via counter-factual comparisons the validity of the Protestant ethic thesis, the contents of the writings subsequently presented as well as the inclusion of several crucial linking essays indicate the problematic had been modified in important ways.[2] *The Religion of China* was Weber's first large-scale study of a non-western religious system, and contains an important concluding essay comparing Confucianism directly with Puritanism. In our view the work played a pivotal role in the transformation of Weber's thought because, in concluding his researches on China, Weber was obliged to confront a much larger question than that of the causal significance of Protestantism. Because of the presence in China of some rational, ascetic, scientific and commercial cultural elements, the issue for him now became to determine the specific and distinctive character of western rationality as such. It was no longer merely a question of demonstrating the absence in China and elsewhere of certain causal factors of relevance to the emergence of western capitalism – the precise form of western rationality had to be explained in contradistinction from that of the east. The grand theme of the rationalization of culture with all the ramifications this entails thus in the end is the real focus of *The Collected Essays on the Sociology of Religion*, a monumental but unfinished work which nonetheless was sufficiently formed for us to understand its essential arguments.

China: the imperial state and the mandarinate

The Confucian outlook, Weber argues, is particularly distinctive because of its close association with magic, as manifest in its preoccupation with the occult forces residing between heaven and earth which somehow guarantee the harmony of the cosmos.[3] Unlike Judaism and certain strains of

---

[2] On these matters, see F. H. Tenbruck, "The Problem of Thematic Unity in the Works of Max Weber," *British Journal of Sociology*, 31 (1980), pp. 13–51; Stephen Kalberg, "The Search for Thematic Orientations in a Fragmented Œuvre: The Discussion of Max Weber in Recent Sociological Literature," *Sociology*, 13 (1979), pp. 127–139; and Helwig Schmidt-Glintzer, "The Economic Ethics of the World Religions" in H. Lehmann and G. Roth (eds.), *Weber's "Protestant Ethic": Origins, Evidence, Contexts*, Cambridge: Cambridge University Press, 1993. Also relevant is my own "Developmentalism in Max Weber's Sociology of Religion: A Critique of F. H. Tenbruck," *European Journal of Sociology*, 34 (1993), pp. 339–369.
[3] A good general introduction to Weber's writing on China is C. K. Yang's Introduction to *The*

Christianity, its teachings have not led to a demanding and rationalized system of social ethics but rather culminated in an behavioral code that in essence seeks adjustment to the world as it is. The basic strategy of Confucianism is to harmonize the inner state of the individual with the external divine order, in particular by subjecting his desires to the exigencies of position in an hierarchical social order.

For Weber the Chinese bureaucratic state could not have arisen without an accompanying set of beliefs of a specific kind to provide legitimation for rulers as well as orientation and meaning for subjects; yet the role of such a belief system is no mere expression or ideological reflection of what might be deemed the real causal factors operating, as it were, at a more fundamental level.[4] Weber is convinced that intellectually cultivated worldviews can be, and often are, decisive forces of historical development – because ideas serve to anchor values, which in turn induce dispositions of action leading to the patterning of cultural life, and in this fashion the course of historical evolution takes its peculiar direction. As he explains on one occasion, "The rational elements of a religion, its 'doctrine,' have an autonomy . . . The rational religious pragmatism of salvation, flowing from the nature of the images of God and the world, have under certain conditions had far-reaching results for the fashioning of a practical way of life" (FMW 286). Weber typically deals with these relations by speaking of social groups who are the *bearers* of a worldview or certain key attitudes. Thus, "The unity of Chinese culture is essentially the unity of that status group which is the bearer of the bureaucratic classic-literary education and of Confucian ethic with its ideal of gentility . . ." (E&S 1050). And again, "The bureaucratic structure of Chinese politics and their carriers has given to the whole literary tradition of China its characteristic stamp. For more than 2000 years the literati have definitely been the ruling stratum in China . . ." (RC 107–108). The history of Confucianism is thus in large part a

---

Religion of China, New York: Free Press, 1964. Also relevant is his *Religion in Chinese Society*, Berkeley, CA: University of California Press, 1961. Further orientation can be gained from Otto B. van der Sprenkel, "Max Weber on China," *History and Theory*, 3:3 (1964). For general historical background I have used Wolfram Eberhard, *A History of China*, London: Routledge & Kegan Paul, 1950, and Jacques Gernet, *A History of Chinese Civilization*, Cambridge: Cambridge University Press, 1982. Invaluable source material is contained in Fung Yu-lan, *A History of Chinese Philosophy*, Princeton, NJ: Princeton University Press, 1952 and Win-Tsit Chan, *A Sourcebook in Chinese Philosophy*, Princeton, NJ: Princeton University Press, 1963. Also useful are the two volumes by Wm. Theodore de Bary *et al.* (eds.), *Sources of Chinese Tradition*, New York: Columbia University Press, 1960 and Dun J. Li (ed.), *The Essence of Chinese Civilization*, Princeton, NJ: D. Van Nostrand, 1967.

[4] "The Social Psychology of the World Religions" (FMW 270–271).

history of this stratum and of the unusual circumstances which kept its adherents in power.

Comparatively, in China the state was already unified at an early date and controlled large areas of territory before cities had advanced much beyond villages. Thus, even when urban growth occurred, Chinese cities did not function as corporate bodies, were never self-governing, and in consequence did not produce charters and other legal protections to guarantee the rights and liberties of their citizens (as in the west). These aspects of state-formation are connected to the fact that in China crucial sources of local power remained intact – "the fetters of kinship were never shattered" (RC 14). Thus, even in the towns residents identified with the native place of their ancestors because of the importance of kinship ties in maintaining their relation to the spirits. A high degree of centralization nonetheless resulted, owing mainly to military and agricultural exigencies. Like Egypt, the great river systems of China required regulation to avoid destructive flooding, and this called forth extensive engineering works on canals, dams and dikes.[5] To facilitate such large-scale works, an elaborate system of taxation, labor service and technical administration was needed, and this came into being around the third century BCE.

For Weber, the peculiarity of the Chinese situation resides in the fact that its bureaucratic structure was not so rational and centralized that all authority came to be concentrated in the hands of the Emperor and his staff, but neither was power so diffused that the situation became quasi-feudal. The considerable measure of local autonomy in some domains such as military recruitment did not as a rule result in self-equipped militia capable of opposing the central government.[6] Local power was dispensed by the sib – Weber's term *Sippe* is often rendered as kinship group or family – and this acted as a fetter on other types of group formation.[7] The central authority maintained control over benefice-holders by preventing the hereditary appropriation of offices, via surveillance by spies (the "censors"), and by ensuring that officials were always appointed for short

---

[5] This aspect of Chinese history was developed to an extreme by K. A. Wittfogel in *Oriental Despotism*, New Haven, CT: Yale University Press, 1957. See the excellent reviews by S. N. Eisenstadt, *The Journal of Asian Studies*, 17:3 (1958), pp. 435–446 and F. W. Mote, "The Growth of Chinese Despotism," *Oriens Extremus*, 8:1 (1961), pp. 1–40.

[6] The large measure of local autonomy is confirmed by T'ung-tsu Ch'u, *Local Government in China under the Ching*, Cambridge, MA: Harvard University Press, 1962, though Otto van der Sprenkel thinks Weber overstates the position: "Max Weber on China," p. 368.

[7] Weber's emphasis on the power position of the sib in rural China has been generally acknowledged as path-breaking and largely correct: see Otto van der Sprenkel, "Max Weber on China," p. 366 and C. K.Yang, Introduction to *RC*, p. xxvi. See also Patricia Ebrey, "Conceptions of the Family in the Sung Dynasty," *Journal of Asiatic Studies*, 43:2 (1984).

periods to positions other than in their home province (so they could not become independently powerful barons).

The underlying thrust of Weber's analysis of Chinese society is that once established this basic socio-political configuration – a classic instance of what he regards as the type "patrimonial bureaucracy" – became thoroughly entrenched and all but unchangeable. But this stability was also a consequence of the hold of the unique worldview that is Confucianism to which we shall now turn.[8]

Confucianism and the literati

Confucius emerged as a figure of significance only after his own time, in the era of the Warring States (480–222 BCE), when feudalism was still significant though in decline. The embryonic elements of a unified state had begun to appear with the Ch'in dynasty, a completely new type of social order not being established till the later Han period. By the time of the Han dynasty, appointment to administrative positions had become dependent not merely on family connection as before but increasingly on knowledge of the classics (that is, on education).[9] Instead of the traditional feudal glorification of martial virtues, Confucian ideas, such as that heaven rewards the ruler whose actions are morally correct and that the cultivated man likewise acts out of concern for propriety (*li*), become the basis of a "status ethic" of ruling officials.[10]

With such self-understanding, the literati gradually achieved a monopoly over office prebends, and officialdom came to be differentiated internally according to the number of examinations passed – access to the higher ranks was only possible by success in the competitive struggle in qualifying to sit and pass the examinations.[11] But, according to Weber, all this severely limited the sense of solidarity that could develop among the literati and prevented their transformation to a form of office nobility even though they enjoyed high status and numerous privileges. In the eyes of the masses,

---

8 On Confucius see D. Howard Smith, *Confucius*, New York: Scribner, 1973 and, his *Chinese Religions*, London: Weidenfeld and Nicolson, 1968; S. Kaizuka, *Confucius*, London: Allen & Unwin, 1956, and H. Fingarette, *Confucius – The Secular as Sacred*, New York: Harper and Row, 1972.

9 According to H. G. Creel, the development of bureaucracy was much more advanced at this point than Weber credits: "The Beginnings of Bureaucracy in China: The Origin of the Hsien," *Journal of Asian Studies* 23 (1964), pp. 158–159.

10 C. K. Yang tells us that it was Tung Chung-shu "who succeeded in enshrining Confucianism as the state orthodoxy": *Religion in Chinese Society*, p. 253.

11 An excellent account of the examination system, albeit concerning late conditions in the nineteenth century, is contained in Chung-Li Chang, *The Chinese Gentry*, Seattle, WA: University of Washington Press, 1955, pt. 4.

however, the literati were highly revered, their literary education (knowledge of esoteric sacred writings) being associated with magical prowess. The literati, however, never became a priestly order of any kind, remaining in essence a status group whose prestige rested solely on writing and knowledge of the sacred texts – a lay education that was "partly of a ritualist and ceremonial character and partly of a traditionalist and ethical character" (RC 126).

The approach of Confucianism to ethics was directly connected to its view of the political order of society, for in Confucian self-cultivation a man is believed to necessarily serve the general order of society: just as inwardly he is at ease and composed, so outwardly he conducts himself with grace and dignity. The decisive virtue this promotes is piety (hsiao), especially that directed towards parents and superiors; for this is the only way in which the tranquility of the social order can be maintained.[12] Weber repeatedly emphasizes how the unconditional discipline this enjoins fits perfectly with the requirements of patrimonial bureaucracy (RC 158).

The way in which Confucianism developed its basic presuppositions shows a complex relation to magic. Although its ethical doctrine arose in the transformation of a concern with good and bad spirits into a more abstract moral framework which construed these forces more subliminally, a magical standpoint was never completely overcome. This was the case despite the later conception of the supreme celestial being as a largely impersonal power presiding over both heaven and earth to ensure the harmony of the cosmos as a whole. As a rule, morally correct behavior is enjoined as a means of placating certain personalized spirits which are deemed capable of upsetting this order. According to Weber, the strength of the interconnection of ethics with animism meant that a thorough-going "demagification" and therefore rationalization of ethical conduct could not take place. This, however, did not prevent Confucianism being oriented in a quite practical way to the pursuit of worldly happiness. According to Weber, it sought the well-being of both the ruler and his subjects in the here and now, though its interest in justice was limited by the framework of the patrimonial welfare state.

Traditionalism and capitalism

Weber's remarks concerning the compatibility of Confucianism with rational capitalism focus on the issue of the dominance of tradition, a

---

[12] According to Weber, "Confucius . . . regarded 'insubordination as more reprehensible than brutality,' which indicates that he expressly interpreted obedience to family authorities very literally as the distinctive mark of all social and political qualities" (E&S 579).

question related to the problem of the persistence of magic to which we have already alluded. Weber argues that the strong interrelation between the patrimonial state and traditional practices in culture, economics and politics precluded the emergence of an autonomous, innovating force that might bring a rupture with the status quo. Besides, the Confucian conception of the cultivated gentleman was incompatible with money-making and completely at odds with the idea of specialized labor in a profession (the "vocation"). This is not to say that Confucianism rejected wealth, for Weber tells us that material wealth was indeed "exalted as the supreme good" as in no other civilized country (RC 237). But "Whereas Puritanism objectified everything and transformed it into a rational enterprise, all communal action [in China] remained engulfed in and conditioned by purely personal, above all, by kinship relations" (RC 241). Thus, "The strength of the truly Chinese economic organization was roughly coextensive with [these] personal associations controlled by piety" (RC 236). All of which did not prevent a commercial orientation emerging to some degree, for as Weber notes, despite the lack of training in calculation during basic education, a reasonably functional number system had nonetheless come into being allowing "a calculative attitude in commercial intercourse" to permeate all strata of the population (RC 125). But the crucial thing was "that out of this unceasing and intensive economic ado and the much bewailed crass 'materialism' of the Chinese, there failed to originate on the economic plane those great and methodical business conceptions which are rational in nature and are presupposed by modern capitalism" (RC 242). The personalism of social life meant that the Chinese could not operate in the economic realm in a purely self-interested and matter-of-fact fashion. And the Confucian ideal of the gentleman meant a man "was an end in himself and not just a means for a specified useful purpose" (RC 246).

The stringency of Confucian moral teaching was modified in Taoism, though not in a practical direction. Lao Tzu (the founder of Taoism) and Confucius shared many of the same ideas. Both taught self-control, the value of education and belief in the notion of tao (the eternal order or law of the cosmos), but differed more in emphasis than in fundamental assumptions (RC 180–181). The Taoists were more oriented to mystical contemplation and to the various popular deities, and promoted withdrawal from the world and the minimization of action and self-assertion (quietism), for involvement in worldly affairs risked the achievement of inner harmony and self-perfection.[13] Ultimately, Taoism sought the avoidance of death (hsien) or prolonged youthfulness through the utilization of

13 On this aspect of Taoism, see A. Waley, Introduction to his The Way and Its Power: A

various magical ideas and practices. This fostered a process Weber some-what paradoxically terms "the systematic rationalization of magic," which led to an increasing dependency on forms of esoteric knowledge like astrology, magical pharmacology and geomancy.[14]

Critical reflections

A considerable body of contemporary literature gives support to Weber's argument and indeed furthers it.[15] But rather than explore this further we shall look briefly at the main critical responses to Weber's *Religion of China*. Most of these have argued that religion, Confucianism in particular, has not been the decisive cause of China's failure to develop capitalism and to modernize. Critics have either maintained that China's modernization was inhibited largely because of economic factors,[16] or they have argued that Confucianism cannot be regarded as an inherently negative factor because, among other things, Confucian-influenced cultures show a much more differentiated response to the challenge of modernity than Weber allows – consider the recent success of Japan and the so-called "Asian tiger" economies.

Perhaps the most searching critique of Weber's position along the latter lines is that advanced by Thomas Metzger who claims Weber has drasti-cally misinterpreted the role of Confucianism, especially in the period of the so-called Chinese Renaissance (the Sung era), by failing to register

Study of the Tao Te Ching and Its Place in Chinese Thought, New York: Grove Press, 1958.

[14] On the relation of Taoism to science, see N. Sivin, "On the Word 'Taoist' as a Source of Perplexity with Special Reference to the Relations of Science and Religion in Traditional China," *History of Religions* (1978) pp. 303–330.

[15] As an illustration of the latter we shall merely cite the excellent study of T'ung Tsu Ch'u, *Law and Society in Traditional China*, Paris: Mouton, 1961, which shows in detail how Chinese law was pervaded by the Confucian doctrine of *li* and how this was linked to the family and social status.

[16] The most drastic criticism of Weber's account of Chinese capitalism is provided by Mark Elvin, "Why China Failed to Create an Endogenous Capitalism," *Journal of Sociology*, 13 (1984), pp. 379–391. Elvin's argument explicitly sets out to provide an explanation of China's failure to create an endogenous industrial capitalism which does *not* rely on what he terms Weberian-type cultural analysis. But this argument is less of a critique of Weber than it appears. Elvin's theory is that China became economically stalled because at a crucial stage there was insufficient demand to bring forth a wave of invention and innovation in the economic field (what he calls a "high-level equilibrium trap"). A glance at Weber's own extensive discussion of the importance of changes in demand for the development of *western* capitalism in his lectures on *General Economic History* shows that he also regarded demand as both a crucial element and a distinguishing feature of western capitalism. Where he differs is in asking for an explanation of the differences in demand themselves.

significant innovations in thought brought by the movement known as Neo-Confucianism. While we cannot do justice to all the issues raised by Metzger's book and the subsequent debates, we shall give a brief survey of the main points of contention. Metzger, contrary to Weber (and others), is eager to show that the Chinese religious tradition, at least in the form of Neo-Confucianism, was quite capable of generating "transformative," and even "revolutionary," impulses. Metzger takes Weber to task for too readily assuming a continuity of Confucianism down the ages, such that the original doctrinal elements dealing with filial piety, ancestor worship, deference to authority, ceremonial and ritual observance and so on are taken to be still decisive in much later times. Weber's assumption of the complete integration of Confucianism with the on-going political and administrative structure meant that its ethical teaching is deemed incapable of providing any tension with the existing order of society (in marked contrast to the Christian west). Metzger summarizes Weber's argument thus:

> Without this tension, Weber went on, the individual lacked an "inward" moral struggle comparable to the Puritan's striving for "systematic control of one's own nature regarded as wicked and sinful" (244), "an autonomous ethic" (142), any "internal measure of value," or any counterweight in confronting the world" (235) . . . Thus the Confucian "deserved neither to be saved from evil nor from a fall of man, which he knew not. He desired to be saved from nothing except the undignified barbarism of social rudeness" (156–157). "Propriety" was his overriding concern. "Controlled ease and correct composure, grace and dignity in the sense of a ceremonially ordered court-salon characterize this man" (156; cf. 244, 162–163, 228). His ultimate goal . . . was "only long life, health, and wealth in this world and beyond death the retention of his good name . . . pious conformism with the fixed order of secular powers reigned supreme" (228) . . . One can easily see how Weber's analysis led to the emphasis, still prevalent today, on the "stagnative" and "authoritarian" character of Confucian orientations.[17]

Metzger suggests that Weber's account of the stagnatively ceremonial culture fostered by Confucianism might well have been adequate had Neo-Confucianism not arisen in imperial China.[18] But the advent of Neo-Confucianism (which is really a "discovery" of scholarship since Weber's time)[19] suggests that Weber's account is overdrawn. Neo-Confucianism

---

[17] Thomas Metzger, *Escape from Predicament: Neo-Confucianism and China's Evolving Political Culture*, New York: Columbia University Press, 1977, note 4, p. 238; references in the quotations are to pages in *RC*.

[18] *Ibid*, note 18, p. 247.

[19] See in particular Wm. Theodore de Bary, *The Unfolding of Neo-Confucianism*, New York: Columbia University Press, 1975.

was built around the pursuit of the goal of sagehood, self-cultivation or "the oneness of heaven and man." This was conceived as a moral and/or spiritual quest which essentially involved overcoming the baseness of selfish interests to realize the inherent nobility of man's status. Having arrived at "the extreme of sincerity" (*chih-ch'eng*), Metzger says, did not allow one to escape the need for continuous moral effort. As the great Neo-Confucian sage Chu Hsi explained, the task is "constantly to envelop and nourish one's spontaneously good feelings (*han-yang*) and eliminate selfish ones (*hsing ch'a*)."[20] Although moral purity was something that in the first instance concerned feelings, cognitive clarity was also enjoined, the idea being to combine thought and action in a total synthesis. Thus the specific aspects of moral life were subsumed under abstract concepts, so that concrete familial and political virtues were comprehended with the aid of more universal categories – such as the major metaphysical concepts of benevolence (*jen*), righteousness (*i*), the rules of moral propriety (*li*), and moral understanding (*chih*).[21] The idea of clarity was connected with a sense of coherence of the cosmic order. A confused and troubled mind was one in which there was a danger that the things of the world would disrupt the self's ability to control itself in accord with moral principles. As Chu Hsi put it, one "must cause the mind of the *tao* constantly to be ruler of one's person . . ."[22]

The shift in emphasis brought by Neo-Confucianism is shown in the fact that the early preoccupation of Chou Confucianism with the ethical principles of the true gentleman and the integration of the Emperor into the moral system of the cosmos have now become somewhat secondary concerns. Instead, Chu Hsi repeatedly emphasizes the gap between the potential and the actual, pointing to the great difficulty of overcoming evil to act morally: "The human mind turns to selfishness with ease but only with difficulty to devotion to the public good."[23] To close the gap a kind of spiritual nurturing is required which involves the cultivation of a reverence through which one becomes more aware of the heavenly principle within oneself as the ideal to which one should be devoted. According to Metzger, these ideas had significant implications for social behavior and political action generally, for they promoted "the ideal of action directed outward and aimed at mastering the political world . . . closing the gap between the ideal and the actual . . . [Chu Hsi glorified] the sage's ability to 'act' (*tso*), changing the outer world . . ."[24]

These features of Neo-Confucianism suggest at the very least we must

---

[20] Quoted in *ibid.*, p. 62.   [21] *Ibid.*, p. 65.   [22] Quoted in *ibid.*, p. 68.
[23] Quoted in *ibid.*, p. 138.   [24] *Ibid.*, pp. 157–158.

qualify Weber's broad assessment of the historical significance of Confucianism. In particular they lead us to question whether Confucian ethical teaching should be understood as merely urging an external observance of ritualistic norms devoid of inner meaning. But though Metzger insists there was a very real scope for innovation and change during the Sung era and afterwards, he does not go so far as to equate the situation of China with regard to the ethicization of social life with that of the west – which seems to leave most of Weber's thesis intact.

Of course, Metzger's claims are themselves debatable. Some critics have argued that he has exaggerated the extent to which Neo-Confucianism generated transformative and revolutionary impulses.[25] Besides, it has to be borne in mind that, despite an implied Neo-Confucian reformation, the trend towards centralization and despotism in China was considerably advanced by developments in the Sung period. All statesmen and thinkers responded to the problems of the day by demanding a strengthening of the power of the sovereign who was to be unencumbered by abstract principles or old ideals. According to F. W. Mote, even "the dominant Neo-Confucian *li-hsueh* school was to demand a totally impractical and vaguely conceived return to antique constitutions, but at the same time to give philosophical foundation to an increasingly rigid application of the moral bonds and restraints with an increasingly authoritarian tone . . ."[26] Other commentators have focused on the return to a more ritualized and stereotyped social order in the late Ming and Ch'ing eras, which indicates that the achievements of Neo-Confucianism were somewhat fleeting and inconsequential. According to Kai-wing Chow, during this later period Confucianism underwent a profound ritualist re-orientation in association with the attempt to purify and recover the classical teachings.

A related set of questions to those of Metzger has been raised by S. N. Eisenstadt. For Eisenstadt too the weakness of Weber's interpretation of Confucianism lies in his view that the absence of transcendental values meant it could not produce tension with the world (*RC* 145).[27] Eisenstadt argues on the contrary that Confucianism "did not deny the existence of this tension, and accordingly there did develop within it a very high level of rationalization . . ." He adduces Benjamin Schwartz's reading of the

[25] See Hao Hang, "The Transformation of Neo-Confucianism as Transformative Leverage," *Journal of Asian Society* (1980), pp. 259–263.

[26] Mote, "The Growth of Chinese Despotism," p. 14.

[27] A typical statement of this is the following: "In Confucianism there prevailed . . . an absolutely agnostic and essentially negative mood opposed to all hopes for a beyond . . . and the absence of any other eschatology or doctrine of salvation, or any striving for transcendental values and destinies" (*RC* 145).

Analects to show that Confucius views heaven not "simply as the immanent Tao of nature and society but as a transcendental will interested in . . . redeeming meaning . . . Beyond this it is already clear that the word Tao in Confucius refers not only to the objective structure of society and cosmos, but also to the inner way of man of *Jen* . . ." While the resolution of the tension between the mundane and transcendental orders could be seen as "simple, traditional and ritual upholding of the existing social arrangements . . . in principle, this was not the case. The major thrust of the Confucian orientations was the conscious taking out of these social relations from their seemingly natural context, and their ideologization in terms of the higher transcendental orientations . . ."[28] Hence the many intellectual and personal tensions that arose, giving rise to a variety of religious and other responses, including the efforts of the great Sung and Ming reformers who attempted to reconstruct the social order in line with the ideal of social and cosmic harmony. But Eisenstadt concedes that these efforts had relatively minor institutional impact, in contrast to that in the west, because the tension between the "world" and the "hinterland" that was central to Confucian thought was worked out in a secular rather than religious direction, which defused potential eschatological implications. Eisenstadt's disagreement with Weber is thus not with the major thrust of his analysis but mainly with its details. The apparent stability of the Chinese imperial system (which Weber overstates because he equates it too readily with the example of ancient Egypt) was not so much a function of its traditionality "but rather the very sophisticated and complex mechanisms of control [of the 'center' over the 'periphery'] which were developed by the ruling coalitions and which attest to the high level of nontraditionality, of reflexivity of Chinese civilization and political order."[29]

The issue of Weber's appreciation of Confucianism has been the basis of further critiques, such as that of William Garrett who along with others has noticed that the success of the present-day economies of countries like South Korea, Taiwan, Hong Kong and Singapore (the "Four Little Dragons") suggests Confucianism is not necessarily as inimical to capitalism as Weber would have us believe. Garrett notes that while Weber readily admits, indeed, insists upon the inner-worldly orientation of Confucianism, he was reluctant to categorize it as ascetic.[30] Garrett argues,

---

[28] S. N. Eisenstadt, "This-worldly Transcendentalism and the Structuring of the World:" Weber's *Religion of China* and the Format of Chinese History and Civilization," *Journal of Developing Societies* (1985), pp. 170, 171.

[29] *Ibid.*, p. 182.

[30] This reluctance stems from Weber's conviction that Confucianism, despite embracing some aspects of self-discipline, remained too focused on "the charm and worth of the elegant

on the other hand, that self-discipline, verging on asceticism, was equally crucial for the Confucian effort to accommodate to the world as prescribed by the mandate of heaven.

A final area of criticism of *The Religion of China* concerns Weber's appreciation of the achievements of Chinese science and the level of economic and technical development attained, especially in the period CE 1100–1500, for it was then that China was probably superior to the west in most areas. It is our view that Weber tends to overstate the debilitating effects of tradition and bureaucracy on the developmental possibilities of Chinese science and does not adequately account for the considerable development which Needham and others have been able to demonstrate. Apart from the obvious inadequacy of Weber's sources, one of the reasons for this deficiency is that he saw Taoism as the key source of Chinese scientific efforts,[31] yet apart from alchemy and medical pharmacology, most of the important developments – printing, gunpowder, the magnetic compass, mechanical clockwork, iron-casting, stirrups and an efficient horse harness, segmental-arch bridges, pound-locks on canals, the stern-post rudder, quantitative cartography – had nothing directly to do with it.[32] Nonetheless, many of Weber's general views on Chinese science are confirmed by Needham, such as the former's claim that systematic natural science failed to mature. For Weber Chinese scientific thought "remained sublimated empiricism" (*RC* 150–151), in part a consequence of the Taoist distrust of the powers of reason and logic owing to their conviction that the cosmic order of things was inscrutable. As for the Confucianists, they had no curiosity about nature outside man himself. According to Needham, insofar as the idea of a law-governed nature was approached, as it was in some Neo-Confucian texts, law was understood in an organic sense only, which included all things in heaven, earth and man and had nothing in common with the mathematical universe of Newton.[33]

In conclusion it should not be assumed that these criticisms overturn Weber's general account. Nevertheless, it is clear that some aspects of his study need qualifying in the light of scholarship since his day. Furthermore,

gesture as the highest possible goal of inner-worldly consummation" (*RI* 342) to be self-denying in a truly ascetic sense.

[31] Weber speaks of the "magic stereotyping of technology" which severely curtailed its rationality: "a superstructure of magically 'rational' [sic] science . . . cloaked the simple empirical skills of early times as well as considerable technical endowments, as is evident from the inventions" (*RC* 199).

[32] Joseph Needham, *The Grand Titration: Science and Society in East and West*, London: Allen & Unwin, 1969, p. 11.

[33] Joseph Needham, *The Shorter Science and Civilization in China*, Cambridge: Cambridge University Press, 1978, vol.I, p. 300.

the modernization process which Weber was among the first to describe has shown itself to have many twists and turns as it works itself out in the global context. Consider, for instance the numerous complications raised by the role of Confucianism in the industrial transformation of Korea and Japan where recent studies show it played a very important modernizing role from the seventeenth century down to the present.[34] But however much still remains valid in Weber's account of the role of Confucianism, it is undeniable that the whole debate on the role of religion in the modernization process continues to be shaped by his pioneering studies.

India: the caste system and the Brahmins

As in his study of China, Weber begins *The Religion of India* with a study of social institutions and only then analyzes religious life proper, dealing in turn with the orthodox doctrines of Hinduism, the oppositional movements of Jainism and Buddhism, and finally with the ramifications of all these for popular religiosity and cultural life generally.[35] Of course, the previous study of China provides a basis for instructive comparisons and contrasts. Generally speaking, whereas China's intellectual elite is characterized by worldliness and a practical rationalism in political affairs, India's tends toward mysticism and a theoretical rationalism and is essentially apolitical.

Weber's starting-point in his analysis of social structure is the all-pervasive character of the caste system, a status order that contrasts with those occurring elsewhere because of its direct connection with religious beliefs. But unlike the kind of social exclusiveness found in sectarianism, caste is an ascribed status and does not depend on individual qualifications. In other words, caste membership is hereditary and marked by the extreme nature of the practices employed to differentiate one group from another. Thus, rules exist which generally prohibit marriage between members of different castes (with some exceptions where hypergamy and polygamy are

---

[34] On Japan, see the important work by Masao Maruyama, *Studies in the Intellectual History of Tokugawa Confucianism*, Tokyo: University of Tokyo Press, 1974. On Japan and Korea, see Wm. Theodore de Bary and Irene Bloom (eds.), *Principle and Practicality: Essays in Neo-Confucianism and Practical Learning*, New York: Columbia University Press, 1979.

[35] For general coverage of Indian history I have used A. L. Basham, *The Wonder that Was India*, London: Sidgwick and Jackson and New York: Columbia University Press, 1954, and Hermann Kulke and Dietmar Rothermund, *A History of India*, London: Croom Helm, 1986. An invaluable source book is Wm. Theodore de Bary (ed.), *Sources of Indian Tradition*, 2 vols., New York: Columbia University Press, 1958, as is R. C. Zaehner (trans. and ed.), *Hindu Scriptures*, London: Dent, 1966. For general orientation of Indian religion I have used Heinrich Zimmer, *Philosophies of India*, Princeton, NJ: Princeton University Press, 1951.

tolerated). There are equivalent prohibitions as regards commensalism. The observance of particular ritual practices, such as those determining from whose hand one can receive food, are usually stricter and more intrusive in everyday life the more a caste is seeking to establish its position *vis-à-is* others. The phenomenon of caste is based on what Weber calls "familial charisma," which means that certain qualities thought to be extraordinary and ultimately connected to magical powers can be acquired only through membership of a particular kinship group.

Weber's account of how the caste system emerged and became entrenched emphasizes on the impact of successive waves of invasion in early times. He maintains that dominant groups in this era typically treated vanquished local tribes, who were often racially distinct, as socially inferior (e.g., they were unsuitable as partners in marriage). Furthermore, the subject peoples were often obliged to render services of various kinds as a group, frequently in despised occupations, to the occupying nobles, and this promoted the development of a division of labor not within, but between, the different ethnic groups and villages. Another factor favoring group solidarity and caste specialization of occupation was the imposition of joint taxation liability by the early central political power.

Once established, Weber argues, the caste system became highly effective in subsuming external bodies such as outside ethnic groups (often native tribes). It achieved this by various methods, such as by appealing to the status ambitions of ruling elites within a tribe who, by adopting high-caste practices and the services of a Brahmin in performing rites, could thereby legitimate their position. Or else, occupationally distinct groups who had lost territories they traditionally held could become "guest peoples" (pariahs), and as such could partake in social life though only in a limited fashion, being excluded from the community of the orthodox by extreme forms of ritual propriety that marked them as inferior (this is the origin of the various untouchable castes assumed by others to be a source of pollution). Castes could also be formed by subdivision whereby sections of an existing caste either adopted ritual duties previously not observed or chose to disregard duties once held as binding. Such changes, leading to the development of a panoply of interconnected castes and sub-castes, could be prompted by such factors as the special requirements of sectarian membership, increases in economic inequality, changes in occupational practices, or differentiations within a caste regarding the strictness of ritual observance.[36]

This account of the caste system is the setting of Weber's analysis of the

[36] Weber's account of the caste system is largely consistent with that of specialist scholars like

various streams of Indian religiosity. To understand Indian religious life one must first grasp the role of the Brahmins, an educated group of high status and political importance which has many parallels with the Confucian literati. Both were minority groups of intellectuals whose power was connected with the magical charisma they derived from knowledge of a classical literature, and as such they played a crucial role in forming the religious culture of an entire civilization. But unlike the Confucian literati who were preoccupied with gaining and exercising administrative power, the Brahmins did not aim for political office as such but rather performed various functions as spiritual advisors, educators and theological authorities, being most influential as priests.

The differing social position of the Brahmins and the Confucian intelligentsia was influenced among other things by the fact that, whereas early in its history China had become a unified state, India never achieved the same level of centralization and internal pacification. Furthermore, Indian kings, no matter how powerful, never took on the function of pontifex, and this meant the Brahmins had a basis for their authority entirely separate from that of the secular rulers. Rather than developing skills in the art of writing, connected in China with the crucial role of the annals and calendar reckoning, the Brahmins were initially distinguished by special capabilities in speech (poetry, storytelling, the oral transmission of sacred truths, court representation and law finding, religious disputations, the exercise of magic), and only subsequently did they become a caste of scribes. Even then, the tendency in Indian commentary to luxurious embellishment and exaggeration and the dependence of their status position ultimately on the effectiveness of magic militated against any scientific appreciation of the empirical processes of nature. And, as magical powers were directly related to the practice of asceticism, the Hindu tradition under the influence of the Brahmins developed in the direction of profound indifference to the world – in marked contrast to Confucianism where the ideal of filial piety was connected in very concrete ways with material prosperity in the world here and now.

The sacred texts of Hinduism originate with the Vedas, but these are not as significant for doctrinal and ritual orientation as the later Upanishads, Mahabharata and Sutras. The Vedas were important, however, for establishing the authority of the Brahmins. Whereas the Confucian literati sought an influential though not supreme place within the order of society headed by the imperial court, the Brahmins insisted on their superiority in

---

J. Duncan Derrett. See his "Law and the Social Order in India before the Mohammedan Conquests," in *Journal of the Economic and Social History of the Orient*, 8:1 (1964).

religious matters and social status. From such a position they developed teachings which prescribed the rights and duties of the princes and, indeed, of all the stations in the world, divine and otherwise, down to the lowest human and even sub-human forms of life. The ultimate outcome, of course, was the great cosmological theory of rank order based on the twin doctrines of *samsara* and *karma*.[37] In this worldview there is no general equality of mankind but an acceptance of the differing states of social existence on the grounds that these represent the rewards and punishments of good and bad deeds accumulated from previous incarnations. As Weber explains it, "each single ethically relevant act has inevitable consequences for the fate of the actor, hence that no consequence can be lost" (*RI* 119). The different styles of life that had developed naturally as a consequence of the social and economic division of labor were thus not only legitimated as reflecting a person's ethical merit, but were pushed in the direction of further specialization as the basis of the normatively binding notion that each rank possesses a religiously sanctioned way of life (*dharma*).

The dogmatic core of Hinduism, as developed by the Brahminical priest-hood and its literature, was decisive in Weber's view in establishing and maintaining the entire social order of Hinduism over many centuries:

> The combination of caste legitimacy with *karma* doctrine, thus with specifi-cally Brahminical theodicy . . . is plainly just the product of rationally ethical thought and not of any economic "conditions". Only the wedding of this product of thought with the empirical social order through the promise of rebirth gave this order its irresistible power over the thought and hopes of those embedded within it . . .   (*RI* 131).[38]

Here one should note two complementary implications of the basic doctrine of Hinduism. First, it endorses a kind of ethical relativism in that a single ethical standard does not apply universally – as is clearly the case with Christianity. And secondly, this allows quite contradictory types of action to find moral justification, as long as they can be construed as forming part of a caste's *dharma*.[39]

According to Weber, the Brahmins came to their elevated position – higher in status even than princes – because of their monopoly over the

---

[37] For Weber this constitutes "The most complete formal solution to the problem of theodicy . . . This world is viewed as a completely connected and self-contained cosmos of ethical retribution. Guilt and merit within the world are unfailingly compensated by fate in the successive lives of the soul . . ." (*E&S* 525).

[38] But note Schluchter's comments, on the basis of Wendy O'Flaherty's criticisms, in *Rationalism, Religion and Domination: A Weberian Perspective*, Berkeley, CA: University of California Press, 1989, p. 156.

[39] We shall critically discuss Weber's understanding of *dharma* below.

position of family priest (*purohita*) to the king. (This is in marked contrast to priesthood in other settings where power usually depends on an elaborate church organization.) On such a basis the Brahmins were able to extend their activities beyond traditional functions connected largely with ritual to become personal advisors to the prince in matters both religious and political, in return for which they typically received "gifts." They further gained decisive influence over all disputes concerning the rank order of society as a whole, as well has taking on various judicial functions.

Weber assumes the key rival of the Brahmins to be the Kshatriyas, classically conceived of as a caste of warriors whose *dharma* was intimately connected to the practice of war – though generally the Kshatriyas were comprised of those who exercised some form of authority from kings and princes down to village leaders. While the Brahmins often received large grants of land, the Kshatriyas were actually the principal landholders. Thus, any understanding of Indian political history must deal with the role of the Kshatriyas in what was essentially, from the point of view of Weber's political sociology, a system of "patrimonial rule."[40] Typically, the Kshatriyas enjoyed considerable local autonomy, being in control of such things as the administration of justice (which they financed from fines and various fees). The central authority made demands on them only as regards the provision of military recruits and the collection of taxes to finance its wars. But India was also affected by feudalism, so that self-equipped knights often fought alongside the ruler's mercenaries and were rewarded by land grants as in medieval Europe. This, of course, tended to undermine the power of the central authority which lacked bureaucratic development as in China; the patrimonial empires of India were frequently fragmented leaving a network of small competing kingdoms.[41]

A turning point in early Indian history for Weber was the rise of the Maurya Dynasty (321–185 BCE), and especially the reign of Asoka who became a devout Buddhist and whose missionary promotion made Buddhism dominant throughout India and beyond.[42] These early events, in a time when the caste system was not yet firmly established, mark the end of the original warrior society, and see the partial demise of both the Kshatriya nobility as well as the Brahmin priesthood. The rapid expansion and

[40] Unfortunately, there are few references to India in Weber's extensive theoretical and empirical discussion of patrimonialism in chs. 12 and 13 of *Economy and Society*.
[41] We analyze Weber's account of patrimonialism below.
[42] For general orientation on Buddhism I have used Trevor Ling, *The Buddha: Buddhist Civilization in India and Ceylon*, London: Temple Smith, 1973; Richard Gombrich, *Theravada Buddhism: A Social History from Ancient Benares to Modern Columbo*, London: Routledge & Kegan Paul, 1988, and Edward Conze, *Buddhist Thought in India*, London: Allen & Unwin, 1962.

consolidation of the empire brings to social pre-eminence new strata like court officials, a professional army, merchants and landlords. According to Weber, these groups are among the first to be attracted to Buddhism, being repulsed by the asceticism and pretensions of the Brahmins. Various concessions made to convention in the code of practice of the monks suggests to Weber that Buddhism underwent a process of popularization in response to the religious needs of the new elite of Maurya society. It must be recognized, however, that the leveling tendencies expressed in the fact that even a layman might gain merit by the mere support of the monks materially was not the beginning of a movement of social reform. Rather, Weber argues, these arrangements for the laity suited the interests of the rulers who sought to use Buddhism as a means of domesticating the masses.[43]

But during this period, the Brahmins continued to carry out their traditional duties in the performance of rites and the like, and were never completely eclipsed. Their survival was assisted by the fact that the two main reform movements, Buddhism and Jainism, did not directly attack the caste system, teaching merely that it be treated with indifference. The Buddhists were oriented to a way of life which was itinerant, mendicant and focused on inner detachment, and unlike the Brahmins asked little of the laity. The Jains, on the other hand, emphasized the path of austerity, and together with Buddhism opposed the synthetic approach of the Brahmins which was being developed at the time in such works as the *Bhagavad Gita*. Both Buddhism and Jainism took as their point of departure the ideas of world renunciation embodied by orthodox Brahminical religiosity in the ideal of the *sramana*, but transformed this by joining the individual virtuosi together in monastic communities. Buddhism differed from Jainism in its practice of world flight by focusing on contemplation as the basic means of salvation, and this it developed in a highly rational fashion.[44] The gradual strengthening of the caste system together with the subsequent emergence of Hindu sects oriented to mass religious tastes, however, saw the reassertion of the Brahmins and the eventual elimination of Buddhism from India.[45]

The most significant feature of Brahminical religiosity for Weber is its

---

[43] Weber's view that Asoka adopted Buddhism for largely expedient reasons to do with the political domestication of the masses is rejected by Heinz Bechert, "Max Weber and the Sociology of Buddhism," *Internationales Asienforum*, 22:3–4 (1991), p. 186.

[44] The issue of whether Jainism approximated the kind of innerworldly asceticism of Puritanism and was therefore conducive to the spirit of capitalism is discussed at some length by Weber (*RI* 199–202).

[45] The Buddhists were finally decimated by the Mohammedans in the twelfth century.

cultivation of asceticism and world renunciation. At the outset, the Brahmins had induced ecstatic states as a way of enhancing their magical prowess, but, in order to differentiate themselves from the more plebeian practice of magic, they increasingly emphasized prayer, sacrifice and austerity as the correct means of achieving holy states. In everyday life the Brahmin was admonished to abstain from alcohol and meat and to practice restraint in sex. These and other austerities were of course only outward signs of the Brahmins' claim to be alone qualified to achieve the highest form of salvation, escape from the cycle of rebirth. It is indicative of the high social standing of the intellectuals who fashioned Brahminical doctrine that the idea of "bliss consciousness" is the focus of holy seeking – in contrast to the more mundane forms of reward typically sought in religious questing. This goal was pursued by techniques such as that of Yoga which, by disciplined concentration and the control of body functions like breathing, aimed at the emptying of consciousness so as to open the way to the experience of the Divine.[46] For Weber these techniques of auto-hypnosis, which cultivated indefinite and inexpressible inner experiences as well as magical states and miraculous powers, were less rationalized than those of classical Brahminism which placed knowledge at the center: the latter sought to achieve states experienced not as emotion but as what Weber calls "gnostic comprehension of the godly" (*RI* 165).

A paradoxical consequence of the Brahminical view of salvation, in Weber's view, is that it has the effect of devaluing the existing world of Hindu religiosity, including caste rituals and the role of individual gods; but, more than that, it places no significance as such on ethical conduct in the world. The ascetic ideal aims at bliss now, by radically separating the individual from all that binds them to the world with its inevitable effects of retribution from previous incarnations. The virtuoso of this kind of holy seeking (the *sramana*) is in a way beyond good and evil, and this raises the issue of whether in classical Hinduism there is any real hope of salvation for the mass of ordinary believers who devoutly follow their caste *dharma*. In fact, a meaningful connection between the ideal of studied apathy and caste *dharma* seems to exist only for the Brahmins, and though the holy man might offer those with inferior religious endowments guidance, the prospect of ultimate salvation for the latter is remote since it would depend on unlikely, almost super-human efforts of individual self-enlightenment.[47]

---

[46] See James Woods (trans.), *The Yoga-System of Patanjali*, New Haven, CT: Harvard University Press, 1914.

[47] As Weber explains, "success [in reaching the goal of salvation, *nirvana*] is not always achieved. In fact, to actually attain possession of the godly was the highest charisma of the blessed. However, how do things stand with the great mass that never attains it? For them,

This problem of the reconciliation of religious interests with the structure of society Weber found to be at the heart of the great religious classic of Hinduism, the *Bhagavad Gita*. In this text the decisive issue concerns the dilemma of the heroic figure of Arjuna who as a Kshatriya is obliged to engage in battle despite his profound misgivings as to the consequences for fellow human beings of his carrying out his duty. The advice from Krishna, his charioteer and at the same time the incarnation of the supreme being, is that Arjuna must not shrink from the obligation of his caste *dharma* even though this seems to bind him more than ever to the material world and the consequences of acting in it. The unique solution of Krishna to this dilemma implies that, while action in the world is inevitable, attachment to its outcome can be avoided, and this is the task of the enlightened man. By becoming detached from the material world, the man who nonetheless engages in it in a minimal fashion merely to maintain his physical existence without hoping for any result does not really act at all, and thus he escapes the effects of *karma* and the wheel of rebirths generally.[48]

But in Weber's view this ideal could not be generalized because the different propensity for religious experience among men and women – the extent to which they are "religiously musical," as Weber on occasion puts it – as well as the various functional requirements that society demands of some individuals, means the ascetic ideal can never capture the mass of ordinary individuals. And so the position actually espoused by the Brahmins is a compromise, and in lieu of austerity demands only detachment from the results of action according to each person's *dharma*. As Wolfgang Schluchter explains, "The conflict between the this-worldly *karma* ethic and the striving for a salvation of world-flight can be defused by a theory of inner-worldly flight."[49] This line of teaching, of course, provided a powerful religious sanction for the caste system.

Critical reflections

There have been two main areas of criticism/commentary on an empirical level concerning Weber's *Religion of India*, namely the problem of Hinduization and the issues arising from the treatment of *dharma*. On Hinduization there has been some agreement that Weber blazed a path in showing the precise mechanisms by which the caste system was able to expand and

---

in a very practical sense, 'the end was nothing, the movement everything' – a movement in the direction of emptying" (*RI* 339).

[48] See the *Bhagavad Gita*, ch. 3, as well as the Introduction by Swami Nikhilanda to the edition published by the Ramakrishna-Vivekananda Center, New York, 1978.

[49] Schluchter, *Rationalism, Religion, and Domination*, p. 159.

envelop such a large societal domain.[50] This work was developed in various ways by subsequent scholars. First, the concept of "Sanskritization" was introduced by M. N. Srinivas and refers mainly to what Weber called "internal" Hinduization, the process whereby low castes improve their position by adopting vegetarianism and teetotalism and by Sanskritizing their ritual and pantheon. But this construction was criticized for emphasizing the imitation of the Brahminical stylization of life as against that of other castes, so Srinivas introduced other models of social change based, for example, on the effort to claim to Kshatriya status. Attention to the more political, "extensive" Hinduization has been the concern of Surajit Sinha who coined the term "Rajputization" to describe the situation where narrow lineage groups from previously egalitarian tribes dissociate themselves from their fellows and claim to have Rajput origins.[51]

Perhaps the most controversial aspect of Weber's study of Hinduism has been his treatment of the concept of *dharma*, which he argues was a major factor in the dominance of tradition in economic affairs. Most commentators have focused on Weber's argument that texts like the *Bhagavad Gita* demand an attitude to work activity that "was rigidly traditionalistic in character and thereby mystically oriented as an activity in the world but not yet of the world" (*RI* 326). Surendra Munshi, for example, has maintained that despite the fact that the *Bhagavad Gita* enjoins every person "to remain 'devoted to his own duty' . . . the manner in which individual caste duty is defined certainly does not in any way imply the preclusion of technological innovation or occupational specialization."[52] But this kind of critique of Weber which seeks to "defend" Hinduism against a presumed charge of being anti-modern has not been very widely accepted.

A more penetrating study of Weber's work on *dharma* is that by Dieter Conrad, and in what follows we largely follow him.[53] Conrad argues that Weber became interested in the unique *dharma* teaching of the *Bhagavad Gita* not only because of its traditionalizing effects in economics but also

---

[50] Some commentators have, however, seen Weber as having completely misunderstood Indian religion in general and Hinduism in particular: see Chaturvedi Badrinath, "Weber's Wrong Understanding of Indian Civilization," in Detlef Kantowsky (ed.), *Recent Research on Max Webert's Studies of Hinduism*, Munich: Weltforum, 1986, p. 52.

[51] These theories are discussed by Hermann Kulke in "Max Weber's Contribution to the Study of 'Hinduization' in India and 'Indianization' in Southeast Asia," in Kantowsky (ed.), *Recent Research*, pp. 103–104.

[52] Surendra Munshi, "Max Weber on India: An Introductory Critique," *Contributions to Indian Sociology* (n.s.), 22:1 (1988), p. 17.

[53] Dieter Conrad, "Max Weber's Conception of Hindu Dharma as a Paradigm," in Kantowsky (ed.), *Recent Research*, pp. 169–192.

because of the way it provided moral justification for the use of violence, and Machiavellian practices generally, in politics. This it could do because of the way *dharma* was conceived only in relation to specific castes, forming an organic specialization that was integrated with the doctrines of *karma* and *samsara*. In other words, there was no *dharma* common to all, and consequently (in marked contrast to the west) no notion of human equality or natural rights of each individual.

Weber was particularly taken by the counsel that each profession must be guided by a discrete of duties (*svadharma*) that are held to belong uniquely to it alone, and he seems to have interpreted the implied idea of the lawful autonomy of each sphere of action (a notion that appears elsewhere in his writing, for example in discussing the duties of the professor in the contemporary German university) as a factor of crucial significance. Weber was so struck by the systematic nature of this compartmentalization of the social order that he even thought (incorrectly according to Conrad)[54] there could be completely socially dysfunctional *dharmas* – thus, for example, for robbers, thieves and prostitutes. The corollary of this view is that Weber either downplayed or ignored altogether the existence of general moral duties (*sadharana dharma*) – though he was fully aware of some general ritual prohibitions such as the killing of cows.[55] On a few occasions, he discusses the presence of moral duties common to all castes – such as the duty not to kill a living being, to tell the truth, not to steal, to live purely, to control the passions, and so forth – but then describes these as "unusually colorless." This judgment Conrad finds unacceptable, especially given that Weber knew that such duties had on occasion led to major social reforms (the reports of kingdoms where capital punishment had been abolished and vegetarianism was official policy) – and besides, these duties would be difficult to distinguish from those of the Decalogue in the western tradition.

According to Conrad, Weber is too focused on the idea of *dharma* as "particularized, individual duty," and even though he knows the notion of *dharma* was also associated with the idea of cosmic order, he does not fully appreciate the way *svadharmas* are derived from the idea of *dharma* understood as "the primary integrating order upholding the universe."[56] Thus, he did not register the importance of the general rule that distributes everyone to his special *dharma*, or that which states that it is better to fulfill

[54] *Ibid.*, p. 176.
[55] On this issue see Wendy O'Flaherty, "The Clash Between Relative and Absolute Duty: The Dharma of Demons," in Wendy O'Flaherty and J. Duncan Derrett (eds.), *The Concept of Duty in South Asia*, New Delhi: Vikes, 1978, pp. 96–106.
[56] Conrad, "Max Weber's Conception of Hindu Dharma," p. 174.

one's own *dharma* imperfectly than another's perfectly.[57] The problem of understanding the function of such a basic *dharma* is connected to the characterization of the *svadharma* of the king (*rajadharma*) as that of upholding the order of *dharmas* as a whole, in particular by preventing the confusion of castes (*varnasankara*). But this gives rise to a special difficulty that attracted Weber's attention and concerns the contradiction which emerges here between the *svadharma* of the Kshatriyas which permits the use of physical force if necessary (*danda*) and the *sadharana dharma* of *ahimsa* (the general duty not to kill living things). This problem of the legitimacy or otherwise of the use of violence in politics is, of course, the central focus of Weber's great essay "Politics as a Vocation."

While early texts (the *Bhagavad Gita* or the *Kautiliya Arthashastra*) do not analyze this dilemma as a specific problem for politics, others like the *Dharmashastra* have done so, and the solution arrived at is that the warrior's violence is justified, and he will incur no sin, if he kills in protection of the community – that is, the *svadharma* of the Kshatriya is superior to the general duty of *ahimsa* when life itself is at stake. Conrad points out that while Weber does not appear to register how close this was to his own position on the relation of ethics and politics, he nonetheless drew from his understanding of the principle of *svadharma* an idea that became crucial for his subsequent interpretation of modernity: the idea of *Eigengesetzlichkeit*, often translated as "lawful autonomy" (from *eigen* = own, proper; *Gesetzlichkeit* = legality, lawfulness).[58] From an ethical point of view, Weber characterized the modern condition using the term "polytheism" to denote the anarchistic predicament faced by the individual in having to deal with the demands of different values which are both incommensurable and incapable of being ordered in a rational way. The individual's values come into irreconcilable conflict with each other because they follow their own "inherent logics" or "laws of development" as a consequence of the drive toward logical consistency, and there is no higher rationality which can be invoked to overcome the contradictions that inevitably develop between the demands of the autonomous spheres.[59] This is why Weber effectively embraces a kind of existentialist position (in the Kierkegaardian sense) by insisting on the ultimately irrational character of action choices, however much the individual may weigh the consequences and try to rationally justify their commitments. Assuming Conrad's

---

[57] *Bhagavad Gita*, ch. 18, 45, 47; *Manu*, X, 97.

[58] Conrad, "Max Weber's Conception of Hindu Dharma," p. 180.

[59] Such a view is the object of the critical response of Jürgen Habermas, *The Theory of Communicative Action, vol. I: Reason and the Rationalization of Society*, Boston, MA: Beacon Press, 1984.

analysis is correct, then, it appears Weber gained insights into the essential character of the modern west on the basis of understandings of a quite different cultural world. While Weber's "solution" is not the same as that arrived at in the Indian philosophy of *dharma*, it owes to it the important idea that social life in complex civilizations cannot be completely ordered by a uniform ethical code.

One further criticism of Weber's work on India concerns his account of the political structure of Indian society and in particular his use of the concept of "patrimonialism." Jakob Rösel has pointed to a number of weaknesses both in the concept as such as well as in its application in the case of India. The concept is in his view too vague because though it is advanced as a kind of transitional stage somewhere between a primitive patriarchalism and the advanced rational-legal state, its precise location and content are not adequately indicated. Emerging out of the patriarchal household, patrimonialism attempts to extend the domain of the ruler by the domination of the weaker households around him, and from here the process may be extended almost indefinitely, to a limit point where collapse is imminent or actually ensues. Weber concentrates on the ways in which the ruler develops his means of administration (i.e., the military and other personnel who obey his commands), and emphasizes the numerous difficulties he may encounter engendering loyalty and thus maintaining the effectiveness of central control. At the most developed stage, patrimonialism enters into complex relations with non-patrimonial forces, such as a citizenry or professional bureaucracy, and this may lead to the formation (often precarious) of a patrimonial state. An added complication is the problem of feudalism, which Weber sometimes sees as an alternative structure altogether involving a decentralized dispersion of power, while at other times he construes it as an extreme corporatist variant of patrimonialism itself.

In looking at how Weber employs the concept of the patrimonial state in India, Rösel points out that although he assumes it to be "a structure of traditional political control operating in the regional context, as well as underlying all major and . . . ephemeral imperial episodes of Indian history,"[60] he never describes the Indian kingdoms in any detail to show in just what ways they exemplified the patrimonial form of traditional domination. (This stands in marked contrast to the study of the Chinese patrimonial state where nearly a hundred pages are devoted to the topic.) In particular, Weber did not explore whether the regional kingdoms

---

[60] Jakob Rösel, "Weber, India and the Patrimonial State," in Kantowsky (ed.), *Recent Research*, p. 137.

developed their own vertical structures with various solidarity groups or merely exploited the existing patterns of group formation (tribes, village communities, castes or craft associations) by integrating them politically and fiscally. The reason for this, according to Rösel, is that, by keeping this concept unclarified in the background, Weber could employ it as a general covering hypothesis to counter those critics who claim that there is considerable evidence that India was already developing an indigenous capitalism before the British occupation, for he could readily dismiss them as missing the point: he could argue that the economic phenomena invoked by such critics testify only to the presence of a "patrimonial capitalism," not the modern, rational variant.[61]

Conclusion

In drawing conclusions from Weber's studies of China and India, it is absolutely essential to take account of the complex bibliographical context, in particular their placement between his two great studies of the Judeo-Christian tradition (*PE* and *AJ*), as well as their being punctuated, as it were, by five seminal essays designed to link and further develop the primary texts ("Confucianism and Puritanism," "The Social Psychology of the World Religions," "The General Character of Asiatic Religion," "Religious Rejections of the World and Their Directions," and the "Author's Introduction").[62] This context indicates that the studies are important elements of what is an exceedingly complex argument concerning the world-historical significance of western rationality. They are designed to demonstrate not merely what socio-economic outcomes occurred in the absence of Protestantism, but the character of the alternative courses of cultural development in such settings. In order to make his case, Weber had to invent and explicate an enormous array of sociological concepts owing to the fact that his central problematic touched on so many interrelated themes. At the heart of the latter was the issue of "demagification" or the "disenchantment of the world," for it was ultimately this phenomenon that facilitated the modernization process in the west, enabling so many further developments to ensue (science, capitalism, democracy and so on). The unbroken magical enchantment of the world in the east correspondingly kept these societies from being rationalized, at least along the lines taken in the west.

---

[61] *Ibid.*, pp. 140–142.

[62] The first and the third of these are presented as the concluding chapters of *The Religion of China* and *The Religion of India* respectively.

To sum up, Weber believes Asiatic religions differed from those of the Christian west because their soteriological interests were so different. In contrast to the emissary prophecy of the Ancient Jews, "Asiatic soteriology knew only an exemplary promise . . . [Connected with this] was the fact that all philosophies and soteriologies of Asia finally had a common presupposition: that knowledge or mystical gnosis is finally the single absolute path to the highest holiness here and in the world beyond" (*RI* 330). This is not knowledge of the empirical world of natural and human events and their laws, but knowledge of the ultimate significance of the world and life as such. This quest was most rationally pursued in India and culminated in the unique worldview of Hinduism; but in China also gnosis was held to be the way to both the highest holiness as well as the only way to correct behavior. Such knowledge, though teachable, is not a product of rational empirical science. "Rather it is the means of mystical and magical domination over self and the world. It is attained by an intensive training of body and spirit either through asceticism or, as a rule, through strict, methodologically-ruled meditation" (*RI* 331). From this two major consequences follow. First, the focus on knowledge leads inevitably to a redemption aristocracy, for the capacity for mystical gnosis requires a charisma not possessed by all. And second, because this knowledge is mystical, it cannot be fully communicated by rational and public means; it is thus essentially asocial and apolitical, and leads its seekers in otherworldly directions. The highest god-like states of holiness are attainable only via a process of "emptying" oneself of worldly experiences. Yet such soteriologies had to confront the actual practices of social life in the Asiatic world. One outcome was that of Vedanta Brahminism, the single, most inwardly consistent solution to the problem of theodicy reached anywhere. Based on its twin teachings of *samsara* and *karma*, it produced an organismic social doctrine in which the various cultivated and distinguished lay strata could find a place only by adopting an extreme traditionalism in all affairs. The main alternative development was in China where the high-status laity became secular officials in a patrimonial bureaucracy and "developed a particular, narrow ceremoniousness, a pure inner-worldly life conduct . . ." (*RI* 338). Even though politically attuned, the Confucians were in essence "aesthetically cultivated literary scholars and conversationalists" (*RI* 338).

In summarizing the whole Asian ethos and comparing it with the west Weber says this:

> The Taoistic Wu wei, the Hinduistic "emptying" of consciousness of worldly relations and worldly cares, and the Confucian "distance" of the spirit from

preoccupation with fruitless problems, all represent manifestations of the same type. The occidental ideal of active behavior . . . centrally fixes on "personality". To all . . . highly developed Asiatic intellectual soteriology this could only appear either as hopelessly onesided philistinism or as barbaric greed for life. (*RI* 338–339)

According to Weber, the key search in the west has been for the individual personality as such, a quest which has been based on "the conception that through simple behavior addressed to the 'demands of the day' one may achieve salvation" (*RI* 342). Under Protestantism this led finally to the emergence of what Weber calls an "ethic of inner conviction" (*Gesinnungs-ethik*) in which the external observance of sacred law is displaced by a more radical and intense cultivation of a sacred inner religious state. Here, he says, "the systematization of religious obligations . . . breaks through the stereotypization of individual norms in order to bring about a meaningful total relationship of the pattern of life to the goal of religious salvation" (*E&S* 578). Herein lies the ultimate source of the west's unique world-transforming potency. Nothing in India or China could match this force which enlists the whole being of man in the service of transcendental goals.

10

JOHN LOVE

Max Weber's *Ancient Judaism*

Ancient Judaism is perhaps Weber's greatest single creation. Nearly 500 pages in length, though unfinished at the time of his death, it is the largest of the three major studies of the three-volume *Gesammelte Aufsätze zur Religionssoziologie* (Collected Essays in the Sociology of Religion) (*GARS*). The work is deeply rooted in Weber's thought.[1] In the *Protestant Ethic* Weber had already emphasized affinities between Judaism and the outlook of Puritanism, suggesting that ascetic Protestantism had inherited the "perfectly unemotional wisdom of the Hebrews" which had seen "the rational suppression of the mystical, in fact the whole emotional side of religion" (*PE* 123). He observed that despite its distinct petty-bourgeois and traditionalistic tendencies, "Old Testament morality was able to give a powerful impetus to that spirit of self-righteous and sober legality which was so characteristic of the worldly asceticism of . . . Protestantism" (*PE* 165).

By the time of *Ancient Judaism*, Weber's appreciation of the significance of the Hebrew legacy had deepened in proportion as his investigations broadened to deal with the origins of western rationality. One can also read the argument of *Ancient Judaism* as Weber's response to Nietzsche on the very large questions of the "genealogy of morals" and the significance of the Judeo-Christian tradition for the fate of western modernity in general.[2] For Weber shared with Nietzsche a preoccupation with the peculiar character of the religious impulse as such, especially insofar as powerful inner forces are unleashed in directions that lead to various "unnatural" and self-denying practices (*FMW* 271–272).

---

[1] On Weber's relation to Sombart, whose book on the Jews and capitalism had been an important stimulus for his work, see H. Lehmann, "The Rise of Capitalism: Weber versus Sombart," in H. Lehmann and G. Roth (eds.), *Weber's Protestant Ethic: Origins, Evidence, Contexts*, Cambridge: Cambridge University Press, 1993.

[2] On this topic see the essay by Wilhelm Hennis, "The Traces of Nietzsche in the Work of Max Weber," in *Max Weber: Essays in Reconstruction*, trans. Keith Tribe, London and Boston: Allen & Unwin, 1988.

Weber's underlying interest is not merely the Protestant appropriation of the Old Testament conception of God and the Law, but the broader sociological phenomenon of the transmission via Christianity of "a highly rational religious ethic of social conduct . . . free of magic and all forms of irrational quest for salvation . . ." (*AJ* 4). This, he believed, was largely an achievement of the period of the Deuteronomic reforms under the influence especially of the pre-exilic prophets from Amos to Jeremiah. From the Exile onwards, however, Weber saw Judaism as developing a legalistic ethic with a highly ritualistic and formal character, culminating in the rabbinic move- ment of the Talmudic period which presupposed the Diaspora and the caste-like transformation of Jewry into a "pariah people."

The social basis of the covenant relation

Weber's analysis in *Ancient Judaism* begins, as do his studies of India and China, with an account of material conditions, emphasizing in addition the geo-political situation of the peasant/tribal culture of ancient Palestine between the two great river-valley civilizations of Egypt and Mesopotamia. These imperial powers were always bent on expansion and domination, and increasingly struck terror into the inhabitants of the regions they conquered (*AJ* 267). Any small-scale independent political association in the region was most precarious, though the transformation of the early Israelite tribal confederacy into a monarchy, culminating in the centralized state of Solomon – a kind of "oriental despotism" – was possible largely as a consequence of a lull in the domination of outside forces between the thirteenth and the tenth centuries BCE.

In Weber's view, many of the key ideas of Judaism were formulated during the period of the confederacy, before being further transformed by the considerable difficulties that subsequently enveloped the Hebrew people. In this formative time, the Israelite conception of God – as a "supra-mundane, personal, wrathful, forgiving, loving, demanding, pun- ishing lord of Creation" – was born (*FMW* 385). For Weber, this involved the gradual sublimation of the original naturalistic idea of God as a "god from afar" associated with the sudden appearance of thunder and with distant mountains and typically invoked in warfare. As He was viewed as "holding sway from his remote mountain seat near heaven and on occasion personally intervening in the course of events" (*AJ* 124), a sense of "distance" was felt which gave the idea of god a special majesty, such that over time God came to be construed as a personal power of heaven at odds with the world (in marked contrast, in particular, to the impersonal power of heaven of China which was always a force for harmony).

A key concern of Weber is the form of cohesion that united the original tribes of Israel and brought them into a political alliance. The separateness of the individual groups was overcome by a shared religious outlook conditioned by the experience of unity in war, somewhat analogous to the "amphictyonic council" of the ancient Greeks (*AJ* 90). Weber traces the crucial idea of the "covenant" (*berith*) to the contractually regulated links between on the one hand the warrior clans who owned the land and on the other those who could not own land, such as the groups of foreigners (*gerim*) who were typically merchants and craftsmen, and the Levites who performed priestly functions (*AJ* 79). At the armed assemblies that took place to organize war campaigns, Weber surmises, charismatic war prophets claiming the authority of God came forward and promulgated the idea that the tribes were bound together in an oath-bound covenant with God. This led to forms of fraternization and cohesion that evidently strengthened military effectiveness. (It is worth noting that the original meaning of the word Israel is probably "people of the God of War.") The notion of a compact between God and his people (not the mere witnessing of oath-taking by the deity) in which both sides freely choose each other is, in Weber's view, unique in history and had manifold implications for subsequent religious developments:

> The fact that various oath-bound confederations under divine protection existed throughout Israelite history *per se* is not peculiar . . . Rather, the peculiarity consists in the first place in the extensive employment of the religious *berith* as the actual (or construed) basis of the most varied legal and moral relations. Above all, Israel itself as a political community was conceived as an oath-bound confederation. (*AJ* 75)

As the course of history unfolded, events were interpreted in the light of the special relationship of partnership between God and His people. God has chosen the people of Israel and vowed to destroy their enemies, as in the case of deliverance from the Egyptians, if in return they will obey His commandments and be faithful to Him. To the original idea of a fearsome God of war, who if provoked can destroy his opponents, is now added a more reasonable and benign side, the idea of a loving God who is also just and merciful. Of course, the worship of Yahwe did not immediately displace other belief systems already present in Palestine, and struggle ensued as the proponents of Yahwe attempted to overcome competing cults. In the original Canaanite society there had been a great variety of religious life, but most threatening were the local Baal cults and foreign-influenced cults of the dead. For the Yahwists the idea of God as partner in the covenant distinguished Him from the typical local gods common throughout the region with their particularistic, functional qualities and magical powers. From Weber's perspective, this was a crucial element which enabled subsequent development in the direction of abstract and universal ethics. Originally, however, religiously sanctioned codes of conduct were predominantly legalistic rather than ethical in character.

Decisive in the transition to the next stage, to what Weber calls ethical rationalization, was the role of a distinct kind of religiously inspired seer the prophet who emerged in the late confederacy on the basis of important changes in the social structure. With settlement, differences began to emerge between the rural-based tribes of peasants and shepherds, and the patrician groups in the towns. The antagonism between rich and poor which typically accompanied urbanization was further exacerbated by the establishment of the monarchy, because only the patricians could afford the expensive armaments upon which military and thus political power rested. The monarchy organized itself like other despotisms in the region, introducing cohorts and bodyguards as warfare was transformed with the use of chariots and horses. At the same time a novel form of administration was put in place with all the paraphernalia of royal officialdom, harem, court priests, etc. Associated with this was the hegemonic rise of an urban patriciate over the *gerim* and small peasants who were progressively demilitarized and proletarianized; the former monopolized court positions and increasingly adopted the status accoutrements of a nobility. According to Weber, the original Canaanite cult of Baal was well adapted to the proud and haughty disposition of the patricians, but their religious and social pretensions provoked the hostile response of plebeian groups. The latter were led by the remnants of the declassed war prophets and Levites, who sought to restore the old ideals of the nomadic past by reinvigorating the original cult of Yahwe.

Weber's *Agrarian Sociology of Ancient Civilizations*

The sociology of these developments had been a major concern of Weber as early as his *Agrarian Sociology* of 1897, in which he had analyzed the social content of the Law of ancient Israel at some length. National unification under Saul had been the unintended outcome of the war of independence against the Philistines, the twelve tribes arising on analogy with ancient Greek states as a mechanism of allocating taxation liabilities. By the time of Solomon, however, the typical features of near-eastern monarchy were established, including labor services, a royal hoard, foreign bodyguard and large-scale public works. Furthermore, the Hebrews had become urbanized and power was monopolized by those families rich enough to supply fully equipped and trained soldiers. (As evidence for this Weber cites the new concern for blood purity and ancestry and a growing interest in the heroic legends of the Patriarchs as found in the Deutero-nomic history writings.)[3]

But the concentration of royal power and religious cult in the citadel of Jerusalem was a fatal flaw for the monarchy. It led to conflict between the old rural-based military families, who wanted the army to remain loyal to their local cults and the urban priestly groups who also sought control of the monarchy and its army, and eventually to civil war. The war led to the division of the state when the old Israelite tribes refused to submit to the labor service of the monarch and seceded, leaving Judah as little more than the city kingdom of Jerusalem. Under Phoenician influence the newly established northern kingdom had allowed pagan cults to flourish and this provoked prophetic reaction, especially that of Elijah. First Israel and then Judah came under the influence of the expanding Assyrian Empire. During this period (the eighth century), as the national aspirations of the Jews suffered numerous setbacks, the great prophets Amos, Hosea and Isaiah countered by interpreting these events as showing God's concern to recall His people to their covenant obligations. With the destruction of Samaria and the deportation of many Israelites to Mesopotamia, religious develop-ment continued in Judah. A unique opportunity arose for the priesthood to assert itself and, eventually, under King Josiah they promulgated a radical set of laws (Deuteronomy) designed to limit royal power as well as to centralize worship in the Temple at Jerusalem. From then on the monarch had to be "legitimate": that is, in the line of David. In Weber's view, this involved an attempt to reconstitute the Jewish state on the basis of ancient law. It was also the most serious attempt thus far to theocratize the social structure, a development that grew out of the increasingly theological elaboration of the law.

The nature of the legislation involved is of particular interest to Weber, though interestingly he does not emphasize the role of the prophets as he does in *Ancient Judaism* and sees elements of class antagonism as being formative. The extensiveness of the social regulations reflect the revulsion of many at the excesses of the Egyptian-style monarchies of Solomon and David (*ASAC* 141–142):

> The essence of *Deuteronomy* . . . is that it seeks to increase the limitations on
> the misuse of power by the rich. Thus in the old law there were restrictions on

---

[3] Weber's work largely predated the dispute that has arisen on the origins of the earliest Israelite community in Canaan between conservatives such as Y. Kaufmann and W. Albright and radicals such as N. Gottwald and G. Mendenhall.

distraint, while in *Deuteronomy* it is absolutely forbidden to distrain a debtor's home or private mill . . . a day's wages must be paid on the day earned; collection of debts on the Sabbath is forbidden . . . and the rule is tightened that all who sold themselves into slavery must be freed in the seventh year. But the most far-reaching provision of all is that which forbids taking interest from fellow Hebrews. (*ASAC* 142)

Deuteronomy and the role of prophecy

If priests alone had been responsible for religious development, could they have shown concern beyond a centralized cult and the radical rejection of other gods? As Weber puts it on one occasion in *Ancient Judaism*, "In general cult priests are not the usual exponents of rational ethical teachings; as a rule they are oriented to ritual" (*AJ* 244). Herein, of course, lies the decisive contribution of the prophets to the course of Judaic history. In his later writings Weber is adamant that the prophets were in large part responsible for the unique ethical strain of the legal formulations of this period.[4] But the central problem is to explain precisely how Israelite law came to be rationalized in this way.

One of the earliest forms of Israelite law developed, as elsewhere, from ancient practices. Warleaders on occasion made pronouncements that gave rise to fixed norms. *Chuk* was the original expression for "the binding custom and legal usage established through precedents" (*AJ* 87). The more thoroughly juridical concept, however, was *mishpat*, which was employed for "judgments" of a more strictly legal kind. But such lawfinding assumed an already valid body of law. For new law to emerge the quite different means of the oracle and the solemn *berith* was needed, and this produced the more categorical form of the commandment (*debar*). According to the tradition, the *berith* was employed in the adoption of the Deuteronomic law book and this testifies to the presence of the novel form of lawmaking, although the extent to which earlier *mishpatim* were also included makes interpretation difficult. According to Weber, the formal structure of Deuteronomy "consists of a fairly systematically ordered code of *mishpatim*[5] to which single *debarim* are unsystematically appended. These are partially moral, and partially cultic in nature. Substantively speaking the *mishpatim*

---

[4] Weber does not deal at great length with the Israelite "judges" who were decisive in these developments, but as Abraham Malamt has shown they represent an ideal-typical form of charismatic leadership from a Weberian point of view. See his "Charismatic Leadership in the Book of Judges," in F. Cross *et al.* (eds.), *Magnalia Dei, the Mighty Acts of God: Essays on the Bible and Archaeology in Memory of G. Ernest Wright*, Garden City, NY: Doubleday, 1976.

[5] Exodus 21:1 to 22:16.

without doubt show Babylonian influence reaching into the distant past" (*AJ* 88). But precisely who produced the great law book? The formal juristic technique displayed in the *mishpatim* indicates those norms did not stem from priestly lawfinding and therefore were borrowed in some fashion. Thus, for Weber, Deuteronomy is neither of juristic nor hierocratic origin but is a work compiled by laymen. With its "reflection on the God-pleasing and reasonable nature of the law to be instituted as valid and the addition of *debarim*," it has the character of a "law book" created in a theological milieu and circulated among the urban populace (*AJ* 88). This was the very same plebeian milieu in which the prophets had made their representations.

Thus, for Weber, the Deuteronomic reforms were brought about by the combined efforts of the pre-exilic prophets and the Levitical teaching priests, who recast the injunctions of the Decalogue in the direction of a unified religious ethic, separating out the ritual and socio-political elements. The prophets were basically concerned with the stance of the individual toward God, especially as revealed in his inner state (the origin of the idea of an "ethic of conviction" to which we shall return), and this was combined with the priests' focus on the conception of God as the supreme master of the world (the advent of monotheism). To the increasingly ethical strain of prophecy there corresponded a sublimation in the conception of God – from a warlord embroiled in local conflicts to a supreme and universal God of world history.

The ethical conception of the law

The interpretation of God's law took on a decidedly ethical coloring as the traditional legal code was progressively sublimated by prophetic enhancement of the covenant relation. For this to occur the early understanding of wrongdoing had to be transformed. The earliest concept of sin had been associated with the purely objective matter of whether a ritualistic transgression (*chatah*) had provoked God's anger. Hence, fear of ritualistic mistakes and their effects was the original motive for seeking expiation.

> But Yahwe was also contractual partner to the *berith* with Israel and the old social law based upon fellowship and brotherly aid in need was considered an obligation to him. The concept of sin, thus, had to extend to substantively ethical, particularly social-ethical stipulations. Yahwistic criticism of the attitude of the kings and of the social changes brought about by urbanism thus led to expansion of the concept of sin beyond the area of ritual to social ethics. (*AJ* 165)

The prophets thus insisted that God had made prerequisite to his ancient promises to Israel the honoring of ritual and ethical obligations, but this had not occurred. The ancient notion of joint liability of the people for individual transgressions and of descendants for the deeds of forefathers, however, created difficulties for a rational theodicy, because the individual inevitably asked the question what good it would do if other's misdeeds could enmesh the innocent anyway. This risked a fatalism detrimental to the individual cure of the soul. Thus, these problems of consistency gave rise to the kind of skeptical speculations about God's conduct found in the wisdom literature.

But while the rationality of the prophets was not sophisticated by the standards of later Hellenistic philosophy, it was sufficient to ensure their contribution in the field of ethics.[6] They were unlike prophets occurring elsewhere because, as independent demagogues who addressed a public, they advanced highly critical views of the political authorities and social conditions of their day (*AJ* 110–117). Against a somewhat idealized picture of conditions under the ancient confederacy, the prophets of the period of the divided kingdom warned of an impending despotism and servitude that would envelop the Jews unless the commands of God were obeyed. In addition to certain cultic infractions, various kinds of injustice, corruption and impropriety were condemned, reflecting the indignation of oppressed groups with the abuses of the monarchical rulers and their knightly patrician supporters (the *gibborim*). The concepts of *mishpat* (justice) and *sdaqa* (righteousness) were crucial foci.[7] But while some prophets enjoyed royal patronage, Weber says we should not assume they had significant popular support, even from depressed strata such as peasants, owing to their opposition to magic and their insistence on demanding standards of moral conduct. Their critical attitude also meant they clashed repeatedly with the priests whom they berated for undue dependence on ritual and cultic authority. In contrast to the scriptural orientation of the latter, the prophets rely on charismatic inspiration as a means of hearing the word of God, for whom they are mere instruments through which the word of God (*debar*) is made manifest (*AJ* 312–113). Unlike religious virtuosi elsewhere, they did not claim to be vessels of the

---

[6] There is a vast literature on the phenomenon of prophecy. Earlier studies of note are S. Mowinckel, *Prophecy and Tradition: the Prophetic Books in the Light of the Study of the Growth and History of the Tradition*, Oslo: Dybwald, 1946, and I. Engnell, *The Call of Isaiah*, Uppsala: Lundquist, 1949. But see now Joseph Blenkinsopp, *A History of Prophecy in Israel*, Louisville, Westminster John Knox, 1995.

[7] See the discussion of these concepts in K. Koch, *The Prophets, vol. I: The Assyrian Period*, Philadelphia, PA: Fortress, 1982, pp. 56–62.

Divine, or to possess exceptional or exemplary qualities as regards their own conduct, but merely claimed to transmit the will of God (Weber's concept of "missionary prophecy").[8]

Not all prophets experienced being seized by God's spirit as a fortunate condition, as did Amos and Hosea; Isaiah and Jeremiah were often weighed down by the awful burden of their mission. The prophets were not oriented to mystical questions in any way, nor to metaphysical speculations as to the meaning of the world (as was common for holy knowledge in India). Nor were they driven to God as a way of finding salvation or perfection of the soul, in opposition to an imperfect world; thus, they could not feel deified, nor be united with the godhead and relieved from the trials of life (*AJ* 315). Rather, their task was to comprehend God's counsels and apply them in their plain and intelligible sense to the situation of the day. "The nature of Yahwe contained nothing supernatural in the sense of something extending beyond understanding. His motives were not concealed from human comprehension" (*AJ* 314). The ultimate religious demand of the prophets was faith (love was not as important, and certainly not loving communion with God). This was connected to the teaching of obedience and humility as decisive virtues, harnessed for the observance of the commandments of the Holiness Code which the prophets largely accepted from tradition (*AJ* 320). The detailed content of their teaching was increasingly focused on correct ethical behavior in the here-and-now, in the realm of everyday affairs, which for Weber means that striving after salvation was pushed in a fundamentally worldly direction.

As we have already noted, the prophets were not alone responsible for this outcome: "the extensive sublimation of sin and god pleasing behavior into ethical absolutism . . . developed out of the cooperation of prophecy and the gradual rationalization of the Levite Torah and the thoughtways of pious, cultured lay-circles" (*AJ* 332). Strictly speaking, the prophets did not contribute new interpretations of the commandments, but set the traditional teachings in a more radical historical framework in which doom and salvation would be played out on a grand scale by God. "Prophecy presupposed the content of the commandments to be familiar. The prophets are far from yielding an even approximate knowledge of Yahwe's ethical demands upon the individual. These demands received their character from quite a different area, namely from the Torah of the Levites" (*AJ* 235). According to Weber, the Levitical Torah teachers achieved their influence

---

[8] On the distinction between missionary and exemplary prophecy, see Weber's discussion in "The Social Psychology of the World Religions," in *FMW* 285–286.

not from their traditional priestly functions but from "the ritualistic and ethical cure of souls" (*AJ* 242).

> A strict separation of *jus* and *fas* could no longer be maintained with their growing importance and with increased consideration given their views by the Yahwistically interested laity . . . This cooperation of devout Yahwistic laymen with ethically reflective priests resulted in the theologizing, on the one hand, of law and the rationalization of religious ethics, on the other.
>
> (*AJ* 243).

At the same time, the majesty and power of God were enlarged in the transformation of Yahwe from a local war god to a god of history. Yet Yahwe remained a god of the confederacy, regardless of how much he was also conceived of as a heavenly king: "he was no God with whom one could seek mystical union by contemplation, but a superhuman, yet understandable personal master whom one had to obey" (*AJ* 225). It was crucial to ascertain how the violation of ethical norms had occurred in order to correct the offending condition. The final result was a theodicy which saw the Deity as simultaneously a universal God of all nations who controls the course of world history, as well as the being the God of the Israelite confederacy with a special relation to her people only.

The fear induced by the pronouncements of the prophets had greatly assisted in transforming the magico-legalistic ethic of the confederacy into a rationalized moral code which more and more required the commitment of the total personality. Weber relates this fear to a kind of "war psychosis" that became all but permanent as a response to the frightening prospect of devastating conquest that threatened all around. A striking innovation of prophetic thought in this connection was the idea that even the calamities of Israel were influenced by Yahwe. The prophets gradually developed a theodicy of misfortune in which Yahwe ascends to the rank of the one supreme God who alone is responsible for the course of historical events. "Amos gave a turn to the *berith* idea which made Yahwe himself the cause of all misfortune" (*AJ* 311). But most important of all, the powerful emotional impact of prophecy "promoted systematic unification, by relating the people's life as a whole and the life of each individual to the fulfillment of Yahwe's positive commandments" (*AJ* 255).

What particularly interests Weber in all this is the long-run historical process he variously calls "de-magification" (*Entzauberung*) or the "disenchantment of the world". The Judaic hostility to magic initially arose because prophets promoted the worship of Yahwe in opposition to the cult of Baal who, as a god of fertility, had to be approached by essentially magical means. Yahwe, by contrast, acts like a human being with a rational will that can be known, and demands obedience to intelligible norms; unlike Baal he cannot be manipulated by magic or other ritual devices.

The ethical teaching advanced thus went beyond the observance of specific norms in fostering "a meaningful total relationship of the pattern of life to the goal of religious salvation" (*E&S* 578). Weber sees in this development an achievement of the greatest significance for understanding later western history. In the teaching of the prophets is the germ of the specific attitude to worldly conduct that was to be eventually taken up and further developed by the Puritans. It is worth recalling Weber's description of this ethic in *The Protestant Ethic and the Spirit of Capitalism*: "The God of Calvinism demanded of his believers not single good works, but a life of good works combined into a unified system . . . The moral conduct of the average man was thus deprived of its planless and unsystematic character and subjected to a consistent method for conduct as a whole" (*PE* 117).

Weber's further discussion on the origins of these novel thoughtways is of considerable interest. He maintains that entirely new religious conceptions have rarely originated where they might be expected, namely at the center of rational culture complexes such as those of Babylon, Athens, Alexandria, Rome and so on, but typically have arisen in quite marginal areas such as pre-exilic Jerusalem, Galilaea of late Jewish times, Roman Africa or New England, though the influence of near-by rational civilizations must also be reckoned with:

> prerequisite to new religious conceptions is that man must not yet have unlearned how to face the course of the world with questions of his own. Precisely the man distant from the great culture centers has cause to do so when their influence begins to affect or threaten his central interests . . . The possibility of questioning the meaning of the world presupposes the capacity to be astonished about the course of events.   (*AJ* 206–207)

The "pariah people" thesis

One key dimension of Weber's study has rightly provoked a quite large literature of critical comment: his thesis that the Jews were fated to become a "pariah people." Associated with this was his view, advanced especially against Werner Sombart, that the Jews did not contribute directly to the development of modern industrial capitalism though they did function as "pariah capitalists." The largely negative response of some scholars to the "pariah-people" thesis has undoubtedly colored the attitude of many to

Weber's *Ancient Judaism* as a whole.[9] To some, Weber has demeaned the historical achievement of the Jews by concluding his study with an account of their national demise and implied degeneration into a caste-like status group located on the margins of society, leaving the dynamic of further social change to other movements such as Christianity. But, as the issues raised here take us well beyond the scope of the present article, we shall confine ourselves to a brief consideration of the telling criticisms of Arnaldo Momigliano on this point.

Although Momigliano acknowledges that much of Weber's treatment of Judaism remains valid and is unaffected by this issue, he argues that the pariah people thesis rests on a confusion between the situation of the Jews and that of certain lower castes in India whom Weber describes as "guest peoples" (*Gastvolk*) because they were ritually separated from their surroundings. In *Economy and Society* Weber describes his concept of "pariah people" as denoting "a distinctive hereditary social group lacking autonomous political organization and characterized by prohibitions against commensality and intermarriage . . . Two additional traits of a pariah people are political and social disprivilege and a far-reaching distinctiveness in economic functioning" (*E&S* 493). Weber had also implied, according to Momigliano, "that an ethic of resentment (*Ressentiment*) is characteristic of the Jews as pariahs." But Weber's view is misleading. First, although the Jews lacked political independence and lived on foreign soil for much of their history, Momigliano insists they never abandoned a belief in both nationhood and ownership of their land. Furthermore, they never accepted an inferior status in the framework of an alien belief system, as did some Indian castes. Indeed, despite the many difficulties encountered throughout their history, the Jews have always presupposed that "loss of political independence does not entail renunciation of self-government . . . Believing Jews never gave up their sovereign rights and never admitted to being without political institutions of their own." Weber had assumed that the ritualistic closure that had begun in

---

[9] Of course, not all those who have had reservations about aspects of the "pariah-people" thesis have dismissed Weber's work as a whole. S. N. Eisenstadt and Arnaldo Momigliano remained extremely appreciative of Weber's work as a whole while criticizing aspects of his treatment (cf. Eisenstadt, *Jewish Civilization: The Jewish Experience in a Comparative Perspective*, Albany, NY: State University of New York Press, 1992, pp. 313–318; Momigliano, "A Note on Max Weber's Definition of Judaism as a Pariah Religion," *History and Theory*, 19 (1980). The whole topic has also been addressed in a comprehensive, balanced and scholarly fashion by Ephraim Shmueli, "The 'Pariah-People' and its Charismatic Leadership: A Revaluation of Max Weber's 'Ancient Judaism,'" *American Academy for Jewish Research Proceedings*, 36 (1968), pp. 167–247, a study which contrasts markedly to Gary Abraham, *Max Weber and the Jewish Question: A Study of the Social Outlook of his Sociology*, Urbana, IL: University of Illinois Press, 1992, which is unreliable and tendentious.

Deuteronomic times and been diffused during the Exile and after meant the Jews had "voluntarily" adopted the status of pariahs. But "Weber confused ritual separation by a sovereign nation (which is what we find in the Bible, in the Talmud and in later legal treatises) with pariah status."[10]

This argument of course does not show that in the period of the Exile and just after resentment was not an important factor. In any case, the origin of the Jews' pariah status for Weber is connected with the self-imposed ritual segregation they began during the Exile when the priests and Torah teachers in the Babylonian community sought to prohibit mixed marriages as a way of avoiding assimilation. For they had seen that absorption into the foreign environment had been the fate of the North Israelites exiled earlier by the Assyrians. They then added increasingly ritualized dietary proscriptions designed to inhibit commensalism, as well as strict observance of the Sabbath. Ritualistic segregation in general gave rise to what Weber describes as "the dualism of in-group and out-group morality." In economics this meant that no attempt was made to ethically rationalize relations with outsiders and so Jews could pursue various forms of "irrational capitalism" without restriction. In this way, according to Weber, they came to play a role in western economic development as "pariah capitalists," rather than in conventional business activities (*AJ* 345). But whether because of this they warrant being classified as a pariah people in general is a debatable question.

The history of the Jewish wars of liberation in the Roman period along with other struggles suggests Weber's view of the Jews as accepting their political inferiority is overdrawn. It remains an open question as to precisely what portions of Weber's analysis of Judaism would need qualification were the concept of pariah to be rejected wholly or in part. Had he been able to fulfill his intention to follow his last writings on the Pharisees and Essenes with studies of early Christianity and Talmudic Judaism, his view on these matters might have been further qualified.[11] But it has to be acknowledged that Weber's treatment of Judaism in these respects is somewhat dated and certainly insensitive to Jewish sensibilities. In his defense, however, it should be said yet again that Weber was not an anti-semite in any form, and wrote in a similar, detached and unsentimental tone about other religions as well.

---

[10] A. Momigliano, "A Note on Max Weber's Definition of Judaism as a Pariah Religion," pp. 314–317.

[11] See the comments of Wolfgang Schluchter, *Rationalism, Religion, and Domination: A Weberian Perspective*, Berkeley, CA: University of California Press, 1989, p. 245.

The origins of the Law

In what follows we shall confine our commentary to Weber's treatment of the origins of the Law. This is a problem which runs through the whole of Old Testament studies since well before Wellhausen, and clearly has many ramifications for theology and religious dogmatics which cannot be pursued here. Of course, the debate on the origins of the Law continues unabated even to this day, but two contributions which complement Weber's approach are worth mentioning. The first is Albrecht Alt's "The Origins of Israelite Law" of 1934. Utilizing the then new form-criticism approach, Alt emphasized the important dichotomy between two fundamental types of law found in the Hexateuch, what he termed the "casuistic" and the "apodeictic," a distinction which enabled each law to be analyzed without having to first establish precise authorship and dating. The distinctive formal characteristic of casuistic law is the fact that its syntactical construction is invariably based on the sequence of a prothesis, which takes the form of a conditional clause which describes the general features of the case in question as well certain limiting conditions, followed by an apothesis in which the penalties to be imposed are specified. (E.g., "Supposing men quarrel and one strikes the other with a stone . . . and [this man] does not die . . . if then . . . [he] can walk the street, he that struck him shall be clear, only he shall pay for the loss of time, and shall have him thoroughly healed.")[12] According to Alt, the range of this type of law was considerable and corresponds to the ordinary secular jurisdiction of ancient Israel. It was administered not by appointed judges or priests but by laymen gathered at the city gate to form a court. Since the discovery of the Code of Hammurabi and other near-eastern legal codes, it is possible to show there is nothing unique to Israel about the contents of this kind of law as it appears in the Old Testament, for it merely regulates the practical relations of society. It is likely, Alt surmises, that the Israelites merely inherited this legal structure from the pre-existing Canaanite law which shared many features with the law of surrounding nations.

In marked contrast to the casuistic is the second type of law, the apodeictic, which knows of no conditions, having the absolute character of the *lex talionis*. As Alt explains, this type of law arises because "it is Yahwe who demands a stern retribution for every drop of blood that is spilt . . . Yahwe demands [the murderer's] life, without regard to the rights of the injured . . . and without giving the criminal the opportunity to make

---

[12] Exodus 21:18–19, quoted in A. Alt, "The Origins of Israelite Law," in his *Essays on Old Testament History and Religion*, Oxford: Blackwell, 1966, p. 89.

satisfaction by paying damages."[13] This type of law, according to Alt, is unique to Israel and reflects the desire to obey the implacable will of God, in contrast to the other legal form which presupposes an almost complete separation of law and religion. The wording and poetic beat of the apodeictic laws is also distinctive, the typical form having a certain weightiness when read aloud and repeated: "Whoever strikes his father or mother shall be put to death. Whoever steals a man and sells him . . . shall be put to death."[14] Alt argues that the form of these laws clearly indicates they were a concern of the whole community, and reflect its interest in regulating social affairs at large. Another version of this kind of law is that which involves the form of direct address introduced with "thou," which usually states categorical prohibitions, the best-known instance being the Decalogue. All these have a more absolute character than the casuistic form of law even where severe penalties are provided for, as the focus is the principle rather than the nature of the individual case.

Alt argues that an account of the origins of these laws must allow for the passionate intensity of their expression, a feature which would not exist if they had arisen in ordinary legal practice. He therefore suggests that

> the internal construction of the lists of apodeictic laws implies they were created and maintained in use in a part of Israelite life distinct from that of a single community administering secular justice. A context is required in which the whole people, and through them their God, could adopt the imperative tone towards individuals, and impose on them absolute prohibitions . . .[15]

Such a context is easy to find in the tradition itself, such as the setting of the curses presented in Deuteronomy 27 where the Levitical priests deliver them to the whole assembled people in the great natural amphitheater at Shechem. Furthermore, it is now perfectly understandable why the authors of the Hexateuch would choose "the lists of apodeictic laws to put into the stories of the first and basic covenant between Yahwe and Israel, on the mountain of God in the desert."[16]

The second major work is Martin Noth's essay "The Laws of the Pentateuch: Their Assumptions and Meaning," which largely accepts Alt's analysis of the origins of the specifically Israelite law, but is more concerned with the complexity of the history of the law in its subsequent phases. Noth rejects the idea that the law could have functioned generally as the

---

[13] *Ibid.*, p. 110.
[14] Exodus 21:15–17, quoted in Alt, "The Origins of Israelite Law," p. 111.
[15] *Ibid.*, p. 125.   [16] *Ibid.*, p. 129.

equivalent of a state form of law akin to those of other states in the region. He argues that the social function of the law changed in stages:

> whereas it had been the presence of [the sacral confederacy] which had provided the necessary prerequisite for the validation of the old laws, it was now the acknowledgment and observance of the law by which individuals constituted the community . . . and the presence of this community appeared to be a sign that the covenant relationship . . . still existed.[17]

This inversion of the usual relationship between the observance of the law and the fact of community led to a new stage in the understanding of the law, for now it became an absolute entity, not connected to a particular community chosen by God – no longer tied to anything, it is now a power in its own right.[18] As evidence of this novel attitude, Noth cites the fondness in the later Old Testament of referring to *the* law and *the* commandments, which "has the effect of making the law as the totality of commandments appear as a complete, firm entity, whose overall validity cannot be doubted."[19] With these developments we enter the era of rabbinic Judaism with its emphasis on the teaching of the Torah and its establishment of a cultic order based on the close observance of an elaborate code of conduct. This account complements Weber's, especially with respect to the transformation of the law into an absolute entity in which the individual emerges as a subject of the sovereign deity.

Conclusion

Weber's unrealized intention to write further on Talmudic Judaism and the origins of occidental Christianity suggests some final comments on his treatment of the process of rationalization and the way he tries to connect developments occurring in late antiquity with those of subsequent eras. The cultural achievements of ancient Judaism, the creation of a rationalized social ethics via the prophets and the understandings achieved in the Psalms and Wisdom literature, are elements that Weber is convinced shaped the modern west in decisive ways (though, of course, in a fashion quite different from the perspectives of conventional theology). Yet a full account of this connection was never written, and only a tentative reconstruction is possible. We have seen, for example, that for Weber Protestantism had rediscovered the spirit of the original Judaic ethic in its demand for the total organization of the personality for worldly conduct pleasing to God.

---

[17] Martin Noth, in Noth (ed.), *The Laws in the Pentateuch and Other Essays*, London: SCM, 1966, pp. 1–107.
[18] *Ibid.*, pp. 86–87.   [19] *Ibid.*, p. 87.

And, obviously, early Christianity was instrumental in transmitting the heritage of Judaism to the Greco-Roman world out of which western society arose.[20] But one would like to know more about the nature of the relationships involved in these broad-ranging developments.

In the concluding sections of *Ancient Judaism* Weber had outlined in some detail the conditions that had simultaneously given rise to rabbinic Judaism as well as to Christianity, the latter being to a certain extent a reaction to the former. He sees rabbinic Judaism as largely a product of the Pharisaic movement of the last two centuries before Christ, and it is worth briefly considering his account.[21] He tells us the Pharisees first appear after displacing the earlier Hassidic movement which had gradually died out as the Maccabeans came to an accommodation with the political realities of Hellenistic domination. The Pharisees had the character of an order or sect-like "brotherhood" (*chaburah*) and obliged members to adopt the strictest Levitical purity. Importantly, this implied separation not only from Hellenes but also from non-observant Jews.

> There developed the contrast between the Pharisaic "saints" and the ʾam haʾaretz, the "countrymen", the "ignorant" who did not know nor observe the law. The opposition was greatly intensified bordering on ritualistic caste segregation. The *chaber* (brother) . . . obligated himself not to share the table with pagans or ʾam ha-arez, to avoid connubium and association with them and, in general, to minimize all intercourse with them.   (*AJ* 387)

For Weber, this sectarianism contributed a large part to the indestructibility of Jewish communities in the Diaspora. To this must be added various community institutions created under the influence of the Pharisees, such as the synagogue. The Sabbath and other traditional religious festivals were gradually transformed into domestic or synagogue occasions, with the effect that the significance of the priesthood was devalued. In the place of the priest a new figure arose, the teacher learned in law, the *sofer*, a precursor of the *rabbi*. The legal decisions of the *soferim* are accommodated to the interests of an essentially urban community and reflect a "practical-ethical rationalism characteristic of petty-bourgeois strata. Practical everyday needs and 'common sense' dominate the discussion and resolution of controversial issues" (*AJ* 389). In opposition to the Sadducees, the Pharisees also begin to

---

[20] Consider these remarks in the opening pages of *Ancient Judaism*, "The world-historical importance of Jewish religious development rests above all in the creation of the *Old Testament*, for one of the most significant intellectual achievements of the Pauline mission was that it preserved and transferred this sacred book of the Jews to Christianity as one of its own sacred books" (p. 4).

[21] The classic study of the subject is Louis Finkelstein, *The Pharisees: The Sociological Background of their Faith*, Philadelphia, PA: Fortress, 1938.

nurture messianic hopes and belief in the resurrection of the dead. It is out of this general religious environment that the two subsequent religious movements of rabbinic Judaism and Christianity arise.

Pharisaic ideas form the basis of rabbinic Judaism. Weber points out that the *rabbi* had no recognized position until after the fall of the Temple, and even then was never a full-time, professional teacher. Rather, a *rabbi* always worked at an ordinary trade and only acted in a religious capacity avocationally, primarily by offering advice and counsel in matters of ritual. The basic orientation of rabbinic teaching was toward strict observance of the law, which meant hostility to all forms of mysticism ("dreaming") and esoteric gnosis. The duty of the Pharisee is to reject all irrational means to salvation and to anchor oneself to the law via continuous study. This did not strictly involve asceticism, accept insofar as the requirement to measure one's conduct by the law with its innumerable commandments enjoined vigilant self-observation and absolute self-control. Weber alludes to the 613 prescriptions that were alleged to have been given by Moses and notes how these were considerably augmented by rabbinical casuistry.

> The technical nature of legal interpretation corresponded to the social nature of the petty bourgeoisie . . . Thus the "ratio" of the stipulations instead of the letter, on the one side, the compelling needs of everyday life, above all the economy, on the other, came into their own . . . [However] the *rabbi* was invariably . . . more strictly bound to the positive divine commandment than the jurist can ever be to positive law . . .   (*AJ* 414)

The alleged "legalism" of rabbinic Judaism thus emerges from the combined effects of ritualistic closure to outsiders and rabbinic casuistry. We shall not consider the responses that Jewish scholars have made to such a "charge" except to note that it obviously coincides to a large degree with the early Christian view of Pharisaic Judaism.[22] Certainly Christ and Paul saw themselves as separating from Judaism on this very question, for they were essentially motivated to overcome the problems that legalism presented. As Weber explains, even though the early Christian ethic in many ways has to be understood as the Pharisaic ethic intensified, with regard to ritualistic (Levitical) purity Jesus took a quite different position. "The monumentally impressive lordly word, 'not that what goeth into the mouth defileth a man; but that which cometh out of the mouth' and out of an impure heart,[23] meant that for him ethical sublimation was decisive, not the ritualistic surpassing of the Jewish purity laws" (*AJ* 411).

---

[22] See for example the discussion of Shaye Cohen in his *From the Maccabees to the Mishnah*, Philadelphia, PA: Westminster Press, 1987, ch. 3.
[23] Matthew 15:11–18f.

Christ's decisive significance for Weber was to radically oppose intellectual access to cultic norms with an ethic of conviction expressed as an inner state of spiritual receptiveness based on faith. As Wolfgang Schluchter puts it, " 'Law' no longer controlled 'spirit'; 'spirit' now controlled 'law.' "[24] The spirit was not to come upon the solitary individual but was "poured out" upon the faithful as a community (*AJ* 292). This transformation of Judaism into a religion of faith involved an intensification of ethical demands, however, because the greater flexibility of applying norms non-ritually required the total involvement of the individual personality. But earliest Christianity was at the same time a retreat from the rationalism of Talmudic Judaism insofar as the latter had evolved an elaborate practical ethics directed to worldly conditions, whereas the former reintroduced magical and demonological elements in response to the needs of the oppressed rural masses (the 'poor in spirit') to whom it was in the first instance oriented.[25]

Paul overcame the unstructured character of the original movement formed around the itinerant charismatic Kyrios Christos in Palestine[26] – which otherwise would have remained a Jewish pneumatic sect or mystery religion – by organizing a network of lay congregations (at first amongst the urban Jewry of the Diaspora in the Mediterranean area). Although a Pharisaic scribe, Paul's sudden transformation of spirit (conversion) with its inner-convictional quality gave his mission a legitimacy that was different in principle to the gnosis of Judaism. But unlike Christ, Paul was not anti-intellectual and directed his proselytizing to educated petty-bourgeois strata, tempering and directing the pneuma of the ecstatic community in a rational way.[27] The rupture with Judaism occurred despite the initial nurturing of Christianity in the synagogues of Diaspora Jewry, though this did not prevent the preservation of the sacred books of the Old Testament for western Christianity. According to Weber, the decisive break occurred in Antioch when Paul reproached Peter for withdrawing from the gentiles after a common meal at the behest of the Jerusalemite Jews: "this shattering of the ritual barriers against commensalism meant a destruction of the

[24] Wolfgang Schluchter, *Rationalism, Religion, and Domination*, p. 206. On the status of law in rabbinic Judaism, see M. Kaplan, "The Legal Foundations of Rabbinic Judaism," in Jacob Neusner (ed.), *Understanding Rabbinic Judaism: From Talmudic to Modern Times*, New York: KTAV Publishing House, 1974, pp. 55–60, as well as other sections in Neusner's volume. Also see Weber's discussion in *E&S* 578.
[25] On Christ's use of magical means, see Morton Smith, *Jesus the Magician*, New York: Harper, 1978.
[26] On the initial reception of Christ in the Palestinian setting, see Gerd Theissen, *Sociology of Early Palestinian Christianity*, Philadelphia, PA: Fortress, 1978.
[27] On Paul, see E. P. Sanders, *Paul and Palestinian Judaism*, Philadelphia, PA: Fortress, 1977.

voluntary ghetto . . . [Christian 'freedom'] meant the universalism of Paul's mission, which cut across nations and status groups . . . [This was] the hour of the conception for the occidental 'citizenry'" (*RT* 37–38).

Using the important study of *The First Urban Christians* by Wayne Meeks, Wolfgang Schluchter has explored how a new religious community organized as a "charismatic congregation" emerged in the voluntary association of households which constituted the early Christian *ekklesia*.[28] Whereas the *rabbis* of Talmudic Judaism were "plebeian religious rational *teachers* of ritual, one can term the Pauline missionaries plebeian religious pneumatic dispensers of *grace*."[29] According to Weber, from this point on the trajectories of Christianity and Judaism diverged irrevocably – indeed, these events constitute the turning point for the "entire cultural development of the West and the Near East."[30] Both were ethical salvation religions and emerged in close connection with the ancient polis, but whereas Judaism became a religion of groups that were socially marginalized, Christianity was ideally adapted to the conditions of the western city. The suitability of Christianity for urban life "holds for the ancient type of piety of the pneumatic congregation, as well as for the mendicant monk orders of the High Middle Ages, and for the sects of the time of the Reformation up to and including Pietism and Methodism."[31] Of course, all this is only the briefest of outlines of some of the developmental courses Weber wanted to investigate.[32] Many additional questions arise and require further study, such as, for example, the precise role of Hellenistic intellectual culture.[33] Also pertinent are the important recent advances in near eastern studies brought by the discoveries of the Dead Sea Scrolls and the Gnostic Gospels found at Nag Hammadi.[34]

In summarizing the general features of religious traditions deriving from the east and near east, Weber pointed to the existence of key differences as

---

[28] Wayne Meeks, *The First Urban Christians*, New Haven, CT: Yale University Press, 1983. See also Alan Segal, *Rebecca's Children: Judaism and Christianity in the Roman World*, Cambridge, MA: Harvard University Press, 1986.

[29] Schluchter, *Rationalism, Religion and Domination*, p. 225.

[30] Quoted in *ibid.*, p. 227.

[31] Quoted in *ibid.*, 228.

[32] A further discussion of this problem of the transition to modernity is found in Wolfgang Schluchter, *The Rise of Western Rationalism: Max Weber's Developmental History*, trans. Guenther Roth, Berkeley, CA: University of California Press, 1981.

[33] On this issue a crucial starting point is the work of Martin Hengel, *Judaism and Hellenism*, 2 vols., London: SCM, 1974 and Elias Bickerman, *The Jews in the Greek Age*, Cambridge, MA: Harvard University Press, 1988.

[34] On these issues, see James Robinson (ed.), *The Nag Hammadi Library*, New York: Harper, 1978 and James Robinson and Helmut Koestler, *Trajectories through Early Christianity*, Philadelphia, PA: Fortress, 1971.

a consequence of the basic presuppositions out of which the various religions emerged. As Christianity developed from Judaism and Buddhism from Hinduism, there was this basic contrast: on the one hand, in the near east a "theocentric" view prevailed in which a religion of ethics and God-directed commands was developed by essentially plebeian strata; on the other hand a "cosmocentric" outlook was typical of Asiatic religions in which intellectuals of high rank were the carriers of a tradition focused on gnostic knowledge and contemplation.[35] One of the results of these differences was that any deliberate procedure oriented to salvation in the west was prevented from attempting self-deification or mystical union with the divine, and salvation generally had the character of "an ethical justification before god, which ultimately could be accomplished and maintained only by some sort of active conduct in the world" (*E&S* 552). As the world was conceived as a "work" of divine creation, it could not be a possible object of radical rejection as often occurred in the orient. Intellectualism in the orient, however, never abandoned the idea of the intrinsic "meaningfulness" of the world, though insight into its ultimate processes paradoxically led in the direction of flight. In the occident, by contrast, intellectualism, confronted by the unsolvable paradox of the creation of a permanently imperfect world by a perfect god, tried to master the world and transform it for god's glory, but this also had unexpected results for it led ultimately to science and the disenchantment of the world.

[35] The concepts "theocentric" and "cosmocentric" are terms coined by Schluchter, *Rationalism, Religion, and Domination*, p. 93.

PART IV

Law and economics

I I

HAROLD J. BERMAN AND CHARLES J. REID, JR.

Max Weber as legal historian

Max Weber was initially trained in both law and history and he drew extensively on examples from legal history in constructing his later sociological works. Yet he was not, properly speaking, a legal historian.[1] In fact, as we shall show, the superimposition upon legal history of his sociological categories of "ideal types" of legal authority resulted in serious distortions at the same time that it led to some important insights. His sharp separation of "fact" from "value," and his relegation of law to the realm of "fact," led him to overlook entirely the importance of legal values in two of his best known socio-historical studies, *The Protestant Ethic and the Spirit of Capitalism* and *The City*. In the background of his entire sociology of law was an oversimplified historiography in which the history of law in the West was viewed as a progression from a "feudal," "traditional," "personal" type to a "capitalist," "formal-rational," and "bureaucratic" type, with the prospect of an emerging "socialist," "substantively rational" type.

Weber's background in the law

Max Weber was born into a family that "was steeped in the intellectual culture of the law."[2] His father was a lawyer as well as a politician, who served as a member of the National Liberal Party in the German *Reichstag*

---

[1] The question whether Weber can be counted a historian has been addressed by Raoul C. van Caenegem, "Max Weber: Historian and Sociologist," in R. C. van Caenegem, *Legal History: A European Perspective*, London: The Hambledon Press, 1991. Van Caenegem answers the question by stating that in his first period of scholarship Weber was a legal historian, in his second a cultural historian, and in his third a sociologist. See also Jürgen Kocka, *Max Weber, Der Historiker*, Göttingen: Vandenhoeck & Ruprecht, 1986. Kocka himself, in a chapter entitled "Max Webers Bedeutung für die Geschichtswissenschaft," denies Weber the status of a professional historian, although he concedes his importance for the development of the historical discipline. Neither of these works treats in detail Weber's uses of legal history.

[2] Stephen P. Turner and Regis A. Factor, *Max Weber: The Lawyer as Social Thinker*, London: Routledge & Kegan Paul, 1994, p. 3.

HAROLD J. BERMAN AND CHARLES J. REID, JR.

from 1872 to 1884. The son pursued a legal education from the time he
first matriculated at Heidelberg University in 1882, where, in his first
semester, he enrolled in a course entitled *Roman Law: Pandects and
Institutes*.[3] He later continued his law studies at the University of Berlin,
under the tutelage of some of the leading lights of the late nineteenth-
century German legal academy. His mother wrote:

> He is taking German Civil Law with Beseler, "whose sound scholarship
> makes up for the dryness of his lectures," International Law with Aegidi,
> German Constitutional Law and Prussian Administrative Law with Gneist,
> and History of German Law with Brunner and Gierke. In addition, he
> attended Mommsen's and Treitschke's lectures on history.[4]

After earning his degree in law in 1886, Weber passed the examination
for *Referendar* and commenced the practice of law while also pursuing
advanced legal studies at the University of Berlin. He subsequently completed a doctoral dissertation, *Zur Geschichte der Handelsgesellschaft im
Mittelalter* ("On the History of the Trading Company in the Middle
Ages"), a work in both legal and economic history supervised by Theodor
Mommsen, among others, and – in accord with German university custom
– immediately embarked upon his *Habilitationsschrift*, an analysis of land
distribution and agrarian practices in imperial Rome.[5]

By 1892, at the age of twenty-eight, Weber had apparently tired of the
practice of the law. He had found himself "performing various clerical
tasks of an essentially mechanical nature,"[6] and his failure to win a
competition for appointment to a legal position in the City of Bremen led
him to decide upon a career in the legal academy.[7] This much had been
predicted for him by his mother, who had written in 1886, while Max was
preparing for his *Referendar's* examination: "I think his other interests will
prevail over this dry-as-dust legal stuff . . . He is by no means practical and
organized enough in his everyday doings to be an official; also, he has
always been more interested in the historical development of the law than
in its application."[8]

Weber was certified to teach Roman, German, and commercial law in
1892, and secured an appointment at the University of Berlin later that
same year, where he taught each of these subjects at different times. In

[3] Marianne Weber, *Max Weber: A Biography*, trans. Harry Zohn, New York: John Wiley and
Sons, 1975, p. 65.
[4] Letter of Helene Weber, reproduced in Marianne Weber, *Max Weber*, pp. 95–96.
[5] *Ibid.*, pp. 113–114, 115.
[6] Anthony Kronman, *Max Weber*, Stanford, CA: Stanford University Press, 1983, p. 190.
[7] Turner and Factor, *Max Weber*, p. 4.
[8] Letter of Helene Weber, reproduced in Marianne Weber, *Max Weber*, p. 106.

1894, however, he left the legal academy to take a chaired position at the University of Freiburg, where he taught political economy, and, in 1896, he accepted a professorship of economics at the University of Heidelberg. It may be conjectured that at the age of thirty Weber had lost interest in both the practice and the teaching of law, although he remained deeply committed to resolving basic questions about the nature and social functions of law as they were revealed in history.[9]

Weber's ideal types of legal order

In evaluating Max Weber's scattered but prolific writings on the history of law, it must be stressed at the outset that he wrote not primarily as an historian or as a lawyer, although he was well versed in both fields, but rather as a sociologist, drawing heavily, however, on historical examples taken from various types of legal systems. Indeed, at the outset of the treatment of law in his *Economy and Society*, Weber distinguishes between sociology and history, stating that "it is with . . . *types* of conduct that sociology is concerned, in contrast with history, which is interested in the causal connection of important, i.e., fateful *single* events."[10]

Weber classified law into four categories, based on the ways in which "legitimate validity" can be ascribed to a legal order by those who participate in it. The following is his succinct statement of the four "ideal types," as he called them, of legal order:

> The order can be recognized as legitimate, *first*, by virtue of tradition: valid is that which has always been. *Second*, the order may be treated as legitimate by virtue of affectual, especially emotional, faith; this situation occurs especially in the case of the newly revealed or the exemplary. *Third*, the order may be treated as legitimate by virtue of value-rational faith: valid is that which has been deduced as absolutely demanded. *Fourth*, legitimacy can be ascribed to an order by virtue of positive enactment of recognized *legality*. Such legality can be regarded as legitimate either (a) because the enactment has been agreed upon by all those who are concerned; or (b) by virtue of imposition by a domination of human beings over human beings which is treated as legitimate and meets with acquiescence.[11]

---

[9] At Heidelberg, Weber suffered a long period of crisis and stress, and he seems to have produced no major writings between 1896 and 1904. His works on the sociology of law, written for the most part after 1908, are collected chiefly in *E&S*, published posthumously.

[10] *Max Weber on Law in Economy and Society*, ed. Max Rheinstein, Cambridge, MA: Harvard University Press, 1954, p. 2 (emphasis in original).

[11] *Ibid.*, p. 8.

Tradition, Weber continues, is "the oldest and most universally found type of orders . . ."[12] Traditional authority is grounded on the normativity sometimes ascribed to institutions whose origins and development are lost in the mists of an essentially static past. Crucial to Weber is the way in which the traditional ruler's authority is exercised:

> The person exercising authority is not a "[bureaucratic] superior," but a "personal chief." His administrative staff does not consist primarily of officials, but of personal retainers. Those subject to authority are not "members" of an association, but are either traditional "comrades" or his subjects. What determines the relations of the administrative staff to the chief is not the impersonal obligations of office, but personal loyalty to the chief. Obedience is not owed to enacted rules, but to the person who occupies a position of authority by tradition or who has been chosen for such a position on a traditional basis. (*TSEO* 341)

Weber associated his second ideal type of legitimacy with religious belief. It is legitimacy "enjoying prophetical sanction" and is based "upon the faith in the . . . prophet."[13] In extreme form, this sort of legitimacy gives rise to the charismatic authority of singular figures who are "treated as endowed with supernatural, superhuman, or at least specifically exceptional powers or qualities" (*TSEO* 358). It is the essence of the charismatic figure to "claim the right to break through all existing normative structures."[14] Ultimately, however, with the passing away of a given prophetic or apostolic age, charismatic authority becomes "routinized" (*TSEO* 363–373).

> If it is not to remain a purely transitory phenomenon, but [is] to take on the character of a permanent relationship forming a stable community of disciples or a band of followers or a party organization or any sort of political or hierocratic organization, it is necessary for the character of charismatic authority to become radically changed . . . [Charismatic authority] cannot remain stable, but becomes either traditionalized or routinized, or a combination of both. (*TSEO* 364)

Weber did not associate his third ideal type, legitimacy based on "value-rational" – in German, *Wertrational*, usually translated "substantively rational" – faith, with any legal order that had ever existed in the past. We therefore postpone discussion of it until after consideration of his fourth ideal type, in which legitimacy is grounded in positive "enactment," or, as he

---

[12] *Ibid.*   [13] *Max Weber on Law in Economy and Society*, p. 8.
[14] Martin E. Spencer, "Weber on Legitimate Norms and Authority," *British Journal of Sociology*, 21 (1970): pp. 124–125. As Weber puts it: "From a substantive point of view, every charismatic authority would have to subscribe to the proposition, 'It is written . . . but I say unto you . . .'" See *TSEO* 361.

states, "acquiescence in enactments which are formally correct and which have been made in the customary manner." Such "legal-rational," or "formal-rational," authority, he writes, is "the most common form of legitimacy" found in contemporary western society.[15] It has as its basis not "the eternal yesterday" of tradition, but "a consistent system of abstract rules which have been intentionally established," that is, "a system of consciously made *rational* rules" (*E&S* 217, 954). By the same token, legal-rational, or formal-rational, authority differs also from authority based on affectual or charismatic foundations. "Insofar as they obey a 'person in authority,' the members of a legal-rational organization 'do not owe this obedience to him as an individual, but to the impersonal order.' This is true even of the highest official in such an organization to the extent that he, too, is subject to the law."[16] Because of its impersonal nature, formal-rational authority was closely associated by Weber with the development of modern bureaucracy, which "operates in a special sense *sine ira et studio*" and "without regard to person" in order to ensure the "calculability of rules."[17]

In contrast to the formal-rational type of legal order, Weber's substantively rational legal order accords predominance to ethical considerations, utility, expediency, and public policy.[18] This was an even more "ideal" type of legal order than the others, for the others all have had some reflection in the "real" legal orders of one or another society, while the substantively rational type was, for Weber, almost entirely a thing of the future,[19] which he saw emerging in the "anti-formalist" tendencies of contemporary legal

---

[15] *Max Weber on Law in Economy and Society*, p. 9.

[16] Kronman, *Max Weber*, p. 46 (quoting Weber, *E&S*, p. 218).

[17] *Max Weber on Law in Economy and Society*, pp. 351 and 350.

[18] *Ibid.*, pp. 63–64. Weber wrote that "the purest type of value-rational validity is represented by natural law ... Its propositions must be distinguished from those of revealed, of enacted, and of traditional law": *ibid.*, pp. 8–9. He does not, however, develop this point, and does not compare his concept of natural law with the natural-law concepts of Greek philosophy, Roman law, or the Christian or humanist west.

[19] Indeed, in a later discussion of the types of legal order he makes no mention of the *Wertrational* type. He there states that "every domination" needs "self-justification through appealing to the principles of its legitimation. Of such ultimate principles there are only three: The 'validity' of the power of command may be expressed first in a system of consciously made *rational* rules ... The validity of a power of a command can also rest, however, upon *personal authority* [which can in turn be] founded upon the sacredness of *tradition* [or] the belief in [the] *charisma* [of a] savior, a prophet, or a hero." Each of these types of legal order then corresponds to the "three possible types of legitimation," which find their "typical expression" respectively in "*bureaucracy*," "*patriarchalism*," and the "authority of a *concrete individual*": *Max Weber on Law in Economy and Society*, pp. 336–337 (emphasis in original).

development,[20] and in a future "social" or "socialist" law that was taking shape in his own time.[21]

In his many writings, Weber draws abundantly on historical examples of the first, second, and fourth of these ideal types of legal order in illustrating his sociological theses, although he asserts that the ideal types of legal order do not as such have exact analogues "in historical reality." This point has been lost on many readers of Weber because he did identify modern Western legal systems with the "formal-rational" type. Nevertheless, his basic thesis was that all legal systems tend to combine the various types. "The forms of domination occurring in historical reality," he wrote, "constitute combinations, mixtures, adaptations, or modifications of these pure types."[22]

Weber's use of legal history

Max Weber's legal history is primarily a search for examples of laws and legal institutions that correspond to the various ideal types which he attributes to the law.[23] In the attempt, he covers a vast expanse of territory, comparing, for instance, Hindu law to Western ecclesiastical law, the German *Sachsenspiegel*, and Islamic and Judaic practices,[24] and, elsewhere, Islamic law to ancient Roman juristic practice.[25] He often draws connections among legal systems that are remote from one another geographically

---

[20] *Ibid.*, p. 303.

[21] Weber did not view such a prospect optimistically. He saw the danger that "[a] (democratically) socialist order" that "rejects coercion" might in fact, if realized, operate by "agreed abstract laws" that would "nonetheless in [their] practical effects facilitate a quantitative and qualitative increase not only of coercion in general but quite specifically of authoritarian coercion" (*ibid.*, pp. 190–191). Elsewhere, Weber subjected to severe criticism as "value-irrationalism" the challenge to legal formalism by proponents of "a 'social law' . . . based upon emotionally colored ethical postulates such as justice or human dignity" and the appeal to "norms which . . . claim as [their] legitimation substantive justice rather than formal legality" (*ibid.*, pp. 308–309, 311–313). Writing in 1916, Weber sharply attacked the Communist view of socialism as historically and economically mistaken, and posed as an alternative the development of a "collective economy" by "a gradual process of evolution." See Max Weber, "Socialism," in *Max Weber: Selections in Translation*, ed. W. G. Runciman, trans. E. Matthews, Cambridge: Cambridge University Press, 1978, pp. 251–262.

[22] *Max Weber on Law in Economy and Society*, pp. 336–337.

[23] Weber at one point does propose in the most general terms a theory of legal development from charismatic law to traditional law to formal-rational law (*ibid.*, p. 303). But he follows this by stating that "[s]ince we are here concerned only with the most general lines of development, we shall ignore the fact that in historical reality the theoretically constructed stages of rationalization have not everywhere followed in the sequence which we have just outlined, even if we ignore the world outside the Occident" (*ibid.*, p. 304).

[24] *Ibid.*, pp. 208–209.   [25] *Ibid.*, pp. 240–241.

and chronologically, in order to illustrate a sociological argument. This practice is apparent, for instance, in his treatment of the tension inherent in modern, westernized formal-rational legal systems between the freedom required for the successful operation of modern capitalist enterprise and survivals of earlier models of charismatic justice, called by Weber "khadi-justice:"[26]

> Above all, those in possession of economic power look upon a formal rational administration of justice as a guarantee of "freedom," a value which is repudiated not only by theocratic or patriarchal-authoritarian groups but, under certain conditions, also by democratic groups. Formal justice and the "freedom" which it guarantees are indeed rejected by all groups ideologically interested in substantive justice. Such groups are better served by khadi-justice than by the formal type. The popular justice of the direct Attic democracy, for example, was decidedly a form of khadi-justice. Modern trial by jury, too, is frequently khadi-justice in actual practice . . . Quite generally, in all forms of popular justice decisions are reached on the basis of concrete, ethical or political considerations or of feelings oriented toward social justice. The latter type of justice prevailed particularly in Athens, but it can be found even today. In this respect, there are similar tendencies displayed by popular democracy on the one hand, and the authoritarian power of theocracy or of patriarchal monarchs on the other.[27]

This is not to say that Weber pays no heed at all to the structure or the development of particular legal systems, but rather that his understanding of legal history is distorted by his attempt to demonstrate the operation of certain pre-existing models by reference to historical sources. His treatment of the canon law of the Roman Catholic Church and of the English common law both illustrate this point. Thus he classifies the canon law as

---

[26] The khadis were judges of the religious courts of Islam, who, in Weber's view, possessed absolute discretion to render substantive justice in the case before them: "Their opinions are authoritative, but they also vary from person to person; like the opinions of oracles, they are given without any statement of rational reasons. Thus they actually increase the irrationality of the sacred law rather than contribute, however slightly, to its rationalization" (*ibid.*, p. 241). More recent studies have challenged this view of the khadi's discretionary authority. See Noel J. Coulson, *Conflicts and Tensions in Islamic Jurisprudence*, Chicago: University of Chicago Press, 1969, pp. 63–64, 69.

[27] *Max Weber on Law in Economy and Society*, p. 229. Another example of this sort of juxtaposition is found at pp. 224–225 of Rheinstein's edition: "To the extent to which the rationality of the organization of authority increased, irrational forms of procedure were eliminated and the substantive law was systematized, i.e., the law as a whole was rationalized. This process occurred, for instance, in antiquity in the *jus honorarium* and the praetorian remedies, in the capitularies of the Frankish kings, in the procedural innovations of the English Kings and Lords Chancellor, or in the inquisitorial procedure of the Catholic Church." Weber's point here is not to illuminate the development of the law, but to use changes in the law to illuminate a sociological pattern, the rationalization of authority.

sacred law, but assigns to it "a relatively special position with reference to all other systems of sacred law," chiefly because of the progress it had made toward attaining a formal-rational structure. He attributes the canon law's commitment to formal rationality partly to the relationship it had developed even during late antiquity with the Roman law, but chiefly to its transformation in the late eleventh century during the pontificate of Pope Gregory VII, when "the Church's functionaries were holders of rationally defined bureaucratic offices."[28]

Although these cryptic insights into the history of the canon law are valuable, Weber understates the enduring significance of the canon law for the development of Western legal concepts and institutions. He acknowledges that the canon law of corporations played a role in the growth of Western rights theories, although he never develops this insight.[29] Elsewhere he states that "apart from a few particular institutions, the main influence of the canon law lay in the field of procedure," where the canonists bequeathed to the West the inquisitorial method of criminal procedure.[30] His underestimation of the very substantial influence of the canon law on secular legal systems as a whole reflected the prevailing view of the legal historians of his time, a view that has only been convincingly refuted in recent decades, but one might have expected him to entertain suspicions, at least, of its validity.

Weber's treatment of the English common law is similarly sophisticated but abbreviated and ultimately flawed. He accepts the prevailing view of his time that modern English law is essentially a continuation of medieval English law, and concludes that therefore it is not a "formal-rational" type of law but an amalgam of traditional and charismatic elements whose "legal rationality is essentially lower than, and of a type different from, that of continental Europe" (*E&S* 890).[31] Thus he misses the progressive element in the English doctrine of precedent. He also misses the "formal-rational" element in the English emphasis on analogy of cases, preferring to see at work in the common-law courts not the close analysis of comparable judicial decisions in order to extract the principles and rule implicit in them, but the personal authority of powerful, charismatic judges such as Lord Mansfield. He states that "up

---

[28] *Ibid.*, pp. 250, 252. Rheinstein's notes make it clear that Weber is here referring to the reform initiated by Pope Gregory VII: *ibid.*, p. 251, note 104. On the importance of Pope Gregory VII to the origin of the western legal tradition, see Harold J. Berman, *Law and Revolution: The Origins of the Western Legal Tradition*, Cambridge, MA: Harvard University Press, 1983, pp. 85–119.

[29] *Max Weber on Law in Economy and Society*, pp. 172–174.   [30] *Ibid.*, p. 254.

[31] Cf. *FMW*, p. 217: "Even today in England . . . a broad substratum of justice is actually Kadi-justice to an extent that is hardly conceivable on the Continent."

to the recent past, and at any rate up to the time of Austin, there was practically no English legal science that would have merited the name of 'learning' in the continental sense" (*E&S* 890), entirely overlooking comprehensive analytical treatises on English law such as those of Matthew Hale and William Blackstone.[32]

Weber's unhistorical use of legal history is also apparent in his treatment of other great legal systems of the world. Roman law, canon law, Jewish law, Germanic law, Hindu law, Buddhist law, and Chinese law all figure prominently in different parts of Weber's scholarship. However, he never analyzes these systems on their own terms, but only draws on them as evidence for his social theories. Canon law is useful for the way it illustrates formal-rational legal reasoning in the context of religious law, while the English law illustrates the tenacity with which traditional methods of legislative enactment and the guild-style of legal education survived "up to the threshold of modern times." A historically sensitive portrait of these and other systems is never presented.

One must distinguish, however, Weber's general sociology of law from his sociology of western law, which he treated somewhat more systematically and whose historical development, he stated, had both a unique character and "universal significance and validity" (*GARS* 1). Only the Occident, he declared, experienced a fully developed system of tribal "folk" justice in the early middle ages, a subsequent legal regulation of status groups under feudalism, constitutional controls over princely power in the sixteenth, seventeenth, and eighteenth centuries, and successive receptions of Roman law. For Weber, Western feudalism, the medieval western city, and other features of "traditional" medieval Western society contained within themselves forces that were lacking in the traditional societies of other world cultures, forces which were ultimately capable of transforming the West. "All these events . . . have only the remotest analogies elsewhere

---

[32] See Harold J. Berman and Charles J. Reid, Jr., "The Transformation of English Legal Science: From Hale to Blackstone," *Emory Law Journal*, 45 (1996), pp. 437–522. Students of Weber have also been troubled by the fact that Weber declares England to be the first home of capitalism in the seventeenth and eighteenth centuries but at the same time characterizes English law as lacking the formal-rational character that is congenial to capitalism. See David Trubeck, "Max Weber on Law and the Rise of Capitalism," *Wisconsin Law Review* (1972), pp. 720, 746–748; and Alan Hunt, *The Sociological Movement in Law*, Philadelphia, PA: Temple University Press, 1978, pp. 122–128 (discussing the "England problem"). In challenging this reading of Weber, Sally Ewing cites several places in which Weber recognizes that the English empirical method may give greater calculability and, in that sense, greater rationality to law than the more formal continental codifications. See Sally Ewing, "Formal Justice and the Spirit of Capitalism: Max Weber's Sociology of Law," *Law and Society Review*, 21 (1987), pp. 487–512, especially 494–497.

in the world," he wrote. "For this reason, the stage of decisively shaping law by trained legal specialists has not been fully reached anywhere outside the Occident."[33]

In addition, Weber's sociology of law led him to the important historical insight that the distinctive thought-processes of the English common law, as contrasted with the thought-processes of other Western legal systems, grew out of the needs and habits of the English legal profession, which as late as the sixteenth and seventeenth centuries retained the character of a medieval guild. He stresses the fact that by the sixteenth century the English common lawyers formed a hierarchy, with sergeants at the top, who alone were empowered to plead cases in the common-law courts and from among whom were selected the judges of those courts. The lower rungs of the hierarchy were occupied by "attorneys" or "solicitors" who managed more routine legal transactions (*E&S* 785–786). He correctly saw in the method of legal education, apprenticeship, and membership of the English common lawyers in the Inns of Court a key to the important role of lawyers' guilds in preserving the characteristically English empirical method of legal reasoning, as contrasted with the more deductive and abstract method of legal reasoning cultivated in the law faculties of German and other European universities. The latter method, in Weber's theory, is appropriate in a bureaucratic legal system based on a coherent body of objective principles and rules. The former method, in his view, was appropriate in a traditional system of precedent that only "moves from the particular to the particular" (*E&S* 787). Thus he failed to see that the empirical method, in law as in the natural sciences, moves beyond particulars to the general principles which they embody.

The neglect of legal history In *The Protestant Ethic* and *The City*

Although in developing his sociological theories Weber drew heavily on examples of various legal institutions at various periods of the history of various societies, he also, in certain of his socio-historical works, neglected to draw on legal developments, and from this neglect something can be learned of his conception of legal history and, more generally, of law and of the role of law in society. Two such works are *The Protestant Ethic and the Spirit of Capitalism*, in which not seventeenth-century capitalism but rather its animating spirit is attributed to a religious ethic which, as he described it, differs sharply from what we know of its accompanying legal ethic; and *The City*, in which the origins of the Western "full urban community" are

---

[33] *Max Weber on Law in Economy and Society*, p. 304.

traced to certain conditions without, once again, any reference to legal concepts and legal values.

The Protestant Ethic and the Spirit of Capitalism

For Weber, the Protestant ethic refers to the set of moral prescriptions which he understood to be grounded in Calvinist predestinarianism, while the spirit of capitalism refers to a set of practices which has as its *summum bonum* "the earning of more and more money, combined with the strict avoidance of all spontaneous enjoyment of life . . ."(*E&S* 53).[34]

It was Weber's thesis that a new attitude toward money and economic accumulation emerged in the late sixteenth and seventeenth centuries. "Time is money . . . Money is of the prolific, generating nature. Money can beget money, and its offspring can beget more, and so on . . . He that kills a breeding sow, destroys all her offspring down to the thousandth generation. He that murders a crown, destroys all that it might have produced, even scores of pounds" (*E&S* 48–49).[35] These and other such maxims of that period are taken by Weber as representing a fundamentally new approach to the question of the importance of economic activity.

The principal source of this ethos, in Weber's view, was the predestinarian theology of John Calvin. Calvin deduced from Scripture "that only a small proportion of men are chosen for eternal grace . . ." Everyone else will be forever damned. "To assume that human merit or guilt play a part in determining this destiny would be to think of God's absolutely free decrees . . . as subject to change by human influence, an impossible contradiction" (*E&S* 103). Calvin avoided an obvious logical consequence of this doctrine – earthly passivity on the part of the believer – by emphasizing that all believers had a spiritual calling to work in the world for its ultimate improvement. It was a necessary sign of one's salvation, of one's inner grace, that one had diligently fulfilled his calling, since the entire social order existed to advance the greater glory of God (*E&S* 108). Indeed, one's whole life had to be rigorously organized to fulfill this calling: "The God of Calvinism demanded of His believers not single good works, but a life of good works combined into a system" (*E&S* 117). Weber called this "asceticism," by which he meant the individual's commitment to self-discipline, austerity, and hard work (*E&S* 53–54,

---

[34] The original German title was *Die protestantische Ethik und der "Geist" des Kapitalismus*, published in two parts in 1904 and 1905. The quotation marks around the word "Spirit" (*Geist*) were omitted from the English translation.

[35] Quoting Benjamin Franklin.

193–194).[36] He distinguished, however, the "other-worldly" asceticism of monastic orders that renounce the earthly city from Calvinist "inner-worldly" asceticism which links salvation of the soul with rational and dispassionate pursuit of material success.

The result of this theology, according to Weber, was an intense individual loneliness, as frail, finite beings were forced to confront the eternal and omnipotent God:

> In its extreme inhumanity this doctrine must have had one consequence . . .
> That was a feeling of unprecedented inner loneliness of the single individual.
> In what was for the man of the Reformation the most important thing in life,
> his eternal salvation, he was forced to follow his path alone to meet a destiny
> which had been decreed for him from eternity. No one could help him. No
> priest, . . . no sacraments . . . no church . . . Finally even, no God. (E&S 104)

It was, then, according to Weber, the obsessive desire continually to prove to oneself and to the community that one is a member of the elect that led the English Calvinists of the seventeenth and eighteenth centuries not only to advance their economic interests with an enthusiasm not previously seen on the world stage but also to create the belief system that supports the social structures of modern capitalism.

Omitted from this history is any reference to the legal institutions that prevailed in the same societies that came under Calvinist influence – especially England and Holland. This omission may be attributed in part to Weber's view that English law was "traditional" and "charismatic" and did not fit in either with the Protestant ethic or with the spirit of capitalism. In addition, however, his sharp distinction between "fact and "value," and his consignment of law to the realm of "fact," led him to disregard the "values" that are inherent in legal institutions.[37] In truth, his thesis is not only not supported but is refuted by seventeenth-century developments in English law, which reflected not an individualist but a communitarian ethic and spirit – indeed, a communitarian ethic and spirit that are at least as firmly rooted in Calvinist Protestantism as its "inner-worldly asceticism."

A striking example is the emergence of the joint-stock company as a device for bringing together a group of prominent persons to constitute a

---

[36] Although Weber placed great stress on the influence of the Calvinist doctrine of predestination, he also traced "asceticism" to the Protestant doctrine of "calling," or "vocation," which was shared by Lutherans and Calvinists alike.

[37] *Max Weber on Law in Economy and Society*, pp. 11–14 (distinguishing between law as fact and law as value and accepting the former as the subject-matter of his study). Cf. John M. Finnis, "On 'Positivism' and 'Legal Rational Authority,'" *Oxford Journal of Legal Studies*, 5 (1985), p. 85 (demonstrating that Weber's fact–value distinction was the product of his neo-Kantian belief that values rest ultimately on non-rational grounds, while facts are capable of rational verification).

business or charitable enterprise, on the one hand, and a large number of shareholders to raise the capital needed to finance it, on the other. In his analysis of the spirit of capitalism, Weber did not take account of the communitarian character of such important seventeenth-century joint-stock companies as overseas trading enterprises, which were designed not only to make a profit but also to serve public causes. An example is the 1692 Act of Parliament granting a corporate charter to a Company of Merchants of London to carry on trade with Greenland, which recited the great importance of such trade, how it had fallen into the hands of other nations, and the need to regain it by the joint efforts of many persons.[38] Similar recitals of a public purpose marked the corporate charters of other joint-stock companies. These were, to be sure, entrepreneurial activities intended to be profitable to the shareholders, and the new corporate form permitted venturers to limit their risks to the proportion of their subscriptions to the jointly held stock. At the same time, the enterprise depended on the close cooperation of many like-minded people, who were motivated partly by a desire to participate with others in a joint venture serving a public cause.

Nothing is more symbolic of the "spirit of capitalism" in England in the late seventeenth century than the creation of the joint-stock company called the Bank of England, which was founded by Act of Parliament in 1694 principally in order to finance the Government's war against France. Under the Act, Commissioners were appointed by the Crown to receive subscriptions, and the Crown was empowered to incorporate "subscribers and contributors, their heirs, successors, or assigns, to be one body politick and corporate . . ."[39] Shareholders were required to identify their collective interests with the welfare of the English economy. Some 1,300 persons subscribed £1,200,000 to support the war – and to receive profits from increases in the value of their shares, which were backed in part by Government subsidies from customs duties. Subscribers included leading merchants and landed gentry, amongst whom were many members of

---

[38] On the act incorporating the Greenland Company, see Samuel Williston, "History of the Law of Business Corporations before 1800," *Harvard Law Review*, 2 (1888), pp. 105–122, at 111. The economic and legal history of the English joint-stock company has been thoroughly canvassed in the existing literature. See William Robert Scott, *The Constitution and Finance of English, Scottish, and Irish Joint-Stock Companies to 1720*, 3 vols., Gloucester, MA: Peter Smith, 1968 [1912]. See also Frank Evans, "The Evolution of the English Joint-Stock Limited Trading Company," *Columbia Law Review*, 8 (1908), pp. 339–361, 461–480. Unfortunately, these works do not discuss, but take for granted, the strong communitarian character – and philosophy – of this form of economic and legal enterprise.

[39] 5 & 6 William & Mary c. 20 (1694).

Parliament. Of the first twenty-six members of the Court of Directors, six subsequently became Lord Mayors of London. The by-laws of the Bank required the Court of Directors to meet every week and the General Court of the shareholders to meet twice a year "for considering the general state and condition of this Corporation and for the making of dividends . . . according to their several shares."[40]

The late seventeenth century also witnessed the creation of another important legal institution which served communitarian as well as private purposes, namely, the modern law of trusts.[41] Like the joint-stock company, the trust device facilitated the formation of business and charitable associations embracing numerous members in common endeavors.

These examples should suffice to establish that had Weber considered legal developments in seventeenth-century England, the thesis of the *Protestant Ethic and the Spirit of Capitalism* would have had to be quite different. When one looks at the lawyers and the institutions they were creating, one does not see ascetic individualists trembling before the prospect of ultimate damnation or salvation. Rather, one sees community-minded men creating communitarian legal institutions such as joint-stock companies, bank credits, and the trust device. This communitarianism, involving large-scale cooperation among landed gentry and merchant elites, itself had Calvinist roots.[42] The spirit of capitalism, to the extent that it

---

[40] See John Giuseppi, *The Bank of England: A History from its Foundation in 1694*, London: Evans Brothers, Ltd., 1966, pp. 9–14 (discussing the origins of the Bank and the social backgrounds of its first investors and directors); *Rules, Orders, and By-Laws for the Good Government of the Corporation of the Governor and Company of the Bank of England*, reprinted in *Bank of England: Selected Tracts, 1694–1804*, Farnborough, Hants: Gregg International Publishers, Ltd., 1968, p. 11 (on the weekly meetings of the Court of Directors) and p. 19 (on the biennial meetings of the General Court of shareholders). As in the case of the joint-stock company, so in the case of banking and other forms of crediting, there exists a large economic and legal literature which traces the origins of the modern forms of these institutions to the latter half of the seventeenth century but which takes for granted, without stressing, their strong communitarian character. See, for instance, Frank T. Melton, *Sir Robert Clayton and the Origins of English Deposit Banking, 1658–1685*, Cambridge: Cambridge University Press, 1986; P. G. M. Dickson, *The Financial Revolution in England: A Study in the Development of Public Credit, 1688–1756*, London: Macmillan, 1967; and James Steven Rogers, *The Early History of Bills and Notes: A Study of the Origins of Anglo-American Commercial Law*, Cambridge: Cambridge University Press, 1995.

[41] On this development, see Charles J. Reid, Jr., "The Seventeenth-Century Revolution in the English Land Law," *Cleveland State Law Review*, 43 (1995), pp. 221–302, at 288–296, and authorities cited therein.

[42] See Harold J. Berman, "Law and Belief in Three Revolutions," *Valparaiso Law Review*, 18 (1984), pp. 569, 604–613 (substantially reprinted in Harold J. Berman, *Faith and Order: The Reconciliation of Law and Religion*, Atlanta, GA: The Scholars Press, 1993, pp. 116–125).

was a seventeenth- and early eighteenth-century phenomenon, was less the product of "asceticism" than what was called at the time "public spirit,"[43] which, in turn, reflected not the "individualist" doctrines of predestination and calling, but the "collectivist" Calvinist doctrines of covenant and covenanted communities.[44]

The City

A second example of Weber's neglect of the role of law in the formation of belief-systems – its role in fusing "fact" and "value" – is found in his urban sociology, in which he starts with an analysis of the structural unity of the Western city at the time of its historical origins in the eleventh to thirteenth centuries. Although the rudiments of theWestern type of city, he writes, may occasionally be found in other cultures, "an urban 'community' in the full meaning of the word appears only in the Occident." He then defines "a full urban community" as a settlement engaged predominantly in commercial relations in which there are five constituent elements: a fortification, a market, a court applying an at least partially autonomous law, a form of association related to these features, and at least partial political autonomy under an administration in whose election the burghers participate (C 54–55). Such a peculiar system of forces, according to Weber, could only appear under special conditions and at a particular time, namely, late medieval Europe.

Here Weber does mention law as a necessary element in the integrated structure of the city, but again, as in his analysis of the relation of the Protestant ethic to the spirit of capitalism, he sees law, as he sees a fortification or a market, as a "fact" and fails to examine the "values" that are represented in law in order to determine how those values contributed not only to the sense of community but also to the community's ongoing development, its consciousness of its ongoing history.

In addition, Weber is stuck, here, with his static conception of tradition. In his general sociology, he defines a "traditional society" as one in which legitimacy is based on "the sanctity of age-old rules and powers," and "traditional law" as law "determined by ingrained habituation." And in his general historiography, he defines the "middle ages" as a traditional society with a traditional body of law derived from political power (*Herrschaft*).

---

[43] On the seventeenth-century English concept of public spirit, see classically Eugen Rosenstock-Huessy, *Out of Revolution: The Autobiography of Western Man*, Providence, RI: Berg Publishers, 1993 [1938], pp. 319–322.

[44] See John Witte, Jr., "'Blest Be the Ties that Bind': Covenant and Community in Puritan Thought," *Emory Law Journal*, 36 (1987), pp. 579–601.

But in fact the law of the new Western urban communities of the late eleventh, twelfth, and thirteenth centuries was not "traditional law" in Weber's sense, but a new law, a dynamic law, a law that balanced continuity with change. And indeed, the most striking and distinctive characteristic of the new Western urban community was its historical consciousness – its consciousness of its own historical movement from past to future, its sense of its own ongoing, developing character as a community or polity. The constituent elements of Weber's full urban community listed above reflect its structural integration but they do not account for its development in time. They do not explain how or why the twelfth-century city developed into the city of the sixteenth and twentieth centuries, many of whose features are continuous with those of the twelfth century while others are substantially different.[45]

If Weber had written a book not on "the Protestant Reformation" but on "the Roman Catholic Reformation and the Rise of the City," he could have shown that what was called in the late eleventh and twelfth centuries "the Gregorian Reformation" (after Pope Gregory VII) had resulted in the creation of new systems of ecclesiastical and secular law, including, in the secular sphere, new systems of urban and royal law, and that those systems embodied new values, including a new sense of the historicity of law, understood as law's capacity to maintain continuity with the past by adapting tradition to new situations. The Western legal "tradition," which originated at that time, was not a tradition in the Weberian sense, which refers only to the past and not to an ongoing continuity from past to future. Weber's tradition is what Jaroslav Pelikan has called traditional*ism* – "the dead faith of the living" as contrasted with "the living faith of the dead."[46] It is historicism, not historicity. It is partly because Weber neglected the dynamics of traditional law in the west that he underestimated the role of law in the revolutionary formation and gradual evolution of the Western city.

Conclusion

From an analytical point of view, Weber's distinctions between four types of authority, with their four types of law, are brilliant: traditional law, based on historicism; charismatic law, based on inspiration; formal-rational

---

[45] See Harold J. Berman, "Some False Premises of Max Weber's Sociology of Law," *Washington University Law Quarterly*, 65 (1987), pp. 758–770 and the literature cited therein (substantially reprinted in Berman, *Faith and Order*, pp. 239–250).

[46] Jaroslav Pelikan, *The Vindication of Tradition*, New Haven, CT: Yale University Press, 1984, p. 65.

law, based on the logical consistency of rules; and substantively rational law, based on fairness and equity. Weber defines them so narrowly, however, that on the surface they appear to be mutually exclusive. In fact the western legal tradition, as it has developed since the late eleventh century, has combined, and therefore transformed, all four of these "ideal" types. Both the "spirit of capitalism" and the "full urban community" owe their origins and their subsequent development to that combination.

Perhaps Weber would agree with this criticism. Perhaps he even said it somewhere. But if so, it remains obscured by his failure to develop a theory of the interaction of these four dimensions of the Western legal tradition. That failure may have been due to the very concept of an ideal-type, which by definition does not correspond to historical reality. It may have also been due to Weber's conflicting belief that the ideal type of formal-rational law had in fact become a historical reality and had triumphed in the West and was doomed by its identification with capitalism.

Finally, Weber's historiography of Occidental law postulated that in the West, starting in the sixteenth century, an earlier "medieval," "feudal," "traditional" type of law was gradually superseded by a "modern," "capitalist," "formal-rational" type of law. To be sure, this conception was contradicted by some of his own historical insights – for instance, that the canon law of the "medieval" Roman Catholic Church had very strong "modern" and "formal-rational" elements, and that the "modern" city had deep roots in the heyday of "feudalism." Nevertheless, Weber for the most part associated "formal-rational" law with the bureaucratic state, and both with the emergence of Protestantism, and all three with the rise of capitalism; and "traditional" law with "patriarchal" ecclesiastical and royal power, and both with Roman Catholicism, and all three with feudalism. This perspective, which came to be very widely shared in the period between the two world wars, was not only congenial to the conventional nationalist historiography of the late nineteenth and early twentieth centuries, but also to the socialist historiography which postulated an historical evolution from feudalism to capitalism to socialism. Only in the last decades of the twentieth century has its ideological character been exposed and its accuracy challenged.

12

WILFRIED NIPPEL

From agrarian history to cross-cultural comparisons: Weber on Greco-Roman antiquity

Weber devoted a large part of his early work to the study of Greco-Roman antiquity. He published a book on Roman agrarian history,[1] an article on the social causes of the decline of ancient culture,[2] surveys of the agrarian history of ancient civilizations (*Agrarverhältnisse im Altertum*) in three successive editions of the encyclopedia *Handwörterbuch der Staatswissenschaften*,[3] and compared the ancient city (-state) with equivalents in European, and non-European cultures (*Die Stadt, The City*).[4] There are numerous, if scattered, references to antiquity in his *Economy and Society* (*E&S*) and his collection of articles on the sociology of world religions (*GARS*).

Despite the considerable quantity of research and writing which Weber did on antiquity in his work prior to 1914[5] he never presented a comprehensive account of his view of antiquity. Rather he approached the subject under various questions and different angles. He started with agrarian history (and was occupied at the same time with current developments in the eastern parts of Prussia),[6] widened his approach to a general view of the ancient economy, and finally used Greco-Roman Antiquity as

---

[1] *Dir römische Agrargeschichte in ihrer Bedeutung für das Staats- und Privatrecht* [*Roman Agrarian History and Its Importance to State and Civil Law*], Stuttgart: F. Enke, 1891; *MWG* I/2.

[2] *Die sozialen Gründe des Untergangs der antiken Kultur*, 1896 (*ASAC* 387–411; *SWG* 289–311).

[3] 1897, 1898, 1909, which in the final version became a text of book length *ASAC* 35–386; *SWG* 1–288)

[4] Published posthumously; see *Archiv für Sozialwissenschaft und Sozialpolitik*, 47 (1921), pp. 621–772; also: *E&S* 1212–1372; *WuG*, 727–814. A new edition (*MWG* I/22–25) by Wilfried Nippel was published in 1999. *Die Stadt*, ed. Wilfried Nippel, Tübingen: Mohr (Siebeck), 1999

[5] Cf. Alfred Heuss, "Max Webers Bedeutung für die Geschichte des griechisch-römischen Altertums," *Historische Zeitschrift*, 201 (1965), pp. 529–556.

[6] Cf. Lawrence A. Scaff, *Fleeing the Iron Cage: Culture, Politics, and Modernity in the Thought of Max Weber*. Berkeley, CA: University of California Press, 1989, pp. 34–72.

one element for the cross-cultural comparisons he concentrated on in his later work.

Weber's *Roman Agrarian History and its Importance to State and Civil Law* of 1891 (the *Habilitationsschrift* by which he qualified himself for the discipline of Civil and Commercial Law; see *MWG* I/2) is the only text which lives up to the usual standards of scholarly work on antiquity by constantly referring (though somewhat casually) to the ancient sources. It nevertheless proved to be highly controversial.

Agrarian history

In the *Roman Agrarian History* Weber reconstructed the development and economic consequences of the Roman land law from its very beginnings to late antiquity on the basis of the manuals for Roman land surveyors (*agrimensores*). He assumed that the different techniques of land surveying corresponded to different legal types of land (according to their liability to taxes) and that this connection, even if it was not pointed out in the sources, could be reconstructed as following from the "objective nature" (*Natur der Sache*) of the phenomena under discussion. Methodologically, he was indebted to the work of contemporary German agrarian historians, especially to August Meitzen, who had reconstructed German agrarian history from the early middle ages onwards on the basis of inferences from eighteenth-century cadastral maps.[7]

The great Theodor Mommsen took Weber's theory very seriously.[8] But at the same time he pointed out that Weber's basic premise of his method of analysis – namely that survey techniques and legal status corresponded – was beyond empirical proof, a challenge Weber could neither ignore nor answer definitely (*ASAC* 300–305, 384; *SWG* 222–227, 287). Weber's analysis also assumed, as others had, development from a sort of primordial agrarian communism to private property of land. This evolutionist assumption came under heavy attack. Works in diverse fields (e.g. on the Russian peasant commune, the *mir*, the south Slavonic house community, *zadruga*, and the Indian village community) had made the idea of an original agrarian communism as a typical stage of development very dubious.[9] In response to these discussions Weber modified his views. In an

---

[7] Jürgen Deininger, Introduction to *Die römische Agrargeschichte* (*MWG* I/2), pp. 1–54; Luigi Capogrossi Colognesi, *Economie antiche e capitalismo moderno. La sfida di Max Weber*, Rome: Laterza, 1990, pp. 292–312.

[8] Theodor Mommsen, "Zum römischen Bodenrecht," *Hermes*, 27 (1892), pp. 79–117.

[9] Cf. Wilfried Nippel, *Griechen, Barbaren und "Wilde": Sozialanthropologie und Alte Geschichte*, Frankfurt: Fischer, 1990, pp. 118–122.

article of 1904 on early Germanic social structure (*Der Streit um den Charakter der altgermanischen Sozialverfassung in der deutschen Literatur des letzten Jahrzehnts* [*SWG* 508–556]), the origins of which had been reconstructed in scholarly literature by interpreting famous remarks of Caesar and Tacitus in the light of this assumed law of evolution, Weber argued that "stages of culture" should not be understood as representing sequences according to historical laws of development but as ideal-types which should only be used for heuristic reasons – a conception which he developed more fully almost simultaneously in his first famous article on methodology ("Objectivity in Social Science and Social Policy," 1904 [*MSS* 49–112; *WL* 146–214]). Thus the emergence of Weber's theoretical and methodological approach was at least partly a result of his ongoing reflections on the proper models to be applied to ancient economic history.[10] He distanced himself from stage models that implied a sequence from nomadism to pastoralism, and in his later writings on antiquity he argued against all attempts to identify historical institutions as survivals of prehistoric stages, for example, in the case of the subdivisions of the *polis*, which he interpreted as units artificially created for military and administrative purposes and not as relics of tribal structures.[11]

Weber's substantive ideas about the economic history of the ancient world also changed. The last chapter of the *Roman Agrarian History* differed considerably in substance and method from the preceding ones. Here Weber used the Roman treatises on agriculture (from Cato the Elder through Varro and Columella to Palladius) in order to depict the structural changes from the Middle Republic to late antiquity. Roman expansion over Italy had fostered the emergence of large estates from the second century BCE onward (especially in those parts of the conquered territories left to occupation by Roman citizens, a system which turned out to be favorable to a wealthy elite) and the development of an unrestrained agrarian capitalism which more and more employed chattel slaves as labor force. This development stopped with the end of expansionist wars in the imperial age: the steady supply of slaves was no longer guaranteed.[12] The conse-

---

[10] Cf. Wilfried Nippel, "Methodenentwicklung und Zeitbezüge im althistorischen Werk Max Webers," *Geschichte und Gesellschaft*, 16 (1990), pp. 355–375.

[11] Cf. Wilfried Nippel, "Eduard Meyer, Max Weber e le origini dello stato," in Beatrice de Gerloni (ed.), *Problemi e metodi della storiografia tedesca contemporanea*. Turin: Einaudi, 1996, pp. 175–193.

[12] Later research on slavery in modern ages suggests that a slave population might be reproduced by breeding, so this is no longer an acceptable argument. But comparative studies cannot establish what had been the case in antiquity; they can, however, discredit the assumption that the maintenance of a slave population presupposes necessarily a constant supply of slaves from abroad. Cf. Moses I. Finley, *Ancient Slavery and Modern*

quence was that hitherto "barracked" slaves were allowed to acquire a precarious property and to live a kind of family life and thus enjoyed a certain degree of status improvement by becoming hereditary serfs of a sort, while formerly free peasants were reduced to a similar status by being bound to the soil as *coloni* of a peculiar type (a tendency which, moreover, was accelerated by fiscal demands).

Large estates no longer produced for the market but aimed towards autarky, which implied a decline of commerce and the money economy. Weber also dwelt on this topic in his 1896 essay "The Social Causes of the Decline of Ancient Culture," adding there that this tendency was in part due to the expansion of a previously coastal civilization into large continental areas, which entailed insuperable problems of transportation. By suggesting these "social" causes Weber distanced himself from all conventional explanations for the "decline and fall of the Roman Empire." He stressed the growing structural tension between a barter economy and a political and military system which still depended on money as a fundamental discrepancy between (as he put it, playing on Marxian vocabulary) "basis" and "superstructure," which in the long run made collapse inevitable. However, Weber focused only on the structural preconditions without actually analyzing the situation of the fourth and fifth centuries CE.

The problem of "ancient capitalism"

In the course of some general remarks on the fundamental structural difference between ancient and modern culture in "The Social Causes of the Decline of Ancient Culture," Weber took sides in a debate on the character of the ancient economy which later was to be known as the "Bücher–Meyer controversy" or the "primitivists versus modernists debate."[13] Leading ancient historians like Eduard Meyer and Karl Julius Beloch took issue with the economic historian Karl Bücher who had presented a scheme of sequence from *oikos* (domestic) economy through urban economy to national economy (*Hauswirtschaft, Stadtwirtschaft, Volkswirtschaft*). Domestic economy should denote a kind of economic system which appeared in antiquity with its basic features and characteristic consequences in a closer approximation to its "pure concept" than anywhere else, without becoming universally dominant in antiquity, either

---

Ideology, London: Chatto & Windus; New York: Viking, 1980, ch. 4; John R. Love, *Antiquity and Capitalism: Max Weber and the Sociological Foundations of Roman Civilization*, London and New York: Routledge, 1991, pp. 30f.

[13] Harry W. Pearson, "The Secular Debate on Economic Primitivism," in Karl Polanyi *et al.* (eds.), *Trade and Market in the Early Empires* (Glencoe, IL: Free Press, 1957), pp. 3–11.

in time or in space. Meyer and Beloch, champions of an anti-classicist, realistic approach to antiquity, (mis)understood Bücher as identifying antiquity with the stage of *oikos* economy, protested against this alleged characterization of the ancient economy and compared it with the early modern period in European history.

Weber developed his own view in the introduction to his enlarged 1909 version of the *Agrarian Sociology of Ancient Civilizations*. He claimed that Bücher's category of *oikos* economy should be understood as an "ideal-type" (*ASAC* 43; *SWG* 7). Weber insisted, *pace* Meyer, on the fundamental difference between manufactures based on slave labor and an industry organized on a qualitative division of labor and making use of a formally free labor force. "Nothing could be more misleading, therefore, than to describe the economic institutions of Antiquity in modern terms" (*ASAC* 45; *SWG* 10). Somewhat surprisingly, Weber nevertheless insisted that one should speak of an ancient capitalism (*ASAC* 48–52; *SWG* 12–17). He asserted that capitalism should be defined in economic terms only, i.e. "property is an object of trade and is utilized by individuals for profit-making enterprise in a market economy" and one should not "needlessly" include the social factor characteristic of modern capitalism, "the exploitation of other people's labor on a contractual basis," in a general definition (*ASAC* 50f.; *SWG* 15).

This abstract definitional suggestion sounds rather peculiar in the context of Weber's own arguments against Meyer's and Beloch's use of terms like "industry" and "factory" as neglecting the decisive criterion of the organization of labor – contractual, free labor in modern and slave labor in ancient times. Apparently Weber wished to preserve a universally applicable category of capitalism so as not to blur the structural differences between cultures and epochs and (as he emphasized subsequently) to enable the differentiation of the phenomena of ancient, premodern and non-European capitalism, based on war and booty, state monopolies, tax-farming, or trade from the specific modern and "rational" capitalism (cf. *GARS* III 359).

Despite the article's title, Weber's final version of the *Agrarian Sociology* was a comprehensive survey of the ancient economy, since ancient agrarian history could not be considered without taking into account changes in political, and that meant primarily, urban structures (*ASAC* 68; *SWG* 34). Although he had previously written only on Roman history, he now not only included ancient Greece but also dealt at length with ancient Egypt, Mesopotamia and Israel. Here Weber obviously derived benefit from Eduard Meyer's monumental work,[14] but he also showed an astonishing

[14] Arnaldo D. Momigliano, "Max Weber and Eduard Meyer: A Propos of City and Country

command of the rapidly growing specialized scholarly production in all parts of his extremely broad subject.

Weber stressed a fundamental difference between the Greco-Roman and the oriental world. He saw two distinct patterns of development, due to fundamental geographical and ecological factors.[15] Within the coastal civilization of the Greco-Roman world, the citizen state could develop, because aristocracies were able to dispose of the gains of commerce and thus reduce monarchy to merely military leadership and finally get rid of it. Later they had to accept the political participation of the bulk of the citizenry who, as hoplites, made up the military. In contrast, the civilizations on the banks of great rivers, which began with similar primordial monarchies, were governed by the necessities of river regulation and irrigation, which fostered the development of a centralized bureaucracy subject to a monarch with an indisputable monopoly in political, military, and economic power. Eventually this led to "the authoritarian liturgical state, in which the state's necessities were met by a carefully contrived system of duties imposed on the state's subjects" (ASAC 74; SWG 39f.). In the end (owing to the factors which Weber had analyzed already in "The Social Causes of the Decline of Ancient Culture") the authoritarian liturgical state, especially as it had been created in Ptolemaic Egypt, also dominated the later Roman Empire.

Weber's scheme was based on two fundamental yet hardly provable assumptions: first, that towns (in the occidental world) were founded primarily for commercial reasons and the profits from trade led to a social stratification with an aristocracy of great landowners at the top of society, and, second, that (in the oriental world) the irrigation problem necessitated a centralized (and not a locally based) solution – a variant of the theory of "oriental despotism" (which would later be further developed by Witt-fogel).[16]

The potential for the development of ancient capitalism was limited by the basic political structures of antiquity. The basic constraints resulted from the monopolistic tendencies of the oriental monarchies (which were powerful, despite differences between Mesopotamia, which permitted some private trade, and Egypt which was understood as the *oikos* [household] of

in Antiquity," in *Settimo Contributo alla Storia degli Studi Classici e del Mondo Antico*, Rome: Edizioni di storia e letteratura, 1980, pp. 285–293.

[15] Jürgen Deininger, "Die politischen Strukturen des mittelmeerisch-vorderorientalischen Altertums in Max Webers Sicht," in Wolfgang Schluchter (ed.), *Max Webers Sicht des antiken Christentums*, Frankfurt: Suhrkamp, 1985, pp. 72–110.

[16] Karl A. Wittfogel, *Oriental Despotism: A Comparative Study of Total Power*, New Haven, CT: Yale University Press, 1957.

the Pharaoh) on the one hand and the exigencies of the military organization of military organization common to the city-states, on the other.
Changes of economic structures in the Greco-Roman world were the
consequences of political developments. Thus the emergence of a concept
of personal liberty and citizenship created a demand for the import of
chattel slaves, and certain restrictions concerning the disposability of real
estate were intended to preserve the peasant household, on which the
supply of citizen warriors depended. Capitalistic enterprises were possible
only through politics and warfare. Tax farming and state contracts of
course depended on the state, but so did agrarian capitalism, which
depended on war for the acquisition of land and on capturing people to be
used as slaves. The bureaucratic structures that emerged in the Roman
Empire "strangled" capitalism by replacing the system of tax farming run
by private entrepreneurs which in late Republican times had been a main
source for the accumulation of large capital by the imperial fiscal administration (*ASAC* 62–65, 361–365; *SWG* 28–31, 274–277). These tendencies
towards bureaucratization, it may be noted, suggested a parallel: that
similar tendencies would almost inevitably undermine modern capitalism
as well (*ASAC* 365f.; *SWG* 277f.).

Weber thus arrived at a developed account of antiquity. Ancient capitalism was "only indirectly economic in character, for the critical factors
were the political fortunes of the *polis* and the opportunities it provided for
profit through contracts for tax farming and wars for human and (especially in Rome) territorial booty" (*ASAC* 358; *SWG* 271). But there were
also inherent causes of the structural weakness of ancient capitalism.
Chattel slavery entailed, apart from the political circumstances with their
consequences as to supply and prices, economic disadvantages in comparison to free labor, since slaves had to be fed continually and the owner had
to take the risk of mortality (*ASAC* 53f.; *SWG* 18f.). The typical ancient
capitalist was no entrepreneur, but (in Rome) was a gentleman *rentier* who
took a steady income as an absentee landlord that allowed him to engage in
politics (*ASAC* 328; *SWG* 248; *E&S* 1293; *WuG* 774; *MWG* I/22–5: 195)
and (in Athens) considered his property in manufacturing slaves as a source
of rental income, and was willing to sell some of them (*ASAC* 44, 208;
SWG 9, 144). Roman law did not provide the banking system and legal
framework necessary for sustained capitalist trade and steady industrial
enterprises: the appropriate legal forms were only developed in Italy during
the middle ages (*ASAC* 45f., 354; *SWG* 9f., 268); the thesis goes back to
Weber's doctoral dissertation of 1889, "On the History of the Trading
Company in the Middle Ages" (*SWG* 312–443). Finally, religion did not
produce any incentives to a rationalized economic behavior in comparison

to the role Protestantism (according to Weber's famous thesis of 1904/5) played in the early modern period. "Businessmen . . . were not sustained by any positive justification of the profit motive . . . In early modern times the rationalization and economization of life were furthered by the essentially religious idea of 'vocation' and the ethic derived from it, but nothing similar arose in Antiquity" (*ASAC* 67; *SWG* 33). All in all, ancient capitalism reached an impasse; thus the preconditions for the emergence of modern capitalism rather have to be looked for in the later middle ages. That is why Weber in the final section of the *Agrarian Sociology* announced that a systematic comparison between antiquity and the middle ages with respect to this question should be undertaken.

The City

Weber embarked on this comparison in *The City* but there it became only part of a wider discussion which reflected the new interest in true universal comparison which Weber had developed in the meantime. The article is obviously incomplete, as is indicated by the abrupt end as well as by a cross-reference to a passage on the Roman Empire (*E&S* 1317; *WuG* 785; *MWG* I/22–5: 122–125, 225f.) which is actually not included in the text. It was apparently left in this form in 1913 or 1914. The text represents a sort of working paper which shifts between quite different systematic contexts. (It had probably originated as a special part – on "non-legitimate domination" – of the sociology of domination intended for *Economy and Society*, but it is far from certain whether Weber would have incorporated the text as it now reads into this work or would rather have instead used at least parts of it in the context of his work on the sociology of religions.)

Weber started with a discussion of the adequate definition of the city (*Stadt*). He tried out, one after the other, definitions based on geographical, economic, social and legal criteria, only to come to the conclusion that with regard to the variety of phenomena all over the world (now including China, India, Arabia, Russia, the middle ages and modern Germany) any comprehensive definition must fail. One may detect, however, a special interest in economic definitions, probably a reaction to an article by Werner Sombart.[17] But in view of recent discussions by ancient historians it is worth stressing that Weber did not associate these types, especially "consumer city" and "producer city," with peculiar periods, that is, the ancient and the medieval world respectively. Moreover, after having abandoned the

---

[17] Werner Sombart, "Der Begriff der Stadt und das Wesen der Städtebildung," *Archiv für Sozialwissenschaft und Sozialpolitik*, 25 (1907), pp. 1–9.

discussion on this sort of typology he did not come back to it in the remainder of the text.[18]

Instead, in the course of his essay Weber concentrated on the city with a distinct political-administrative status, the commune as a self-governing body (*die Stadt im Rechtssinne, die Gemeinde*). There is a certain ambiguity in this definition since Weber wanted to cover different legal types of cities: the fully autonomous ancient city-states and the great Italian city-republics as their equivalents as well as those self-governing medieval cities which as subjects of a kingdom, principality or the Holy Roman Empire could not claim sovereignty. By using self-governance as the core of his definition he could include the ancient and Italian city-republics *a fortiori*.[19]

Only the occidental city, in which the military system was based on the self-equipment of citizens, could possess this specific quality. In oriental societies, especially India and China, the basic structures did not allow such a development. As a result of his concurrent work in comparative religion, i.e. on Confucianism, Hinduism and Buddhism (to be published in a series of articles from 1915 to 1917), Weber now stressed the importance of religiously constituted social structures (in addition to the factors of irrigation works and bureaucracy) in preventing commune-building in oriental societies. The distinctiveness of the occidental city is due to its character as a confraternity (*Verbrüderung*), a community based on artificially created and freely willed mutual ties, and not on consanguinity. This meant that the community depended on equal rights, solidarity against non-members, *connubium* and a common cult symbolically expressed in communal cult meals (*E&S* 1241; *WuG* 744; MWG I/22–5: 122–125, 170f.). In Asia the taboos between sibs (as in China) or castes (as in India) prevented such confraternal structures, and therefore a community of citizens.

In pre-Christian antiquity religion did not inhibit confraternity, though neither did it particularly encourage it. Confraternity materialized to a

---

[18] See Hinnerk Bruhns, "De Werner Sombart à Max Weber et Moses I. Finley," in Philippe Leveau (ed.), *L'Origine des richesses dépensées dans la ville antique*, Aix-en-Provence: Lafitte, 1985, pp. 255–273 for a rectification of Moses I. Finley, "The Ancient City: From Fustel de Coulanges to Max Weber and Beyond," *Comparative Studies in Society and History*, 19 (1977), pp. 305–327 (reprinted in: *Economy and Society in Ancient Greece*, London: Chatto & Windus, 1981, pp. 3–23), which unfortunately has passed almost unnoticed: Weber did not, as assumed by Finley, qualify the ancient city as a "consumer city." See now Hinnerk Bruhns, "Max Weber, l'économie et l'histoire," *Annales*, 51 (1996), pp. 1259–1287.

[19] Weber was well aware that with respect to antiquity only the cities within the Hellenistic monarchies and the Roman Empire that had once had, but then lost, true autonomy could be properly regarded as *Gemeinden*, communes of self-governing bodies (*E&S* 1243; *WuG* 745; *MWG* I/22–5: 122–125, 172).

certain degree in the union of heads of sibs or clans that originally constituted the city-state by means of *synoikismos*, i.e. either the real "housing together" in an urban center or the constitution of a singular political center for hitherto separate communities. But the patrician clans tried to keep up their ritual exclusivity towards the plebeians, which was only abolished in the courses of struggles of the orders. According to Weber, the ancient city-states did not reach the intensity of confraternity which later was to be achieved in the medieval commune, where burghers constituted the community by individually taking an oath. (That the commune originated in *coniurationes* as a sort of revolutionary uprising against feudal overlords applied especially to the Italian, but partly also to the German, case.) In the European middle ages confraternity had a positive religious basis since all members of the community did already belong to the same church, as symbolized in the community of the Eucharist.

The treatment of medieval European cities as in effect the model case obscures the cases from Greco-Roman antiquity. Weber sees constitutive acts of founding a commune in antiquity (by *synoikismos*) and in the middle ages (by *coniuratio*) as equivalents, but this leads him to regard community-building within the ancient city as somewhat deficient, something he might not have considered had he concerned himself with the modes of confraternity which materialized in the religious festivals of the city-state and its subdivisions rather than with the act of foundation of the city.[20] The approach leaves open the question how and when the emergence of Christianity changed the social and cultural character of the cities in the Roman Empire.

Weber referred (here and on several other occasions) to the breakthrough in Antioch praised by St. Paul[21] when the community of the Lord's Supper was practiced for the first time between circumcised and uncircumcised Christians, which meant that the Judeo-Christians were no longer bound to the Jewish ritual law. This event, Weber claimed, was the hour of conception of the citizens' association, which, however, saw the light of the day only in the *coniurationes* of city dwellers in the medieval cities a thousand years later (*GARS* II: 39f.). He did not enter into the complicated historical and theological questions as to the respective controversies in the early Christian community[22] but was only interested in the fact that the "Incident

[20] Cf. Wilfried Nippel, "Max Weber zwischen Althistorie und Universalgeschichte. Synoikismos und Verbrüderung," in Christian Meier (ed.), *Die okzidentale Stadt nach Max Weber*, Munich: Oldenbourg (Historische Zeitschrift, Beiheft 17), 1994, pp. 35–57.

[21] Galatians 2.

[22] Cf. e.g. James D. G. Dunn, "The Incident at Antioch (Gal. 2:11–18)," *Journal for the Study of the New Testament*, 18 (1983), pp. 3–57.

at Antioch" could retrospectively be perceived as the turning point which led to the universality of Christianity. The argument thus had to fill the great gap between the beginning of the Christian era and the high middle ages, which was not treated in the historical parts of Weber's work.

Weber instead embarked on a comparison of the structural similarities in the constitutional development in antiquity and the middle ages, which went from domination by patrician families to more popular regimes. The rationalization of the political systems (by the establishment of magistracies with restricted terms of office and clearly defined competencies, codification of laws and rules for the creation of new laws) was achieved in the course of these developments. The comparison relates the "classical" ancient city-states, Sparta, Athens, Republican Rome on the one hand, to the Italian city-states on the other hand, and takes up *inter alia* similarities between the Roman *plebs* and the Italian *popolo* and their respective representatives or between ancient tyranny and Italian *signoria*. But Weber warned that parallels as to the political superstructures should not be misunderstood as indicating an identical economic basis. (It should be mentioned that the comparison always starts with the middle ages and that the medieval examples are presented with much more detail than the ancient ones.) The fundamental difference lay in the relationship between city and hinterland: the political unity of the two in the ancient world implied that the peasants made up the majority of citizens, whereas the legal distinction between the two spheres in the middle ages meant that peasants were excluded from urban political life.

In the last part of this essay (at least as we have it) Weber returned to the question of economic rationality which had originally led him to the comparison between antiquity and the middle ages. Here we meet the famous distinction between the ancient *homo politicus* and the medieval *homo oeconomicus*:

> The specifically medieval city type, the artisan inland city, was altogether economically oriented . . . Whereas in Antiquity the hoplite army and its training, and thus military interests, increasingly came to constitute the pivot of all urban organization, in the Middle Ages most burgher privileges began with the limitation of the burgher's military duties to garrison service. The economic interests of the medieval townsmen lay in peaceful gain through commerce and the trades, and this was most pronouncedly so for the lower strata of the urban citizenry . . . The political situation of the medieval townsman determined his path, which was that of a *homo oeconomicus*, whereas in Antiquity the polis preserved during its heyday its character as the technically most advanced military organization. The ancient townsman was a *homo politicus*.   (E&S 1353f; WuG 805; MWG I/22–5: 274f.)

The representative medieval city on which this distinction was based was the artisanal inland city (*bürgerliche gewerbliche Binnenstadt*) of Europe north of the Alps. These cities were embedded in a power structure which did not allow them to play an independent military role. Consequently they neither offered their citizens opportunities for material gain by military and political means nor burdened them with more than a minimum of military service. Thus they stood in sharp contrast to the ancient city-republics. The Italian city-states were located between these extremes. The maritime republics of Venice and Genoa were closer to the ancient example; and some of the Italian inland city-states also showed some characteristics comparable to the ancient ones because of their ability to pursue an expansionist policy and because their elites still showed the mentality of knighthood, which prevented them in a certain degree from taking on the role of the entrepreneur. But the bulk of the citizens, craftsmen, were, like their northern European counterparts, interested in an economic policy that promoted their commercial interests.

The new element in Weber's consideration of the different levels of economic rationality in antiquity and the middle ages is the focus on the lower strata of citizens. In antiquity, the typically declassed citizen was a dispossessed farmer; in the middle ages it was an unemployed craftsman. The character of class struggles as well as the direction of the cities' economic policy thus differed: only in the middle ages did the municipal authorities seek to protect the interest of local producers. An ancient *demos* who participated in the gains of an expansionist policy by colonization, booty, soldier's pay and grain distributions was not inclined to an economic orientation properly speaking, but they were interested in keeping up the exclusivity of a status, citizenship, that itself provided material rewards. Therefore the "warrior guilds" of antiquity kept a "closed shop" policy with respect to citizen status (which especially in the Greek case implied an inability to build up stable empires). Maintaining status distinctions against metics, freedmen and slaves meant that groups such as metics and freedmen were the only ones truly oriented towards the pursuit of peacefully acquired profit through commerce and trade. And it also implied that there could be no guilds in the proper sense.

The organization of labor on the basis of formally free contract, the most productive type of labor organization known in history, appears for the first time in the middle ages. That is why the foundations for the emergence of rational capitalism could be laid only in the later middle ages, and not in antiquity. However, two crucial test cases are missing, namely the cities within the Hellenistic and Roman Empires. If, as Weber had said himself, in a "unified and pacified" Mediterranean world "the ancient city became the center of exclusively economic interests" (*ASAC* 358; *SWG* 271), these structures would have needed a more thorough analysis, something more than the statement that the bureaucratic monarchy and the shift from coastal to continental civilization precluded dynamic economical development.

Because Weber believed that the political structures of antiquity limited economic rationalization and that ancient politics distracted the bulk of the citizenry from a rationalized economical orientation, he never properly appreciated the political life of ancient cities. This comes out clearly in his one-sided, gloomy picture of Athenian democracy.[23] The political participation of citizens, service in the political institutions and in military campaigns "of proportions which no other differentiated culture in history has ever experienced before or after" is seen not as a positive achievement, but as an impediment to "pacific economic acquisition based on rational and continuous economic activity." The liturgies, a mixture of compulsory duties and volunteer engagement, by which wealthy citizens contributed to the financing of the fleet and of public festivals, are seen as subjecting any accumulation of wealth to outmost instability. The system of the popular courts in which even civil trials were decided by hundreds of lay jurymen implied an "arbitrariness of justice" which "imperiled the safeguards of the formal law so much that it is the mere continued existence of wealth which is to be marveled at, rather than the violent reversals of fortunes which occurred after every political mishap" (*E&S* 1361f.; *WuG* 810; *MWG* I/22–5: 286f.). The demands of the *polis* as a military association also implied that "any kind of behavior which might endanger the military and political morals and discipline" would be punished, and that "as a matter of principle, thus, there was no freedom of personal conduct . . ." (*E&S* 1360; *WuG* 809; *MWG* I/22–5: 285.).

Weber followed a tradition of criticism of Greco-Roman antiquity as cultivating an omnipotence of the state and at the same time preventing economic progress which had deep roots. It goes back to authors of the Scottish and French Enlightenment, then was taken up in the French post-revolutionary debate, summarized in 1819 by Benjamin Constant with the distinction between the freedom of the ancients and the moderns, and was dwelt upon by late nineteenth-century authors like N. D. Fustel de Coulanges and Jacob Burckhardt.[24] But Weber's attitude to ancient politics

---

[23] Cf. Moses I. Finley, "Max Weber and the Greek City-State," in *Ancient History, Evidence, and Models* (London: Chatto & Windus, 1985), pp. 88–103, 122–125.

[24] Cf. Nicole Loraux and Pierre Vidal-Naquet, "La Formation de l'Athènes bourgeoise. Essai d'historiographie 1750–1850," in Robert R. Bolgar (ed.), *Classical Influences on Western Thought, A. D. 1650–1870*, Cambridge: Cambridge University Press 1979, pp. 169–222

also corresponded to his own political conviction that direct democracy was impossible in the long run and that the rationale of modern parliamentary democracy had to be that it enabled the election of a responsible and competent leadership (a criterion which, in Greco-Roman antiquity was met by the Roman nobility, but not the Athenian demagogues, as Weber emphasized at the end of his article).

Though Weber in the course of his work distanced himself more and more from conventional ancient history, it cannot be said that his work had no influence on the scholarly debate among the classicists of his time. There were a number of repercussions in dissertations on, for example, Roman agrarian law,[25] the management of large estates,[26] the emergence of the colonate,[27] the bureaucracy in Ptolemaic Egypt,[28] the liturgical corporations of late antiquity,[29] the (limited) rationalization in Greco-Roman agriculture,[30] the organization of overseas trade in classical Greece and the role of state intervention which was only aimed at the furtherance of grain imports.[31] But impressive as the list may appear, it should not obscure the fact that in the course of time, mainly owing to the monumental works of Rostovtzeff[32] on the economics of Hellenistic times and the Roman Empire, and their overall approach, a modernistic interpretation of the ancient economy came more and more to prevail.[33] Certain exceptions

---

(English trans. in Vidal-Naquet, *Politics, Ancient and Modern*, Cambridge: Polity; Cambridge, MA: Blackwell, 1995, pp. 82–140).

[25] Richard Maschke, *Zur Theorie und Geschichte der römischen Agrargesetze*, Tübingen: J. C. B. Mohr, 1906.

[26] Rudolf His, *Die Domänen der römischen Kaiserzeit*, Leipzig: Veit, 1896; Herman Gummerus, *Der römische Gutsbetrieb als wirtschaftlicher Organismus nach den Werken des Cato, Varro und Columella*, Leipzig: Dieterich, 1906; Aalen: Scientia, 1963.

[27] Michael Rostowzeff (=Rostovtzeff), *Studien zur Geschichte des römischen Kolonates*, Leipzig and Berlin: B. G. Teubner, 1910; William L. Westermann, "The Economic Basis of the Decline of Ancient Culture," *American Historical Review*, 20 (1915), pp. 723–743.

[28] Friedrich Oertel, *Die Liturgie. Studien zur ptolemäischen und kaiserlichen Verwaltung Ägyptens*, Leipzig: B. G. Teubner, 1917.

[29] Gunnar Mickwitz, *Die Kartellfunktion der Zünfte und ihre Bedeutung bei der Entstehung des Zunftwesens. Eine Studie in spätantiker und mittelalterlicher Wirtschaftsgeschichte*, Helsingfors (Helsinki): Societas Scientiarium Fennica, 1936; New York: Arno Press, 1979.

[30] Gunnar Mickwitz, "Economic Rationalism in Greco-Roman Agriculture," *English Historical Review*, 52 (1937), pp. 577–589.

[31] Johannes Hasebroek, *Staat und Handel im Alten Griechenland*, Tübingen: J. C. B. Mohr, 1928 (English trans. *Trade and Politics in Ancient Greece*, New York: Biblo and Tannen, 1965).

[32] Michael Rostovtzeff, *The Social and Economic History of the Roman Empire*, Oxford: The Clarendon Press, 1926 [2nd edn. 1957]; Michael Rostovtzeff, *The Social and Economic History of the Hellenistic World*, Oxford: The Clarendon Press, 1941.

[33] Cf. Edouard Will, "Trois-quarts de siècle de recherches sur l'économie grecque antique," *Annales*, 9 (1954), 7–22.

notwithstanding, this tendency can be ascribed to most ancient historians from the late 1920s to the early 1970s.[34]

The situation changed with the publication of Moses Finley's seminal *Ancient Economy*[35] and the fresh debate on the character of ancient economics it provoked. There can be no doubt that Finley's work, with its key themes – the fundamental importance of agriculture, the limited level of economic rationalization, the political unity of city and hinterland, the lack of trade and commercial policy, the predominance of war and politics and the effects of this on the economic mentality of citizens, etc. – was highly indebted to Weber's pattern.[36] The acknowledgement of this intellectual tradition and also the declining impact of Marxism on the intellectual climate (in Italy and France),[37] as well as the new accessibility of Weber's relevant texts in translation (into English and other languages) led to a renewed interest in Weber's work on antiquity. All in all, one may say that the, so to speak, Weber–Finley model of ancient economy has now carried the day. In recent years, there has, however, been a growing tendency to criticize this model.[38] Insofar as the criticism concentrates on the question of the "consumer city" it is, with respect to Weber though not Finley, misplaced.[39] The substantial question that is still unanswered is whether,

---

[34] The accompanying decline of interest in Weber was partly also a consequence of the increased specialization of disciplines, especially the widening of the gap between an economics that lost its interest in historical problems and the historical disciplines. In more recent times, two more factors have contributed to this development: the image of Weber as a founding father of a sociology of the modern world (cf. Reinhard Bendix, *Max Weber. An Intellectual Portrait*, New York: Doubleday, 1960; London: Methuen, 1959) and not as a scholar having worked in close touch with the ongoing debates within the established older, historically orientated, disciplines; and, especially since the second world war, a decline in the knowledge of German, which has led to Weber's texts, – written in a highly complicated style and using an idiosyncratic terminology – becoming almost inaccessible.

[35] Moses I. Finley, *The Ancient Economy*, London: Chatto & Windus; Berkeley, CA: University of California Press, 1973 [2nd edn. 1985].

[36] Cf. Wilfried Nippel, "Finley and Weber. Some Comments and Theses," *OPUS*, 6–8 (1987–1989) [published 1991], pp. 43–50.

[37] Cf. Emanuele Narducci, "Max Weber fra antichità e mondo moderno," *Quaderni di storia*, 14 (1981), pp. 31–77; and Paul Veyne, *Le Pain et le cirque: Sociologie historique d'un pluralisme politique*, Paris: Seuil, 1976 (abridged English trans. *Bread and Circuses: Historical Sociology and Political Pluralism*, London: Allen Lane, 1990).

[38] Cf. Jean Andreau, "Présentation: Vingt ans après *L'Economie antique* de Moses I. Finley," *Annales*, 50 (1995), pp. 947–960; and Raymond Descat, "*L'Economie antique* et la cité grecque, Un modèle en question," *Annales*, 50 (1995), pp. 961–989.

[39] Cf. note 18 above and, for recent examples of this misapprehension, Donald W. Engels, *Roman Corinth: An Alternative Model for the Classical City*, Chicago: University of Chicago Press, 1990; Henry Willy Pleket, "Wirtschaft," in Friedrich Vittinghoff (ed.), *Europäische Wirtschafts- und Sozialgeschichte in der Römischen Kaiserzeit* (Handbuch der europäischen Wirtschafts- und Sozialgeschichte, vol. I), Stuttgart: Klett Cotta, 1990, pp. 35f.; Charles R. Whittaker, *Land, City, and Trade in the Roman Empire*, Aldershot,

and, if so, with which modifications, a model that is highly suitable for the time of the autonomous city-states can be expanded to cover adequately the Hellenistic and the Roman Imperial times.[40]

Thus far, the new interest in Weber has concentrated on his importance for ancient economic history. But there are other subjects in respect to which recourse to Weber might be fruitful for ancient historians. Take, for example, the concept of confraternity, which could serve as a starting point for a discussion on the correspondence between constitutional structures and civic rituals, lead to a typology of citizenry in the ancient world,[41] and finally might be brought into a comparison with the diverse types of community in the middle ages.[42] And of course, any attempt to analyze the peculiarities of European culture since antiquity in a perspective of universal history presupposes a critical evaluation of Weber's work.[43]

Hants, and Brookfield, VT: Variorum, 1993, pp. 1–20, 110–117; Helen M. Parkins (ed.), *Roman Urbanism. Beyond the Consumer City*, London, New York: Routledge, 1997.

[40] Cf. Keith Hopkins, "Taxes and Trade in the Roman Empire (200 B.C.–A.D. 400)," *Journal of Roman Studies*, 70 (1980), pp. 101–125; Henri Willy Pleket, "Agriculture in the Roman Empire in Comparative Perspective," in *De Agricultura. In Memoriam Pieter Willem de Neeve (1945–1990)*, Amsterdam: J. C. Gieben, 1993, pp. 317–342; Whittaker, *Land, City, and Trade in the Roman Empire*, pp. 49–75, 163–180.

[41] Cf. Walter G. Runciman, "Doomed to Extinction: The *Polis* as an Evolutionary Dead-End," in Oswyn Murray and Simon Price (eds.), *The Greek City from Homer to Alexander*, Oxford: The Clarendon Press; New York: Oxford University Press, 1990, pp. 347–367.

[42] Cf. Anthony Molho, Kurt Raaflaub, and Julia Emlen (eds.), *City-States in Classical Antiquity and Medieval Italy*, Stuttgart: F. Steiner, 1991; Peter Burke, "City-States," in John A. Hall (ed.), *States in History*, Oxford and New York: Blackwell, 1986, pp. 137–153.

[43] John A. Hall, *Powers and Liberties: The Causes and Consequences of the Rise of the West*, Oxford: Blackwell, 1985; Michael Mann, *The Sources of Social Power, vol. I: A History of Power from the Beginning to A.D. 1760*, Cambridge, New York: Cambridge University Press, 1986.

13

STANLEY L. ENGERMAN

Max Weber as economist and economic historian

Max Weber's publications and his intellectual influence were both enormous and wide-ranging. He was educated in the law, held two chairs in economics, and became one of the founders of the discipline of sociology. For his work in economic history he was considered to be one the major figures of the Younger Historical School in Germany, along with Arthur Spiethoff and his frequent intellectual disputant, Werner Sombart, with whom he often disagreed while sometimes working on similar historical problems. As a scholar, the nature of his concerns broadened over time, and shifted to what may be described as economic sociology. His contemporary Joseph Schumpeter described him as "a sociologist with a penchant for things that are primarily concerned with economics." Schumpeter's laudatory and insightful memorial was written at the time of Weber's death.[1] He later indicated that, although Weber's academic career began with chairs in economics, "he was not really an economist at all," but rather a sociologist. Schumpeter distinguished between economic analysis, which "deals with the questions how people behave at any time and what the economic effects are they produce by so behaving," and economic sociology, which "deals with the question how they came to behave as they do." Economic sociology, according to Schumpeter, included the "analysis of economic institutions."[2] A recent collection of essays in economic sociology describes its core propositions as: "(1) economic action is a form of social action; (2) economic action is socially situated; and (3)

I wish to thank Robert E. Gallman for comments on an earlier draft.
[1] Joseph A. Schumpeter, "Max Weber's Work," in R. Swedberg (ed.), *Joseph A. Schumpeter: The Economics and Sociology of Capitalism*, Princeton: Princeton University Press, 1991, p. 225.
[2] Joseph A. Schumpeter in E. Broody Schumpeter (ed.), *History of Economic Analysis*, New York: Oxford University Press, 1954, pp. 21, 819.

economic institutions are social constructions."[3] The present thrust of economic sociology is, while focusing on the study of familiar economic problems, to describe those factors that can lead to inefficient outcomes, unlike, it is argued, contemporary neoclassical economics. The claim that only economic sociology includes a social dimension may, as discussed below, overstate the differences between the two approaches in dealing with specific questions. The development by Weber of economic sociology, in reaction to economic theory, reflected his historical interests, as both economic sociology and economic history emerged in contrast with the abstract nature of the economic theory that had developed in the nineteenth and twentieth centuries. Although economic sociology and economic history represent different approaches and, at times, ask different questions, both are clearly distinguished from the thrust of atemporal economic theory. Nevertheless, despite his originating role in economic sociology, the importance of Weber's contributions to the disciplines of economics and economic history is substantial, and I will concentrate on these.

Some of Weber's most important work endures even when there may be disagreement about his specific conclusions, because of the significance of the questions asked. Given his range of topics, issues, and approaches, and his influence in so many different areas, it is difficult to evaluate Weber's intellectual contributions. And many of his points and arguments have become standard in intellectual discourse, even when the original source may by now have been forgotten. Some scholars draw upon his methods (for example, the role of ideal-types, or, as they have come to be called, models), on his concepts (for example, the nature of bureaucracy, which has had a major impact on recent developments in business history), or on his historical analysis (for example, his exploration of the link between Protestantism and capitalism in western Europe). Thus, to describe Weber's contribution to economics and to economic history is neither simple nor straightforward, so that only some of the key points will be touched upon here.

Basic principles

If we restrict contributions to economics to central analytical contributions to the corpus of contemporary micro or macro theory, Weber's role in economics would be nil. There are few mentions of Weber in any of the basic textbooks in economic theory and applied economics, with the

---

[3] R. Swedberg and M. Granovetter, "Introduction," in M. Granovetter and R. Swedberg (eds.), *The Sociology of Economic Life*, Boulder, CO: Westview Press, 1992, pp. 6–19.

possible exception of economic history. And those mentions are mainly related to *The Protestant Ethic*. Yet even if he had not been the sole proponent of these basic arguments, Weber laid out much of the methodological underpinning to what is conventionally called neoclassical economics. By underpinning I mean the material that usually goes into the first chapter of a Principles of Economics textbook, describing the basic assumptions to be used in economic analysis. He did so in his influential works on methodology, which apply not only to economics, but to the other social sciences as well.

Weber pointed to the importance of what he called the "ideal-type" as a necessary heuristic device for analysis. The ideal-type isolates those variables central to the study of a problem, putting aside those aspects of the reality which seem inessential to the analysis. While clearly subject to debate and disagreement, given the underlying difficulty in determining what is and what is not to be regarded as a central variable, the ideal-type has continued to be extensively used in economics and other social sciences, under the name of "model." Since it is impossible to ever capture all of reality, some abstraction must be used to examine (or assume) the key relationships. An ideal-type or model differs from what Weber's contemporary, Arthur Spiethoff, called a "real type." The "real type" reflected an intention to capture all of reality, and not just a part of it, or, as described by Frederic C. Lane, "a real type is a general statement of what phenomena really occurred regularly together with a causal connection between them." But, as Lane comments, "the distinction between real type and ideal-type is indeed likely to be blurred in any extensive historical analysis."[4] It seems clear that Spiethoff's method has not been followed up to the same extent as has Weber's.

Another basic analytical concept of the present economic approach, methodological individualism, was seen by Weber as a necessary starting point for analysis. He pointed to the methodological importance of the assumption of rationality in models of action, necessary to allow for the analysis of significant issues. Without that initial assumption of rationality, attempts at meaningful analysis would be limited (*TSEO* 92).[5]

In response to possible misinterpretations, he pointed out that this did

---

[4] Frederick C. Lane, "Some Heirs of Gustav von Schmoller," in J. T. Lambie (ed.), *Architects and Craftsmen in History: Festschrift für Abbott Payson Usher*, Tübingen: J. C. B. Mohr, 1956, pp. 16–22.

[5] Weber did not assume all actions were rational, but believed that it was useful to begin an ideal-type analysis by asking what would happen if behavior had been rational, and then "to introduce the irrational components as accounting for the observed deviations from this hypothetical course."

not imply that everyone was always purely selfish and were not influenced by other individuals as well as external conditions. Rather it is meant to argue that actions are taken by specific individuals, and that a "subjectively understandable orientation of behavior exists only as the behavior of one or more *individual* human beings" (*TSEO* 101). Although individuals are open to external influences (called "collective entities," but the result of actions of individual persons) and have concerns for others, it remains methodologically important to understand the nature of the beliefs and actions of individuals (*TSEO* 101–107).

Weber was greatly interested in achieving an objective, value-free, analysis of issues. He presented a useful, but still debated, discussion of the role of tastes (or preferences or values) in theoretical and empirical analysis. For Weber, values played a primary role in influencing the choice of the specific problems to study. Once the problem to be examined was selected, however, the basic analysis would presumably be the same for all scholars, as would be the conclusions to the study. The choice of empirical data to be used, and the basic form of the analysis, should not be influenced by personal tastes and prejudices. Correspondingly, values cannot be validated, being regarded as items of individual taste. This aspect of rationality, and its divorce from ethics, applies not only to the choice of scholarly problems, but is also one of the key postulates of the behavior of economic actors, underlying the economists' models of consumer choice and behavior.

The concern with rationality of human behavior was one of Weber's major interests, and has played a key role in modern economics. This issue is discussed in great detail by Jon Elster, above, and I will only briefly mention the uses of the concept of rationality in economics and in economic history. Weber distinguished four types of human social action: two based on rationality, two not (*TSEO* 115–118). The former are rationality in seeking chosen ends, and rationalities of belief in some absolute value. The latter two are affectual (emotional) and traditionally oriented, the result of "habituation of long practice." Traditional behavior may be described as rational in an important sense, since it can lower the costs of "appropriate" behavior. Rationality may be goal-oriented in the sense that it seeks means to an end which is an "absolute value," which may mean that it becomes "irrational" in the failure to consider alternatives, or else rational action may involve the "choice between alternative and conflicting ends" (*TSEO* 117). In describing the varieties of rational actions, Weber drew a sharp analytic distinction between means and ends. The ends selected by individuals have no inherent rationality, and cannot be ranked, since people's preferences differ and comparisons of the choices of ends remains, for the most part, outside any rational analysis. What can be studied rationally is the choice of means to achieve specific ends. The central economic problem is how to maximize, given desired ends, and it is the failure to use appropriate means to achieve these ends at minimal cost that is to be regarded as irrational. This does not mean, when discussing ends, that the social context should not be considered. It does not mean that the profit motive be considered more highly (or lowly) than other ends, nor does it exclude the importance of non-market considerations (*TSEO* 164–166).[6]

Weber gave some attention to the importance of non-pecuniary tastes in actions within the economy. Following a strand of argument raised by a member of the Older German Historical School, Karl Knies, he argued that people did not necessarily profit-maximize at all times.[7] Non-economic factors do play a role in human behavior. Weber believed that it was certainly possible that there may be less extensive attempts at the maximum degree of maximization within a market economy, at least as a short-term goal, than in other forms of social organization. Weber argued that "the notion that our rationalistic and capitalistic age is characterized by a stronger economic interest than other periods is childish," and claims that while Cortez and Pizarro had strong economic interests, they certainly did not have "an idea of a rationalistic economic life" (*GEH* 261). Weber distinguished between economic interests, found in many past societies, and a rationalistic, capitalistic channeling of those interests. To Weber, the market system was not an idealized means of solving social problems. He recognized the conflicts that existed within the market system, suggesting that price and market outcomes should be seen as the result of conflict, since people disagreed over the use of the economic surpluses that could exist (*E&S* 107–109). But to Weber the market, with its various difficulties, seemed to provide a reasonable way to resolve conflicts and to allocate resources with some limitations on destruction and loss of freedom (*E&S* 635–40; *TSEO* 212–218).

The unique rise of the west

Weber's concerns within economic history, particularly in *The Protestant Ethic and the Spirit of Capitalism*, fit well into the general interests of the

---

6 Jacob Viner in *Religious Thought and Economic Society: Four Chapters of an Unfinished Work*, ed. J. Melitz and D. Winch, Durham, NC: Duke University Press, 1978, pp. 151–152, argues that something as "irrational and unnatural" as the spirit of capitalism required the "support and sanction of certain religious doctrines."

7 Wilhelm Hennis, "A Science of Man: Max Weber and the Political Economy of the German Historical School," in W. J. Mommsen and J. Osterhammel (eds.), *Max Weber and his Contemporaries*, London: Allen & Unwin, 1987.

turn-of-the-century historical schools in Germany and in England. These scholars were concerned with explaining the rise of modern economies, as well as with the examination of the institutions and conditions which influenced the development and operation of economies and societies. Weber, unlike others in the German School, spent little time describing the role played by economic policies of governments in economic change. He focused, as did Sombart, more on the study of modern capitalism, its nature and the causes of its rise. As the interest in this topic waned, the interest in Weber's work was lessened, a pattern that existed for several decades.

Many of Weber's works dealt with topics in the area of economic history. One book was devoted exclusively to the study of world economic history, *General Economic History*, based on the transcripts of Weber's lectures in 1919–1920, taken from student notes. The English language version, published in 1927, was based upon the translation made by the distinguished economic theorist Frank H. Knight, who was to spend most of his influential academic career at the University of Chicago. Knight made a number of important contributions to economic theory, including his book *Risk, Uncertainty, and Profit,* which dealt with the adjustments of business firms and markets to unexpected events. There, is, however, little apparent evidence of a direct influence of Weber on Knight's theoretical work, even when, later in his career, Knight's work took a more philosophical bent. Knight did teach a graduate seminar on Weber at Chicago in the 1930s, and wrote one article in 1928 on modern capitalism, dealing with Sombart as well as Weber, much to the benefit of Weber.[8]

General Economic History is an overall survey of economic developments, from ancient times to the modern world. It provides summary statements (in some cases, revisions) of key arguments found in earlier writings, useful descriptions of the pattern of western economic development, and insightful brief views of major economic changes that are sometimes detailed in other writings. Its major contentions include the claim that forms of what could be considered capitalism had long existed, leading to earlier accumulations of wealth, but it was only with the development of capital accounting and rational commerce, and with the

---

[8] Frank H. Knight, "Historical and Theoretical Issues in the Problem of Modern Capitalism," *Journal of Economic and Business History,* 1 (1928), pp. 119–136. Knight contributed an essay, "Liberalism and Christianity," in F. H. Knight and T. W. Merriam, *The Economic Order and Religion* New York: Harper & Brothers, 1945. He is described by the series editor as "perhaps the best-known writer in the field of ethics in relation to modern economics" (p. vii). Knight does not refer to Weber in his essay, his concern here being contemporary religion and ethics.

need for rules and trust that arise when there are continued transactions among individuals, that the modern form of capitalism emerged in western Europe. This development was unique to that particular geographic region. In describing this evolution Weber also provides discussions of the changing organization of the manor, the stages in the rise of industry, the impacts of slavery and other forms of labor organization upon the economy as well as the reasons for their transformations over time, and numerous other topics that are still covered, often in a quite similar manner, in today's textbooks in European economic history.

Nevertheless, Weber's major contribution to the study of economic history no doubt remains his classic study *The Protestant Ethic and the Spirit of Capitalism*, first published in 1904–1905. This is discussed in more detail above, so it will be only touched on here. Weber did not originate the thesis linking Protestantism and capitalism, as he himself pointed out. Jacob Viner, among others, has indicated that this idea of linking religion to the onset of capitalism had a long history in regard to Protestantism and to other religions prior to Weber's writings.[9] Some of this linking was made by earlier writers such as William Petty.[10] What Weber did was to provide the specifics for the argument, with the details of the mechanism by which the belief in a "calling" and in worldly asceticism developed, leading to modern capitalism. Nevertheless, Weber argues that these behavioral changes alone could not bring about modern capitalism as it required the appropriate set of conditions in the economic sphere.

To clarify his contention on the uniqueness of the west, Weber undertook several major studies in the sociology of religions in different areas, particularly Asia, in order to understand why other religions did not generate the emergence of a modern capitalism. These comparative religious studies have yielded insights into the impact of these different religious systems in China, India, and elsewhere, and their impacts on behavior. To some scholars, however, it was the political nature and openness to new beliefs and innovations in those countries of northwest Europe that led to those developments in science, business, and political freedom that permitted economic and scientific progress to take place.

The issue of the relation of Protestantism and capitalism remains an historical perennial, frequently cited and necessarily discussed and evaluated in all works dealing with its general time period. Weber clearly had raised a central issue for historical studies. The general question and

---

[9] Viner, *Religious Thought*, pp. 151–189.

[10] William Petty, "Political Arithmetick, or A Discourse," in *The Economic Writings of Sir William Petty*, ed. C. H. Hull, 2 vols., Cambridge: Cambridge University Press, 1899, pp. 260–264.

Table 13.1. *Per capita incomes, 1750–1970 (in 1960 US dollars and prices)*

Year	Western Europe	Third World
1750	190	188
1860	379	174
1950	928	203
1970	2098	308

Source: Paul Bairoch, "The Main Trends in National Economic Disparities since the Industrial Revolution," in P. Bairoch and M. Lévy-Leboyer (eds.), *Disparities in Economic Development since the Industrial Revolution*, London: Macmillan, 1981, pp. 3–17.

Weber's approach have remained important to recent works by economic historians for several reasons. First, it has made central the question of the uniqueness of western civilization and the nature of its economic and social development. Whatever might have been the relative incomes of different parts of the world before 1700, it is clear that since then economic growth has been much more rapid in western Europe and its overseas offshoots than in other parts of the world. (See Table 13.1.)

Modern economic growth has taken place with a quite different economic and social structure from that which had existed earlier. Economic growth occurred at roughly the same time, or soon after, these areas experienced the rise of Protestant religions. Some may hold this similarity to be of completely independent occurrences, but for many such a non-relationship would seem difficult to understand and accept. Second, Weber has pointed to the significance of non-pecuniary (or what some would call non-economic) factors in influencing economic change, at least in conjunction with some appropriate set of conditions. For Weber, the key non-pecuniary factor was based on a particular religion and set of religious codes; to others it was a religious influence, but from a different religion; while to several scholars it has been some different factor leading to behavior changes, such as rationalism, individualism, or the development of an economic ethic. And, to still other scholars, the major factor has been the nature of a minority group of penalized outsiders in society. These

[11] Petty, "Political Arithmetick"; W. Sombart, *The Jews and Modern Capitalism*, New York: Burt Franklin, 1969 [1913]; Thorstein Veblen, "The Intellectual Pre-eminence of Jews in Modern Europe," in M. Lerner (ed.), *The Portable Veblen*, New York: Viking Press, 1958 [1919]; Alexander Gerschenkron, *Europe in the Russian Mirror: Four Lectures in Economic History*, Cambridge: Cambridge University Press, 1970. For a recent study that casts doubt on religious arguments, but points to the role of outside groups experiencing new tensions, see Everett E. Hagen, *On the Theory of Social Change: How Economic Growth Begins*, Homewood, IL: Dorsey, 1962.

scholars include William Petty, who looked at several different areas in the seventeenth century, Sombart and Thorstein Veblen who wrote on the Jews, and Alexander Gerschenkron who examined the Russian Old Believers.[11] Each of these explanations has been advanced in the attempt to describe the primary cause of those changes in economic behavior that have led to the distinction between the modern and pre-modern worlds.

The recent literature by economic historians, dealing with "How the West Grew Rich," "The Rise of the Western World," "The European Miracle," "The Unbound Prometheus," and related titles, has begun, as did Weber, with the perceived uniqueness of the western European economy.[12] These studies, by such leading economic historians as Nathan Rosenberg (with William Birdzell), Douglass North (alone, and with Robert Paul Thomas), Eric Jones, and David Landes, with the related writings by Fernand Braudel, Immanuel Wallerstein, and J. R. Hicks, focus on somewhat different explanatory factors from Weber's, but the problem to be analyzed is identical. Posited answers include the role of political freedom, the development of property rights, changes in technology and organization of workers, the changing ratio of land to labor, the reactions to different environmental conditions, the emergence of markets, the rise of rational thought, the inflow of specie – and various others. Some focus more on what might be regarded as economic factors, while others are more in the Weberian tradition, even if there is no unanimity concerning specific causal factors. Rather curious, however, is that several of these recent works by economic historians do not refer to Weber's work on the Protestant ethic, and in those that do his work is not seen as central to explaining the rise of the west. Nevertheless, it is clear that as long as there is a belief that the economic performance of western Europe has been unique, Weber has presented an argument that must be confronted. Early in the second half of the twentieth century a non-western nation, Japan, as well as, somewhat later, several east Asian nations, have come to experience some of the characteristics of modern economic and social change, with the developments of a pattern of thrift and of a work ethic (even if cooperative not individualist), but with a different form of religion. This seems, however, to have done more to reawaken interest in Weber's arguments than to lead to their dismissal.

Thus, despite the sharpness and frequency of the criticism, the Weber thesis remains central to posing questions about the onset of modern

---

[12] See Stanley L. Engerman, "The Big Picture: How (and When and Why) the West Grew Rich," *Research Policy*, 25 (1994), pp. 547–559 for citations to and discussion of the works mentioned in this paragraph.

economic growth and social and religious change in seventeenth- and eighteenth-century western Europe. In addition to the debates on economic growth there are subsidiary questions about related aspects of western development, which might be regarded either as substitutes for or complements to the Weber thesis. These include debates on the rise of individualism, the causes of the development of a more deliberate and rational approach to economic and other behavior, and the link between the emergence of modern capitalism and modern science. Weber discussed the role of those climatic and geographic factors that have interested such present-day economic historians as Eric Jones, arguing that the development of firstly cities, and then nation-states, left Europe, unlike Asia, with rational states and rational law. This set of developments reflected, according to Weber, initial differences in natural forces.[13]

Many of the disagreements about Weber's linking of Protestantism and capitalism contain a distinct moral flavor. To those who find capitalism and the modern world morally distasteful, linking capitalism's rise to religious beliefs places an unfortunate and unfair burden upon the religion, which can lead to a denial of any relationship between the two. Presumably those more sympathetic to modernism and capitalism would find a relationship more acceptable. Weber, himself, believed that capitalism generated important problems, and he did not believe that capitalist growth could continue indefinitely. The decline of capitalism was anticipated because of the development of rigid institutions and the rise of a bureaucratic state, posing a threat to political freedom as well as causing economic stagnation. Weber's use of the image of the "iron cage" to describe modern society reflected his belief that certain cultural problems emerged because of capitalist development. And while Weber did not describe the same scenario for capitalism's demise as that later presented by Schumpeter, it was similarly based on the impact of increasing bureaucracy and rationalism on the belief system in society.[14]

While attention was given to the cultural problems due to capitalism, in Weber's view the rise of capitalism was related to favorable changes in the distribution of economic resources within society. It was what Weber called the "democratization of luxury" that was the key source of early market demand, rather than "War and luxury, the military administration and

[13] See Daniel Chirot, "The Rise of the West," *American Sociological Review*, 50 (1985), pp. 181–195.
[14] See Mommsen and Osterhammel (eds.), *Max Weber*, pp. 68–84. For a more general argument on the role of social rigidities in economic decline, see Mancur Olson, *The Rise and Decline of Nations: Economic Growth, Stagflation, and Social Rigidities*, New Haven, CT: Yale University Press, 1982.

court requirements" (*GEH* 228–231). None of these, important as they may have seemed at the time or to subsequent scholars (for example, Sombart), had led to prolonged economic growth anywhere. That was the result of growth of the mass market which arose with capitalism, and which lowered prices permitting the broad masses to imitate the consumption patterns of the rich. Weber argued that "first the prices fell relatively and then came capitalism," the price declines being due to preceding shifts in technology and economic relations. And Weber, as do the later economic historians who stress the role of property rights, Douglass North and Robert Thomas, points to the importance of the English patent act of 1623.[15] To North and Thomas "the role of patents in developing a system of property rights instrumental in encouraging invention and innovation and its spread (particularly from the continent to England) was the result of the Statute of Monopolies."[16] Weber similarly notes that "without the stimulus of this patent law the inventions crucial for the development of capitalism in the field of textile industry in the eighteenth century would not have been possible" (*GEH* 231–232).

The history of pre-modern economies

Weber's contributions to the study of economic history include both methodological approaches and substantive conclusions. His general questions on the role of changing institutions and human behavior have again come into vogue, as has his interest in the law, legal rationality, and the process of historical development. Thus, in a number of ways, Weber reads very much like a present-day economic historian, a development taking place after a long period in which Weber was relatively ignored by economic historians. In part his loss of influence was due to a shift in questions, to those mainly dealing with only a relatively short, recent period in the history of the west. As it became clear that the process of economic growth was rather more complex than believed in the mid-twentieth century, and that its understanding was based on happenings over a much longer time span than was being looked at, Weber's analysis again became more central. Here I will deal with only a few of the many issues related to Weber's work as an economic historian, to highlight some aspects of interest.

As other chapters, notably Nippel's, have shown, many of Weber's early

---

[15] Douglass C. North and Robert P. Thomas, *The Rise of the Western World: A New Economic History*, Cambridge: Cambridge University Press, 1973, pp. 146–156.
[16] *Ibid.*, pp. 152–153.

writings dealt with the economics of the ancient world. These writings included a discussion of the problem of slavery, a problem that Weber wrote on at other times in his career. Weber asked why slave societies were not capable of continued development. His arguments are those still widely in use in the economic condemnation of slavery, not just for the ancient world but for other times as well, including the United States South and elsewhere in the Americas. Indeed, much of what has come to be called the Marxian critique of slave economies can be found most clearly spelled out in Weber. Slave economies were, according to Weber, necessarily irrational since the owners could not adjust labor time and costs in response to fluctuations in prices and demands, as could the hirers of free workers. Slaves were capital goods, requiring considerable investment, making them more costly than free workers, and the fact that slaves were given no incentives, had no sense of responsibility, and lacked appropriate self-interest meant that their work habits were poor and that they would not use tools appropriately.[17] Political factors made slave ownership risky, while the inability to keep slaves in families lowered the reproduction rates of slaves, making slave societies dependent on external sources for slaves. Slave societies, because of their large slave populations and low labor costs, had limited incentives for technical change. Further, the nature of slave work served to discredit the idea of labor, and degrade free workers. More generally, Weber argued that slavery provided a limited capacity for long-run growth of wealth and economic development. Not that slavery was always unproductive, since Weber, following John E. Cairnes, H. J. Nieboer, and W. E. B. Du Bois, pointed to the possibilities for profitable use of slave labor when the following conditions held: labor was cheap; there was a well-supplied market for slave labor, and large-scale plantations could be used for producing marketable goods. He provided a demographic argument to explain why slavery in the United States was doomed and also to explain why it would have been replaced by share tenantry without a civil war, arguments resembling those he presented earlier to account for the decline of Roman slavery.[18] While recent research on modern slavery has raised questions about almost all of Weber's statements on the

---

[17] Weber also argues that blacks were "unsuitable for factory work" and machine operations because of "tangible racial distinctions," and "American Indians were entirely unsuitable for plantation labor" (*GEH* 275, 222).

[18] See *GEH* 75–76. The decline would occur, according to Weber, when slave importation was prohibited, and "when the available land threatened to become inadequate." The shift from plantations to small farms also explained the decline of Roman slavery, reflecting "an acute shortage of labor" once slave imports dried up, and the resulting need for families to encourage reproduction. See *ASAC* 397–400.

economics of slavery, most still retain a powerful hold on present-day scholars.

While pointing to the drawbacks of slavery, Weber expressed some reservations about the meaning of free labor in contrast with slavery He cited the Mesopotamian code that stated that for free men "the period of work was regarded as temporary slavery" (*ASAC* 96). Free workers were described as being in a position of "masterless slavery" (*E&S* 1186). Thus Weber's approach to labor institutions has views in common with the ideas recently presented by labor historians, which emphasize the constraints upon labor mobility and the controls exercised by employers in the work place. Rather than accept a sharp dichotomy between free and slave labor, there is seen to be a spectrum between the polar cases, with some over-lapping characteristics and similarities in legal and non-legal constraints. While free labor need not be seen as "wage slavery," its freedom was not without some socially imposed limits.

As Hamilton shows in his chapter in this volume, some of Weber's writing developed as part of an ongoing debate with Werner Sombart which extended more generally to the problems of the causes and nature of capitalism.[19] Weber and Sombart perceived themselves as intellectual rivals, judging from sources of topics and the infighting in footnotes. Sombart was about the same age as Weber, and the two had certain overlapping concerns, but Sombart died two decades after Weber. Where Weber argued for the role of Protestantism in the rise of capitalism, Sombart, writing several years later (in a book that is a mixture of scholarship and imagination) pointed to the role of Jews. Where Sombart argued for the role in economic growth of wars and luxury expenditures, Weber claimed that these could not lead to long-term growth, which could be based only on mass markets. While both agreed on the role of religion in the development of the spirit of capitalism, therefore, they did point to different timing and different religions, although some scholars argue that Sombart attributes to the Jews the same set of ideas that Weber accords to the Protestants. The current historical consensus would be that Weber has stood up better on these key questions than has Sombart.

One of the major substantive legacies of Weber is his description of the

---

[19] See Arthur Mitzman, "Personal Conflict and Ideological Options in Sombart and Weber," in Mommsen and Osterhammel (eds.), *Max Weber*. The two books of Sombart noted in this paragraph are *Jews* and *Luxury and Capitalism* (Ann Arbor: University of Michigan Press, 1967 [1913]), though there was considerably more written by Sombart. For a useful summary statements of Sombart's views as to the nature of capitalism, see Werner Sombart, "Capitalism," in Edwin R. A. Selgman (ed.), *Encyclopedia of the Social Sciences*, vol. III, New York: Macmillan, 1930.

characteristics of modern capitalism. Weber regarded capitalism as an evolving system, so that present-day capitalism has some features rather different from those at the onset of modern capitalism. He did not, however, regard commercial and capitalist activity as something new in the modern era, since such behavior had existed in most societies in earlier times, as well as in other societies considered non-capitalist at the present time. Under modern capitalism, however, activities of a somewhat different pattern and nature occurred from those in the other forms of capitalism.

The principal characteristics of modern capitalism that Weber points to are the centrality of rationality and those measures that help to implement rational behavior. The emergence of a rationally organized formally free labor market to replace the various forms of labor institutions that had characterized earlier forms of capitalism, the development of rational law and administration in large firms and governments, the evolution of forms of rational bookkeeping and capital accounting, and the growth of bureau-cracies in the public and private sectors to order the behavior of the larger-scale units in economic society – all these represent those factors developed out of Protestantism which permit continued capitalist growth. Other characteristics of the modern capitalist economy include the use of accounting procedures to separate business and household capital in the interests of rational decision making, and the increased number of business leaders whose leadership is based upon their personal charisma, not on either traditional or legal influences. This concept of charisma in business leadership is consistent with Schumpeter's discussion of the "creative response" in entrepreneurship. Moreover, both Weber and Schumpeter have similar arguments, not only for the successful development of capitalism but also for its weakening as a system over time. Weber's argument that charisma weakens with the growth of bureaucracy resembles Schumpeter's contention of the decline of the entrepreneurial function in modern capitalism, leading to a declining social appeal of capitalism. Recently, however, the concept of charisma in the past has had its most frequent use as applied to political and religious, rather than economic, leadership. Recent studies of leadership in management, however, have focused upon so-called "change agents" and shapers of corporate culture, leading to attempts to determine what are the crucial characteristics of successful business leaders and what they have done to achieve their success. Thus more attention has been given in the business community to the concepts of Weber and of Schumpeter.

In terms of distinguishing modern from pre-modern capitalism and governments, Weber's discussion of bureaucracy has been rather fruitful. As firms grew in size, new mechanisms of control were required to permit successful expansion. Central to the rise of the large, modern corporation has been this bureaucratic expansion, with a large administrative staff and detailed procedures to plan and implement policies. This concept has been central to the developments in business history through the writings of Alfred D. Chandler, Jr., of the Harvard Business School.[20] Chandler, who is the most influential business historian of his generation, had remarked that in studying the growth of the large corporation he found Weber's work on bureaucracy to be more useful than the micro-economic theory of markets. Chandler's description of big business emphasizes the internal operation of firms based on a "visible hand," rather than placing the emphasis on external considerations and the constraints of the market with its "invisible hand." As Chandler's influence upon the study of economics and economic and business history has spread, in the U.S. and elsewhere, so has the importance of Weber's concept of bureaucracy. Thus, in business history as in economic history, a shift in questions asked, to now deal with the internal operations of firms, has made Weber's work more central.

Conclusion

The later studies of Weber are generally considered under the rubric of economic sociology, a field of which he was one of the originators. The basic issues discussed were how various economic and social institutions evolved and how they influenced human behavior over time. Thus this work would fit into what has come to be called "the new institutional history," with its focus on institutions, legal changes, the role of property rights and rules in providing the setting for economic change, and with its interests in such broader aspects as culture and religion and their economic influences. As with Weber, the influence of non-pecuniary factors on economic behavior now plays a large role in economic and historical analysis. Also central to study are the causes of those differences in political and economic systems that set the background conditions for economic change.

In summary, while Weber's work may not have fit in well with economic history when the influence of cliometrics was at its peak, his work fits in extremely well with today's analysis of questions and issues in economic

---

[20] Alfred Chandler, Jr., *The Essential Alfred Chandler: Essays toward a Historical Theory of Big Business*, ed. T. K. McCraw, Boston, MA: Harvard Business School Press, 1988, pp. 296–297, 304–305. For a discussion of the use of the concept of bureaucracy in American business and economic history, see M. A. Yeager, "Bureaucracy," in G. Porter (ed.), *Encyclopedia of American Economic History: Studies of the Principal Movements and Ideas*, Vol. III, New York: Charles Scribner's Sons, 1980, pp. 894–926.

history, with the asking of broader questions about the process and nature of long-term economic growth. It is not that Weber's work had been disproved and held to be intellectually inadequate: this cannot explain the lack of attention to his scholarship for several decades. It is mainly the shift in questions deemed important that can explain first his neglect and then his revival in economic history. And probably most important in explaining these recent changes has been the increased awareness of the great complexities in generating economic development in what used to be called the Third World, and the much broader range of changes required than formerly in the less developed nations.

FURTHER READING

Several Weber bibliographies are available, dating to the forties. They are far too extensive to usefully duplicate here. Weber's works, including newspaper articles and extant letters, are being published in the *Max Weber Gesamtausgabe*. A bibliography of Weber's own writings is available in Dirk Kaesler, *Max Weber: An Introduction to His Life*. The most recent and extensive bibliography of writings on Weber in English is in Alan Sica, *Max Weber and the New Century*. An extensive and valuable bibliography on Weber's economic sociology has been assembled by Richard Swedberg, in *Max Weber's Economic Sociology: A Bibliography*, Working Paper 61, Department of Sociology, Stockholm: Stockholm University, 1998. In this list of further reading I have included texts in English, and the English translations of the works of major contributors to the Weber literature, with a few exceptions for German texts that have no English language version. Much of what is written on Weber appears in edited volumes, and in this list, rather than citing each chapter separately, I have created a section for edited volumes.

Primary texts

The Agrarian Sociology of Ancient Civilizations, trans. R. I. Frank, London: New Left Books; Atlantic Highlands, NJ: Humanities Press, 1976 [contains the 3rd edition of *Agrarverhältnisse im Altertum* and *Die sozialen Gründe des Untergangs der antiken Kultur*].

Ancient Judaism, trans. and ed. Hans H. Gerth and Don Martindale, Glencoe, IL: Free Press, 1952.

The City, trans. and ed. Don Martindale and Gertrud Neuwirth, New York: Free Press, 1966 [1958].

Critique of Stammler, trans. Guy Oakes, New York: Free Press, 1977 [1907].

Economy and Society: An Outline of Interpretive Sociology, 3 vols., ed. Guenther Roth and Claus Wittich, Berkeley and Los Angeles, CA: University of California Press, 1978 [1968].

From Max Weber: Essays in Sociology, trans. H. H. Gerth and C. W. Mills, New York: Oxford University Press, 1946.

General Economic History, New York: Collier Books, 1961 [1927], New Brunswick, NJ: Transaction, 1981.

Gesammelte Aufsätze zur Religionssoziologie, 3 vols., (1920/1), reprinted Tübingen: Mohr (Siebeck), 1988 [1920].

Gesammelte Aufsätze zur Sozial und Wirtschaftsgeschichte, reprinted Tübingen: Mohr (Siebeck), [1924] 1988.

Gesammelte Aufsätze zur Soziologie und Sozialpolitik, ed. Marianne Weber, Tübingen: Mohr (Siebeck), 1924.

Gesammelte Aufsätze zur Wissenschaftslehre, 7th edn., ed. J. Winckelmann, reprinted Tübingen: Mohr (Siebeck), 1988 [1922].

Max Weber Gesamtausgabe, Tübingen: Mohr (Siebeck).

The Methodology of the Social Sciences, trans. E. Shils and H. Finch, New York: Free Press, 1949.

Political Writings, ed. Peter Lassman and Ronald Speirs, Cambridge: Cambridge University Press, 1994.

The Protestant Ethic and the Spirit of Capitalism, trans. Talcott Parsons, New York: Scribner's, 1958.

The Rational and Social Foundations of Music, trans. D. Martindale *et al.*, Carbondale, IL: Southern Illinois Press, 1958.

Religion of China: Confucianism and Taoism, New York: Free Press, 1964.

The Religion of India: The Sociology of Hinduism and Buddhism, New York: Free Press, 1958.

Roscher and Knies, New York: Free Press, 1975.

The Russian Revolutions, trans. G. Wells and P. Baehr, Ithaca, NY: Cornell University Press, 1995.

The Theory of Social and Economic Organization, ed. Talcott Parsons, Glencoe, IL: Free Press, 1947.

Wirtschaft und Gesellschaft. Grundriss der verstehenden Soziologie, 5th edn., ed. J. Winckelmann, Tübingen: Mohr (Siebeck), 1976.

Secondary literature

Books

Albrow, Martin, *Max Weber's Construction of Social Theory*, New York: St. Martin's Press, 1990.

Antoni, Carlo, *From History to Sociology: The Transition in German Historical Thinking*, trans. Hayden White, Detroit, MI: Wayne State University Press, 1959; London: Merlin Press, 1962.

Beetham, David, *Max Weber and the Theory of Modern Politics*, London and Boston: Allen & Unwin, 1974; 2nd edn. Cambridge: Polity Press; Oxford: Basil Blackwell, 1985.

Bendix, Reinhard, *Max Weber: An Intellectual Portrait*, New York: Anchor Books, 1962 [1960].

Bologh, Roslyn Wallach, *Love and Greatness: Max Weber and Masculine Thinking – A Feminist Inquiry*, London: Unwin Hyman, 1990.

Breiner, Peter, *Max Weber and Democratic Politics*, Ithaca, NY: Cornell University Press, 1996.

Brennan, Catherine, *Max Weber on Power and Social Stratification: An Interpretation and Critique*, Aldershot, Hants. and Brookfield, VT: Ashgate, 1997.

Brubaker, Rogers, *The Limits of Rationality: An Essay on the Social and Moral Thought of Max Weber*, London: George Allen & Unwin, 1984.

Bruun, H. H., *Science, Values, and Politics in Max Weber's Methodology*, Copenhagen: Munksgaard, 1972.

Burger, Thomas, *Max Weber's Theory of Concept Formation*, Durham, NC: Duke University Press, 1976.

Eden, Robert, *Political Leadership and Nihilism: A Study of Weber and Nietzsche*, Tampa, FL: University Presses of Florida, 1983.

Eisenstadt, S. N. (ed.), *The Protestant Ethic and Modernization: A Comparative View*, New York: Basic Books, 1968.

Goldman, Harvey, *Max Weber and Thomas Mann: Calling and the Shaping of the Self*, Berkeley, CA: University of California Press, 1988.

Honigsheim, Paul, *On Max Weber*, trans. Joan Rytina, New York: Free Press, 1968.

Horowitz, Asher and Maley, Terry (eds.), *The Barbarism of Reason: Max Weber and the Twilight of the Enlightenment*, Toronto: University of Toronto Press, 1989.

Jaspers, Karl, *Max Weber: Ein Gedenkrede*, Tübingen: Mohr (Siebeck), 1989.

Kaesler, Dirk, *Max Weber: An Introduction to His Life*, trans. Phillipa Hurd, Chicago: University of Chicago Press, 1988.

Kronman, Anthony, *Max Weber* (Jurists: Profiles in Legal Theory), Stanford, CA: Stanford University Press, 1983.

Liebersohn, Harry, *Fate and Utopia in German Sociology, 1870–1923*, Cambridge, MA: MIT Press, 1988.

Love, John, *Antiquity and Capitalism: Max Weber and the Sociological Foundations of Roman Civilization*, London: Routledge, 1991.

Löwith, Karl, *Max Weber and Karl Marx*, ed. and Introduction by Tom Bottomore and William Outhwaite, new preface by Bryan Turner, New York: Routledge, 1993.

MacFarlane, Alan, *The Origins of English Individualism: The Family, Property and Social Transition*, New York: Cambridge University Press, 1978.

Marshall, Gordon, *In Search of the Spirit of Capitalism: An Essay on Max Weber's Protestant Ethic Thesis*, New York: Columbia University Press, 1982.

Mayer, Jacob Peter, *Max Weber and German Politics: A Study in Political Sociology*, 2nd revised and enlarged edn., London: Faber and Faber, 1956.

Mitzman, Arthur, *The Iron Cage: An Historical Interpretation of Max Weber*, New York: Grosset and Dunlap, 1971.

Mommsen, Wolfgang J., *Max Weber and German Politics, 1890–1920*, trans. Michael S. Steinberg, Chicago: University of Chicago Press, 1984 [1974].

Nelson, Benjamin, *The Idea of Usury: From Tribal Brotherhood to Universal Otherhood*, Chicago: University of Chicago Press, 1969.

Oakes, Guy, *Weber and Rickert: Concept Formation in the Cultural Sciences*, Cambridge, MA: MIT Press, 1988.

Outhwaite, William, *Understanding Social Life: the Method Called* Verstehen, New York: Holmes and Meier, 1976.

Parsons, Talcott, *The Structure of Social Action*, New York: McGraw-Hill Book Co., 1937; reprinted in paperback, 2 vols., New York: Free Press, 1968.

Poggi, Gianfranco, *Calvinism and the Capitalist Spirit: Max Weber's "Protestant Ethic,"* Amherst, MA: University of Massachusetts Press, 1983.

Portis, Edward Bryan, *Max Weber and Political Commitment, Science, Politics, and Personality*, Philadelphia, PA: Temple University Press, 1986.

Rheinstein, Max, Introduction to *Max Weber on Law in Economy and Society*, trans. and ed. Edward Shils and Max Rheinstein, Cambridge, MA: Harvard University Press, 1954.

Roth, Guenther and Schluchter, Wolfgang, *Max Weber's Vision of History: Ethics and Methods*, Berkeley, CA: University of California Press, 1979.

Scaff, Lawrence A., *Fleeing the Iron Cage: Culture, Politics, and Modernity in the Thought of Max Weber*, Berkeley, CA: University of California Press, 1989.

Schluchter, Wolfgang, *The Rise of Western Rationalism: Max Weber's Developmental History*, trans. Guenther Roth, Berkeley, CA: University of California Press, 1981.

    Rationalism, Religion, and Domination: A Weberian Perspective, trans. Neil Solomon, Berkeley, CA: University of California Press, 1989.

    Paradoxes of Modernity: Culture and Conduct in the Theory of Max Weber, trans. Neil Solomon, Cambridge: Polity Press; Stanford, CA: Stanford University Press, 1996.

Schroeder, Ralph, *Max Weber and the Sociology of Culture*, London: Sage, 1992.

Sica, Alan, *Weber, Irrationality, and Social Order* (revised paperback edition 1990), Berkeley, CA: University of California Press, 1988.

Sica, Alan, *Max Weber and the New Century*, Oxford and Cambridge, MA: Blackwell, forthcoming.

Swedberg, Richard, *Max Weber and the Idea of Economic Sociology*, Princeton, NJ: Princeton University Press, 1998.

Turner, Bryan S., *Weber and Islam: A Critical Study*, London and Boston: Routledge and Kegan Paul, 1974.

    For Weber: Essays on the Sociology of Fate, London: Routledge and Kegan Paul, 1981.

Turner, Charles, *Modernity and Politics in the Work of Max Weber*, London: Routledge, 1992.

Turner, Stephen P. and Factor, Regis A., *Max Weber and the Dispute over Reason and Value: A Study of Philosophy, Ethics, and Politics*, London: Routledge and Kegan Paul, 1984.

    Max Weber: The Lawyer as Social Thinker, New York: Routledge, 1994.

Weber, Marianne, *Max Weber: A Biography*, trans. Harry Zohn, with an Introduction ("Marianne Weber and her Circle") by G. Roth, New Brunswick, NJ: Transaction Press, 1988 [1926].

Zeitlin, Irving M., *Ancient Judaism: Biblical Criticism from Max Weber to the Present*, Cambridge: Polity Press, 1984.

Collections

Bendix, Reinhard, and Guenther Roth, *Scholarship and Partisanship: Essays on Max Weber*, Berkeley, CA: University of California Press, 1968.

Giddens, Anthony, *Politics and Sociology in the Thought of Max Weber*, London: Macmillan Press, 1972, reprinted in Giddens, *Politics, Sociology, and Social Theory: Encounters with Classical and Contemporary Social Thought*, Cambridge: Polity Press; Stanford, CA: Stanford University Press, 1995.

Green, Robert W. (ed.), *Protestantism and Capitalism: The Weber Thesis and Its Critics*, Boston: D. C. Heath, 1959.

Hennis, Wilhelm, *Max Weber: Essays in Reconstruction*, trans. Keith Tribe, London and Boston: Allen & Unwin, 1988.

Lash, Scott and Sam Whimster (eds.), *Max Weber, Rationality, and Modernity*, London: Allen & Unwin, 1987.

Lassman, Peter, Irving Velody, and Herminio Martins (eds.), *Max Weber's "Science as a Vocation,"* London: Unwin Hyman, 1989.

Lehmann, Hartmut and Guenther Roth (eds.), *Weber's "Protestant Ethic": Origins, Evidence, Contexts*, Cambridge: Cambridge University Press, 1993.

Mommsen, Wolfgang J. and Osterhammel, Jürgen (eds.), *Max Weber and His Contemporaries*, London: Allen & Unwin, 1987.

Seyfarth, Constans and Schmidt, Gert (comps.), *Max Weber Bibliographie: Eine Dokumentation der Sekundärliteratur*, Stuttgart: Ferdinand Enke Verlag, 1977.

Stammer, Otto (ed.), *Max Weber and Sociology Today*, New York: Harper Torchbooks, 1972.

Tribe, Keith (ed.), *Reading Weber*, London: Routledge, 1989.

Articles and chapters not included in collections listed above

Abraham, Gary A., "Max Weber on 'Jewish Rationalism' and the Jewish Question," *Politics, Culture, and Society*, 1:3 (1988), pp. 358–391.

Abramowski, Guenter, "Meaningful Life in a Disenchanted World: Rational Science and Ethical Responsibility (A Study of Max Weber)," *The Journal of Religious Ethics*, 10:1 (1982), pp. 121–134.

Albrow, Martin, "Legal Positivism and Bourgeois Materialism: Max Weber's View of the Sociology of Law," *British Journal of Law and Society*, 2 (1975), pp. 14–31.

Ashcraft, Richard, "Marx and Weber on Liberalism as Bourgeois Ideology," *Comparative Studies in Society and History*, 14 (1972), pp. 130–168.

Baehr, Peter, "Weber and Weimar: The 'Reich President' Proposals," *Politics*, 9:1 (1989), pp. 20–25.

Barkawi, Tarak, "Strategy as a Vocation: Weber, Morgenthau and Modern Strategic Studies," *Review of International Studies*, 24 (1998), pp. 159–184.

Bary, William T., "Neo-Confucianism in Modern East Asia," in Tu Wei-Ming (ed.), *The Triadic Chord: Confucian Ethics, Industrial East Asia, and Max Weber*, Singapore: Institute of East Asian Philosophies, 1991.

Bellah, Robert, "Max Weber and World-Denying Love: A Look at the Historical Sociology of Religion," *Journal of the American Academy of Religion*, 67 (1999), pp. 277–304.

Ben-David, Joseph, "Max Weber on Universities," Review Essay, *American Journal of Sociology*, 80:6 (1975), pp. 1463–1468.

Benhabib, Seyla, "Rationality and Social Action: Critical Reflections on Weber's

Methodological Writings," *The Philosophical Forum*, 12:4 (1981), pp. 356–374.

Berman, Harold J., "Some False Premises of Max Weber's Sociology of Law," *Washington University Law Quarterly*, 65:4 (1987), pp. 758–770.

Birnbaum, Norman, "Conflicting Interpretations of the Rise of Capitalism: Marx and Weber," *British Journal of Sociology*, 4 (1953), pp. 125–141.

Blegvad, Mogens, "'Value' in Turn-of-the-Century Philosophy and Sociology," *Danish Yearbook of Sociology*, 26 (1991), pp. 51–96.

Cahnman, Werner J., "Ideal-Type Theory: Max Weber's Concept and Some of Its Derivations," *Sociological Quarterly*, 6:3 (1965), pp. 268–280; reprinted in Werner J. Cahnman, *Weber and Tönnies: Comparative Sociology in Historical Perspective*, ed. J. B. Maier, J. Marcus, and Z. Tar, New Brunswick, NJ: Transaction Publishers, 1995.

Camic, Charles, "Charisma: Its Varieties, Preconditions, and Consequences," *Sociological Inquiry*, 50:1 (1980), pp. 5–23.

Davis, Winston, "Max Weber on Religion and Political Responsibility," *Religion*, 29 (1999), pp. 29–60.

Drysdale, John, "How are Social-Scientific Concepts Formed? A Reconstruction of Max Weber's Theory of Concept Formation," *Sociological Theory*, 14:1 (1996), pp. 71–88.

Finley, Moses, "Max Weber and the Greek City-State," in *Ancient History: Evidence and Models*, London: Chatto & Windus, 1985.

Fulbrook, Mary, "Max Weber's 'Interpretive Sociology': A Comparison of Conception and Practice," *British Journal of Sociology*, 29:1 (1978), pp. 71–82.

Gellner, David, "Max Weber, Capitalism, and the Religion of India," *Sociology*, 16:4 (1982), pp. 526–543.

Habermas, Jürgen, "Max Weber's Theory of Rationalization," in *The Theory of Communicative Action*, vol. I, trans. T. McCarthy, Boston: Beacon Press, 1984.

Hennis, Wilhelm, "Max Weber's 'Central Question,'" *Economy and Society*, 12:2 (1983), pp. 136–180; reprinted in *Max Weber: Essays in Reconstruction*, trans. Keith Tribe, London and Boston: Allen & Unwin, 1988.

Kalberg, Stephen, "Max Weber's Types of Rationality: Cornerstones for the Analysis of the Rationalization Process in History," *American Journal of Sociology*, 85:5 (1980), 1145–1179.

Lehmann, Hartmut, "Ascetic Protestantism and Economic Rationalism: Max Weber Revisited after Two Generations," *Harvard Theological Review*, 80:3 (1987), pp. 307–320.

Liebersohn, Harry, "Max Weber's Historical Interpretation of Judaism," *Publications of the Leo Baeck Institute, Year Book IX* (1988), pp. 41–68.

Momigliano, Arnaldo, "New Paths of Classicism in the Nineteenth Century [From Mommsen to Max Weber]," *History and Theory*, 21:4 (1982), pp. 1–64.

Oakes, Guy, "The *Verstehen* Thesis and the Foundations of Max Weber's Methodology," *History and Theory*, 16:1 (1977), pp. 12–29.

O'Neill, John, "The Disciplinary Society: From Weber to Foucault," *British Journal of Sociology*, 37:1 (1986), pp. 42–69.

Parsons, Talcott, "'Capitalism in Recent German Literature: Sombart and Weber" [Parts I and II], *Journal of Political Economy*, 36:6 (1928), pp. 641–661; 37:1

(1929); reprinted in Talcott Parsons, *The Early Essays*, Introduction and ed. by Charles Camic, Chicago: University of Chicago Press, 1991.

Pipes, Richard, "Max Weber and Russia," *World Politics*, 7:3 (1955), pp. 371–401.

Ringer, Fritz, "Max Weber on the Origins and Character of the Western City," *Critical Quarterly*, 36:4 (1994), pp. 12–18.

Roth, Guenther, "Weber's Political Failure" [Review of Weber's *Zur Neuordnung Deutschlands*, vol.XVI of *Max Weber Gesamtausgabe*], *Telos*, 78 (1988/89), pp. 136–149.

Scaff, Lawrence A., "Max Weber's Politics and Political Education," *American Political Science Review*, 67:1 (1973), pp. 128–141.

Shils, Edward, "Some Observations on the Place of Intellectuals in Max Weber's Sociology, with Special Reference to Hinduism," in S. N. Eisenstadt (ed.), *The Origins and Diversity of Axial Age Civilizations*, Albany, NY: SUNY Press, 1986.

Shinohara, Koichi, " 'Adjustment' and 'Tension' in Max Weber's Interpretation of Confucianism," *Comparative Civilizations Review*, 15(1986), pp. 43–61.

Simey, T. S., "Weber's Sociological Theory of Value: An Appraisal in Mid-Century," *Sociological Review*, 14:3 (1966), pp. 303–327.

Singer, Milton, "Max Weber and the Modernization of India," *Journal of Developing Societies*, 1:2, (1985), pp. 150–167.

Steeman, Theodore, "Max Weber and the Lutheran Social Congress: The Authority of Discourse and the Discourse of Authority," *History of the Human Sciences*, 7:4 (1994), pp. 21–39.

Stone, Norman, "The Religious Background of Max Weber," in W. J. Sheils (ed.), *Persecution and Toleration*, Oxford: Basil Blackwell and Ecclesiastical History Society, 1984.

Swedberg, Richard, "Max Weber's Manifesto in Economic Sociology," *Archives européens de sociologie*, 39:2 (1998), pp. 379–398.

Torrance, John, "Max Weber: Methods and the Man," *Archives européens de sociologie*, 15:1 (1974), pp. 127–165.

Tronto, Joan, "Law and Modernity: The Significance of Max Weber's *Sociology of Law*" [Review essay on Kronman's *Max Weber*], *Texas Law Review*, 63:3, (1984), pp. 565–577.

Trubek, David M., "Max Weber on Law and the Rise of Capitalism," *Wisconsin Law Review*, 1973:3 (1972), pp. 720–753; also as Working Paper No.12, Program in Law and Modernization, New Haven, CT: Yale University Law School.

Ulmen, G. L., "The Sociology of the State: Carl Schmitt and Max Weber," *State, Culture, and Society*, 1:2 (1985), pp. 3–57.

Wagner, Gerhard and Zipprian, Heinz, "The Problem of Reference in Max Weber's Theory of Causal Explanation," *Human Studies*, 9:1 (1986), pp. 21–42.

Warner, R. Stephen, "The Role of Religious Ideas and the Use of Models in Max Weber's Comparative Studies of Non-Capitalist Societies," *Journal of Economic History*, 30:1 (1970), pp. 74–99.

Warren, Mark, "Max Weber's Liberalism for a Nietzschean World," *American Political Science Review*, 82:1 (1988), pp. 31–50.

INDEX

Index

Cato the Elder, 242
causality, 9, 11–14, 27, 28, 72, 74
  and spirit of capitalism, 154
  legal, 11, 12
Chandler, Alfred D., 270
Chapman, Stanley, 123
character, 34, 112
charisma, 94–95, 140, 191 n.47
  and democracy, 135, 141, 144, 146, 147
  and early Christian communities, 219
  and legitimate rule, 91, 96, 141, 142, 226
  entrepreneurial, 121
  familial, 186
  personal, 230, 269
  see also prophets
Chicago, University of, 261
Ch'in dynasty, 176
China, xiii, 173–187, 196, 197, 198, 199,
  201, 247, 248, 262
Ch'ing era, 182
Chow, Kai-wing, 182
Christ, 217, 218
Christian ethic, 85
Christianity, 17, 18, 94, 110
  and urban life, 219
  vs. eastern "meaningfulness" of the world,
  220
  vs. Judaic legalism, 217–219
Christliche Welt, xii
Coca-Cola, 44
Collins, Randall, 52
Columella, 242
Communists, 147
community, 160, 248, 249
  and communitarian ethic, 234
  and joint stock company, 236
  history and tradition, 237, 238
Confucianism, 152, 173, 176–185, 187,
  248
  and Hinduism, 187, 198
  and magic, 173
  and Puritanism, 173, 178, 180, 197
Confucius, 176, 178
Conrad, Dieter, 193, 194, 195
Constant, Benjamin, 252
Cortez, Hernando, 260
Coulanges, N. D. Fustel de, 252
Counter-Reformation, 167
covenant, 168, 204, 205, 206, 207 n.6, 237
  and Calvinism, 237
  and Judaism, 201–202
Cromwell, Oliver, 165
Cunningham, William, 161

Darwinism, 70
  Social, 126
David, King, 204
Davidson, Donald, 27
de Gaulle, Charles, 140, 146
de Man, Paul, 56
democracy, 139, 140, 146, 147, 148
  see also caesarism; charisma
democratization, 106, 107, 141, 145
  of luxuries, 265
  of Russia, 127
  leadership democracy, 95, 133–134, 142
Deuteronomy, 214
  Deuteronomic reforms, 201, 204–206,
  212
Deutsche Gesellschaft für Soziologie
  (German Society for Sociology), xiii
Deutsche Bank, 120, 122
dharma, 188, 189, 191, 192, 193, 196
  and cosmic order, 194–195
  rajadharma, 195
  sadharana dharma, 194, 195
  svadharma, 194, 195
Diaspora, Jewish, 201, 216, 218
Diederichs, Eugen, 106
Dilthey, Wilhelm, 72
disenchantment of the world (*Entzauberung*),
  85, 105, 209, 220
  and legitimacy, 97
  and pre-Socratic Greece, 98
  and rationalization, 95, 97–98, 113
  and western modernity, 197
Dostoevsky, Fyodor, 103
Du Bois, W. E. B., 267
Durkheim, Emile, 25, 151

economic ethics, 263
economic history, 6, 72, 240, 242, 243,
  257–258, 260–264, 266, 270
economic rationalism, 260
economic sociology, 256–257, 270
economics
  ancient, 268
  of slavery, 268
  vs. psychology, 74
Egypt, 175, 183, 201, 244, 245–246, 253
Egyptians, 202
Ehrenberg, Hans, 139
Ehrenberg, Richard, 64
Ehrenfelt, Christian von, 77
Eigengesetzlichkeit, 195
Eisenstadt, S. N., 182–184
Eisner, Kurt, 133, 133 n.8

Index

Russian Old Believers, 263

Sadducees, 216
samsara, 188, 194, 198
Samuelsson, Kurt, 168
Sanskritization, 193
Sappho, 46
Sartre, Jean Paul, 3
Saul (King of Israel), 203
Scaff, Lawrence, 5, 46
Schäffle, Albert, 70
Schluchter, Wolfgang, 5, 47, 172 n.1, 192,
    218, 219
Schmidt, Helmut, 1
Schmitt, Carl, 147, 148
Schmoller, Gustav, 62, 63, 64
Schneckenburger, Matthias, 153
Schubert, Hans von, 161
Schulze-Gaevernitz, Gerhard von, 161
Schumpeter, Joseph, 256, 265, 269
Schwartz, Benjamin, 182
self-interest, 22, 24, 25, 28
shame, 34
Shils, Edward, 3
sib, sippe (*sib* – kinship group or family), *see*
    kinship
Sica, Alan, 5
Siebeck, Paul, xiii
Siemens, Georg von, 120, 122
Simmel, Georg, 107
Singapore, 183
Sinha, Surajit, 193
slavery, 242, 242 n.12, 243, 246, 262, 267
    and Deuteronomy, 205
    demise of, 267
    economics of, 268
    Roman, 267
    United States, 267
    vs. free labor, 244, 268
Social Democrats, 128
sociology
    interpretive, 70, 75
Solomon, 203, 204
Sombart, Werner, xiii, 107, 162, 200 n.1,
    210, 247, 256, 261, 262, 268
Sonderweg, 134
Souchay family, 119, 122, 123
South Korea, 183
Spain, 151, 162, 163
special path (*Sonderweg*), 134
Spiethoff, Arthur, 258
spirit of capitalism, 121, 154, 162, 170, 170
    n.36, 234, 236, 239

and Protestant ethic, 237
and religion, 163–165
see also Protestant ethic thesis; joint-stock
    company
Srinivas, M. N., 193
Stammler, Rudolf, 24
Staatslehre, 90
status ethic, 175
status groups, 42
Steiner, George, 56
Stinchcombe, Arthur, 3
Strauss, Leo, 3
subjectivism, 106, 130
Sung era, 179, 183
Sutras, 187
Swedberg, Richard, 6, 257 n.3
Switzerland, 153
    Geneva, 167

Tacitus, 242
Taiwan, 183
Talmud, 162, 212, 215, 218
    Talmudic period, 201
Taoism, 152, 173, 174, 178, 198
Tauler, John, 156
Tawney, R. H., 166–167
Tenbruck, Friedrich H., 47
Thomas, Robert Paul, 264, 266
Thompson, E. P., 38
Tobler, Mina, 131
Tocqueville, Alexis de, 106
Toller, Ernst, 133 n.8
Tolstoy, Leo, 103, 107
Tönnies, Ferdinand, 107
Torah, 215
    Levite, 208
tradition, 237, 238
    Chinese, 178, 184
    religious, 17
    see also ideal-type
Treitschke, Heinrich von, 11
Trevor-Roper, Hugh, 167, 171
Troeltsch, Ernst, 132, 132 n.5, 161, 162
Turner, Stephen, 148
typifications (models), 9–10, 13, 258
    see also ideal-type

United States, 101, 118, 119, 122, 123, 132,
    153, 159, 164, 170
    immigrants, 128 n.21
    compared with Russia, 127–128
    slavery, 267
Upanishads, 187